COMMUNICATION AND LAW

Multidisciplinary Approaches to Research

COMMUNICATION AND LAW

Multidisciplinary Approaches to Research

Edited by

Amy Reynolds
Indiana University

Brooke Barnett
Elon University

Routledge
Taylor & Francis Group
NEW YORK AND LONDON

This edition published 2011 by Routledge

Routledge
Taylor & Francis Group
711 Third Avenue
New York, NY 10017

Routledge
Taylor & Francis Group
2 Park Square, Milton Park
Abingdon, Oxon OX14 4RN

First issued in paperback 2012

Routledge is an imprint of the Taylor & Francis Group, an informa business

Cover design by Tomai Maridou

ISBN13: 978-0-415-64682-6 (PBK)
ISBN13: 978-0-805-84942-4 (HBK)

Library of Congress Cataloging-in-Publication Data

Communication and law : multidisciplinary approaches to research / edited by
Amy Reynolds & Brooke Barnett.
    p. cm. — (LEA's communication series)
Includes bibliographical references and index.

1. Mass media—Law and legislation—United States—Research. 2. Freedom of
speech—United States—Research. 3. Mass media—United States—Research.
I. Reynolds, Amy. II. Barnett, Brooke, Ph. D. III. Series.

KF2750.C65   2006
343.7309'9—dc22   2005049846
                                                                      CIP

For Tad and Chase

A. R.

For Tom, Lily, and Jack

B. B.

Contents

Preface   xi

Introduction: The Benefits of a Multidisciplinary Approach
in Communication Law   xiii
Amy Reynolds and Brooke Barnett

I THEORETICAL PERSPECTIVES AND APPROACHES

1 Charting the Future of Interdisciplinary Scholarship
in Communication and Law   3
Jeremy Cohen and Timothy Gleason

2 Method in Our Madness: Legal Methodology
in Communications Law Research   9
Fred H. Cate

3 Social Science Research in Judges' First
Amendment Decisions   23
Anthony L. Fargo

Introductory Comments to Chapter 4   39
David Pritchard

4 A New Paradigm for Legal Research   43
David Pritchard

5 The Intersection of Legal Practice and Social Science
on the Issue of Pretrial Publicity   61
Jon Bruschke

6 Pornographic Knowledge, the Law, and Social Science   87
Robert Jensen

7 Creating Meaning, Creating Citizens: The U.S. Supreme
Court and the Control of Meaning in the Public Sphere   109
David S. Allen

Introductory Comments to Chapter 8   139
Sandra Braman

8 Information and Socioeconomic Class
in U.S. Constitutional Law   161
Sandra Braman

II MULTIDISCIPLINARY METHODOLOGICAL
APPROACHES

Introductory Comments to Chapter 9   181
Bill F. Chamberlin

9 Merging Legal Research and the Practices of
Social Science: Comparing State Access Laws   183
Bill F. Chamberlin, Cristina Popescu,
and Michael F. Weigold

Introductory Comments to Chapter 10   201
Robert M. Entman

10 Blacks in the News: Television, Modern Racism, and Cultural Change 205
Robert M. Entman

Introductory Comments to Chapter 11 229
Glenn Leshner

11 The Effects of Dehumanizing Depictions of Race in TV News Stories 233
Glenn Leshner

Introductory Comments to Chapter 12 253
Robert Drechsel and Tom Grimes

12 Word-Picture Juxtaposition, Schemata, and Defamation in Television News 257
Tom Grimes and Robert Drechsel

Introductory Comments to Chapter 13 273
Brooke Barnett

13 The Stories They Couldn't Tell: How Journalists Use Public Record Databases 275
Brooke Barnett

Introductory Comments to Chapter 14 295
Amy Reynolds

14 The Impact of *Walker's Appeal* on Northern and Southern Conceptions of Free Speech in the Nineteenth Century 301
Amy Reynolds

Introductory Comments to Chapter 15 329
Constance Ledoux Book

15 The People and the Cable Guy: Federally Empowered Public Interest Standards 333
Constance Ledoux Book

Introductory Comments to Chapter 16   349
Michael Hoefges and Kent Lancaster

16 Utilizing Mass Media Advertising for Legal Notice
       in Class Action Lawsuits   353
       Michael Hoefges and Kent Lancaster

Contributors   371

Author Index   379

Subject Index   389

Preface

This volume brings together scholars from law and communications to talk both specifically and broadly about the different theoretical and methodological approaches one can use to study the First Amendment and general communication law issues. Our hope is that this book will help graduate students, new scholars, and established scholars think about new approaches to questions about communication and law. It offers a survey of the kind of multidisciplinary work that is now available. It is designed to challenge the conventional notion that traditional legal research and social science methodological approaches are mutually exclusive enterprises. The scholars with whom we collaborated to produce this volume present, in our view, the best argument in favor of considering multidisciplinary avenues for the study of communication law, in addition to the traditional approaches that have helped shape our field.

The book is divided into two parts: The first focuses on multidisciplinary theoretical approaches, and the second focuses on methodology. We believe that you can never separate theory and methodology when conducting research, but we think it is important to highlight these two primary areas of importance on their own merits. When one begins to consider a multidisciplinary approach to the study of communication law, that approach is grounded in theory and an appropriate methodology. We suggest in this book that the sources of the theory and methodology are plentiful and diverse and also provide a multitude of ways to study a variety of communication and the law questions.

This volume begins with reflections from Jeremy Cohen and Timothy Gleason (chap. 1), whom we believe provide much of the intellectual energy and force behind this strand of inquiry in our field. Their chapter focuses on the future of multidisciplinary work in communication and law and sets up the chapters and studies that follow.

The book contains a few reprinted articles that have made a significant contribution to a better understanding of how a multidisciplinary approach to the study of communication and law works. For the two reprinted articles in the first part of the book, the authors wrote new introductions that reflect on the significance of their original work and how they came to their original research designs and questions.

In the second part of the book, which highlights a variety of methodological approaches, contributors wrote a brief introduction to their research. The aim of these introductions is to give the reader snapshots into the thinking of the scholar who is, in some instances, paving a new way to explore communication and law.

We would like to thank all of our contributors for their willingness to collaborate on this project and for providing insightful, innovative, and thought-provoking ideas and research that we think will encourage more people to consider, and perhaps employ, multidisciplinary approaches to the study of communication and law. We also thank Linda Bathgate at Lawrence Erlbaum Associates for her encouragement, guidance, support, and patience with this project. We are grateful for the supportive reviewer comments that came to us when this volume was simply a prospectus, particularly from Jennings Bryant and our three anonymous reviewers for LEA.

Finally, we each would like to thank the numerous colleagues, friends, and scholars who have supported, encouraged, and guided our academic endeavors at this early stage in our careers. Although there are too many people to single out, we would particularly like to acknowledge Bob Jensen, Jim Tankard, and David Rabban at the University of Texas; and Fred Cate, Dan Drew, and Betsi Grabe at Indiana University. We thank you for your inspiration and hope you know how much you have helped shape our academic inquiries and intellectual journeys thus far. We hope that this volume stimulates new ideas and directions for research in communication and law that will lead to long-term programs of study into how free expression functions in society.

—*Amy Reynolds*
Brooke Barnett

Introduction: The Benefits of a Multidisciplinary Approach in Communication Law

Amy Reynolds
Brooke Barnett

In 1986, legal scholar and judge Richard Posner observed that, "After a century as an autonomous discipline, academic law in America is busily ransacking the social sciences and the humanities for insights and approaches with which to enrich our understanding of the legal system" (p. 1351). That same year, communication scholar Everette Dennis wrote,

> We are witnessing the development of at least three strains of legal scholarship in mass communication today: first, the continued articulation of traditional, documentary research; second, socio-behavioral methods; and finally, the critical-qualitative method. There is much dissatisfaction with the singular focus in communication law studies and with the notion that media law scholars should be boosters for media industries. (p. 10)

Although these statements from Judge Posner and Professor Dennis suggest a new era of collaboration among disciplines, in reality the fields of law and communication are still quite separate. In 1990, Jeremy Cohen and Tim Gleason suggested in *Social Research in Communication and the Law* that

> ... freedom of expression is an area of research especially appropriate to the discipline of communication studies. Yet while freedom of expression may be anchored well within our discipline, understanding clearly requires familiarity with a variety of substantive fields and methodological approaches beyond the usual concerns of communication theory, such as le-

gal studies, history, and jurisprudence. . . . A communication and law approach must distinguish itself from research generally recognized as within the traditional purview of law or legal studies. It should add to the literature of communication. It should be generated from the perspective of the communication scholar, not in competition with the legal scholar, but in recognition of the objectives of communication research. (p. 8)

We agree with Cohen and Gleason and would argue that more than 15 years after the publication of *Social Research in Communication and the Law* a number of innovative scholars are connecting the academic disciplines of communication and law in some of the ways they envisioned. For a few years, we have believed that an edited collection of work that showcases the "communication and law" approach is greatly needed. That is one of the purposes of this volume.

We became familiar with the challenges of navigating both the law and the field of mass communication when we began our doctoral studies at two slightly different times in two different places (Reynolds at the University of Texas, 1995–1998; Barnett at Indiana University, 1998–2001). The process of learning how to become legal scholars within the field of mass communication left us feeling torn between the two fields. We learned about mass communication theory and social science methodologies as well as general approaches to research and writing in our home doctoral programs. Most doctoral programs (ours included) offer at least one graduate-level mass communication law course. This was as close to a merging of the two disciplines as we would see in our graduate studies. Although we found solid training in the mass communication theories and methods in our communication classes, we learned more about First Amendment theory, history, the broader legal theories, legal methodology, and how to write for law reviews in law school courses. The only merger of our two research interests happened in that sole graduate mass communication law course, and it was really a repurposing of the law school approach, rather than a social science mass communication approach to law.

How does one bridge this gap? We knew even in graduate school that we wanted to explore the law in connection with mass communication theory and that we wanted to discover how media work within a First Amendment theoretical framework. We saw connections everywhere in our heads, but in our physical locations we found mostly separations— separate buildings, separate faculties, separate libraries, separate scholarly publications, separate graduate training, and separate paths that only sometimes crossed.

As we collaborated on a few research projects, we started to talk about the connections we saw between our two chosen areas of study. We started to think about all of the scholars we have admired who have challenged the separation that so many of us have experienced in our graduate training. We knew, of course, that academics who study the law reside in many different departments, schools, and colleges at universities across the country. We knew that some solely employed traditional legal research methodology to examine purely legal questions. This made sense to us, and we believe it is valuable, but we thought that other avenues for research that embraced a multidisciplinary approach could also add to our understanding of communication and law in different and perhaps more complete ways.

As we began to think about our own work and the work of scholars like Cohen and Gleason, we observed that over the past 40 years or so scholars from across disciplines have increasingly started to ask legal questions and seek answers using traditional legal research as well as social science methodologies. Their work was informed by a variety of theories that come from a variety of disciplines. Within the past two decades, these kinds of multidisciplinary approaches have become more creative and a little bit more common—traditional legal research combined with surveys, content analysis, experiments, or participant-observations, for example, as methodologies that answer questions and hypotheses that try to connect the law and mass communication rather than separate them.

We find this trend encouraging. Despite the emergence of innovative and significant multidisciplinary approaches to the study of communication law in recent years, little of this work is appearing in primary mass communication peer-reviewed journals. The journals, after all, mirror the field, and work that combines these two areas does not have an obvious fit anywhere.

Empirical data bear this out. In a 2003 article about research trends in mass communication from 1980 to 1999, Rasha Kamhawi and David Weaver found so little legal research in 10 primary communication journals that they collapsed it into other categories. Traditional legal research or historical legal research was considered qualitative, whereas multidisciplinary approaches were categorized as quantitative if they employed a content analysis, experiment, survey, or other quantitative approach.[1] The Kamhawi and Weaver study only looked at general communication journals, not specific topical journals like *Communication Law & Policy*. This is important to note because had they added topical journals to their sample they would likely have found more work in the area

---

[1] This information is based on personal conversations with Kamhawi and Weaver and on the findings from their study (see Kamhawi & Weaver, 2003). For detailed information about legal research published in a smaller sample of communication journals between 1974 and 1983, see Cohen (1986).

of communication law.[2] Still, we think the Kamhawi and Weaver data are compelling because the journals they studied are the most widely read and are considered the most prestigious general multidisciplinary journals in the communication field. At our request, Kamhawi and Weaver produced separate legal research data for us (the data they had prior to collapsing categories). It shows that, of the 889 studies published between 1980 and 1999, only 60 involved communication law topics (about 6%). Of those, 57 utilized traditional legal research or historical legal research methodologies.

MASS COMMUNICATION SCHOLARSHIP THAT INFORMS LAW

Although communication law scholars tend to look to each other's work for potential models of multidisciplinary theoretical and methodological approaches, a true multidisciplinary approach in these two fields extends beyond that produced by self-identified communication law scholars. Many researchers in the field of mass communication are studying communications questions that are clearly linked to legal issues, although they would not necessarily associate themselves with communication law. For example, in Robert Entman's (1992) *Journalism Quarterly* framing study, "Blacks in the News: Television, Modern Racism and Cultural Change," Entman concluded that routine crime and political reporting may indirectly promote racism in the ways that Blacks are depicted on TV news. This has clear "free press/fair trial" implications that some legal scholars have started to explore. Yet Entman does not consider himself a scholar who explores legal issues.

The communication law area with perhaps the longest history of study by both traditional mass communication as well as legal scholars is in the area of pretrial publicity. Some of the leading scholars in mass communication have, during their academic careers, looked at questions of pretrial publicity, and yet none of these scholars is widely or commonly identified with the law or legal scholarship. Part of this may come from the brevity of their exploration of the topic, or part may spring from these studies emerging as purely communication studies—that is,

---

[2]The journals included in the Kamhawi and Weaver study were *Communication Monographs, Communication Quarterly, Communication Research, Critical Studies in Mass Communication, Human Communication Research, Journal of Broadcasting and Electronic Media, Journal of Communication, Journalism and Communication Monographs, Journalism and Mass Communication Quarterly,* and *Public Opinion Quarterly.*

they lack any meaningful legal research to accompany the social science. Whatever the reason, we think the mass communication scholar's general interest in communication law from a nonlegal perspective provides some anecdotal evidence of the potential for collaboration and multidisciplinarity that is often overlooked.

Joseph T. Klapper, one of the founding fathers of media effects research, published a 1949 content analysis that examined one of the early questions tied to issues of pretrial publicity—whether press coverage of crime is biased against defendants (Klapper & Glock, 1949). Klapper is most widely recognized for his book, *The Effects of Mass Communication* (1960); his academic training was in English. President Lyndon Johnson appointed Klapper to the government's Commission on Obscenity and Pornography (1966–1970). In a completely different area of First Amendment law, Klapper "played a major role in the preparation of policy documents advocating the importance of scientific study to replace popular prejudice and mythology in the assessment of the effects of pornography and violence on the audience" (Maisel & Cisin, 1984, p. 658).

Other examples of leading mass communication scholars who have published at least one study in the area of pretrial publicity include:

- Steven H. Chaffee. In a 1966 publication, Chaffee and Mary Dee Tans crafted an experiment using simulated news stories to try to explore the effect media could have on creating jury bias, specifically negative attitudes toward defendants (Tans & Chaffee, 1966).

- Maxwell E. McCombs. During the 1960s, McCombs wrote a few articles (although not all were published) about pretrial publicity and the role the media plays in potentially prejudicing a jury. One study was an experiment co-authored with Walter Wilcox that was similar in design and purpose to the Tans and Chaffee study mentioned earlier (Wilcox & McCombs, 1967; see also McCombs, 1966). Another article offered three general hypotheses that could be used in structuring and guiding empirical research in the area of pretrial publicity (McCombs, 1969).

- James W. Tankard. Tankard and two co-authors conducted a content analysis of crime stories in newspapers to see whether those stories complied with American Bar Association (ABA) guidelines (first developed in 1968). The ABA guidelines were designed to help the press understand what kind of information released before a trial is most prejudicial to a defendant (Tankard, Middleton, & Rimmer, 1979).

- David H. Weaver. In a 1981 report prepared for the Modern Media Institute with Judith M. Buddenbaum, Ralph Holsinger, and Charlene

Brown, Weaver and his colleagues reviewed available empirical studies to find out whether pretrial publicity did have "scientifically measurable effects upon jurors and jury verdicts" (Buddenbaum, Weaver, Holsinger, & Brown, 1981, p. 1).

In an introduction to the Buddenbaum et al. article, the authors noted the tension between the two different ways one could view the issue of pretrial publicity:

> The issue of pretrial publicity is both old and vexing. In the legal literature the issue is usually referred to as fair trial versus free press, while in the field of journalism and mass communication the issue becomes one of free press versus fair trial. The difference in the terminology underscores the nature of the problem, for both sides take as their starting point important rights and freedoms guaranteed by the Bill of Rights. (p. 1)

Although the legal side of the issue in the prior passage could refer (and probably does refer) to scholars concerned with Sixth Amendment issues and not First Amendment ones, it does suggest that the law and communication come at overlapping questions in different ways. Yet the existence of these mainstream mass communication studies that date back more than 50 years suggests that communication law and social science can be quite compatible despite a long history of separation.

Bunker and Perry (2004) observed that,

> The intersection of social science and the law has long been controversial. The extent to which social scientific methods and theoretical structures can or should contribute to the law has been contested in American legal thought since the early twentieth century. (p. 1)

Bunker and Perry suggested that much of the resistance to the incorporation of social science comes from basic philosophical disagreements that are often traced back to legal scholars who still embrace law as an autonomous discipline.[3] Throughout the 20th century, this formalist, autonomous view of the law weakened—as evidenced first by the scholarship and arguments put forth by the legal realists (and others, such as those espousing sociological jurisprudence); the sporadic and then more

---

[3]Bunker and Perry (2004) explained that the autonomous view of the law is frequently credited to Christopher Langdell, Harvard Law School Dean in the latter 19th century, and assumes that "the common law had generated definitive and wise legal rules that could be applied deductively to all later cases, without the need for the contributions of other disciplines" (p. 2).

continual inclusion of social science evidence within court decisions; and, more recently, with the development of critical legal theory (see, e.g., Allen & Jensen, 1995; *Brown v. Board of Education*, 1954; Holmes, 1897; *Muller v. Oregon*, 1908; White, 1972). Despite this century-long weakening of the view that law in general is autonomous, First Amendment law is still considered by some legal scholars as "the last bastion" of formalism (Bunker & Perry, 2004; Delgado, 1994). Free speech theory as well as jurisprudence have resisted interdisciplinary efforts more so than most other areas of the law, although much more interdisciplinary work has emerged in recent years (Bunker, 2001; Bunker & Perry, 2004; Cohen, 1986; Delgado, 1994; Dennis, 1986; Posner, 1986).

The use of social science methodology and theory in communication law research, and the use of social science by the courts, are the two primary arenas in which discussions about multidisciplinarity occur. Yet as Cohen (1986) pointed out, values tied to journalism education also inform this debate and might also help explain why journalism as a field sometimes inadvertently undermines the promotion of multidisciplinary approaches that might lead to more elaborate research questions and designs—and ultimately to theory-building. Cohen (1986) noted that communication law as a field of study within journalism established its roots in the training of journalists. We suggest that a communication law orientation that is focused more squarely on the training of reporters, whether at the undergraduate or graduate level, could promote more microlevel/narrowly focused approaches to research. Cohen (1986) cited a 1986 Berkeley study of graduate communication law courses that, to us, highlights the problems a microlevel approach (i.e., topical vs. theoretical) create:

> The [Berkeley survey] instrument included boxes to check when a graduate media law class studies libel, copyright, advertising, the history of press freedom, and a dozen other topics. Missing, however, was any mention of topics such as communication law research, jurisprudence, or the study of media law as a communication phenomenon. This does not mean that media law courses do not go beyond basic orientations to the law of the press and freedom of expression. It does underline the need to examine our research priorities. (p. 12)

Ultimately, all of this suggests that the separate disciplines of communication and law and the scholars who navigate both worlds understand the different dimensions of communication law as a distinct area of study. There is a pragmatic and philosophical history to the separation of the two fields, but

at the end of the day, the intersection of First Amendment thought and social science may not result in irreconcilable conflict. . . . It is one that scholars and judges must grapple with, while doing their best to ensure that
valuable First Amendment freedoms are respected. (Bunker & Perry, 2004,
p. 23)

Over the past three or four decades, some mass communication scholars, judges, and legal scholars have created in their own research and
writing some potential resolution to the conflict. We find Cohen and
Gleason's approach most notable, particularly when they wrote in their
ground-breaking 1990 book that,

[this] is an attempt to encourage distinctions that recognize the relationships among communication theory, freedom of expression, history and
law and place them squarely within the identifiable domain of communication scholarship. Contextual understanding of communication and law can
only benefit from familiarity with, and respect for, the integrity of each of
these disciplines. (Cohen & Gleason, 1990, p. 7)

This volume was created with the Cohen and Gleason framework in
mind, and it operates under the assumption that, as Bunker and Perry
noted, the "intersection of First Amendment thought and social science"
can result in ground-breaking scholarship and meaningful contributions
to our discipline, as opposed to irresolvable conflict.

COMMUNICATION AND LAW: MULTIDISCIPLINARY
APPROACHES TO RESEARCH

In devising a structure for this book, we decided to begin with the two
scholars cited so often in this introduction. The first chapter offers reflections from Cohen and Gleason that expand on the program of interdisciplinary approaches to communication and law that they laid out in *Social Research in Communication and Law*. In that 1990 book, Cohen and
Gleason invited scholars to join them in an endeavor that would help all
of us better understand the interactions of communication and law. We
hope this project fosters a better understanding of the interaction between communication and law. We also hope it encourages more scholars to consider how to engage in theory building and long-term research
programs that reinforce the Cohen and Gleason approach.

The chapters that follow the Cohen and Gleason chapter fit into one of
two parts within the book. The first part of the book focuses on theory,
social science, and the law, and the broader multidisciplinary advances

and questions within specific topical areas of communication law. The second part offers a glimpse of a variety of methodological approaches, all of which are accompanied by author introductions that help contextualize the individual and collaborative research projects.

PART I: THEORETICAL PERSPECTIVES AND APPROACHES

The second chapter in this volume offers a law school perspective on methodology from Fred Cate, a professor at the Indiana University School of Law. Cate explains his quest (after years of avoiding the subject altogether) to find out whether the law as an academic discipline has a meaningful methodology that contributes to social science research. Cate suggests that legal methodologies are useful for communication researchers, and in his chapter he outlines the major legal schools of thought and their accompanying methodologies.

One of the questions that often arises when people discuss the role of social science in the study of law is the applicability of social science research within the judicial system. One of the arguments in favor of conducting social science research connected to law is that such research could and should be useful to the courts. This is a normative statement on which we do not want to take a position, but it does raise interesting questions. Do judges use social science research when deciding cases, particularly in the realm of First Amendment jurisprudence, and, if so, how?

Anthony Fargo (chap. 3, this volume) demonstrates that, although many communication law scholars study effects, that research is not having an effect on free speech law. According to Fargo, the U.S. Supreme Court appears to be more accepting of social science research today, but this acceptance has not played out in a meaningful way for First Amendment cases. Fargo notes that media effects studies rarely make it into court, and when lower courts use these data higher courts often overturn those decisions. He suggests that conducting longitudinal studies, publishing studies that show no effects, and preparing for judicial scrutiny of studies would make social science research more attractive in First Amendment cases.

In 1986, David Pritchard (chap. 4, this volume) argued for a new paradigm for legal research in communication. He noted that research conducted under the traditional, existing paradigm was built around legal institutions and focused almost exclusively on the study of courts, judges, administrative bodies, and legislatures. Pritchard suggests that this approach offers no information about how important social forces interact with and affect the legal system. In putting forth an argument for what he calls a "dispute-focused" paradigm, Pritchard says that these social forces (political, cultural, etc.) are important legal variables. In re-reading and commenting on his original article, Pritchard still believes the dispute-focused paradigm has something to offer to scholars in both their research and teaching of law.

Jon Bruschke (chap. 5, this volume), who recently co-authored a book about the impact of publicity on trial outcomes, provides an overview of this issue in the context of social science research. Bruschke explains why there is limited interdisciplinary effort in this area that seems ripe for multidisciplinary study. He also demonstrates how social science and legal findings coincide and differ and suggests that, in their evaluation of potentially prejudicial materials, "both social science and the law need to develop a more complete sense of what content in the media is of concern." Bruschke concludes his chapter by outlining five areas in need of study if either the law or social science wants to untangle the real effects of pretrial publicity.

Bruschke's overview of free press/fair trial issues is followed by an alternative approach to the study of pornography. Robert Jensen (chap. 6, this volume) argues that both legal and social science scholars have failed to ask the right questions about pornography and that this has resulted in damaging silences. Jensen describes pornography as a system of oppression that needs to be debated and discussed. He addresses some of the standard arguments against the regulation of pornography and concludes that neither the law nor social science research in their current form is helpful in challenging the capitalist patriarchy that creates the silences that surround pornography.

David Allen (chap. 7, this volume), whom we consider one of the nation's experts on the application of critical theory to First Amendment jurisprudence, uses critical theory to better understand how the U.S. Supreme Court struggles to control and establish meaning. His chapter highlights court decisions that limit public action from the community and examines the Supreme Court's practice of controlling meaning and how this in turn controls the public sphere and limits activism among citizens. Allen suggests that if new First Amendment theory were developed, it may allow the Court to move away from the need to establish societal order at the expense of quelling disagreement and dissent. The Court might then find ways to promote a more democratic society with a more active public sphere.

Sandra Braman (chap. 8, this volume) ends Part I with a thorough discussion of the process of explication, specifically in the context of information policy research. She describes the evolution of the theoretical and methodological innovation of her ground-breaking 1989 article, "Information and Socioeconomic Class in U.S. Constitutional Law," in the introduction to a reprint of the article.

PART II: MULTIDISCIPLINARY METHODOLOGICAL APPROACHES

Bill Chamberlin, Cristina Popescu, and Michael Weigold (chap. 9, this volume) begin Part II of the book with a detailed overview of a sophisticated and innovative methodological approach to rating state public record and access laws. The chapter focuses on the Marion Brechner Citizen Access Project at the University of Florida (www.citizenaccess.org). This research is a good example of how a multidisciplinary approach can not only help produce enlightening scholarship, but also contribute something tangibly useful to the profession of journalism and to citizens interested in participating in self-governance or keeping a watchful eye on what government does.

We see the next two chapters as good examples of how social science research in mass communication can inform and inspire communication law research. Robert Entman's (1992) well-known study about "Blacks in the news" on TV has led many scholars to consider the impact of racist images on potential jurors. Entman's study concluded that routine crime and political reporting may indirectly promote racism in the ways that Blacks are depicted on TV news. This has clear and important free press/ fair trial implications that could never have emerged from a traditional legal research study. In his introduction to a reprint of the original article, Entman (chap. 10, this volume) discusses the implications of his original study (and those that have followed) on potential jury bias.

Glenn Leshner (chap. 11, this volume), another scholar from mass communication who does not specifically devote his research to legal issues, puts Entman's findings to an experimental test. His chapter explores the effect of dehumanizing depictions of race in TV news on viewers. Leshner's experiment "is meant to forge the link between content and effects by assessing the relationship among types of depictions of alleged criminals (black and white) in television news stories and subsequent social judgments of the target suspects." Leshner's experimental findings "corroborate Entman's suspicions that dehumanizing depictions of African American males in television news crime stories encourage stereotyping in judgments about those suspects." Both of these social science studies make a meaningful contribution to a better understanding of media content and its effect on legal processes.

Another experiment follows Leshner's, but this one focuses on the juxtaposition of voice-over and video in TV news stories and asks whether

TV is more vulnerable to legal claims as a result of this juxtaposition that might create unintended defamatory meaning. Tom Grimes and Robert Drechsel (chap. 12, this volume) found that a viewer's gender and schemata can be used to help determine whether potential libel plaintiffs can reasonably claim to be harmed and identified by audio and video juxtaposition, even if nothing defamatory was communicated literally.

The Grimes and Drechsel study first appeared in *Journalism Quarterly* in 1996. The authors' introductory commentary emphasizes what is one of the main thrusts of this volume—that mass communication and legal scholars can work hand in hand to produce meaningful research that combines the theoretical and methodological expertise of both areas. Grimes and Drechsel write in their introduction that their experiment emerged precisely because of the inherent multidisciplinary nature of the field of mass communication. Their original study concluded by observing that their juxtaposition experiments "confirm the value of applying communication theory to legal issues."

Brooke Barnett (chap. 13, this volume) provides another good example of a study that merges traditional legal research with social science methodology to look at a relevant question, beyond just employing what Pritchard calls the institutional paradigm. Barnett uses a survey to determine how the federal Driver's Privacy Protection Act impacted journalists' use of public record databases. This study focuses on a legal issue (access to public records) and looks beyond cases and statutes to determine not what the law is saying, but rather to explore issues of impact. Also noteworthy about Barnett's chapter is the fact that this study was written two different ways—for a law school audience (this version of the study was printed in the *Federal Communications Law Journal*) and for a social science audience. Barnett's chapter offers the social science version of the piece, and her introduction discusses how these two different target outlets influenced her writing.

In the chapter that follows, a look at a more common qualitative approach to the study of communication law is offered. Amy Reynolds' (chap. 14, this volume) study of the impact of *Walker's Appeal* on how states in the North and South treated abolitionist speech in the early 19th century offers an example of legal historical work. Legal history is certainly not new, nor is the methodological approach employed by Reynolds. Yet as she notes in her introduction, this particular article (which appeared in *Communication Law & Policy* in 2004) is heavily reliant on historical primary sources rather than legal primary sources, which is less common in legal-historical endeavors. As with contemporary, traditional legal research, much of the historical work done in the area of law is heavily reliant on court opinions and statutes as well as judicial interpretation. Reynolds' article includes some of this, but the focus is shifted to the social realm in an effort to better understand how factors beyond the law might have influenced perceptions of the dangers of abolitionist speech.

Continuing in the qualitative realm, Constance Ledoux Book (chap. 15, this volume) offers insight into the use of focus groups to aid in the identification of the public interest as it is understood in broadcasting. Although Book's study does not actually employ focus groups, it provides a helpful overview of the ways in which focus groups aid both the Federal Communications Commission (FCC) as well as cable companies in their ascertainment of what public interest actually means. This has implications for the study of broadcast regulation law and its relationship to the citizens it serves.

The last methodological chapter offers a good example of traditional legal research that maintains a multidisciplinary focus. Michael Hoefges and Kent Lancaster (chap. 16, this volume) approach the study of mass media advertising plans as a way to provide legal notice in class action lawsuits. They suggest that their research can provide important insights to legal professionals and scholars by further advancing an understanding of "advertising media planning theories, methods and data."

The following chapters offer a wide range of models for multidisciplinary work. As suggested throughout our introductory comments, we hope that this project will stimulate new ideas and directions for research in communication and law that will lead to long-term programs of study into how the First Amendment functions in the society in which we live.

REFERENCES

Allen, D. S., & Jensen, R. (Eds.). (1995). *Freeing the First Amendment: Critical perspectives on freedom of expression.* New York: New York University Press.

Brown v. Board of Education, 347 U.S. 483 (1954).

Buddenbaum, J. M., Weaver, D. H., Holsinger, R. L., & Brown, C. J. (1981). *Pretrial publicity and juries: A review of research.* Bloomington, IN: School of Journalism Research Report.

Bunker, M. D. (2001). *Critiquing free speech: First Amendment theory and the challenge of interdisciplinarity.* Mahwah, NJ: Lawrence Erlbaum Associates.

Bunker, M. D., & Perry, D. K. (2004). Standing at the crossroads: Social science, human agency and free speech law. *Communication Law & Policy, 9,* 1–23.

Cohen, J. (1986). Degrees of freedom: Parameters of communication law research. *Communications and the Law, 8,* 11–21.

Cohen, J., & Gleason, T. (1990). *Social research in communication and law.* Newbury Park, CA: Sage.

Delgado, R. (1994). First Amendment formalism is giving way to First Amendment legal realism. *Harvard Civil Rights-Civil Liberties Law Review, 29,* 169–174.

Dennis, E. E. (1986). Frontiers in communication research. *Communication and the Law, 8,* 3–10.

Entman, R. (1992). Blacks in the news: Television, modern racism and cultural change. *Journalism and Mass Communication Quarterly, 69,* 341–362.

Holmes, O. W. (1897). The path of the law. *Harvard Law Review, 10,* 457–469.

Kamhawi, R., & Weaver, D. (2003). Mass communication research trends from 1980 to 1999. *Journalism and Mass Communication Quarterly, 80,* 7–28.

Klapper, J. T. (1960). *The effects of mass communication.* Glencoe, IL: The Free Press.

Klapper, J. T., & Glock, C. Y. (1949). Trial by newspaper. *Scientific American,* pp. 16–21.

Maisel, R., & Cisin, I. H. (1984). In memoriam: Joseph T. Klapper, 1917–1984. *Public Opinion Quarterly, 48,* 658–659.

McCombs, M. E. (1966). Research study probes trial by newspaper. *The Iowa Publisher, 14,* 6–7.

McCombs, M. E. (1969). *Behavioral research on pre-trial publicity.* Unpublished report, University of North Carolina at Chapel Hill.

Muller v. Oregon, 208 U.S. 412 (1908).

Posner, R. A. (1986). Law and literature: A relation reargued. *Virginia Law Review, 72,* 1351–1392.

Pritchard, D. (1986). A new paradigm for legal research. *Communications and the Law, 8,* 51–67.

Tankard, J. W., Jr., Middleton, K., & Rimmer, T. (1979). Compliance with American Bar Association fair trial-free press guidelines. *Journalism Quarterly, 56,* 464–468.

Tans, M. D., & Chaffee, S. H. (1966). Pretrial publicity and juror prejudice. *Journalism Quarterly, 43,* 647–654.

White, G. E. (1972). From sociological jurisprudence to realism: Jurisprudence and social change in early twentieth-century America. *Virginia Law Review, 58,* 999.

Wilcox, W., & McCombs, M. E. (1967). *Crime story elements and fair trial/free press.* Unpublished report, University of California at Los Angeles.

Part I

THEORETICAL PERSPECTIVES AND APPROACHES

Charting the Future of Interdisciplinary Scholarship in Communication and Law

Jeremy Cohen
Penn State University

Timothy Gleason
University of Oregon

The United States is engaged in what the president refers to as "a war on terrorism," as we pause from our work as university and journalism school administrators to reflect on freedom of expression, on how we come to understand it as scholars, and on what the work of social research in communication and law may hold for the future. As in other times of military and social conflict, there are implications for the flow and veracity of information, for the ability of the government to hold and interrogate prisoners outside of the public's view, for the efficacy of public calls to question official policy, for the ways in which journalists may gather information and report it to citizens, and for the privacy of individuals. For much of the last half of the 20th century, there was a fragile consensus about the value of freedom of expression in a democratic society. Nonetheless, although most Americans say they favor our constitutional freedoms of speech, Stanford law professor Kathleen Sullivan (1994) noted that many are willing to roll back or trade those rights to achieve other goals. The freedoms of expression take on particular salience when ideologies clash. There will be no lack of work for the foreseeable future for those interested in the interactions of communication and law.

We shared our program of interdisciplinary approaches to communication and law more than two decades ago with the publication of *Social Research in Communication and Law* (Cohen & Gleason, 1990), in which we offered an invitation to others to join us. They felt like halcyon days.

For Gleason, historical examination of the watchdog concept (1990), of libel law (1988, 1993), and of the Fairness Doctrine (1991), and for Cohen, *third-person effects* and social science studies of libel (1987, 1988, 1989, 1990), cameras in the courtroom (1982), First Amendment jurisprudence (1989), and communication and law (1986) suggested inroads toward deeper understanding of the links among expression, democracy, and communication behaviors. The Association for Education in Journalism and Mass Communication held a panel discussion of social science approaches to media law—its first—that included many of the authors represented in the current volume.

It was our belief then, and it remains so now, that communication scholars have the opportunity to add greatly to the understanding of freedom of expression by developing lines of research that examine free speech issues "from the perspective of the communication scholar, not in competition with the legal scholar, but in recognition of the objectives of communication research" (Cohen & Gleason, 1990, p. 8). We noted then that to do so added the need for increased scholarship. Contributors would need expertise in multiple disciplines. Thorough familiarity with law and expertise in communication would be the minimum credential before the work could be held up to the peer review of disciplinary scholars in law or colleagues in communication. To do less would risk confusion, the formulation of unsound theory, and the creation of unrealistic expectations. We tried to make it clear that, in the end, law is not science. Legal and scientific theory are not the same. The work of the communication and law scholar requires deep disciplinary awareness of the distinctions between these sometimes conflicting ways of knowing and framing human discourse.

We set out in 1990 to describe a framework for communication and law. We identified three different issues ripe for research:

- The theoretical and methodological elements that distinguish among law, freedom of expression, and communication, and the conceptual approaches needed to bridge these disciplines.
- The validation or (invalidation) of assumptions about communication embedded in law.
- The use of social research to identify and examine the impact of law on communication.

Today, the task feels particularly daunting. We do not have a crystal ball. We cannot predict the work of future communication and law scholarship. Yet little at present suggests the emergence of unified or cohesive communication and law research programs. By and large, studies have remained *ad hoc* research ventures that provide intriguing glimpses into law, but that have yet to bring a larger field into focus. No communication graduate program has yet established itself as a leader in the manner that some have developed deserved reputations for work in First Amendment law, children and media, or the study of journalism institutions.

It may be that part of what makes communication and law so difficult as a field is the fundamental difference between science and law. Recognizing that the field of communication includes a wide range of approaches including but not limited to social science, a distinction nonetheless remains between the purposes of law and communication.

Law is a system of regulation. Its purpose is to set, interpret, and enforce rules of conduct by which people will live—or, at least, be held accountable. Communication as an academic discipline, whether the scholarship of critical theorists, historians, or social scientists, is a search for *understanding* of individuals, events, institutions, and other phenomena.

Law is not science. Oliver Wendell Holmes (1881) made this clear in the opening paragraph of *The Common Law* when he wrote, "The life of the law has not been logic; it has been experience" (p. 1). Holmes understood that the "felt necessities of the time, the prevalent moral and political theories, intuitions of the public . . . even the prejudices which judges share with their fellow men" (p. 1) had more to do with judicial decision making than did science. Science, of course, is not always a desirable basis for law. The "best" science of the first half of the 19th century viewed Black men and women as inferior. It was this *scientific* view that generated the legal logic the Supreme Court relied on in *Dred Scott* (*Scott v. Sandford*, 1857), one of the most shameful cases in American history. If Blacks were inferior to Whites, then the subtleties of citizenship were not relevant. *Inferior* races (the accepted scientific view at the time) could not be citizens. The citizenship question before the Court was moot.

Science has never been an easy fit for the courts, a point Hastings College law professor David Fairman (2004) illuminated in his history of the Supreme Court's "200-year struggle" to integrate science and law. Science remains a hit-and-miss proposition for the courts, as Chief Justice William Rehnquist's opinion for the Supreme Court in *City of Renton v. Playtime Theaters, Inc.* (1986) demonstrates. The case rested in part on an empirical question. Did the presence of adult entertainment in Renton, Washington, lead to increased crime, which was the rationale for the ordinance under consideration? "The First Amendment does not require a city . . . to conduct new studies or produce evidence independent of that already generated by other cities so long as whatever evidence the city relies upon is reasonably believed to be relevant," Rehnquist wrote (*City of Renton v. Playtime Theaters, Inc.*, 1986, p. 51). In other words, the courts may accept the reasonable views of legislators over scientific evidence re-gardless of whether a question may be subject to empirical verification. The felt necessities of the time, as well as empirical evidence, are at the heart of legal decision making. Understanding how communication con-tributes to the felt necessities of the public, and the ways in which those necessities interact with law, is a task for communication and law schol-ars.

In *City of Renton*, the Court found little use for an empirically produced factual basis. Are the courts ready for the even more difficult lead of crafting doctrine around social science discovery? Bunker and Perry (2004) concluded that, although interdisciplinary legal scholarship is on the rise in areas such as law and economics, "the [o]ne area of legal thought in which the social scientific world view has gained little traction . . . is free speech theory and doctrine" (p. 3).

We do not propose applied research as the single justification for com-munication and law. Nonetheless, it should give each of us pause to re-consider the larger picture and to ask: What is the purpose of the research at hand? How does it contribute to freedom of expression and democratic practice? Are we building a body of work as members of a community of scholars that will make a difference in the formulation and application of law?

On a more positive note, the following chapters and studies indicate constructive growth. Interest in communication and law has increased. Research scholars are regularly working beyond the limits of the single discipline approaches of law, history, psychology, and communication to develop richly textured portraits of the environments—legal, social, and cognitive, among others—that influence and are influenced by the regulation, practices, and philosophies of expression. Psychology and law courses, and, on occasion, communication and law are now widely avail-able to undergraduate as well as graduate students.

For scholars interested in understanding freedom of expression, the present offers a profusion of challenges sufficient to establish the direc-tion of a body of work for many years to come. The work will be impor-tant if it holds implications for citizens and others who feel called on to engage in the democratic process through the First Amendment freedoms that underlie the American constitutional democracy.

There appeared to be strong protection for journalists claiming limited constitutional, statutory, or administrative rights to conceal the identity of their sources when we began teaching media law. Today, several jour-nalists are facing prison sentences for refusing to reveal the names of confidential sources. As scholars, we would like to know: What has changed? Is there more than a simple correlation between the public's de-creasing trust in news organizations and prosecutorial zeal? Does the public think about freedom of expression differently now than during other times of national crisis?

Today, the contours of the Patriot Act and the architecture of information technology are altering the boundaries of privacy and shrinking the zone of individual privacy, once taken for granted. Communication and law scholars will contribute to the policy realms of law if full-fledged programs of scholarship are mounted to develop an understanding of the phenomena. Likewise, legal scholars such as Stanford University law professor Lawrence Lessig (2004) are asking new questions about what it means to own information. Of course more familiar questions remain that will benefit from careful interdisciplinary study. Communication effects, media ownership and distribution, intellectual ownership, privacy, and national secrecy are among a multitude of phenomena subject to law and regulation, and to deeper understanding through communication scholarship.

Legal scholar Frederick Schauer (2004) argued that the definition of the First Amendment cannot be explained by examining only the law. Its limits, he wrote, "turn out to be a function of a complex and seemingly serendipitous array of factors that cannot be (or at least have not been) reduced to or explained by legal doctrine or by the background philosophical ideas and ideals of the First Amendment" (Schauer, 2004, p. 1768).

Lacking a crystal ball, we will nonetheless hazard a prediction—the task the editors of this volume have asked us to perform. The work of communication and law scholarship will only find influence beyond the laboratory and library when the protocols of our studies exchange ad hoc scholarship for long-term programs of study. The presence in the journals of unrelated research developed because scholars followed esoteric personal interests will not generate enlightened consideration among others. It is time to follow our colleagues in other social, biological, and physical sciences, and to identify realms of study that will produce useful understanding. It is time to focus our limited resources on questions for which the answers can make a difference. To do so, we have to adopt a new sense of what it means to be collegial, and we have to work pragmatically, as well as with an interdisciplinary vision.

REFERENCES

Bunker, M. D., & Perry, D. K. (2004). Standing at the crossroads: Social science, human agency and free speech law. *Communication Law & Policy, 9,* 1–23.

City of Renton v. Playtime Theaters, Inc., 475 U.S. 41, 50 (1986).

Cohen, J. (1982). Cameras in the courtroom and due process: A proposal for a qualitative difference test. *University of Washington Law Review, 57,* 277–291.

Cohen, J. (1986). Degrees of freedom: Parameters of communication law research. *Communication and the Law, 8*, 11–21.

Cohen, J. (1989). *Congress shall make no law: Oliver Wendell Holmes, the First Amendment, and judicial decision making.* Ames, IA: Iowa State University Press.

Cohen, J., & Gleason, T. W. (1990). *Social research in communication and law.* Newbury Park, CA: Sage.

Cohen, J., & Gunther, A. (1987). Libel as communication phenomena. *Communication and the Law, 9*, 9–30.

Cohen, J., Mutz, D., Nass, C., & Mason, L. (1989). Testing some notions of the fact/opinion distinction in libel. *Journalism Quarterly, 66*, 11–17, 247.

Cohen, J., Mutz, D., Price, V., & Gunther, A. (1988). The impact of defamation on reader perceptions: An experiment on third-person effects. *Public Opinion Quarterly, 52*, 167–173.

Cohen J., & Spears, S. (1990). Newtonian communication: Shaking the libel tree for empirical damages. *Journalism Quarterly, 67*, 51–59.

Fairman, D. L. (2004). *Laboratory of justice: The Supreme Court's 200-year struggle to integrate science and the law.* New York: Times Books.

Gleason, T. W. (1988). The fact/opinion distinction in libel. *Hastings Journal of Communications and Entertainment Law, 10*, 763.

Gleason, T. W. (1990). *The watchdog concept: The press and the courts in nineteenth century America.* Ames, IA: Iowa State University Press.

Gleason, T. W. (1991). Killing "gnats with a sledgehammer"? The fairness doctrine and KAYE broadcasters. *Journalism Quarterly, 68*, 805–813.

Gleason, T. W. (1993). The libel climate in the late 19th century: A survey of libel litigation: 1884–1899. *Journalism Quarterly, 70*, 893–906.

Holmes, O. W. (1881). *The common law.* Boston: Little, Brown.

Lessig, L. (2004). *Free culture: How big media uses technology and the law to lock down culture and control creativity.* New York: Penguin.

Schauer, F. (2004). The boundaries of the First Amendment: A preliminary exploration of constitutional salience. *Harvard Law Review, 117*, 1765–1809.

Scott v. Sandford, 60 U.S. 393 (1857).

Sullivan, K. M. (1994). Free speech wars. *Southern Methodist University Law Review, 48*, 203–214.

Chapter 2

Method in Our Madness: Legal Methodology in Communications Law Research

Fred H. Cate
Indiana University

As a law professor specializing in communications law, I often find myself as the external member of qualifying examination and dissertation committees for doctoral students in journalism and telecommunications. Having grown up in a field in which the JD, rather than the PhD, is the teaching degree, I have never fully understood all of the rites of this process. Without question, the most mysterious parts deal with methodology. I have read countless essays and participated in dozens of dissertation defenses that discuss, seemingly without end or purpose, independent and dependent variables, inductive and deductive reasoning, regression analysis, and standard deviations.

Occasionally, a colleague who works in the social sciences, but has training or an interest in law, will ask a candidate a question about "legal methodology." This is one of the moments I fear most—when I must exert the greatest energy to ensure that my face does not look as blank as the candidate's. Fortunately, with a little preparation, the occasionally sagacious nod, and vigilant silence, I usually can keep my fellow committee members—not to mention the candidate—from catching on to how completely lost I am.

This worked relatively well until the qualifying exam of Brooke Barnett, one of the editors of this volume. In her exam, she was asked—not by me, to be certain—how a scholar would approach a certain problem using legal methodology. Her written response—that there really was not any such thing as legal methodology—struck me as vaguely sensible even if something of a slight to my academic discipline. My immediate concern, however, was that the issue might come up when the committee met with her to discuss her responses.

Sure enough it did. The faculty member who had posed the initial question—an obvious troublemaker—asked Brooke to comment on her dismissal of legal methodology. Whatever she said as I was busy trying to look thoughtful and nod sagaciously, its effect was to reiterate that law did not have many analytical tools to contribute to social science research.

"I am sure Professor Cate wouldn't agree," Brooke's inquisitor retorted, as he and the other committee members turned their eyes on me. My worst nightmares were realized as a blank look replaced my mask of wisdom. "I think she may have been a little harsh," I stammered, and then took the road of all professorial cowards and asked Brooke to expand on her answer.

The underlying question—Does law have any meaningful methodology to contribute to communications or other social science research?— was left unanswered and surprisingly, given how much lawyers like to write about everything, appears largely unexamined. Methodology is just not a subject legal scholars tend to address explicitly, either in the classroom or in published research. Our failure to do so not only threatens to undermine the rigor and reliability of legal research, it also obscures the fact that legal scholarship does, in fact, use a variety of methodologies, which are indeed useful for communication researchers.

In the pages that follow, I describe, briefly and in broad terms, some of the major schools of legal thought, each of which involves different methodologies. In fact, it would be no exaggeration to say that one of the characteristics that most distinguishes each of these schools from the others is their different methodologies. I conclude by addressing four specific analytical tools that are crucial to legal scholarship and relevant to communication and other social science research.

SCHOOLS OF LEGAL ANALYSIS

Common and Civil Law Systems

The early Western legal systems, on which the U.S. legal system has drawn most heavily, are generally divided into those based on civil (also called Roman or code) law and those based on common (or case) law. Civil law, which the Romans spread throughout continental Europe, relied on extensive written codes—what today we would call statutes, rules, and regulations. In theory, albeit admittedly oversimplified, the answer to any legal problem was codified somewhere. The role of the civil law system, therefore, was primarily to ensure that the facts of any dispute or issue were correctly adduced and the right codified law applied.

Common law, by contrast, although not devoid of written laws, relied far more heavily on the resolution of specific disputes to create precedents that could then be applied to future legal disputes. Therefore, the common law system placed great emphasis on the adversarial role of attorneys to help hone factual and legal disputes and determine which of potentially many conflicting precedents applied to the case at issue. Whereas the raw material of the civil law system was complex codes, the raw material of the common law system was a constantly expanding array of precedents, each of which was highly fact-specific. These precedents might conflict among each other and from jurisdiction to jurisdiction, and they might even include divergent legal interpretations within a specific case. In House of Lords decisions, for example, each law lord might write his own opinion for why a case should be decided a certain way, none of which would be labeled as *majority* or *dissenting* opinions. Common law was uniquely English and exerted far greater influence on the early development of U.S. law; only the legal system of Louisiana, with its French origins, was explicitly based in civil law.

As can easily be imagined, the methodologies of these two systems—the ways in which they analyze and solve questions or disputes—are quite different. Although both systems require some way of determining facts that are in dispute, the civil law system relies heavily on judges to be fact-finders. Once the facts become clear, application of the law is really a matter of looking it up. In the common law system, by contrast, judges are more like referees or umpires between attorneys who fight not only about the facts, but also about which precedents should be applied and why. Categorization, as my colleague Professor Don Gjerdingen has noted, is therefore one of the key tools of the common lawyer.

In the United States, the two systems have blended significantly. Although scholars usually describe the U.S. legal system as being based in common law, most states have codified the widely accepted principles of common law precedents into statutes and regulations. By the start of World War II, the U.S. legal system, although often still referred to as a common law system, had evolved millions of statutes and regulations necessary, or at least more appropriate, for regulating an industrial economy.

Legal Formalism and Positivism

Moreover, both common and civil law systems contribute to the development of law as a set of fairly technical rules and procedures, and of lawyers as experts trained in the intricacies of legal argument and set apart from the population at large. Sometimes characterized as legal formalism or positivism, this understanding sees law and legal rules—procedural and substantive—as important in their own right and requiring compliance without much regard for what their effect might be in practice. For example, a litigant might be barred from court because he failed to comply with a filing technicality or neglected to respond to a complaint in the precise time or manner required by court rules or precedent. Or a statute might be applied to an individual without regard for whether the result of its application appeared fair or just. One criticism leveled against the legal system is that its methodologies have become more important than its effect or outcome—that process trumps substance.

Natural Law and Utilitarianism

One of the earliest responses to this perception of law was reliance on some notion of natural law, which in turn often reflected theological principles. The founders relied heavily on such an approach in justifying rebellion against England. Recourse to natural law requires some shared understanding as to what values are natural and when they should be applied. Few truths are, in fact, self-evident, and both lawyers and legal scholars have found recourse to natural law methodologically problematic as a result.

Another early and often related response to legal formalism or positivism emphasized a more utilitarian approach to law. Thomas Jefferson, for example, wrote in 1810:

> A strict observance of the written laws is doubtless *one* of the high duties of a good citizen, but it is not *the highest*. The laws of necessity, of self-preservation, of saving our country when in danger, are of higher obligation. To lose our country by a scrupulous adherence to written law, would be to lose the law itself, with life, liberty, property and all those who are enjoying them with us; thus absurdly sacrificing the end to the means. (Thomas Jefferson to John B. Colvin, Sept. 20, 1810; cited in Ford, 1904–1905, p. 146)

Utilitarianism, like reliance on natural law, raises all manner of methodological issues for both practitioners and scholars because it requires agreement on what desirable outcomes are and when formal law may be evaded to achieve those. As Jefferson noted: "The line of discrimination between cases may be difficult; but the good officer is bound to draw it at his own peril, and throw himself on the justice of his country and the rectitude of his motives" (cited in Ford, 1904–1905, p. 146).

The 20th century saw the evolution of additional responses to legal formalism or positivism that offer more interesting (and, arguably, more useful) methodologies and are largely distinguished by their methodologies.

Legal Realism

The earliest of the modern responses—legal realism—tends to reject both formalism and natural law as the basis for legal decision making or scholarship. Instead legal realists see law as seldom being as precise or infallible as lawyers and judges might portray it; legal realists focus on factors such as judicial experience and bias, desirable public policy goals, and even social science research as better explanations of trial outcomes. Methodologically, legal realists abandon the concept that law is objective or neutral, or that codified law or common law precedents can be applied to achieve predictable, consistent results. For legal realists, analysis of the law requires looking outside of the legal system to results, effects, and context.

Like many of the 20th-century schools of legal thought, the primary contributions of legal realists might be characterized as *negative*: They criticize an established order and question the infallibility of laws, legal procedures, and legal decision makers. Legal realism thus helped lay the groundwork for many of the other schools of legal thought to follow. It also helped to legitimize critiques from broader perspectives than just analyzing how accurately facts are adduced and legal precedents applied.

Economic Analysis of Law

Law and economics—or the economic analysis of law—brings a more quantified or scientific approach to utilitarianism. This school of legal thought accepts as the goal of law *wealth maximization*. What constitutes wealth may be determined by allowing voters or litigants to actually value different outcomes (e.g., Would you pay more to have cleaner air or cheaper products?). Law and economics proponents then focus on the economic efficiency of various ways to achieve the desired end and to identify, avoid, or reduce transaction costs. Cost–benefit analysis is the key tool of law and economics proponents. Law and economics thus supplies a distinctive method both for determining the goal of a law or legal decision and for evaluating how that goal is achieved.

Although many adherents are careful to note that not all problems are capable of economic analysis and that economic analysis does not always consider all competing values (e.g., How do you value clean air for future generations?), this school of analysis is often criticized for ignoring non-monetary values (e.g., liberty or equality).

Critical Legal Studies

The critical legal studies movement emerged in the 1970s largely in response to law and economics, although the *crits*, as its proponents are called, also viewed the movement as building on the more radical aspects of legal realism. Critical legal studies focuses on the indeterminacy of law and legal process and argues that legal outcomes significantly or even predominantly reflect bias, ideology, politics, wealth, power, status, and other extralegal factors. Thus, law is often seen as a tool of legitimizing wealth and injustice and oppressing individuals, especially those who are less powerful or farthest removed from the social norm.

The methods of crit analysis, therefore, are far less quantitative than those of law and economics and far less concerned with legal precedent or procedure than any of the prior schools of legal analysis. After all, if the system is corrupt, applying its rules precisely and efficiently would only further the corruption. Instead crit methods are far more concerned with identifying bias, measuring impact on disenfranchised populations, and enhancing social justice.

Feminist Legal Studies

Over the past three decades, the critical legal studies movement has given birth to a number of related, but distinct, strands of legal analysis. One of the most distinctive is feminist legal studies. This label covers a wide array of thinking, but the common element they share is some focus on the questions of whether there are intrinsic differences between men and women and, if so, to what extent the legal system does or should reflect those differences.

For example, some feminist scholars argue that there are inherent differences between men and women—that women have distinct perspectives and approaches to problems that are often ignored by the legal system. As a result, these scholars urge reform of the legal system to accommodate women's ways of approaching problems and seeing the world and remove biases that favor male voices. Another strain of feminist legal thinking rejects the claim that there are inherent differences between men and women, and argues instead that the legal system, dominated by men, has created and perpetuated differences, allowing male-dominated society to subjugate women (e.g., by denying them the right to vote or failing to take domestic violence seriously).

Critical Race Theory

Another powerful offshoot of the crit movement is critical race theory. Professor Brian Bix describes critical race theory as presenting two strands of analysis. The first is that racism is pervasive in the legal system. The second is that people of minority ethnic groups have "distinctive views, perceptions, and experiences which are not properly recognized or fully discussed in mainstream of conventional discussions of the law" (Bix, 1999, p. 215).

The methodologies of feminist legal and critical race scholars, like those of most crit scholars, involve the extensive application of disciplinary approaches and analytical tools external to the law and legal system. These schools of legal analysis are inevitably concerned with context as much or more than with the content of law and legal institutions. They are also more likely to be interested in the impact of the legal system in operation, the nature of the people acted on, and, significantly, the identity, demographics, and experiences of the observer or scholar.

Law and Society

Law and society builds on—and, to some extent, includes—many of the previous schools of legal thought to focus on how law and legal institutions operate in society. What is distinctive about this movement, and most relevant to this chapter, is that law and society is dominated by *nonlawyers*: anthropologists, economists, historians, political scientists, psychologists, sociologists, and others who study the operation and impact of law from the perspective of other disciplines. These scholars thus apply the tools of their disciplines to their analysis of broad questions about law in society. Those same tools and a broad interdisciplinary approach are often adopted by legal scholars active in the law and society movement. The reverse, however, has proved true as well: Legal methodologies are increasingly infiltrating the work of nonlawyer law and society scholars.

This brief and incomplete survey of some of the major schools of legal thought does not begin to do justice to the richness, diversity, or complexity of ways in which legal practitioners and scholars think about the law and analyze legal problems. However, it does suggest the range of legal approaches and tools available to both legal and social science scholars.

TOOLS OF LEGAL ANALYSIS

This final section highlights four of the most pervasive tools—four methodologies, if you will—that are clearly applicable to communications law and other social science research.

Precedent

One of the oldest and most widely used analytical tools in the common law is precedent: How well does a current or proposed application of the law comport with past decisions? This is one of the most basic tools used by judges, attorneys, and scholars every day, and it has the advantage of limiting the inquiry to a fixed body of law—no matter how large and complex that body may be.

Communications law research is often concerned with precedent: How did the Federal Communications Commission (FCC) apply its past decisions in similar areas? What is the new technology or media most like—how do we categorize it? This question has dominated the debate over the First Amendment status of cable and satellite TV for decades: Is cable more like over-the-air broadcasting, which gets limited First Amendment protection, or more like print, which gets full First Amendment protection?

Similarly, courts will often ask about FCC decisions: Did the Commission adequately follow its past precedent or justify departing from it? If the reviewing court concludes that the Commission ignored precedent or finds the justification for departing from it is inadequate, it will often reverse the Commission or remand the case for further consideration. As a result, precedent often acts to slow the pace at which communications law evolves and tends to keep both the practice and scholarship of communications law backward-looking.

Precedent is focused almost wholly *within* the legal system: It is concerned with the identity of the decision maker and the affected parties only to the extent necessary to determine whether they are bound by prior decisions (e.g., a lower court bound by the decision of an appellate court or a litigant bound by a decision in a prior case involving the same facts in a different jurisdiction). Precedent is rarely concerned with the identity of the observer at all and takes into account other contextual factors only as necessary to evaluate whether past precedent was applied correctly or how the current case might be applied as precedent in the future.

It is difficult to overstate the importance of precedent in communications law—not only because of its prevalence, but because precedent often plays a key role in applying other analytical tools—for example, in interpreting statutes or determining jurisdiction. Yet precedent is not the only tool used by communications law researchers.

Codified Rules

As the legal system has evolved in the United States, constitutional, statutory, and rule-based analyses have grown increasingly important: Did a court or other decision maker act as commanded by legislation or administrative rule? This type of analysis has proved especially vital in communications law, where the First Amendment to the Constitution has played a critical role and where Congress has passed a number of major statutes and the FCC has engaged in hundreds of rule-making proceedings in recent years.

Statutes and, to a lesser extent, rules are exceptionally important because they can overturn in an instant all but constitutional precedent. For example, the deregulatory approach that Congress adopted in the Telecommunications Act of 1996 led to the overturning of dozens of Commission rules governing broadcasting and telecommunications.[1]

Codified rules are thus far more likely than precedent to precipitate change. The two methods of analyzing communications law problems are otherwise quite similar: focused almost exclusively within the legal system and not particularly concerned with parties or outcomes. Moreover, precedent is used to interpret codified rules and to judge whether those rules were applied appropriately. This can be particularly vexing in situations where the codification took place years before substantial advances in the social or economic activity that is the subject of the rules. (For example, the Communications Act that created the FCC and governed the entire structure of communications industries in the United States into the 21st century was adopted in 1934 and was based largely on an earlier law enacted in 1927.) Nowhere is the difficulty inherent in interpreting aging codified law clearer than in courts' and agencies' interpretation of the Constitution—the United States' earliest and most authoritative source of codified law.

Policy Analysis

A third and increasingly prominent methodology used in communications law research is policy analysis. Policy analysis focuses on outcomes

---

[1]Section 202(h) of the Telecommunications Act of 1996 requires the Commission to review its broadcast ownership regulations every 2 years to "determine whether any of such rules are necessary in the public interest as a result of competition" and to "repeal or modify any regulation" that the FCC determines no longer serves the public interest. By the end of the Commission's third biennial review, completed in June 2003, it had eliminated the newspaper–TV cross-ownership ban, which had been in place since 1975 in markets with nine or more stations. The Commission raised the national limit on the percentage of TV viewers that any one person could own stations reaching from 35% to 45% (Congress later lowered it to 39%) and raised the limit on the number of stations that could be owned in any one market from one to three in the largest markets and to two in medium-sized markets. The Commission relaxed its rules limiting cross-ownership of TV and radio stations in the same market. The FCC modified the dual network rule, which prohibited common ownership of two or more TV networks, to permit the four largest networks—ABC, CBS, NBC, and Fox—to merge with smaller networks such as United Paramount or Warner Brothers. Some of the Commission's efforts have been stalled by the U.S. Court of Appeals for the Third Circuit (Franklin, Anderson, & Cate, 2004).

and asks whether the result of a particular legal decision or enactment is fair, efficient, or consistent with what the decision maker intended.

Many of the more recent schools of legal analysis argue that policy analysis is the key tool of legal decision makers and therefore should be an essential tool of legal scholars. In communications law, for example, some of the most significant Supreme Court cases appear capable of rational explanation only by focusing on their outcome, not their application of precedent or codified law. The landmark defamation case of *New York Times Company v. Sullivan* (1964) is an excellent example, making little sense in its application of either case law or statutes, but achieving the dramatic—and, many observers would argue, desirable—outcome of prohibiting southern states' high courts from stifling media coverage of the civil rights movement.

As this example suggests, the policy at issue may be unrelated to the four corners of an existing body of common or civil law; it may reflect social or political policy, the preferences of individual legal decision makers, or even explicit bias. As a result, focusing on policy objectives as a means of explaining or evaluating legal decision making is intrinsically responsive to the broader context of an issue: the impact on the parties involved, the implications for future generations, and the identity and experiences of the decision maker or observer. Policy analysis almost always refers to some broad principle or standard by which to evaluate outcomes, such as morality, justice, or social stability. This only heightens the need for the researcher to be aware of the range of contextual issues presented in a specific case or legislative enactment.

Policy or outcome analysis is perhaps the most common methodology used by nonlegal specialists engaged in legal research. Such scholars may be unaware of, or uninterested in, the minutiae of whether a court or administrative body correctly applied prior precedent, ignored key relevant precedent, or followed written statutes or rules. Instead their research focuses on the impact—both immediate and longer term—of whatever they are studying and the desirability of that effect.

For example, a social science researcher might ask whether TV coverage of a crime scene affects the likelihood of the defendant receiving a fair trial. All manner of traditional social science methodologies may be brought to the problem, especially if empirical research is involved, but at the end of the day the researcher will have to consider what makes a trial fair and whether exposure to pretrial publicity has a legally significant impact on the likelihood of achieving that goal.

One of the great challenges of policy-based research is the need to attempt to identify, articulate, and correct for researcher bias. This can be difficult to do. Yet this challenge should not obscure the desirability of policy-based research because such research may be perceived as being more interesting and, in the long run, more valuable because it attempts to answer important, relevant questions concerning the structure and governance of our society.

Procedural Analysis

Finally, a word should be said about procedure as a tool of legal analysis. Procedure may in fact be the most important tool for legal practitioners, although the one least used by scholars. Procedural analysis focuses on a variety of questions involving the authority and competence of the decision maker, the process employed in arriving at the decision, and the impact that process has on the substantive outcome of a legal question or dispute. Did the court have jurisdiction over the parties and the dispute? Did the administrative agency provide appropriate opportunities for the public to comment on a proposed rule? Was the burden of proof or standard for reaching a decision correctly identified? Were other important procedural rules followed?

In law, a procedural violation is sometimes fatal to a decision. For example, decisions by courts that lack jurisdiction to hear the case are invalid and treated as if they never existed. Other procedural violations may not render the ultimate decision invalid, but may give rise to judicial or public challenges to decisions that shape the course and resolution of a case.

Procedural issues form the basis for many—perhaps most—challenges by lawyers to a law, regulation, or a judicial decision. This is especially true in communications law and other forms of administrative law, where agencies often fail to comply with one or more of the many rules contained in the Administrative Procedures Act, the main federal law governing how administrative agency authority is to be exercised. Even if that failure does not automatically render the agency's decision invalid, it may require that the agency reopen its proceedings or reconsider its decision, which gives attorneys a second chance to plead their case while delaying the effective date of an objectionable outcome. Delay is often sufficient, especially in cases involving the press or access to government documents because the need for, and sensitivity of, the information is likely to decrease with the passage of time.

To scholars of communications law, especially those not trained in the law, procedural analysis is often overlooked or dismissed, although procedure may have been dispositive in the outcome of the case. For example, pretrial motions—motions to dismiss a case before it gets to trial—are decided under standards that greatly favor the nonmoving party, standards that are much harder to satisfy than those used at trial. So knowing whether an appeal is from a decision on such a motion or from a full trial on the merits is critical to evaluating its long-term significance.

Moreover, procedural issues have proved particularly significant in at least the constitutional dimensions of communications law because it is often these issues that the Supreme Court interprets as being most affected by First Amendment protections for speech and press. *New York Times Company v. Sullivan* (1964) not only established the now-famous "actual malice" standard for public plaintiffs to recover for defamation, it also required that actual malice be proved with "convincing clarity"—a procedural standard that makes actual malice virtually impossible to demonstrate. In *Philadelphia Newspapers, Inc. v. Hepps* (1986), the Supreme Court ruled that defamation plaintiffs must prove the falsity of allegedly defamatory speech (rather than defendants being required to prove truth), at least where the speech concerned matters of public concern and the defendant was the media. This shift in the burden of proof has made defamation cases involving expression on public issues virtually unwinnable because of the great difficulties inherent in proving falsity. These are only two of many examples where the high Court's tinkering with procedural requirements has had a dramatic and lasting effect on the outcome of cases.

One final example of the importance of procedural analysis is the impact of the procedural posture in determining outcomes in defamation cases. During the 1980s, plaintiffs brought about 1,000 defamation cases. Three fourths of these were terminated by decisions on motions in favor of the defendants. Of the 254 cases that actually made it to trial, however, plaintiffs won three fourths. Defendants appealed 147 of those decisions. The appellate courts ruled in favor of the defendants and reversed the lower court's decision in 53% of those cases and reduced damages in another 17% (Franklin, Anderson, & Cate, 2000).

Defamation scholars have long noted that only about 10% of defamation plaintiffs win their cases. What this new research taught us was much more informative than just that bare percentage: Few plaintiffs ever get to trial; if they do, they tend to win; but if the case is appealed, they tend to lose on appeal. The implications of this research are beyond the scope of this chapter, but notably this work has led to a number of proposals for reforming the defamation system.

Moreover, as this type of research amply demonstrates, procedural issues are not just a topic for communications law research, they are also a method for analyzing communications law problems. Procedural analysis helps make greater sense of existing case and statutory law, and it makes predictions about future decisions more precise.

CONCLUSION

Law is not as devoid of methodologies as generations of doctoral students and I may have surmised, although law's analytical tools may not be as clearly defined as in the social sciences. There are a variety of available explanations for this relative lack of definition, ranging from the fact that legal methodologies continue to emerge and evolve, to the fact that legal methodology is given little attention as such in most law schools. To be sure, we try to teach law students—especially in their first year—to "think like a lawyer," but we rarely are explicit about what this means or the methodological tools available to help lawyers think. Even when we teach those tools, we seldom conceive of them as methodologies. As a result, legal scholarship is more often recognized as borrowing methodologies from other disciplines—perhaps the most prominent example being in law and economics—than contributing to them. But this perception is incomplete and, increasingly, incorrect.

ACKNOWLEDGMENTS

The author gratefully acknowledges the generous help of his colleagues Beth Cate, Aviva Orenstein, Alex Tanford, and especially that of Don Gjerdingen.

REFERENCES

Bix, B. (1999). *Jurisprudence: Theory and context* (2nd ed.). London: Sweet & Maxwell.
Ford, P. L. (1904–1905). *The works of Thomas Jefferson*. New York and London: G. P. Putnam's Sons.
Franklin, M. A., Anderson, D. A., & Cate, F. H. (2000). *Mass media law* (6th ed.). New York: Foundation Press.
Franklin, M. A., Anderson, D. A., & Cate, F. H. (2004). *Mass media law—2004 supplement*. New York: Foundation Press.
New York Times Company v. Sullivan, 376 U.S. 254 (1964).
Philadelphia Newspapers, Inc. v. Hepps, 475 U.S. 767 (1986).

Chapter 3

Social Science Research in Judges' First Amendment Decisions

Anthony L. Fargo
Indiana University

In 1994, Professor Richard Delgado wrote that in legal scholarship we were witnessing an end to what he called "First Amendment formalism" and the rise of "First Amendment legal realism." Professor Delgado argued that long-held beliefs about speech as a "near-perfect instrument for testing ideas and promoting social progress" (p. 170) were being seriously undermined by feminist scholars, critical race theorists, and others. Professor Delgado argued that the new paradigm would allow the law to view equality as just as important as free speech, thus clearing the way for regulations on pornography and hate speech that, under First Amendment formalism, could not pass constitutional muster.

Professor Delgado was not the first or the last legal scholar to suggest that the traditional safeguards for freedom of speech contributed to silencing women, minorities, and other "outgroups" instead of broadening the marketplace of ideas (Fiss, 1996; MacKinnon, 1993). It is beyond the scope of this chapter to debate whether Professor Delgado and others are right that First Amendment jurisprudence has contributed in some way to discrimination against, or the silencing of, women, minorities, and others. However, if Professor Delgado were right that the new trends in legal scholarship would lead to changes in judicial decision making, such changes would seem to bode well for the use of social science research in First Amendment jurisprudence.

Although it is not possible to list all of the studies that have attempted to show relationships between media content and audience behavior—media effects, in other words—a glance at random issues of three leading communications journals indicates that media effects literature is abundant (Arpan & Raney, 2003; D'Alessio, 2003; Eveland, 2003; Gross & Aday, 2003; Lang, Schwartz, Chung, & Lee, 2004; Lasorsa, 2003; Ravaja, 2004; Tsfati & Cohen, 2003; Young, 2004). Of course, there are many more such studies reported in academic and popular journals devoted to psychology and other behavioral sciences (Bunker & Perry, 2004).

Despite the abundance of literature on media effects and the surge in legal scholarship criticizing traditional First Amendment jurisprudence, there has not been a major movement in the courts in the last 20 years to change traditional free-speech protections. At the same time, the Supreme Court, which sets the tone and direction for all other U.S. courts, has appeared of late to put more faith in social science findings than in the past, leading Professor Timothy Zick (2003) to say that "[c]onstitutional law . . . is becoming an empirical enterprise" (p. 118). Professor Zick, citing a number of cases from the Supreme Court and other federal courts, argued that federal judges increasingly did not have "any overarching normative theory of constitutional interpretation" and were turning more often to empirical data and scientific conventions to help them decide constitutional questions (p. 118).

Other legal scholars have suggested that the only roadblock to more favorable judicial notice of social science theories and findings is a lack of adequate research. Professors John Monahan and Laurens Walker (1991) said that empirical questions were increasingly at the "heart of law," but they noted that courts were often frustrated by a lack of empirical data on some issues. Given what seems like a mountain of empirical data about media effects, it would seem that First Amendment law, at least, does not suffer from that defect. Yet the uses of empirical data to inform judicial decisions about free-speech rights are scant, at least at the appellate level.

So we are left with a conundrum. Legal scholars tell us it is time to put aside old ways of deciding at least some First Amendment cases. Hundreds of studies are available regarding the effects of media content on various audiences. The Supreme Court appears to be more accepting of social science data as evidence than in the past. But First Amendment law appears to be largely immune from these trends. Why?

The rest of this chapter attempts to answer that question and suggests what can be done to make social science research more useful in solving First Amendment problems.

THE ROLE OF LEGAL PHILOSOPHY

Both legal scholarship and judicial decision making appear to go through various phases. Some of these phases throughout American legal history have been more amenable to social science or real-life information than others. What follows is a brief exploration of the various legal philosophies that have been identified by legal scholars.

Legal scholars tend to focus on the period after the Civil War in describing the evolution of American law mostly because antebellum courts seemed to focus largely on natural rights rather than positive law. Shortly after the war ended, Christopher Columbus Langdell became dean of Harvard's law school and is generally credited with inventing the case study method (Feldman, 2000). Langdell in effect turned the study of law into an academic specialty that was separate from the rest of the academy and unconcerned and uninterested with other academic disciplines. The case study method focused on a mixture of inductive and deductive reasoning: Students examined cases to identify abstract principles and rules that had guided the decisions in those cases and then deduced from those principles and rules the proper outcome of similar cases (Feldman, 2000). The philosophy behind the case method, at least in its early incarnation, is known as formalism. Formalism emphasizes the idea of law as an autonomous discipline free of influences from the rest of society, with its own logic and principles (Posner, 2003). In practice, formalism can be described as being primarily concerned with three things: procedure, rules, and legal categories (Lempert & Sanders, 1986). Formalists often insist that proper procedures be followed even at the expense of substantive justice; that rules established by constitutions, precedents, and legislation be adhered to; and that parties to a case and their actions be made to fit into familiar legal forms or descriptions (Lempert & Sanders, 1986).

One obvious characteristic of formalism is that it is largely backward-looking. This did not sit well with Progressives and others in the late 19th and early 20th centuries who wanted to use the law to improve the lot of people victimized by laissez-faire economic policies while also elevating their morals (Feldman, 2000). At the same time, some in the legal community, most notably Oliver Wendell Holmes, questioned the Langdellian emphasis on legal decision making as purely logical and deductive. In one of his most famous lines, Holmes (1881/1991) bluntly stated that, "[t]he life of the law has not been logic: it has been experience" (p. 1). He explained that many things went into judicial decision making and had had more to do with the development of law than deductive syllogisms: "The felt necessities of the time, the prevalent moral and political theories, intuitions of public policy, avowed or unconscious, even the prejudices which judges share with their fellow-men. . . ." Law, he said, could not be discussed "as if it contained only the axioms and corollaries of a book of mathematics" (p. 1).

Holmes is regularly identified as one of the pioneers of the American legal realism movement, along with Roscoe Pound, Karl Llewellyn, and Jerome Frank (Lempert & Sanders, 1986). Pound, among others, has also been identified with the sociological jurisprudence movement that also arose in the early 1900s and that criticized Langdellian reasoning as "mechanical jurisprudence" (Feldman, 2000). The sociological jurisprudents believed, like the formalists, in legal principles, order, and organization, but they also believed that legal truths could not be discovered through deduction and that justice sometimes demanded that judges had to make law for the good of society (Feldman, 2000). Together, Holmes' skepticism about the impartiality and cold rationality of judges and the sociological jurisprudents' desire that law be used as a force for social good combined into the realist movement, which flourished in the 1920s and 1930s in the legal academy.

The legal realists have been credited with recognizing the potential of social science to lay foundations for legal decision making. By suggesting that judges should act to improve society by making law, they also provided a philosophy that would help the courts back away from Lochner-era thinking and expand the power of the government to intervene in the economic system during the Great Depression (Feldman, 2000). Yet American legal realism, which suggested that there were no hard-and-fast rules governing legal decision making, proved too relativistic for a world caught up in a war with totalitarian and fascist regimes in World War II. Legal scholars began to emphasize the things that made America different from the countries it was fighting, which in turn led to a new emphasis on democratic ideals, American consensus, and a concern for the rule of law. Scholars, assuming a shared American consensus about the superiority of democracy to other forms of government, began examining what processes were needed to make democracy work. In turn, legal scholars began to examine the conditions necessary for the rule of law to work effectively. For the most part, these scholars, such as Lon Fuller, began to focus on the legal processes that would ensure that law had an "inner morality" (Feldman, 2000).

Legal process theorists shared with realists a disdain for the Lochner-era Supreme Court, but for different reasons. Realists believed that the Lochner Court had ignored outcomes in its decisions and failed to promote social justice. Legal process theorists were concerned with defining the processes that made institutions unique and able to survive. The Lochner Court had stepped out of its proper role and intruded on the legislative function. To process theorists, the proper process of judicial decision making is "reasoned elaboration," which calls for judges to give reasons for a decision based on precedent and the appropriate rule of law (Feldman, 2000). In short, the legal process school of thought rejected realists' empiricism and their belief that judges were arbitrary and returned the focus to the law as it was and as it should be, but not in the formalists' value-free way. Law was seen as an instrument of democracy and should reinforce democratic principles.

The changes in American life in the 1960s and 1970s, epitomized by the civil rights movement, the women's movement, the antiwar movement, and other social movements, as well as government reactions to those movements, cast serious doubt on the idea that Americans were united by their love of democracy, democratic process, and the rule of law. Gradually, the legal process train of thought derailed, along with the idea that there was any one correct legal philosophy or theory. Feminist theory, critical race theory, the law and economics movement, and other collaborations between law and other disciplines emerged and existed in the academy—and in practice—side by side (Feldman, 2000). Some suggest that this fragmentation of legal thought has now led to a postmodern period that encourages multidisciplinary approaches to law and questions the validity of all previous ideas (Feldman, 2000). Others argue, along similar lines, that the practice of law should become more pragmatic. Federal appellate judge and prolific author Richard A. Posner (2003) said that pragmatism could lead judges through bewildering times by forcing them to focus on common-sense solutions to problems. Legal pragmatism, Judge Posner said, is forward-looking, empiricist, and open to empirical theory while hostile to "abstract moral and political theory" when it comes to judicial decision making. In other words, it is antiformalist.

It would be short-sighted to believe that these schools of thought were the only influences on legal scholarship and practice after the Civil War, and it also would be wrong to think that there are clear lines of delineation between one period and another. The case study method still thrives in American law schools despite its formalist tendencies. Legal realists did not cease to exist after the 1930s, and there are echoes of the realists' beliefs in feminist and critical race theories that suggest that law favors the status quo and so is not value-free. Pragmatism, too, sounds a lot like realism, but as Judge Posner (2003) defined it, pragmatism also accepts the power of precedent, even formalist precedent—for purely pragmatic reasons, of course.

Another problem with tracing trends in jurisprudential philosophy is that the trends in scholarship often do not align with trends in judicial decision making. The next section explores the connection between legal decision making and social science by focusing on the Supreme Court's embrace of empirical data as evidence.

THE COURTS AND SOCIAL SCIENCE

Social science research has made sporadic and sometimes dramatic cameo appearances in Supreme Court decisions until recently, when such evidence has been cited more often. Those cameo appearances have been few and far between.

One of the first cases in which the Supreme Court cited social science data favorably was in 1908 in *Muller v. Oregon*. The Court upheld an Oregon law that limited the number of hours per week that women could work. This result was in direct opposition to many of the Court's decisions on economic legislation from the 1880s to the 1930s—the so-called Lochner Era. In *Lochner v. New York* (1905), the paradigm case for the period, the Court struck down a New York law limiting bakers to 60 hours of work per week on the grounds that the law interfered with the Fourteenth Amendment substantive due process rights of bakers and their employers to negotiate freely and equally with each other. In dissent, Justice Holmes took the majority to task for, in his view, hiding behind a mask of judicial impartiality while in fact advancing a particular economic theory, Herbert Spencer's "Social Darwinism" (*Lochner v. New York*, 1905).

In *Muller*, Louis Brandeis, Oregon's attorney (and later a Supreme Court justice), invented the "Brandeis brief" by attaching two pages of legal argument to more than 100 pages of statistics and other data showing the alleged ill effects of long work hours on women's health, safety, and morals (Mason, 1956; Paper, 1983). But one of Brandeis' biographers noted that the case did not mark a wholesale embrace of social science evidence by the Court, and in fact the Court usually was openly hostile to such evidence until the 1930s (Urofsky, 1981). *Muller* was an exception rather than the rule, and one that could be explained by the Court's general attitude toward its role during the so-called Lochner Era. One legal historian argued that the Court from the late 1800s to the 1930s saw itself as having two main functions: protecting the laissez-faire economic system from the government and protecting womanhood (Graber, 1991). In this case, faced with a conflict between the two roles, the Court may have allowed itself to be swayed by Brandeis' evidence of the dangers of long work hours for women.

Despite the ascendancy of legal realism in American legal thought during the first quarter of the 20th century, social science findings did not gain popularity as evidence until after the legal realists had been eclipsed to some extent by legal process theorists. Even then, any use of social science data remained controversial. Just as Justice Holmes' dissent in *Lochner* provides a glimpse into the conflict between formalism and realism—a conflict that was momentarily put aside in *Muller* in part because of the power of the data in that case—we can also see competing philosophies at work in the wake of one of the Supreme Court's most famous decisions.

In a remarkably brief opinion given its importance, a unanimous Court in *Brown v. Board of Education* (1954) declared that racial segregation of public schools violated the Fourteenth Amendment's guarantee of equal protection under the law for all citizens. For its decision, the Court relied in part on a Brandeis brief from the appellants that detailed the findings of dozens of sociological and psychological studies on the effects of school segregation (Appendix to Brief for Appellants, 1954). Based on evidence in the studies indicating that African-American children suffered serious consequences from segregation, the Court found that segregation was inherently discriminatory even if the separate schools were indeed equal facilities.

Five years later, Professor Herbert Wechsler (1959) took issue with the way the Court decided the case. Professor Wechsler took great pains in a law review article to say that he felt the outcome in *Brown* was the right one morally. But in Wechsler's view, the courts should be transcendent, far removed from the political frays over choices between competing values or desires that characterize legislative and executive branch actions. Although courts may consider whether legislative and executive actions are lawful, the courts must do what legislatures and executives do not have to do—support their choices by reasoned explanation. Courts could not act as "naked power organs" in deciding cases, Wechsler argued, but instead had to reach decisions that were principled—that rested on "reasons that in their generality and their neutrality transcend any immediate result that is involved" (Wechsler, 1959, p. 19). In other words, court decisions rest on principles that can be applied in any similar case, but the principles do not necessarily dictate that one side or the other should always win. This advocacy of "neutral principles" may explain how Wechsler could state, apparently without irony, that he believed the internment of Japanese Americans during World War II was an abomination even though he argued for the legitimacy of the internment as a government lawyer (Wechsler, 1959, p. 27; *Korematsu v. United States*, 1944).

In *Brown*, Wechsler struggled and failed to find a neutral principle at work. If one assumes that the separate school facilities for the different races are equal, he said—hardly a safe assumption—then segregation is not really a Fourteenth Amendment issue at all, but a freedom of association issue. How does one then choose between the African Americans who presumably want to associate with Whites and the Whites who would find such associations "unpleasant or repugnant"? Wechsler's argument is that the Court does not choose; this is a political decision that rests with the other branches of government. Wechsler, then, can be seen as making a legal process argument against what appears to be a decision that would make legal realists happy.

Wechsler's argument that the *Brown* case is really a First Amendment freedom-of-association controversy is intriguing because it seems to completely discount the social science data. The data are what make the case a Fourteenth Amendment issue because they show a pattern of discriminatory effect. Wechsler, in effect, said that the data do not exist in any legitimate way. The Court, he argued, should have looked to principles of law alone to solve the legal problem before it. If there were no principles that could lead to a neutral decision, the Court should have left the case alone and let legislative bodies deal with school segregation.

SOCIAL SCIENCE AND THE FIRST AMENDMENT

We see different legal philosophies at work in another debate over social science research in the sharply divided 1972 Supreme Court decision in *Branzburg v. Hayes*. In that case, the Supreme Court by a 5–4 vote rejected the idea that the First Amendment press clause required that journalists be excused from testifying before grand juries investigating crimes if that testimony would reveal the identity of a confidential source. Among other things, the Court said that the First Amendment did not create special rights for journalists that were not created for all citizens. The Court emphasized that all citizens had a duty to provide evidence when called, journalists included. Also, the Court worried that creating a qualified journalist's privilege grounded in the First Amendment would tie up the courts in frequent pretrial hearings over how to decide whether someone was a journalist and whether the government had proved that the material it sought was relevant to a case, important to the case, and unavailable elsewhere (*Branzburg v. Hayes*, 1972).

In support of its decision, the majority in *Branzburg* stated that it had not been shown any compelling empirical evidence to indicate that forcing journalists to testify before grand juries would harm relationships between reporters and sources (*Branzburg v. Hayes*, 1972). The word *compelling* is important here because the Court actually had been shown empirical data. A study by law professor Vince Blasi, combining both quantitative and qualitative methods—surveys and individual interviews— had found that most reporters did not perceive that the threat that they might be subpoenaed had any effect on their relationships with confidential sources. However, reporters who covered various activist and radical groups reported, anecdotally, that subpoenas or their specter did scare away their sources, who feared government repression (Blasi, 1971).

In his dissent in *Branzburg*, in which he was joined by Justices William Brennan and Thurgood Marshall, Justice Potter Stewart did not dispute the majority's interpretation of the Blasi study or suggest that its findings about the relationship between reporters and radicals should have been given more weight. Instead he questioned why the majority was even bringing up the question of empirical evidence:

The impairment of the flow of news cannot, of course, be proved with scientific precision, as the Court seems to demand. Obviously, not every news-gathering relationship requires confidentiality. And it is difficult to pinpoint precisely how many relationships do require a promise or understanding of nondisclosure. But we have never before demanded that First Amendment rights rest on elaborate empirical studies demonstrating beyond any conceivable doubt that deterrent effects exist; we have never before required proof of the exact number of people potentially affected by governmental action, who would actually be dissuaded from engaging in First Amendment activity. (*Branzburg v. Hayes*, 1972, p. 733)

Justice Stewart appeared to be making a somewhat formalist argument against using social science methods or theory to determine the extent of someone's rights. But looks can be deceiving. Elsewhere in the dissent, Justice Stewart sounded more like a realist or pragmatist when he described the logic that led him to dissent from the majority opinion. Journalists should have a qualified privilege to avoid compelled disclosure of their sources to protect the free flow of information to the public, he wrote. If a journalist's source cannot be confident that the journalist will keep a promise of confidentiality, the source will not provide information to the journalist. If the journalist does not receive information from the source, the journalist cannot share that information with the public. Thus, the free flow of information is, literally, cut off at the source.

Justice Stewart's objection to the *Branzburg* majority's decision and its reliance on a lack of empirical evidence is both grounded in the real world of journalists and in the real world of the law. The decision would hurt journalists in the search for truth and, by extension, the public, according to Justice Stewart. At the same time, the decision was not grounded in precedent: Never before, Justice Stewart argued, had the court sought empirical evidence to prove a First Amendment right should exist. His dissent shows flashes of both legal process theory and legal realism.

One striking feature of the Stewart dissent in *Branzburg* is the cast of characters attached to the dissent. All three justices who signed on to the dissent were members of the Warren Court (1953–1969), which welcomed social science evidence in *Brown v. Board of Education*. In fact, in the early 1950s, Justice Thurgood Marshall was an attorney and one of the authors of the Brandeis brief on behalf of the appellants. Given those credentials, how could Stewart, Brennan, and Marshall argue that the majority was wrong to look to empirical data for help in solving the legal problems posed in *Branzburg*?

Part of the answer may be found in the other *Branzburg* dissent by Justice William O. Douglas. In a passionately written argument, Justice Douglas argued that there should be an absolute privilege to prevent the government from subpoenaing journalists. He argued that such an absolute privilege was needed to preserve journalists' "preferred position" in the Constitution, which enabled them to inform the public about government activities (*Branzburg v. Hayes*, 1972).

Although the idea that journalists had a preferred position under the First Amendment was a minority viewpoint, the idea that the First Amendment was among a preferred set of rights was not. The famous footnote 4 in *United States v. Carolene Products* (1938), which suggested that the Supreme Court should be more protective of rights that aided people in fulfilling their political obligations, undoubtedly helped inspire Meiklejohn (1948) and others to write about the close connection between free speech and self-government and between all the expressive freedoms and the need to keep government in check (Blaşi, 1977). Without Meiklejohn there might not have been *New York Times v. Sullivan* (1964), the Supreme Court's landmark libel decision. In that case, according to Kalven (1964), the Court discovered the central meaning of the First Amendment: It protected people from being punished for criticizing their government or its leaders.

The idea that the First Amendment has a core of settled meaning in regard to political speech is respected even by those, like Judge Posner of the Seventh Circuit, who find fault with the way the courts have insulated speech from restrictions (Posner, 2003). What is not always clear is whether a particular utterance or activity falls within that settled meaning. For that reason, the issue before the Court in *Branzburg* may, in fact, not have an empirical answer, although other courts have demanded one as well (*United States v. Smith*, 1998). What the majority and dissenters are really arguing about is whether protecting journalists from having to reveal the names of sources to grand juries is necessary to safeguard the core values of the First Amendment. Deciding whether a particular claim or activity is a vital part of that settled meaning is not something easily determined by a survey or focus group. Such a decision is a matter of legal reasoning in its more traditional sense.

Yet once that initial decision has been made about whether a particular activity is closely related to the core of settled First Amendment meaning, there may be work for social science to do. If an activity is found not to be part of the core, and therefore not highly protected, social science data may be useful in determining how to strike a balance between the speech activity and competing values. Outside of the core, there is a wealth of speech activity that does not get the same protection as social and political speech. The Supreme Court has said that the First Amendment protects commercial speech (*Virginia State Board of Pharmacy v. Virginia Citizens Consumer Council*, 1976), corporate speech (*First National Bank of Boston v. Bellotti*, 1978), indecent speech (*Pacifica Foundation v. FCC*, 1978), and even hate speech (*R.A.V. v. City of St. Paul*, 1992) up to a point

(*Virginia v. Black*, 2003), but that all of these types of speech can be regulated to protect competing interests.

As Bunker and Perry (2004) pointed out, social science studies are often most useful when the degree of regulation of speech depends on its effect on the audience. But Bunker and Perry noted that, in regard to free speech, we often run into another philosophical problem: Are human beings exercising free will or is their behavior determined by outside forces? If humans use reason and free will to guide their actions, then regulation of speech and press to avoid bad behavior makes little sense, so we do not need studies trying to show a link between speech and behavior to decide whether regulation of speech is constitutional.

As Bunker and Perry noted, these issues were at the heart of two cases in which federal courts considered whether violent entertainment content was protected by the First Amendment. Courts considering whether movie and video game producers could be held partially liable for a student's deadly shooting spree in Kentucky determined that such entertainment was protected speech and that the plaintiffs could not collect damages unless they proved that the movie and game producers intentionally or negligently incited the shooting (*James v. Meow Media*, 2002). The U.S. Court of Appeals for the Sixth Circuit and the district court in that case largely ignored social science research about the effects of violent entertainment content and focused instead on the limitations of tort law regarding foreseeable harms (Bunker & Perry, 2004).

In the second case, a federal district court upheld an ordinance in St. Louis County, Missouri, that required parental consent before minors could buy, rent, or play violent video games (*Interactive Software Association v. St. Louis County*, 2002). The court in that case held that video games were not protected by the First Amendment, but assumed, for the sake of argument, that they were and applied strict scrutiny to the content-based regulation. Based in part on the testimony of two doctors and social scientific studies that the doctors cited noting a correlation between violent programming and violent acts, the court found that the county had a compelling interest in passing the ordinance (Bunker & Perry, 2004). However, the U.S. Court of Appeals for the Eighth Circuit reversed (*Interactive Digital Software Association v. St. Louis County*, 2003). The appellate court determined that video games were protected speech under the First Amendment and the ordinance could not survive strict scrutiny. In particular, the appellate court found that the lower court's reliance on social science data was faulty. A psychologist's testimony about a study he had done—finding that children viewing violent video games demonstrated more aggressive thoughts and behavior—was a "vague generality," the court said (*Interactive Digital Software*, 2003, pp. 958–959). Other studies cited by the county were "ambiguous, inconclusive, or irrelevant," the Eighth Circuit panel said (*Interactive Digital Software*, 2003, p. 959).

The violent-game cases point to a way in which social science research might be useful for people who want to restrict some types of content if the studies provide clear results. However, the problem with much of the empirical data on media effects is that there are conflicts and discrepancies, which are normal in research but disturbing to courts. For example, the U.S. Court of Appeals for the Seventh Circuit, in agreeing with a lower court that struck down an Indianapolis, Indiana, ordinance that barred the sale or production of pornography that "subjugated" women, said that it accepted the city's proposition that pornography contributed to a social climate in which women were discriminated against and made victims of sexual assaults (*American Booksellers Association, Inc. v. Hudnut*, 1985). However, in a footnote, the court noted that it meant only to say that it accepted the city's resolution of "disputed empirical questions" and noted that studies on the effects of pornography on its audience were contradictory and difficult to interpret (*American Booksellers Association*, 1985, p. 329). Although the court was sympathetic to the city's aims for intuitive reasons, that did not save the ordinance from being found impermissibly content-based. Whether clearer direction from the empirical data would have saved the ordinance is speculative, but it seems unlikely. Accepting empirical data in this case would have required the court to believe that men are not in control of their own actions, and other language in the court's opinion indicates that it would not have agreed with that supposition. For example, while noting that various other forms of "insidious" speech exist and have influences on the culture, the court said that such forms of speech had to be protected from government control so that government would not become the "great censor" of all thought (*American Booksellers Association*, 1985).

Although the uncertain nature of social science research often works in favor of those who want to protect a certain speech activity, it should be noted that the Supreme Court has been willing to accept, on much weaker empirical evidence (or none), restrictions on nonobscene sexual expression. For example, the Court has been willing to accept, without empirical proof of harm to property values or community morals, government restrictions on where adult businesses can set up shop (*City of Renton v. Playtime Theatres, Inc.*, 1986), nude dancing (*Barnes v. Glen Theatre*, 1991; *City of Erie v. Pap's A.M.*, 2000), and indecent material on the broadcast airwaves (*Pacifica Foundation v. FCC*, 1978). The Court has accepted on faith the idea that material that may be sold to adults legally may be obscene if shown to children (*Ginsberg v. New York*, 1968). Protecting children from exposure to sexual material and sexual exploitation has been at the heart of much of the court's jurisprudence without any particularized empirical findings to back up the concern. The Court recently indicated it was confining its concerns about children to the effects of viewing or making pornography when it struck down a federal law punishing those who produced Internet porn depicting sex acts involving digitally created images of minors (*Ashcroft v. Free Speech Coalition*, 2002). For that decision, the Court did not consider whether viewing such images might encourage pedophiles to act out their fantasies with real children. The Court confined its concerns about pornography's effect on children to the effect on children who actually participate in making sexually explicit material, not any possible effects that arise from an adult's viewing of works that do not depict real children. In none of this discussion does the Court majority consider citing or seeking empirical evidence about the effects of viewing child pornography on pedophiles.

In short, First Amendment law does not seem to be fertile ground for the discussion of social science data about media effects. Even when lower courts find empirical evidence persuasive, higher courts often dismiss such evidence in favor of more traditional considerations of First Amendment values and traditions. But is there a way to make social science data more attractive as evidence in First Amendment cases? This chapter concludes with a consideration of that question.

MAKING SOCIAL SCIENCE DATA ATTRACTIVE TO JUDGES IN FIRST AMENDMENT CASES

Traditional First Amendment jurisprudence is based on the concept that speech is an important individual right that needs broad protection from government restriction. This is particularly true of speech about political and social issues that resides at the core of settled meaning about First Amendment rights. Other types of speech are also protected by the First Amendment, but not to the same extent. Regulation of commercial, corporate, and indecent speech, among other types of expression, is allowed as long as the regulation does not cross certain jurisprudential lines in the sand, which vary according to type of speech.

How could social science research help change the way that judges view restrictions on speech? Conversely, how could such research help those who wish to protect speech from regulation? So far First Amendment law has been relatively immune to social science influences because many assumptions underlying First Amendment law—for example, that people have rational control over their own behaviors regardless of what media content they encounter—are in direct conflict with ideas underlying much of social science research. But there are ways that empirical data can be helpful for all sides in First Amendment disputes.

For those supporting regulation of speech activities, such as violent content in movies, TV shows, or games, longitudinal studies may be useful. Judges are skeptical of research data that show immediate changes in attitude after viewing violent content but do not address long-term effects on behavior. Likewise, in regard to the effect on viewers of sexual content, an inability of most studies to show long-term effects on behavior, rather than attitudes, dooms most studies from being useful.

Likewise, for those who oppose regulation of speech, research that shows no effects, or only slight effects, on behavior after the viewing of violent, sexual, or otherwise questionable media content would be helpful. If such research shows a lack of long-term effects from exposure to media content, that would refute claims of those seeking regulation or at least produce a stalemate that the courts would be reluctant to break one way or the other.

Of course social science data are already useful in the policymaking process of legislatures and regulatory agencies partly because those bodies can decide which data to rely on and find that one argument backed by research is stronger than another. But if the resulting regulation is challenged in court, judges may seek evidence stronger than disputed, weak, or contradictory empirical findings, as the U.S. Court of Appeals for the Seventh Circuit did in the Indianapolis pornography statute case. Attorneys who do not prepare for judicial challenges to empirical data may find that the data will not survive judicial scrutiny.

The good news for those who believe that social science should be used more often to help resolve legal problems is that many in the legal community apparently agree. Heise (2002) noted that a growing number of law schools are offering courses on social science research and interpretation. As already noted, Professor Timothy Zick noticed an increase in the number of Supreme Court opinions that favorably cite social science data. Although those trends have had little effect on First Amendment cases so far, it is likely that this trend will change over time, if for no other reason than that new communication technology continues to create the need for new policies. Those policies are often supported by research and, at the same time, challenged in the courts. If the quality of the research and legal arguments that back it improve, the Supreme Court will have to take notice. That will send an important signal to the lower courts. Whether that signal strengthens protection for free speech or weakens it depends, of course, on what the research shows.

REFERENCES

American Booksellers Association, Inc. v. Hudnut, 771 F.2d 323 (7th Cir. 1985).

Appendix to brief for appellants, *Brown v. Board of Education,* 347 U.S. 483 (1954) (Nos. 8, 101, 191, October 1952 term).

Arpan, L. M., & Raney, A. A. (2003). An experimental investigation of news source and the hostile media effect. *Journalism & Mass Communication Quarterly, 80,* 265–281.

Ashcroft v. Free Speech Coalition, 535 U.S. 234 (2002).

Barnes v. Glen Theatre, 501 U.S. 560 (1991).

Blasi, V. (1971). The newsman's privilege: An empirical study. *Michigan Law Review, 70,* 229–284.

Blasi, V. (1977). The checking value in First Amendment theory. *American Bar Foundation Research Journal, 3,* 521–649.

Branzburg v. Hayes, 408 U.S. 665 (1972).

Brown v. Board of Education, 347 U.S. 483 (1954).

Bunker, M. D., & Perry, D. K. (2004). Standing at the crossroads: Social science, human agency and free speech law. *Communication Law and Policy, 9,* 1–23.

City of Erie v. Pap's A. M., 529 U.S. 277 (2000).

City of Renton v. Playtime Theatres, Inc., 475 U.S. 41 (1986).

D'Alessio, D. (2003). An experimental examination of readers' perceptions of media bias. *Journalism & Mass Communication Quarterly, 80,* 282–294.

Delgado, R. (1994). First Amendment formalism is giving way to First Amendment legal realism. *Harvard Civil Rights-Civil Liberties Law Review, 29,* 169–174.

Eveland, W. P., Jr. (2003). A "mix of attributes" approach to the study of media effects and new communication technologies. *Journal of Communication, 53,* 395–410.

Feldman, S. M. (2000). *American legal thought from premodernism to postmodernism.* New York: Oxford University Press.

First National Bank of Boston v. Bellotti, 435 U.S. 765 (1978).

Fiss, O. M. (1996). *The irony of free speech.* Cambridge, MA: Harvard University Press.

Ginsberg v. New York, 390 U.S. 629 (1968).

Graber, M. (1991). *Transforming free speech.* Berkeley: University of California Press.

Gross, K., & Aday, S. (2003). The scary world in your living room and neighborhood: Using local broadcast news, neighborhood crime rates, and personal experience to test agenda setting and cultivation. *Journal of Communication, 53,* 411–426.

Heise, M. (2002). Empirical and experimental methods of law: The past, present, and future of empirical legal scholarship, judicial decision making and the new empiricism. *University of Illinois Law Review,* pp. 819–850.

Holmes, O. W. (1991). *The common law.* Mineola, NY: Dover. (Original work published 1881)

Interactive Digital Software Association v. St. Louis County, 329 F.3d 954 (8th Cir. 2003).

Interactive Software Association v. St. Louis County, 200 F. Supp. 2d 1126 (E.D. Mo. 2002), *rev'd,* 329 F.3d 954 (8th Cir. 2003).

James v. Meow Media, 300 F.3d 683 (6th Cir. 2002).

Kalven, H., Jr. (1964). New York Times v. Sullivan and the "central meaning" of the First Amendment. *Supreme Court Reporter,* pp. 191–221.

Korematsu v. United States, 323 U.S. 214 (1944).

Lang, A., Schwartz, N., Chung, Y., & Lee, S. (2004). Processing substance abuse messages: Production pacing, arousing content, and age. *Journal of Broadcasting & Electronic Media, 48,* 61–88.

Lasorsa, D. L. (2003). Question-order effects in surveys: The case of political interest, news attention, and knowledge. *Journalism and Mass Communication Quarterly, 80,* 499–512.

Lempert, R., & Sanders, J. (1986). *Law and social science.* New York: Longman.

Lochner v. New York, 198 U.S. 45 (1905).

MacKinnon, C. A. (1993). *Only words.* Cambridge, MA: Harvard University Press.

Mason, A. T. (1956). *Brandeis: A free man's life.* New York: Viking.

Meiklejohn, A. (1948). *Free speech and its relation to self-government.* New York: Harper.

Monahan, J., & Walker, L. (1991). Empirical questions without empirical answers. *Wisconsin Law Review,* pp. 569–594.

Muller v. Oregon, 208 U.S. 412 (1908).

New York Times v. Sullivan, 376 U.S. 254 (1964).

Pacifica Foundation v. FCC, 438 U.S. 726 (1978).

Paper, L. J. (1983). *Brandeis*. Englewood Cliffs, NJ: Prentice-Hall.

Posner, R. A. (2003). *Law, pragmatism, and democracy*. Cambridge, MA: Harvard University Press.

Ravaja, N. (2004). Effects of image motion on a small screen on emotion, attention, and memory: Moving-face versus static-face newscaster. *Journal of Broadcasting & Electronic Media, 48*, 108–133.

R.A.V. v. City of St. Paul, 505 U.S. 377 (1992).

Tsfati, Y., & Cohen, J. (2003). On the effect of the "third-person effect": Perceived influence of media coverage and residential mobility intentions. *Journal of Communication, 53*, 711–727.

United States v. Carolene Products, 304 U.S. 144 (1938).

United States v. Smith, 135 F.3d 963 (5th Cir. 1998).

Urofsky, M. I. (1981). *Louis D. Brandeis and the progressive tradition*. Boston: Little, Brown.

Virginia State Board of Pharmacy v. Virginia Citizens Consumer Council, 425 U.S. 748 (1976).

Virginia v. Black, 538 U.S. 343 (2003).

Wechsler, H. (1959). Toward neutral principles of constitutional law. *Harvard Law Review, 73*, 1–35.

Young, D. G. (2004). Late-night comedy in election 2000: Its influence on candidate trait ratings and the moderating effects of political knowledge and partisanship. *Journal of Broadcasting & Electronic Media, 48*, 1–22.

Zick, T. (2003). Constitutional empiricism: Quasi-neutral principles and constitutional truths. *North Carolina Law Review, 82*, 115–221.

Introductory Comments to Chapter 4

David Pritchard*

University of Wisconsin–Milwaukee

I had not re-read "A New Paradigm for Legal Research" in more than a decade before I sat down to write this introduction. I was curious to see whether its central argument—that research about media law should focus on the behavior of participants in communication-related disputes, rather than on interpretation of formal legal rules—had stood the test of time.

By most traditional measures, the article has not fared well. It was published in an out-of-the-way journal, it was not cited by another scholar until 12 years after it was published, and its call for bottom–up research about the lived experience of media law has had little impact. Nonetheless, I still like the article's point of view. A more sociological approach to media law would provide an understanding of how ordinary citizens and media workers act and react when media-related disputes arise. Such an understanding, in turn, would create the possibility of media-law courses that were more relevant to students who plan to seek careers in the media industries.

I will not rehash "A New Paradigm" here. However, I provide a few thoughts about how a more sociologically focused body of research

*"A New Paradigm for Legal Research" (Pritchard, 1986) originally appeared, without the author's introductory comments, in *Communications and the Law, 8*, 51–67. In the original article that follows, "the author acknowledge[d] his gratitude to Everette Dennis, Robert Drechsel, and Bradford Scharlott for comments and suggestions on an earlier version of this article."

39

might change how media law is taught in journalism and mass communication programs in the United States.

An often overlooked point is that we know very little about the kinds of legal questions mass communicators encounter most frequently. Large chunks of media-law textbooks are devoted to censorship and libel. The implication is that censorship and libel often surface in the lives of people who work in the media.

But they probably do not. One of the few scholars to have asked media workers about the legal issues they deal with most commonly is Craig Sanders, who found that Indiana daily newspapers consulted lawyers far more frequently about access-to-information issues than they did about libel (Sanders, 2000). Censorship was barely on the radar screen. Given that there are about 120,000 journalists in the United States (Weaver & Wilhoit, 1996) and only 14 libel trials in 2003 (Libel Defense Resource Center, 2004), it is difficult to make the case that libel is a central concern of today's American journalists.

Granted, Sanders' study was limited to daily newspapers in one state. Broader studies of the most common legal problems in other forms of journalism and other forms of media work such as advertising and public relations are needed. Unfortunately, few scholars are conducting research in these areas.

Although libel may not be a fixture in the daily lives of media workers, when libel does strike it can be very serious. Because of the potential impact of a libel suit on media organizations, there have been some efforts to understand libel sociologically. The most prominent among these is the Iowa Libel Research Project (Bezanson, Cranberg, & Soloski, 1987), which analyzed all of the libel and privacy cases reported over a 10-year period. Perhaps the most innovative aspect of the Project's research was its interviews with plaintiffs and defendants to find out why the plaintiffs had decided to file a lawsuit and what, if anything, the media could have done to avoid the lawsuit.

The beauty of studying court cases is that their participants are named and relatively easy to locate. However, studies of people involved in court cases cannot avoid excluding all of the potential libel plaintiffs who were harmed by something they considered to be false in a media report, but who did not sue.

Such people are hard to locate; research involving them can be costly and time-consuming. I conducted a small study of these potential plaintiffs (Pritchard, 2000), finding them to be upset at how they had been portrayed in the media, but also finding that in many cases they blamed themselves for the harm the story had caused to them and to relationships with friends and family members. A related study by Nemeth (2000) examined how a daily newspaper dealt with the kinds of complaints that the Iowa Libel Research Project said could erupt into libel suits.

The studies I mentioned are limited in various ways, but each contributes to a greater understanding of the legal context of news. In addition, the studies have implications for how media law might be taught, if indeed one of the goals of teaching media law is to prepare students for careers in the media industries. Libel might merit a smaller role in media-law textbooks and syllabi than is now the case. Access-to-information issues, especially those dealing with state law regarding open meetings and public records, might merit more attention.

The barriers to a more sociologically oriented understanding of media law are many. The research required to gain such an understanding is costly. The institution-centered paradigm is well entrenched, both in doctoral programs and textbooks. There is more status in interpreting decisions of the U.S. Supreme Court than in talking to average citizens or media workers.

However, those barriers are not insurmountable, and perhaps a new generation of scholars will find this volume's republication of "A New Paradigm" to be thought-provoking.

REFERENCES

Bezanson, R., Cranberg, G., & Soloski, J. (1987). *Libel law and the press: Myth and reality.* New York: The Free Press.

Libel Defense Resource Center. (2004). *Annual study of media law trials shows 14 trials in 2003, with media winning 57 percent* (Press release). Retrieved August 27, 2004, from www.ldrc.com/Press_Releases/bull2004-1.html

Nemeth, N. (2000). How a typical American newspaper handles complaints. In D. Pritchard (Ed.), *Holding the media accountable: Citizens, ethics, and the law* (pp. 42–54). Bloomington, IN: Indiana University Press.

Pritchard, D. (2000). Why unhappy subjects of news coverage rarely complain. In D. Pritchard (Ed.), *Holding the media accountable: Citizens, ethics, and the law* (pp. 27–41). Bloomington, IN: Indiana University Press.

Sanders, C. (2000). Newspapers use of lawyers in the editorial process. In D. Pritchard (Ed.), *Holding the media accountable: Citizens, ethics, and the law* (pp. 138–153). Bloomington, IN: Indiana University Press.

Weaver, D. H., & Wilhoit, G. C. (1996). *The American journalist in the 1990s: U.S. news people at the end of an era.* Mahwah, NJ: Lawrence Erlbaum Associates.

A New Paradigm for Legal Research

David Pritchard

"The Parisian police," he said, "are exceedingly able in their way. They are persevering, ingenious, cunning, and thoroughly versed in the knowledge which their duties seem chiefly to demand. Thus, when G detailed to us his mode of searching the premises at the Hotel D, I felt entire confidence in his having made a satisfactory investigation so far as his labors extended."

"So far as his labors extended?" said I.

"Yes," said Dupin. "The measures adopted were not only the best of their kind, but carried out to absolute perfection. Had the letter been deposited within the range of their search, these fellows would, beyond a question, have found it."

I merely laughed, but he seemed quite serious in all that he said.

"The measures, then," he continued "were good in their kind and well executed; their defect lay in their being inapplicable to the case and to the man. . . ."

—from "The Purloined Letter" by Edgar Allan Poe[1]

Communication-law scholars whose interests extend beyond legal doctrine and philosophy to real-world problems have a problem similar to that of G, the unnamed prefect of police in "The Purloined Letter."

---

[1]Edgar Allan Poe, *The Purloined Letter*, in FOURTEEN GREAT DETECTIVE STORIES (Vincent Starrett ed. 1928).

In each case, the (re)search method rests upon questionable, often-implicit assumptions about behavior. For example, G assumed that thieves store contraband in secret places. Had the assumption been correct, the police search of all possible hiding spots in the Hotel D would have turned up the purloined letter.

A similarly questionable, but typically implicit, assumption is often made by communication-law scholars: that formal law and formal law-making institutions influence in important ways the behavior of a significant number of journalists and other mass communicators, their organizations, and the people they deal with (news sources, subjects of stories, other audience members, and government officials, to name a few). To the extent that this assumption is valid, traditional communication-law research can help describe, explain, and predict the behavior of mass communicators and the people they deal with. To the extent that the assumption is invalid, however, traditional communication-law research adds little to the understanding of mass communication behavior.

Accordingly, it is important to examine the validity of the empirical assumptions, implicit or explicit, that provide the framework for communication-law research. After all, such assumptions determine not only where to look for answers to research questions, but also what methods are appropriate to the search.

This article suggests that the set of postulates and assumptions that guide traditional communication-law research can be considered—at least heuristically—a paradigm in the Kuhnian sense.[2] The article also offers an alternate paradigm. Specifically, the first section attempts to sketch the paradigm that structures most teaching and research in communication law. The second section points out some of the flaws of the current paradigm and outlines the alternative. The third section discusses some theoretical and methodological implications of a paradigm shift and suggests ways the alternate paradigm could be applied to pressing questions in communication law.

Underlying this article's arguments is the notion that legal research in mass communication should be scientific. Research methods should be grounded in theory; theories should be based upon available knowledge about how the world works. It is knowledge about how the world really works, rather than opinions about how it could or should work, that lead to a more profound understanding of how law and society influence each other. In addition, such research would be all the more useful to

---

[2]THOMAS S. KUHN, *The Structure of Scentific Revolutions* (2d ed. 1970).

communication-law scholars' constituencies in the journalistic and legal professions.

In other words, this article has an empirical bias, which seems like a reasonable prejudice for people who hope to make correct statements about the role law plays in mass communication. As fellow scholar Sherlock Holmes said to the befuddled Dr. Watson in "A Scandal in Bohemia": "It is a capital mistake to theorise before one has data. Insensibly one begins to twist facts to suit theories, instead of theories to suit facts."[3]

Facts suggest theories, which can be tested by research methods appropriate to the question at hand. The results of such tests may lead to modification of theory, with the ultimate goal of greater understanding of how the world works.

I. THE EXISTING PARADIGM

Kuhn's concept of "normal science" is cited fairly often these days. Legal scholars[4] as well as communication researchers[5] talk about normal science, generally disparagingly.

Kuhn defines normal science as "research firmly based upon one or more past scientific achievements, achievements that some particular scientific community acknowledges for a time as supplying the foundation for its further practice."[6] This means that the research methods and the often-implicit theoretical assumptions that have led to the past achievements will continue to be the tools of normal science. As such, they constitute the received paradigm of a given discipline.

Research and instruction in communication law are guided by such a paradigm. Traditionally, such activity focuses on the work of formal legal institutions—especially appellate courts. The typical research method is textual analysis of legal rules, although quantitative analysis of various attributes of legal institutions and legal decision-makers is not uncommon.

---

[3]Arthur Conan Doyle, *A Scandal in Bohemia*, in THE ADVENTURES OF SHERLOCK HOLMES (1982).

[4]*E.g.*, Mark V. Tushnet, *Deviant Science in Constitutional Law*, 59 TEX. L. REV. 815-28 (1981).

[5]*E.g.*, John L Hochheimer, *Reductionists and Political Communication Research: The Gaps Between Conduct and Utility*, 8, No. 1 JOURNAL OF COMMUNICATION INQUIRY 1-19 (1984); W. Lance Bennett, Lynne A. Gressett, and William Haltom, *Repairing the News: A Case Study of the News Paradigm*, 35, No. 2 JOURNAL OF COMMUNICATION 50-68 (1985).

[6]Kuhn, *supra* note 2, at 10.

That legal institutions provide the framework for research under the existing paradigm is apparent from how law and legal research methods are taught in journalism and mass communication programs. Such considerations are revealing, because textbooks and graduate training in research methods are the principal means by which a paradigm is passed from one generation of scholars to the next.[7]

The leading texts in communication law[8] focus almost exclusively on court opinions to teach students about what the law is and what it means. Four of the texts are more or less casebooks along the traditional law-school model;[9] they rely heavily on excerpts from appellate court opinions. In addition, instructors of mass communication law courses generally use the case-law approach outlined in the texts, according to a recent survey of how law is taught in American journalism programs.[10] And the two texts that offer sections on legal research (or a variant of that theme such as "Finding the Law") do little more than tell students how to find the opinions of courts and other judicial bodies.[11]

In short, teaching in communication law follows an institution-centered paradigm. The paradigm defines as appropriate subjects for study the work of society's formal law-making or law-interpreting institutions—generally courts or judges, but also administrative bodies and legislatures. As such, communication law is taught the same way basic subjects are taught in most American law schools.[12]

As might be expected, graduate training in communication law research methods also follows the traditional law-school model. Students in many graduate communication law classes are advised to buy methods books written for students in law schools,[13] despite the fact that such

---

[7]*Id.* at 10-11.

[8]T. Barton Carter, Marc A. Franklin, and Jay B. Wright, The First Amendment and the Fourth Estate (3d ed. 1985); William E. Francois, Mass Media Law and Regulation (3d ed. 1982); Marc A. Franklin, Cases and Materials on Mass Media Law (2d ed. 1982); Donald M. Gillmor & Jerome A. Barron, Mass Communication Law: Cases & Comment (4th ed. 1984); Harold L Nelson & Dwight L Teeter, Jr., Law of Mass Communications: Freedom and Control of Print and Broadcast Media (4th ed. 1982); Wayne Overbeck & Rick D. Pullen, Major Principles of Media Law (2d ed. 1985); and Don R. Pember, Mass Media Law (3d ed. 1984).

[9]Carter *et al.*, *supra* note 8; Franklin, *supra* note 8; Gillmor & Barron, *supra* note 8; Nelson & Teeter, *supra* note 8.

[10]Copies of the survey are available from Judy Lynch, Graduate School of Journalism, University of California, Berkeley, California.

[11]Gillmor & Barron, *supra* note 8; Overbeck & Pullen, *supra* note 8.

[12]John Henry Schlegel, Searching for Archimedes—Legal Education, Legal Scholarship, and Liberal Ideology, 34 Journal of Legal Education 103-10 (1984); Mark Tushnet, Legal Scholarship: Its Causes and Cure, 90 Yale L. J. 1205-1223 (1981).

[13]Morris L. Cohen, Legal Research in a Nutshell (3d ed. 1978); William P. Statsky, Legal Research, Writing and Analysis: Some Starting Points (2d ed. 1982).

books do not deal specifically with communication law and despite the fact that students in graduate programs in mass communications are not being trained to practice law.

The best overview of research methods in communication law can be found in book chapters by Gillmor and Dennis.[14] Although Gillmor and Dennis define their subject in a traditional manner, they take a broad view of acceptable methods of analyzing legal materials. They devote several pages of the 1981 chapter to what they call "empirical and behavioral legal research in mass communication."[15]

The quantitative strategies mentioned in those several pages, however, hew closely to the existing paradigm's focus on formal legal institutions. For example, Gillmor and Dennis discuss studies that attempt to explain the behavior of judges[16] and that examine news coverage of judicial institutions.[17] Other communication-law scholars who have advocated quantitative methods also hang on to the institution-centered approach.[18]

Accordingly, it is no surprise that much of the quantitative research in communication law has focused on the judiciary or other law-making institutions.[19] Also closely related to the institutional paradigm

---

[14]Donald M. Gillmor & Everette E. Dennis, *Legal Research and Judicial Communication*, in POLITICAL COMMUNICATION: ISSUES AND STRATEGIES FOR RESEARCH (Steven H. Chaffee ed. 1975); Donald M. Gillmor & Everette E. Dennis, *Legal Research in Mass Communication*, in RESEARCH METHODS IN MASS COMMUNICATION (Guido H. Stempel III and Bruce H. Westley eds. 1981). The 1981 chapter largely supersedes the earlier one.

[15]Gillmor & Dennis, Legal Research in Mass Communication, *supra* note 14, at 330-37.

[16]*Id.* at 334.

[17]*Id.* at 330.

[18]*E.g.*, George E. Padgett, *First Amendment Research: Data Analysis Reduces the "Guess-work."* 10 No. 3 MASS COMM. REVIEW 2-5, 22 (1983); Thomas Schwartz, *A Call for Alternative Approaches to Research in Communication Law.* 11, No. 4 MEDIA LAW NOTES 1-3 (1984). For general overview on how quantitative methods can be used to shed light on traditional legal issues, see WALLACE D. LOH, SOCIAL RESEARCH IN THE JUDICIAL PROCESS: CASES, READINGS, AND TEXT (1984) and JOHN MONAHAN & LAURENS WALKER, SOCIAL SCIENCE IN LAW: CASES AND MATERIALS (1985).

[19]*E.g.*, Douglas A. Anderson & Marianne Murdock, *Effects of Communication Law Decisions on Daily Newspaper Editors*, 58 JOURNALISM QUARTERLY 525–28, 534 (1981); Marc A. Franklin, *Winners and Losers and Why: A Study of Defamation Litigation*, AMERICAN BAR FOUNDATION RESEARCH JOURNAL 455–500 (1980); Marc A. Franklin, *Suing the Media for Libel: A Litigation Study*, AMERICAN BAR FOUNDATION RESEARCH JOURNAL 795–831 (1981); Cecilie Gaziano, *Relationship Between Public Opinion and Supreme Court Decisions: Was Mr. Dooley Right?* 5 COMMUNICATION RESEARCH 131–49 (1978); F. Dennis Hale, *State Press Law Provisions and State Demographics*, 6, No.3 COMMUNICATIONS AND THE LAW 31–38 (1984); Achal Mehra, *Newsmen's Privilege: An Empirical Study*, 59 JOURNALISM QUARTERLY 560–65 (1982); Gerald R. Miller *et al.*, *Methodological Issues in Legal Communication Research: What Can Trial Simulations Tell Us?* 50 COMMUNICATION MONOGRAPHS 33–46 (1983); and Guido H. Stempel III, *A Guttman Scale Analysis of the Burger Court's Press Decisions*, 59 JOURNALISM QUARTERLY 256–59 (1982).

are empirical studies focusing on problems defined as significant by major legal institutions. Very little empirical research on the effects of pretrial publicity was conducted before the Supreme Court's decision in the
Sam Sheppard case.[20] In the years immediately following, however,
scores of studies on the topic were published.[21] A similar phenomenon,
though on a much smaller scale, took place with respect to cameras in
the courtroom after states began widespread experiments in the mid-
1970s.[22]

The point of this quick and admittedly incomplete review is to demonstrate that the existing paradigm for teaching and research in communication law limits scholarly inquiry to matters that deal directly with the
work of society's formal law-making institutions. Gillmor and Dennis
reinforce the point. While acknowledging that research focusing on areas
other than formal institutions might result in "a better understanding of
law and legal institutions," they nonetheless contend that "this is not legal research per se."[23]

In stark outline, then, there is the existing paradigm. Legal rules and
the institutions that produce them are worthy of study by communication-law scholars. Specifically defined as *outside* the field of the communication-law scholar are areas of research that could add to an understanding of how law actually works.

II. AN ALTERNATIVE PARADIGM

If communication-law research were intended to be nothing more than
the study of philosophy or moral principles, its focus on legal rules
and institutions would be appropriate. This article assumes, however,

---

[20]*Sheppard v. Maxwell*, 384 U.S. 333 (1966).

[21]For reviews of the research, *see* Judith M. Buddenbaum *et al.*, "Pretrial Publicity and
Juries: A Review of Research," SCHOOL OF JOURNALISM RESEARCH REPORT 11, Indiana University, 1981; FREE PRESS AND FAIR TRIAL SOME DIMENSIONS OF THE PROBLEM (Chilton R. Bush ed.
1970); Mary M. Connors, *Prejudicial Publicity: An Assessment*, 41 JOURNALISM MONOGRAPHS
(1975); Walter Wilcox, *The Press, the Jury and the Behavioral Sciences*, 9 JOURNALISM
MONOGRAPHS (1968).

[22]Susanna Barber, *The Problem of Prejudice: A New Approach to Assessing the Impact of
Courtroom Cameras*, 66 JUDICATURE 248–55 (1983); James L. Hoyt, *Courtroom Coverage: The
Effects of Being Televised*, 21 JOURNAL OF BROADCASTING 487–95 (1977); Dalton Lancaster,
Cameras in the Courtroom: A Study of Two Trials, SCHOOL OF JOURNALISM RESEARCH REPORT 14,
Indiana University, 1984; Kermit Netteburg, *Does Research Support the Estes Ban on Cameras
in the Courtroom?* 63 JUDICATURE 466–75 (1980); and Dan Slater & Valerie P. Hans, *Method-
ological Issues in the Evaluation of Experiments with Cameras in the Courts*, 30 COMMUNICATION
QUARTERLY 376–80 (1982).

[23]Gillmor & Dennis, *Legal Research in Mass Communication*, supra note 14, at 321.

that communication-law scholars want to do—and should do—more, such as contributing to basic knowledge about how law and society affect each other, for example, and helping journalists and others avoid media-related disputes (or at least resolve them before they get to court).

A close look at the reality of how media-related disputes arise will help set the context for this article's discussion of the flaws of the existing paradigm. The process will be illustrated by reference to a situation in which someone is unhappy about something that has been published about him or her. In theory, such a situation could lead to a lawsuit alleging libel, invasion of privacy, intentional or negligent infliction of emotional distress, or a combination of those or related torts. It is important to note, though, that the process to be outlined is not limited to libel-like situations. It could easily be adapted to other kinds of media-related disputes (e.g., access to information, Fairness Doctrine matters).

A dispute must be born and then survive a complex process of dispute definition and processing before it can reach a court of law. Although the prelitigation phases of the disputing process have received some attention from communication-law scholars, the descriptive work[24] has jumped quickly from the initial grievance to consulting an attorney. Other work has been prescriptive in nature.[25] And though some journalism texts have diagrams of the legal process in them,[26] such diagrams focus only on the formal legal process. In sum, communication law's current emphasis on the formal stages of the disputing process obscures the subtlety and complexity of what people do when they are unhappy with how they have been portrayed by the media.

Recent scholarship in nonmedia contexts, however, reveals several stages in the disputing process that have been ignored by communication scholars.[27] These stages of the process are worth considering in some de-

---

[24]E.g., MARC A. FRANKLIN, THE DYNAMICS OF AMERICAN LAW: COURTS, THE LEGAL PROCESS, AND FREEDOM OF EXPRESSION 1-191 (1968); Randal P. Bezanson, Gilbert Cranberg, and John Soloski, Libel Law and the Press: Setting Record Straight, 71 IOWA L. REV. 215-33 (1985).

[25]E.g., Everette E. Dennis, The Press and the Public Interest: A Definitional Dilemma, 23 DE PAUL L. REV. 937-60 (1974).

[26]E.g., GEORGE S. HAGE et al., New Strategies for Public Affairs Reporting: Investigation, Interpretation & Research 321-25 (2d ed. 1983).

[27]William L. F. Felstiner, Richard L. Abel, and Austin Sarat, The Emergence and Transformation of Disputes: Naming, Blaming, Claiming. .. 15 LAW & SOCIETY REV. 631-54 (1981); Jeffrey Fitzgerald, A Comparative Empirical Study of Potential Disputes in Australia and the United States, Working Paper 1982-4, Disputes Processing Research Program, University of Wisconsin Law School, 1982; Jack Ladinsky, Stewart Macaulay, and Jill Anderson, The Milwaukee Dispute Mapping Project: A Preliminary Report, Working Paper 1979-3, Disputes Processing Research Program, University of Wisconsin Law School, 1979; Jack Ladinsky & Charles Susmilch, Conceptual and Operational Issues in Meas-

tail. As we move through the several steps of the process, which is dia-
grammed in [Figure 4.1], keep in mind the hypothetical potential plaintiff
in a possible libel-like situation.

Step 1. Unless a media organization publishes information about the
potential plaintiff, no actionable dispute of the kind mentioned above
arises. Before such a dispute can arise, then, material about the potential
plaintiff must be published by a news organization.

Step 2. If a media organization publishes an item about a person, a
potential dispute is born only if the person has some kind of problem
with the item. A "problem" occurs when the subject of a published item
"senses that something is amiss."[28] This is the stage of the disputing
process that Felstiner *et al.* call "naming."[29] In other words, the person is
somehow unhappy with how he or she has been portrayed by the media
organization. Of course, if the person mentioned in the item has no problem with how he or she was portrayed, there is no dispute.

Step 3. People who are unhappy with how they have been portrayed
in the media may or may not perceive that they have a *grievance* against
the media organization. A grievance, according to Ladinsky and
Susmilch, is "a belief that one has a right, an entitlement, to corrective action with regard to a problem."[30] It is the stage of the process that
Felstiner *et al.* call "blaming."[31]

Step 2 and Step 3 are conceptually distinct; there are all sorts of reasons why people who are unhappy with how they have been portrayed
in the media might not perceive that they have a grievance. For example,
they may perceive that the problem is their fault, not the fault of the media, or they may perceive that they have no right to second-guess media
judgments about how to portray people. Felstiner *et al.*[32] and Coates and
Penrod[33] discuss these and similar theoretical issues in some depth.

---

uring Consumer Disputing Behavior, Working Paper 1981-3, Disputes Processing Research
Program, University of Wisconsin Law School, 1981; Jack Ladinsky & Charles Susmilch,
Community Factors in the Brokerage of Consumer Product and Service Problems, Working
Paper 1983-14, Disputes Processing Research Program, University of Wisconsin Law
School, 1983; Lynn Mather & Barbara Yngvesson, *Language, Audience, and the Transforma-
tion of Disputes*, 15 LAW & SOCIETY REV. 775-821 (1981); and Richard E. Miller & Austin
Sarat, *Grievances, Claims, and Disputes: Assessing the Adversary Culture*, 15 LAW & SOCIETY
REV. 525-65 (1981).

[28]Ladinsky & Susmilch, Conceptual and Operational Issues, *supra* note 27, at 2.

[29]Felstiner, Abel, and Sarat, *Naming, Blaming, and Claiming . . .* , *supra* note 27.

[30]Ladinsky & Susmilch, Conceptual and Operational Issues, *supra* note 27, at 2.

[31]Felstiner, Abel, and Sarat, *Naming, Blaming, and Claiming . . .* , *supra* note 27.

[32]Id.

[33]Dan Coates & Steven Penrod, *Social Psychology and the Emergence of Disputes*, 15 LAW &
SOCIETY REV. 655-80 (1981).

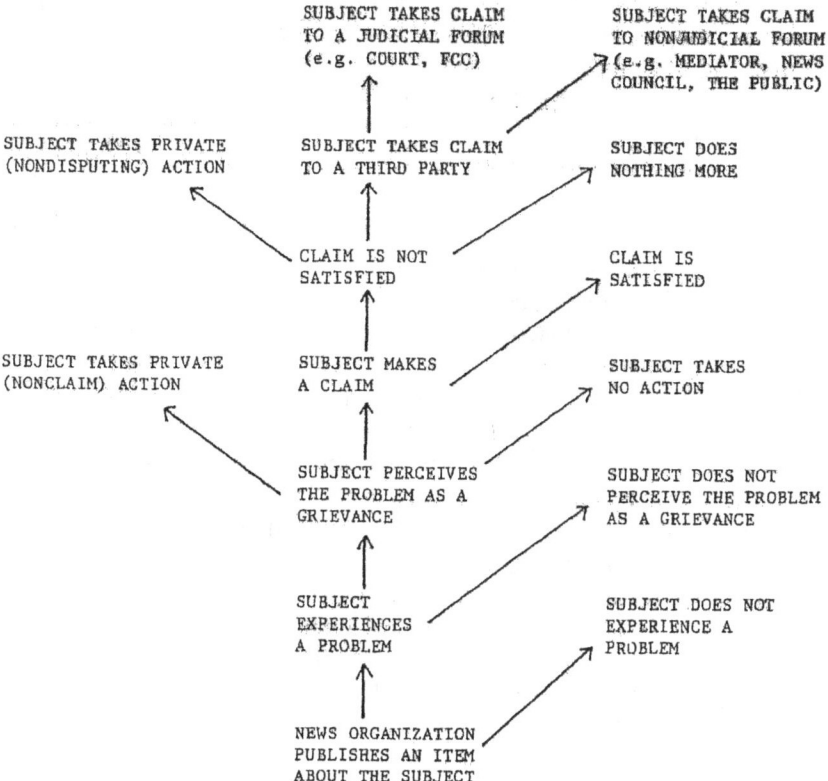

FIG. 4.1. Possible path from being mentioned in a news story to asserting in a judicial forum that the story injured you.

Step 4. It cannot be assumed that all people who perceive that they have a grievance against the media will actually make a *claim* for redress of that grievance. Making a claim (by seeking a correction, retraction, or other compensation from the media organization) is only one of three possible courses of action: taking no action at all and taking private (nonclaim) action are the other two possibilities.

Taking no action needs little explanation. The person who thinks he or she has a grievance may decide (for whatever reason) not to pursue the matter. Ladinsky and Susmilch use the phrase "lumpits" to describe such people.[34]

Taking private, or nonclaim, action happens when people who perceive they have a grievance do something on their own to gain satisfaction. Examples might include canceling their subscriptions to the news-

---

[34]Ladinsky & Susmilch, Conceptual and Operational Issues, *supra* note 27.

paper that portrayed them in a way they didn't like, stealing issues of the offending newspaper from a coin-operated box, or merely making disparaging comments about the media organization to friends and acquaintances.

In any case, a dispute dies if the person who perceives himself or herself as aggrieved fails to make a claim. It should be noted that consumer research suggests that most people do not distinguish between the grievance and the claiming stages of the process.[35] Because the two are conceptually distinct, however, both have been kept in this model.

Step 5. If a person makes a claim against the offending media organization and receives satisfaction, the dispute ends. Satisfaction does not mean that the person who made a claim received exactly what he or she asked for. It means only that the aggrieved subject would say he or she was satisfied with the media organization's response to the claim. Only if the person is unhappy with the organization's response to the claim does the dispute stay alive.

Step 6. If the media organization fails to satisfy the subject's claim, any of three things may happen. First, the subject may decide not to pursue the matter. Ladinsky and Susmilch call such people "clumpits," because they have made a claim before deciding to "lump it."[36] Second, the subject may take private action, similar to the private action described in Step 4 above. Third, the subject may take his or her unsatisfied claim to a third party for resolution. It is only such unsatisfied claims that survive to the next step in the disputing process.

Step 7. People who take unsatisfied claims to third parties for resolution must choose the forum in which they want their claims to be heard. The choices can be viewed either as governmental forums (courts, administrative agencies, etc.) or as nongovernmental forums (news councils or appeals to the public).

Unsatisfied claims that are taken to private third parties seldom find their way into law books. Only the disputes that survive the several informal stages of the disputing process end up in courts, thus becoming acceptable grist for the communication-law-research mill.

No research is available to tell us what proportion of media-related disputes survive past Step 7 of the process and find their way to the courts, although the proportion probably is "tiny."[37] Empirical research

---

[35]Id.

[36]Id.

[37]Herbert v. Lando *et al.*, 441 U.S. 153 (1979).

in areas not related to mass communication, however, suggests that the proportion of disputes that gets to court is quite small.[38] There is no reason to believe that media-related disputes are so different from other kinds that a large proportion of them gets to court.

Nor is there any research to indicate how representative of all media-related disputes are those that actually get to court. But research in other areas indicates that formally litigated disputes are systematically different from disputes that do not go to court,[39] and there is no reason to believe similar differences do not exist with media-related disputes.

Research suggests that whether disputes survive to the litigation stage of the disputing process depends on a variety of nonlegal factors, including the nature of the relationship between the disputants;[40] the power differential between the disputants;[41] the differences between the resources available to each;[42] and the nature of the dispute itself, among other factors.[43] Even in the relatively rare cases when disputes do end up before a court, there is no guarantee that judges and/or juries will follow

---

[38]Arthur Best & Alan R. Andreasen, *Consumer Response to Unsatisfactory Purchases: A Survey of Perceiving Defects, Voicing Complaints, and Obtaining Redress*, 11 LAW & SOCIETY REV. 701-42 (1977); Fitzgerald, A Comparative Empirical Study of Potential Disputes, *supra* note 27; Ladinsky & Susmilch, Community Factors, *supra* note 27; David M. Trubek *et al.*, *The Costs of Ordinary Litigation*, 31 UCLA L REV. 72-127 (1983).

[39]Felstiner, Abel, and Sarat, *Naming, Blaming, and Claiming . . .* , *supra* note 27; Fitzgerald, A Comparative Empirical Study of Potential Disputes, *supra* note 27; Ladinsky & Susmilch, *Community Factors*, *supra* note 27; and David M. Trubek *et al.*, *The Costs of Ordinary Litigation*, *supra* note 38; See also LAWRENCE M. FRIEDMAN & STEWART MACAULAY, LAW AND THE BEHAVIORAL SCIENCES (2d ed. 1977); Marc Galanter, *Reading the Landscape of Disputes: What We Know and Don't Know (and Think We Know) About Our Allegedly Contentious and Litigious Society*, 31 UCLA L. REV. 4-71 (1983); Herbert Jacob, *Trial Courts in the United States: The Travails of Exploration*, 17 LAW & SOCIETY REV. 407-23 (1983); Stewart Macaulay, *Law and the Behavioral Sciences: Is There Any There There?* 6 LAW AND POLICY 149-87 (1984); George L. Priest & Benjamin Klein, *The Selection of Disputes for Litigation*, 13 JOURNAL OF LEGAL STUDIES 1-55 (1984); C. Neal Tate, *The Methodology of Judicial Behavior Research: A Review and Critique*, 5 POLITICAL BEHAVIOR 51-82 (1983); and EUGENE J. WEBB *et al.*, UNOBTRUSIVE MEASURES: NONREACTIVE RESEARCH IN THE SOCIAL SCIENCES (1966).

[40]FRANKLIN, THE DYNAMICS OF AMERICAN LAW, *supra* note 24, at 190; Sally Falk Moore, *Law and Social Change: The Semi-Autonomous Social Field as an Appropriate Subject of Study*, 7 LAW & SOCIETY REV. 719-46 (1973)·

[41]Stewart Macaulay, An Empirical View of Contract, Working Paper 1984-8, Disputes Processing Research Program, University of Wisconsin Law School, 1984.

[42]For a candid view of resource power from a lawyer for a media corporation, see George Freeman, *A Lawyer in the Newsroom*, Times Company Report (News about the People of The New York Times Company), August 1985, at 6, 8.

[43]See Felstiner, Abel, and Sarat, *Naming, Blaming, and Claiming . . .* , *supra* note 27; Ladinsky & Susmilch, Community Factors, *supra* note 27; and David M. Trubek *et al.*, *The Costs of Ordinary Litigation*, *supra* note 38, for in-depth discussions of factors that influence whether a dispute takes a judicial trajectory.

the applicable legal rules.[44] And at the appellate court level, knowledge of how a court acted in one situation is not of much help in predicting how another court will act when faced with a similar dispute.[45]

Finally, it is fairly clear that most Americans lack basic knowledge of the legal system,[46] that a surprising number of reporters are ignorant of such fundamental information as whether their states have shield laws,[47] and that the social and legal impact of court decisions cannot be assumed.[48] In short, existing research in dispute processing and other areas suggests:

- That Americans generally, and journalists specifically, are not particularly knowledgeable about the laws that apply to them;
- That relatively few disputes end up in courts;
- That those that do end up in courts are not representative of disputes generally;
- That the reasons some disputes end up in court, but others do not, have little to do with legal rules;
- That, in the few cases that do go to court, judges and/or juries may not follow established legal rules;
- That *stare decisis* is an uncertain predictor of future outcomes; and
- That the impact of court decisions will vary from case to case.

If these conclusions are correct, then the existing paradigm's exclusive focus on legal rules and the institutions that make them fails to account for factors that are vitally important to understanding the reality of disputes. As Macaulay notes: "The received picture may reassure those who do not look closely, but empirical inaccuracy is a poor base for serious thought about the system."[49] Even such a traditional scholar as Thomas Emerson has noted that "(t)hose who warn us not to rely too much on legal forms are entirely correct that excessive emphasis can easily be placed on the role of law."[50]

---

[44]OVERBECK & PULLEN, *supra* note 8; PEMBER, *supra* note 8.

[45]JEROME FRANK, COURTS ON TRIAL: MYTH AND REALITY IN AMERICAN JUSTICE (1949); David Kairys, *Legal Reasoning*, in THE POLITICS OF LAW: A PROGRESSIVE CRITIQUE (David Kairys ed. 1982).

[46]THE AMERICAN PUBLIC, THE MEDIA & THE JUDICIAL SYSTEM: A NATIONAL SURVEY ON PUBLIC AWARENESS AND PERSONAL EXPERIENCE (1983).

[47]Vince Blasi, *Press Subpoenas: An Empirical and Legal Analysis*, 70 MICH. L. REV. 229-89 (1971).

[48]See F. Dennis Hale, *Impact Analysis of the Law Concerning Freedom of Expression*, in this issue of *Communications and the Law*.

[49]Stewart Macaulay, An Empirical View of Contract, *supra* note 41, at i.

[50]Thomas I. Emerson, The System of Freedom of Expression 5 (1970).

Despite such warnings, communication-law teachers and researchers continue to focus on appellate courts and legal rules. For example, although Carter *et al.* acknowledge that Supreme Court cases are the result of atypical disputes, their text emphasizes them.

> If Supreme Court cases are so relatively rare, one might ask, why not study the "ordinary" cases instead? The answer, of course, is that the way journalists and attorneys assess their chances of winning or losing a suit, and thereby decide whether to pursue it in court or to settle, is by applying the principles from decisions in the major cases.[51]

The only problem with that line of reasoning is that journalists and attorneys do not necessarily—or even often—make their decisions in such a fashion.[52] The *New York Times*, for example, refuses to settle libel suits for money, a nonlegal factor that "deters many cases from being brought."[53]

The relationship of legal rules to behavior, in other words, cannot be assumed. The influence of legal rules is seldom immediate and direct; rather, if the rules have any influence at all, that influence tends to be subtle and indirect.[54] Legal rules, in short, are not a sufficient explanation for how disputes evolve and are resolved.

Accordingly, communication-law scholars are confronted with an anomaly: the existing paradigm provides no theoretical or methodological tools to explain how most media-related disputes are resolved. This is not to say that legal rules play *no* role in determining the paths disputes will take. Even the most ardent opponents of the institution-centered approach to legal scholarship acknowledge that legal rules can have some influence in some situations. That influence, however, tends to be indirect and variable rather than direct and constant, according to legal sociologists. As Cavanagh and Sarat note: "Thinking about (courts') competence

---

[51]CARTER, FRANKLIN, AND WRIGHT, *supra* note 8, at 2.

[52]*See, e.g.,* Herbert M. Kritzer, Formal and Informal Theories of Negotiations: The Form of Negotiation in Ordinary Litigation, Paper presented to the annual meeting of the Law and Society Association, San Diego, California, June 6–9, 1985; Stewart Macaulay, *Lawyers and Consumer Protection Laws: An Empirical Study,* 14 LAW & SOCIETY REV. 115–71 (1979); Michael Massing, *The Libel Chill: How Cold Is It Out There?* 24, No.1 COLUMBIA JOURNALISM REV. 31–43 (1985); Steve Weinberg, *Libel: The Press Fights Back,* 22, No.4 COLUMBIA JOURNALISM REV. 65–8 (1983).

[53]Freeman, *A Lawyer in the Newsroom, supra* note 42, at 8.

[54]Macaulay, *Law and the Behavioral Sciences: Is There Any There There? supra* note 39. Even when legal rules directly influence behavior, the outcomes of disputes do not necessarily change. For example, though Dennis (in this issue's *Frontiers in Communication Law Research)* is correct that the criminal defendant cases of the 1960s influence police behavior, there is considerable evidence that the cases had no significant impact on the allocation of social justice. See Abraham S. Blumberg, *The Practice of Law as Confidence Game: Organizational Cooptation of a Profession,* 1 LAW & SOCIETY REV. 15–39 (1967).

in terms of the ability of courts to reach and enforce decisions misses perhaps their most important function: providing a framework within which parties negotiate and bargain."[55] The phrase many legal sociologists use to describe the typical mode of resolution of disputes is "bargaining in the shadow of the law."[56]

In short, the effect of formal legal rules—essentially, state-centered law[57]—is conditioned in important and complex ways by a variety of social (writ large: political, cultural, economic, psychological, etc.) forces. Scholars cannot begin to understand how and why media-related disputes are resolved until they consider the effects of such forces. Macaulay points out that "scholars often have failed to see the importance of private social control as it interacts with and affects the formal legal system."[58]

As Friedman and Macaulay said in *Law and the Behavioral Sciences:*

> If any part of the legal process has been overstressed, it is the world of statutes and cases. There is a large body of legal scholarship—some of it quite brilliant—concentrating on doctrine and philosophy, but much of it rests on highly questionable assumptions about the connections between, say, the Uniform Commercial Code or the Supreme Court's decisions in the school prayer cases, and the behavior of those who use the law, or who are charged with enforcing and obeying it. . . . People do not simply obey; they interact with legal officials. Law is made and carried out through a process of give and take. To make formal rules and formal institutions the center of attention, and to ignore the way events, values, and people affect them would distort the picture badly.[59]

An attractive alternative to the institution-centered perspective on communication law is a disputes-focused approach, which would use disputes and disputants rather than court cases and judicial institutions as the principal units of analysis. It is important to realize, of course, that the disputes-focused paradigm incorporates the existing paradigm. No theory of dispute resolution would be complete without an understanding of the role formal institutions play in shaping and resolving the relatively few disputes that come their way. For the most part, however, research carried out under a disputes-focused paradigm would concentrate

---

[55]Ralph Cavanagh & Austin Sarat, *Thinking About Courts: Toward and Beyond a Jurisprudence of Judicial Competence,* 14 LAW & SOCIETY REV. 371-420 (1980). *See also* Stewart Macaulay, Private Government, Working Paper 1983-6 (revised), Disputes Processing Research Program, University of Wisconsin Law School, 1983.

[56]Robert H. Mnookin & Lewis Kornhauser, *Bargaining in the Shadow of the Law: The Case of Divorce,* 88 YALE L. J. 950-97 (1979).

[57]For a discussion of this concept, see Marc Galanter, *Justice in Many Rooms: Courts, Private Ordering, and Indigenous Law,* 19 JOURNAL OF LEGAL PLURALISM 1-47 (1981).

[58]Macaulay, Private Government, *supra* note 55, at 2.

[59]FRIEDMAN & MACAULAY, *supra* note 39, at 32.

on the early stages in the disputing process, which is where most disputes are settled.

The disputes-focused paradigm has appeal for several reasons. Among them:

(a) The existing paradigm focuses exclusively on the disputes at the top end of the process outlined in [Figure 4.1]. Researchers who have democratic ideals may prefer a "bottom-up" approach that deals with representative disputes to the "top-down" approach of the existing paradigm.[60]

(b) A disputes-focused approach would allow researchers to make use of the knowledge that has been accumulated over the years about how journalists and the people they cover actually interact.[61] That picture, of course, is far different from the idealized portrait of the journalists as fearless, objective heroes in pursuit of the truth, whatever the cost. Also illuminating to the communication-law researcher might be the substantial amount of sociological research into the legal profession. It turns out that lawyers seldom act out the adversary ideal epitomized by Perry Mason. In fact, there is some evidence that lawyers are not always familiar with the law.[62]

(c) By focusing on representative disputes—the kind journalists and the people they write about routinely face—the disputes-focused paradigm makes communication-law research more relevant to the professional constituencies of many communication-law researchers. The disputes-focused paradigm also offers the possibility of explaining why some disputes take a judicial trajectory but others do not. That clearly would be information useful to journalists and to lawyers who are practitioners of communication law, and may also have policy implications for the alleged crisis of litigation in the United States today.[63]

III. THEORETICAL AND METHODOLOGICAL ISSUES

The disputes-focused paradigm offers communication-law scholars the theoretical tool they have lacked for predicting and explaining the out-

---

[60]The terms are borrowed from Ladinsky and Susmilch, Community Factors, *supra* note 27, at 2.

[61]ROBERT E. DRECHSEL, NEWS MAKING IN THE TRIAL COURTS (1983); DELMER DUNN, PUBLIC OFFICIALS AND THE PRESS (1969); HERBERT J. GANS, DECIDING WHAT'S NEWS (1979); TODD GITLIN, THE WHOLE WORLD IS WATCHING: MASS MEDIA IN THE MAKING AND UNMAKING OF THE NEW LEFT (1980); CHARLES PETERS, HOW WASHINGTON REALLY WORKS (1980); BERNARD ROSHCO, NEWSMAKING (1975); LEON V. SIGAL, REPORTERS AND OFFICIALS: THE ORGANIZATION AND POLITICS OF NEWSMAKING (1973); GAYE TUCHMAN, MAKING NEWS: A STUDY IN THE CONSTRUCTION OF REALITY (1978).

[62]Macaulay, *supra* note 52.

[63]For a critique of the notion that there is such a crisis, see Galanter, *supra* note 39.

comes of all media-related disputes, not just those that end up in appellate courts. That in itself is a significant advance.

But the disputes-focused paradigm does more. It suggests that social forces are important *legal* variables. In so doing, the new paradigm helps rescue legal research from its "intellectual marginality," as critical legal scholar Mark Tushnet, writing in the *Yale Law Journal*, put it.[64]

The theoretical advantages of the disputes-focused paradigm are one thing; whether disputes can be researched in any systematic way is a separate issue. Court decisions and statutes, of course, are relatively easy to research. The raw data have already been gathered and await examination in the local law library.

Disputes, on the other hand, are hard to research. The researcher must gather much of the pertinent data from participants in disputes.[65] The perils of interview-based research are many (*e.g.*, faulty recall, refusal to participate, imperfect questionnaire construction, sampling problems). Some information about disputes is available from institutional records, but the data in such documents are also imperfect.[66]

That communication-law scholars traditionally have relied on available data such as court decisions is not surprising, given the nature of the existing paradigm. As Kuhn notes, "in the absence of a reason for seeking some particular form of more recondite information, early fact-gathering is usually restricted to the wealth of data that lie ready to hand."[67] However, the disputes-focused paradigm generates hypotheses that can be tested only with empirical data, the kind that are not "ready to hand." Obtaining such data may be difficult, but the payoff—in terms of understanding how people use law—promises to be substantial.

What might a piece of new-paradigm research look like? This article does not pretend to offer a well-developed set of concepts and hypotheses. But a typical hypothesis generated by the new paradigm might be this: The more entwined disputants are in a semi-autonomous social field,[68] the earlier in the disputing process (the one outlined in [Figure 4.1]) they will solve their disputes.

Data to test such a hypothesis might come from content analysis of the news media (to identify potential disputes), interviews, and participant observation (to see how disputants really act, in contrast to how they say they act).

[64]Mark Tushnet, *Legal Scholarship: Its Causes and Cure*, 90 YALE L. J. 1205-223 (1981).

[65]Felstiner, Abel, and Sarat, *Naming, Blaming, and Claiming . . .* , *supra* note 27.

[66]For discussions of data-collection strategies, see Herbert M. Kritzer, *Studying Disputes: Learning from the Civil Litigation Research Project Experience*, 15 LAW & SOCIETY REV. 503-24 (1981); and Ladinsky & Susmilch, Conceptual and Operational Issues, *supra* note 27.

[67]KUHN, *supra* note 2, at 15.

[68]The concept comes from Moore, *supra* note 40.

IV. CONCLUSION

This article is not a call for a revival of Legal Realism. The Realists were concerned with the gap between legal rules and human behavior; that is not a central concern here.[69]

But a great concern is that many communication-law scholars' acceptance of the institution-centered paradigm of legal research—"a kind of legal Ptolemaism"[70]—has seriously harmed their ability to explain how the law works in practice. Although some communication-law scholars acknowledge that legal rules may not be a central determinant of behavior,[71] such an awareness has been the exception, rather than the rule. Just as traditional cops-and-robbers thinking prevented G— from seeing the purloined letter that was in plain sight, the traditional legal-research paradigm has prevented communication-law scholars from perceiving the great bulk of media-related disputing activity. The disputes-focused approach offers researchers theoretical and methodological tools that would enable them to describe and explain a wider range of legal phenomena than is now the case.

---

[69]For a discussion of why the gap between legal rules and human behavior need not be a central concern, see Richard L. Abel, *Law Books and Books About Law*, 26 STAN. L. REV. 175-228 (1973).

[70]Galanter, *supra* note 57, at 1.

[71]John D. Stevens, *Freedom of Expression: New Dimensions*, in MASS MEDIA AND THE NATIONAL EXPERIENCE-. ESSAYS IN COMMUNICATIONS HISTORY (Ronald T. Farrar & John D. Stevens eds. 1971).

Chapter 5

The Intersection of Legal Practice and Social Science on the Issue of Pretrial Publicity

Jon Bruschke

California State University, Fullerton

The topic of this volume is interdisciplinary approaches to the study of law. Few areas of law are more ripe for interdisciplinary analysis than pretrial publicity, if only because it smoothes our worst interdisciplinary turf wars. Social scientists, a terrific lot I count myself a member of, can often get carried away with themselves and begin to insist that they are doing pure science. Remembering too well their graduate school research methods textbooks, they can summon derision for applied research (generally because it lacks some vital component of research design) as a lesser form of labor, ranking somewhere between dishwasher and dog catcher. Not so with pretrial publicity: The topic is thoroughly applied. Although grand theories about things like nonverbal communication and decision-making schemas and agenda setting can explain the issues that arise, and although even the snootiest "pure" social scientist will begrudgingly admit that practice informs theories, the research into pretrial publicity is generally directed at improving courtroom practice and only to a much lesser extent testing theories.

Meanwhile, legal practitioners do not often take social science seriously. This may be because they cling to some long-discredited notion that the law is some pure, abstract, perfect form that need not rely on ugly things like facts and data, or because social scientists seem like a generally confused and confusing lot who do weird things with numbers and rarely agree with one another—or because, as one lawyerly friend of mine once explained, experts who testify for fees are the whores of the legal system. Others have explored these reasons in more depth than I (Lindman, 1989; Melton, 1987). No matter how hard courts try to ignore them, when issues of pretrial publicity come up, they undeniably involve empirical questions that require a little social science. How much coverage was there? How many people saw it? What sorts of things will create bias? Can bias be put out of the minds of jurors? Media researchers, psychologists, and those holding PhDs in nebulous fields like communication seem better trained to research and pursue these questions than those drilled in case law.

Thus, there is a deep need for some interdisciplinary interaction when courts hear cases that involve pretrial publicity, and a number of scholars have issued the call for more of it (Carroll et al., 1986; Lindman, 1989; Ogloff, 2002; Riley, 1973; Studebaker & Penrod, 1997; Vidmar & Judson, 1981). Despite this need, the exchange of information between the legal discipline and social science has been halting (Moran & Cutler, 1991; Ogloff, 2002; Rollings & Blascovich, 1977). This chapter explores three questions about the interaction of disciplines in the area of pretrial publicity. First, what are the tendencies of each field that frustrate better interdisciplinary effort? Second, in terms of substance, where do the findings of social science comfortably support legal practice, where do the findings of social science diverge from legal practice, and on what issues do both fields seem to be flying blind? Third, how does all the work in both areas relate to the broader goal of social justice?

THE TENDENCIES OF FIELDS

Given that a considerable gap exists between legal practice and social science research, what are the tendencies of each field that keep them at a distance from one another? This is not a treatise on the relationship between social science and the law in general, but is limited instead to pretrial publicity. Within this narrowed focus, some intriguing patterns emerge. For its part, the social science literature does at least two things that make it hard for any court to take seriously: It reports consensus when there is none, and it conducts research in laboratory settings that seem artificial to the legal community.

It is common to report that social science literature has conclusively proved that pretrial publicity biases the outcome of trials (e.g., Gibson & Padilla, 1998; Kerr, 1994; Steblay, Besirevic, Fulero, & Jiminez-Lorente, 1999; Studebaker & Penrod, 1997). In 1997, Studebaker and Penrod synthesized the research findings this way:

> In sum, it appears that the effects of pretrial publicity can find their way into the courtroom, can survive the jury selection process, can survive the

presentation of trial evidence, can endure the limiting effects of judicial instructions, and cannot only persevere through deliberations, but may actually intensify. (p. 445)

Steblay et al. (1999) came to a similar conclusion 2 years later at the conclusion of a meta-analysis. Fulero (2002) published an affidavit that he submitted to the court in a local murder case and noted that it was similar to the affidavit Penrod submitted in the well-publicized Timothy McVeigh trial. The affidavit began by stating that pretrial publicity could bias the outcome of a trial; noted that voir dire, jury instructions, and continuance all failed as remedies; and concluded that a change of venue or change of jurors were the only remedies likely to be effective. These are recent opinions, but a decade earlier reviewers were declaring that enough evidence had piled up to state a consensus (Fulero, 1987).

Elsewhere, my colleague Bill Loges and I have taken pains to demonstrate that the literature has never been so conclusive (Bruschke & Loges, 2004). In fact roughly an equal number of studies show a pretrial publicity effect, fail to show an effect, and produce mixed results. There is good reason to believe that pretrial publicity may not make any difference at all. There are at least two possible explanations for the divergence in findings. First, other reviews count studies that did not include trial evidence. This is bad. Studies generally show that trial evidence is more important than any other factor in a jury decision (J. Freedman & Burke, 1996; Kaplan & Miller, 1978; Kramer & Kerr, 1989; Visher, 1987), and, more profoundly, a defendant tried without evidence has problems much more troubling than publicity before the trial. Other reviews also include studies that favor defendants as proving a pretrial publicity effect, although these findings can hardly be interpreted as impeding a fair trial for the defendant. Second, reviewers examining what is ostensibly the same literature base strangely review a much different collection of studies. In the particular case of the Studebaker and Penrod article, of the seven studies Loges and I found that did not demonstrate a pretrial publicity effect, four were not cited at all and two studies were published after the review was completed. One article (Simon, 1966) was cited, but no mention was made of the fact that Simon discovered that all differences between publicity and no publicity groups disappeared after trial evidence and deliberation. In their meta-analysis, Steblay et al. reviewed five unpublished articles Loges and I chose not to, did not review 10 of the published studies we did cite (one study was reviewed in its unpublished form), and reviewed six studies that we chose not to review because they did not include trial evidence. Thus, our review and that of Steblay et al. reviewed 13 studies in common, we reviewed 10 studies they did not, and they reviewed 11 studies we did not include.

Law reviews tend to compound the problem, making odd choices about which reviews to select or making empirical conclusions without any reference to empirical literature. For example, Kulish (1998) tackled the question of pretrial publicity and its application to military law and cited all the case law, but not a single social science study. In a rare criticism of the Florida court for liberal excesses, Newsom (2000) faulted the Florida Supreme Court for its decision to require individual voir dire in highly publicized cases. The concern was that the individual questioning would take too long and that "if his name is sufficiently publicized in the news media, any criminal defendant will arguably be entitled to conduct individual voir dire" (p. 1071). Setting aside the unexamined question of how much time individual voir dire would add to a trial, anyone familiar with media patterns and plea bargain rates would immediately recognize what a ludicrously small number of cases would be "sufficiently publicized" for the remedy to affect. Newsom cited no research on the point one way or the other. Strauss (1998) cited social science research to prove that jurors could set aside biases, but oddly cited Simon's (1977) rather dated and limited literature review (it reviewed only five studies) despite the fact that three reviews of social science research had been published at the time, which were all much more extensive, at least a decade more recent, and much more on-point to the topic Strauss was addressing (Carroll et al., 1986; Fulero, 1987; Studebaker & Penrod, 1997). Strauss cited three other sources as support—all law reviews.

Readers interested in the details of the reviews are directed to our extensive chapter dedicated to the subject (Bruschke & Loges, 2004, chap. 2); readers interested in the interdisciplinary issue should have no trouble understanding why courts have difficulty understanding what the social science literature really says when reviewers cannot agree on it. The remedy is simply better social science. Speaking broadly, the peer review process does a rigorous job of honing data analysis and the conclusions that any researcher can draw from his or her findings. It is less meticulous about demanding that the literature review portion of the study be complete and carefully worded to identify limitations and omissions. In fact my experience has been that editors will often suggest cutting the literature review to expand space for the discussion of data. Reviews that are more thorough, identify why articles were or were not included, and focus on key elements of different studies that could explain seemingly contradictory findings would advance social science and also aid courts in figuring out what the state of the field is.

A second tendency of social science is to conduct research in laboratory settings that lack realism or are dissimilar from actual courtroom settings in obvious ways. Although many recognize the need to maximize realism (Jones, 1991; Kovera, 2002; Moran & Cutler, 1991; Padawer-

Singer & Barton, 1975; Padawer-Singer, Singer, & Singer, 1977; Studebaker & Penrod, 1997; Studebaker et al., 2002; Vidmar, 2002), and most agree that there are inherent limitations in laboratory studies that make generalizability difficult (J. Freedman, Martin, & Mota, 1998; Hans & Doob, 1976; Otto, Penrod, & Dexter, 1994; Rollings & Blascovich, 1977; Wilcox & McCombs, 1967), opinion divides on how research that deviates from actual courtroom experience should be evaluated. One camp holds that the research is totally "phony" and should be disregarded altogether (Pember, 1984) or has limitations that are "serious" (J. Freedman & Burke, 1996) or "critical" (Jones, 1991). A second view holds that the lack of realism means scholars should be cautious when extrapolating findings to actual courtrooms (J. Freedman & Burke, 1996; Jones, 1991). A final group is relatively unconcerned about the lack of realism (Fulero, 1987; Studebaker & Penrod, 1997) and cites evidence that laboratory studies generally match actual practice to reach the conclusion that simulation research is typical of actual trials (Kerr, 1994; Wilson & Bornstein, 1998). There is reason to believe the cited research does not prove the point (see Bruschke & Loges, 2004). The divergences of opinion are sharp. Some have concluded the lack of realism has underestimated pretrial publicity effects (Studebaker et al., 2002), whereas others have concluded the opposite and believe it has overestimated the influence of publicity (J. Freedman et al., 1998).

Whatever social scientists think about laboratory research, questions about realism have caused the legal community to turn away from social science research as a source of information (Bornstein, 1999; Carroll et al., 1986; Davis, 1986; Jones, 1991; Padawer-Singer & Barton, 1975; Padawer-Singer et al., 1977; Pember, 1990; Studebaker et al., 2002). I am an advocate for the position that realism and control trade off (see Carroll et al., 1986; Riley, 1973) and there is a need for both field and laboratory research (see also Carroll et al., 1986; Studebaker, Robbennolt, Pathak-Sharma, & Penrod, 2000; Vidmar, 2002). At present, laboratory studies outnumber field studies by a vast ratio. A fair summary of field research is that there is not much of it. Most of the field research that examines trial outcomes has been done by Loges and me. Our field studies, by and large, demonstrate that there is no pretrial publicity effect—at least not anything like that described by Studebaker and Penrod. Whether scholarly research occurs in the field or whether it simply goes to greater lengths to simulate actual trial conditions (e.g., Kramer, Kerr, & Carroll, 1990), an increase in realism can only narrow the interdisciplinary gap between academic research and legal practice.

Meanwhile, courts have their own tendencies that keep academic research from the halls of justice, even when it could considerably assist the decision-making process. First, courts, appellate courts especially, almost never cite academic research. Ever. The occasional law review article finds its way into a footnote, but social science research is almost never cited. Instead courts cite other courts on what are essentially empirical questions. The U.S. 8th Circuit, in *United States v. Allee* (2002), decided that content was critical and, rather than relying on social science evidence, which has a lot to say on the point, cited its own decision in *United States v. Blom* (2001). The *United States v. Blom* decision, in turn, cited the U.S. Supreme Court in *Dobbert v. Florida*, a case decided in 1977. Needless to say, there has been a sizeable amount of academic inquiry into the question of content, and a big pile of it has been published after 1977. When the U.S. 6th Circuit was trying to decide how much publicity was too much in *Ohio v. Ritchie* (1997), they compared coverage to the Ohio Supreme Court's decisions in *Ohio v. Lundgren* (1995) and *Ohio v. Nobles* (1995) and made no effort to consult media scholars, who might be expected to have informed opinions about the volume of media coverage.

The issue seems to be one of occupational blinders: Judges are trained to research and examine case law and they are good at it. Social science is difficult to read for those untrained in its minutiae, and it is much less well indexed and more difficult to research exhaustively. It is fairly easy to Sheppardize a court case, but tracking down all the social science research on pretrial publicity cannot really be done without consulting four or five different indexes and then tracking down a bunch of footnotes that are not in any of them. There are other reasons social science has a hard time creeping into the courtroom, to be sure, but whatever the cause, social science evidence will never inform court decisions so long as it is never read, cited, or considered. It would seem unusual for a court to decide, say, a mercury poisoning case without at least examining evidence concerning whether mercury is poisonous and in what amounts. Mercury poisoning is largely a question of dosage, and such is surely a question for science and not case law. It is unclear why courts seem more comfortable deciding questions of pretrial publicity dosage without any reference to the underlying science.

Neither is the underlying logic similar across cases. In *United States v. Blom* (2001), the court ruled that, because 37 of 72 jurors were struck for cause, voir dire must have been effective; striking a large number of jurors because they had been exposed to publicity was taken as evidence that the remedy was working. In *Ohio v. Yarbrough* (2002), however, the court ruled that the large number of jurors struck for cause called into question the answers of the jurors who claimed they were not biased. Striking a large number of jurors because they had been exposed to publicity was taken as evidence that the remedy was not working. The confusion is juxtaposed poignantly in the *United States v. Faul* (1984) decision: The majority concluded that if 90% of the potential jurors were exposed to the publicity it would be too much, after some calculation concluded that only 26% of the potential jurors in Faul's case had been exposed, and ruled the number acceptable. The dissent recalculated the figure excluding excused jurors and came up with a figure of 50% of the jury pool exposed to publicity and then argued that even the 26% figure was high enough to overrule. It is not surprising that many observers characterize pretrial publicity case law as incoherent (Kramer et al., 1990; Surette, 1992; Walton, 1998). Of course consistency of case law and logic is the *sine qua non* of legal practice, as well as its bain, but the issue raised in this paragraph highlights several key points: Deciding empirical questions solely on case law is fraught with danger, and consulting social scientists on how figures are best calculated and what numbers are acceptable (something courts are evidently doing anyway) is likely to improve the process.

In summary, the interdisciplinary gap is exacerbated by social scientists when contradictory conclusions are reported in what are ostensibly equally complete literature reviews and when laboratory methods are the dominant mode of research for what is an obviously applied area. On the legal side, the gap is widened by a general judicial reluctance to consider social science, and confusion in the logic courts apply to the issue. To some extent, the gap can be closed if each field simply does what it does better: If social scientists are able to produce more thorough and consistent literature reviews, there will be clearer findings to present to the legal system. If courts develop more coherent case law, social scientists will have a better idea of what questions should be researched. To an equal extent, each field could do more to reach out to the other. Social scientists will find a warmer reception to their work if they recognize that applied questions require field research, and that claiming generalizability from laboratory work is not generally persuasive either in or outside the social sciences. Legal practitioners will improve their own case law if they recognize that on empirical questions it does no harm to consult empirical evidence. Of course that evidence might not be completely uncontroversial nor completely consistent, but little evidence presented to courts ever is. There is little to be gained by ignoring it completely.

SUBSTANTIVE ISSUES

There are a number of substantive issues that have been addressed by both courts and social scientists. Some accounting of areas of agreement and disagreement is useful to set an agenda for better interdisciplinary engagement. It is probably not surprising to anyone familiar with either the law or social science that areas in need of more study and better answers are far more common than areas of settled empirical regularity.

Areas of Agreement

Loges and I (Bruschke & Loges, 2004) recently proposed a concept we call the *cumulative remedy hypothesis*, which holds that "remedies working in combination with one another might be more powerful than remedies studied in isolation, and additionally that pretrial publicity can have an effect only when all remedies fail simultaneously" (p. 17). Another way to put it is that a bunch of cheap remedies applied together will often work as well as big, expensive ones. A large part of our argument is that our field studies could not find higher conviction rates in extensively covered trials compared with trials with no coverage at all. The concept is in need of a lot more study, but there is some compelling research on the point at present (Kerwin & Shaffer, 1994; London & Nunez, 2000). One finding of social science research is this: If courts conscientiously apply a large number of cheap remedies, the effects of pretrial publicity can largely be held in check.

By and large, trial courts do exactly that, and appellate courts recognize that the care given to the application of multiple remedies is evidence of a job well done. The comments in *United States v. Blom* (2001) are typical:

> The district court took many precautions designed to assure the selection of an unbiased jury—moving the trial . . . assembling a jury pool of 196, three times the normal size; expanding the area from which the pool was drawn . . . mailing questionnaires to the prospective jurors inquiring about their exposure to pretrial publicity; and increasing the number of peremptory strikes. (p. 804)

Pruett v. Norris (1998) provided another sampling: "Such influences can normally be effectively neutralized by the curative procedural safeguards employed in this case, including a change of venue from the county in which the crime occurred and a thorough, individual voir dire of potential jurors" (p. 19). These two cases each granted a change of venue; these remedies are more rare because they are more expensive. Even without venue change, trial courts do seem to be sensitive to potential bias and generally seek to remedy publicity in a variety of overlapping ways (see also *United States v. Blom*, 2001; *United States v. Faul*, 1984; *United States v. Nelson*, 2003).

This point is the shining ray of light on the pretrial publicity issue: Case law and social science often diverge and are fraught with their own failings, the coverage is excessive and often inaccurate, the defense is underresourced, the instructions are confusing, the jury is uninformed, and the right to a speedy trial might mean a 4-year delay. Yet in the end, there is not a large number of criminal defendants who are wrongly convicted because of pretrial publicity. This is not a cause for relaxation, but vigilance. The pernicious effects of pretrial publicity do not seem to generate bias precisely because of the conscientious work that trial courts do. Continually applying those remedies and constantly refining them is important work (if not, as is argued next, the top priority for the legal system).

Areas of Disagreement

For all its divergence and questionable coherence, there are important areas of agreement in the social science literature. In fact debate and discord are not the character flaws of a disagreeable collection of social scientists, but are probably key elements of a healthy and emerging science. Debate is central to the advance of knowledge, not its rival. There are three areas where social science findings tend to coalesce with one another, but diverge from courtroom practice: (a) jurors cannot set aside their preexisting knowledge, (b) factual information is not less damaging than other sorts, and (c) overall levels of coverage are not irrelevant to individual defendants.

The first area where social science seems to have produced consistent findings concerns the ability of jurors to "set aside" their preexisting knowledge and decide a case solely on the basis of information at trial. Research clearly indicates that jurors will generally do their best to come to a fair conclusion based on the evidence presented at trial and behave as optimal decision makers (see Bornstein & Rajki, 1994; London & Nunez, 2000; Sommers & Kassin, 2001). Despite, and sometimes because of, this, exposure to pretrial publicity complicates their efforts. In a Canadian fraud case (Vidmar & Judson, 1981), publicized trials in California (Constantini & King, 1980–1981), and drug/homicide cases in Illinois and Florida (Moran & Cutler, 1991), those who had seen pretrial publicity were more likely to presume guilt than those who had not. Using slightly different methods, other studies have come to similar conclusions (Ogloff & Vidmar, 1994; Riley, 1973; Shaffer, 1986; Simon & Eimermann, 1971; Sohn, 1976; Tans & Chaffee, 1966). Loges and I have called this the *knowledge–guilt hypothesis*—the more potential jurors know about the facts of a case, the more they will presume guilt. Research on cases involving multiple charges similarly demonstrates that jurors do not easily compartmentalize their knowledge about a defendant (Tanford & Penrod, 1982). The same is true of information about a prior criminal record (Hans & Doob, 1976). Furthermore, potential jurors will not be especially good at recognizing their own biases (Fein, McCloskey, & Tomlinson, 1997; Moran & Cutler, 1991; Newman et al., 1997; Ogloff & Vidmar, 1994; Sue et al., 1975). The findings are clear and relatively unequivocal: Jurors who gain knowledge about a case from the media are more likely to presume guilt than jurors who do not, and asking jurors whether they are biased will not provide many accurate answers.

The remaining question is whether this bias can be remedied. Generally speaking, there is reason to believe that it can be. Instructions used along with deliberation have been shown to eliminate bias (Kerwin & Shaffer, 1994; London & Nunez, 2000), and some defense strategies can sharply shift opinion in favor of defendants even if pretrial publicity is negative (Fein, McCloskey, & Tomlinson, 1997). As is often the case, however, things are not always that simple. Bipolar thinking might lead to the conclusion that either pretrial publicity biases trials or it does not, and remedies either work or they do not. I suggest a more nuanced view: Most potential jurors never see publicity, and if they do they do not remember it. If they have seen it, they will be biased before the trial. Yet a combination of jury instructions, evidence, delay, and deliberation usually offsets the effects.

Across the board, there is not an overall pretrial publicity effect that results in higher conviction rates in cases that receive a considerable degree of publicity. Nonetheless, there may remain situations where, especially when the evidence at trial is not decisive, jurors trying hard to reach a just decision will rely on the best information at their disposal and will not be too finicky if the source of that information comes from somewhere other than the witness box. This nuanced view recognizes that publicity does produce pretrial bias, but also identifies that the use of multiple and carefully applied remedies seems to work effectively. To the maximum extent possible, courts should probe potential jurors individually and seek to discover what specific information they have come to prior to the trial. If the pool is sufficiently large, there is no reason to allow a juror with any exposure to sit on the panel. At a minimum, exposed jurors should be questioned carefully, and any claims to a freedom from bias should be carefully interrogated; particular means of finding out what jurors know, and when it is too much, have been outlined elsewhere (Bruschke & Loges, 2004, chap. 3).

In contrast to the behavioral science conclusion that juror claims that they can set aside information should be mistrusted and trigger further examination, courts, and especially appellate courts, place a great deal of faith in the statement (e.g., *United States v. Nelson*, 2003; *Ohio v. Nobles*, 1995). The Pruett decision is especially telling. The defendant won an appeal at the district court level because the trial judge "erred in accepting at face value the belief of the jurors impaneled that they could ignore what they had read in the newspapers, seen on television and heard and give Marion Albert Pruett the fair trial that was his right" (*Pruett v. Norris,* 1998, p. 584). The U.S. 8th Circuit overruled, saying "each juror expressly affirmed that he or she could be impartial and render a verdict based solely on the evidence presented at trial" (*Pruett v. Norris,* 1998, p. 25). The legal system's repudiation of the knowledge–guilt hypothesis was put succinctly by the U.S. 6th Circuit in *Ritchie v. Rogers* (2002): "Extensive knowledge in the community of either the crimes or the putative criminal is not sufficient by itself to render a trial constitutionally unfair" (pp. 9–10). The point is not that either court ruled incorrectly, but that the legal system gives great deference to juror claims of impartiality and flatly rejects the knowledge–guilt hypothesis. Contrary opinions tend to be overruled (as was the district court in *Pruett v. Norris*) or find their way into dissenting opinions (see the dissent in *United States v. Faul,* 1984). Although they seldom act on this issue, it should be noted that courts recognize that there are times courts should not accept a potential juror's claim that he or she is free from bias (e.g., *Ohio v. Ritchie,* 1997; *Pruett v. Norris,* 1998; *United States v. Bieganowski,* 2002; *United States v. Blom,* 2001). The issue is one of presumption: Courts tend to presume that a juror's claim of impartiality should be given deference, whereas social science research suggests the opposite.

In summary, many trial courts do an excellent job of applying a number of remedies very carefully. However, trial court judges are given extraordinary discretion to pick and choose which remedies to apply and how to apply them, and appellate courts are reluctant to overrule the trial judge's decisions. Needless to say, not all trial judges do an equally good job of using their vast discretion. At both the trial and appellate levels, the court system seems to put more faith in a juror's claim to be able to put aside information than behavioral science evidence suggests is warranted. A better approach is a consistently rigorous interrogation of jurors who have been exposed to pretrial publicity and an appellate review standard that ensures a thorough probing of exposed jurors at the trial level. At a minimum, the existence of admissibility standards makes it clear that courts do believe that there are some sorts of information that jurors are unable to "set aside." If a juror cannot be expected to set aside information about, say, a prior criminal record, it is hard to imagine why he or she can be expected to discount all pretrial publicity.

A second area where social science findings diverge from legal practice concerns the type of information that might be damaging. As discussed in greater depth later, both social science and the law need to develop a more complete sense of what content in the media is of concern. At present, at least some courts have ruled that factual pretrial publicity is not harmful, arguing that the jury has the opportunity at trial to evaluate the evidence and its credibility for itself (*United States v. Blom*, 2001). A court can also rely on case law to conclude that "we must distinguish between largely factual publicity and that which is invidious or inflammatory" (*United States v. Faul*, 1984, p. 17). Other courts have reasoned similarly (*Demouchette v. Texas*, 1979; *Hill v. Ozmint*, 2003) and ruled that factual publicity is not damaging. Social science points to an opposite conclusion. If jurors are primarily motivated to behave as optimal decision makers (Bornstein & Rajki, 1994) and can, therefore, be expected to draw on any source of solid information, the case will literally be tried in the media because that is where jurors draw information. In addition, research on primacy effects and the finding of social judgment theory both give reason to believe that the timing of the information is crucial, and exposure to facts prior to trial makes them more complicated for the defense to contend with at trial. In fact one study discovered that potential jurors who had seen coverage but could not recall any facts were less likely to prejudge guilt than jurors who had seen factual information (Riley, 1973). Put another way, a defendant facing a jury who has seen the facts of the case through the media before the trial is disadvantaged relative to a defendant who has to deal with an identical set of facts at trial with an unexposed jury. Finally, although there is some research evidence pointing the other direction, more recent research does not find emotional publicity more damaging than factual publicity (Wilson & Bornstein, 1998). Whether content is a crucial variable and what content might be especially damaging is largely unknown, but there is little reason to believe that factual publicity is less damaging than any other sort, and some reason to believe it may be more prejudicial.

Third, the issue of general publicity seems to separate the law from the lab. Courts tend to focus narrowly on media attention to a specific defendant and are not impressed by the overall amount of crime coverage, coverage of similar crimes, or coverage that implies the defendant was involved in cases other than the one before the bar at a given moment (see *Kelly v. Texas*, 2003). Social science research provides many reasons to believe that general pretrial publicity, or exposure to cases similar to the one at trial, could be the most important type. Most generally, scholars of media effects have discarded the search for a "magic bullet" in the media—an individual message that can have a specific effect on particular audience members. If the media were capable of such a thing, everyone would buy an advertised product after seeing a commercial for it, and Madison Avenue salaries would be even higher than they are. Instead, attitudes tend to be shaped by repeated exposure to the same message over time—called a *cultivation effect* (Gerbner, Gross, Morgan, & Signorielli, 1986)—or by agenda-setting functions (Kovera, 2002). An extended argument for this approach to pretrial publicity has been offered by Surette

(1992). In more particular terms, a good deal of research has demonstrated that exposure to other, related media cases does have an influence (Greene & Loftus, 1984; Greene & Wade, 1988; Mullin, Imrich, & Linz, 1996; Riedel, 1993). In one study, mock jurors exposed to different stories about an unrelated rape reacted quite differently to evidence in a rape trial (Kovera, 2002). Exposure to the unrelated case altered the evidence jurors gave the most weight and attention, as well as credibility appraisals and assessments of what a typical rape scenario was.

In our own research, Loges and I (2004) found a series of complex relationships between levels of crime coverage in different cities and conviction rates and sentence length. The relations varied depending on the stage of the trial and interactions with other variables, particularly fear of crime. At the pretrial level, a high amount of coverage is good for defendants if fear of crime is low, but bad for defendants where fear of crime is high. At the trial conviction stage, the pattern reverses entirely, and coverage plus fear of crime actually improves a defendant's chances. At the trial sentence stage, coverage appears to be good for most defendants, but extremely bad for a very few of them. Our explanations for these findings—which are all educated guesses—generally have to do with the motivations of court actors. A clear, easy-to-understand pattern is difficult to arrive at, but the results show effects that are at least as compelling as the case for an influence of specific pretrial publicity.

In short, there are good theoretical reasons to believe that general levels of crime coverage and media use will be better predictors of juror prejudgment than exposure to specific coverage of a case. Research evidence reveals powerful and provocative, if occasionally counterintuitive and perplexing, effects for general coverage. It is odd to focus so much attention on the remedy of specific exposure while ignoring entirely the equally important influence of general publicity.

Areas That Need More Research

Human knowledge is frail, scientific principles are in constant dispute, conclusions change with each new research study, and even legal precedent changes over time. Thus, it is not surprising to find that, on any given issue, the amount unknown exceeds that which is verified or at least contingently agreed on. Five areas that are fairly critical to untangling pretrial publicity effects need a lot more study: (a) the amount of pretrial publicity that is damaging, (b) content that might be damaging, (c) whether a delay is a sufficient remedy, (d) how evidence interacts with publicity, and (e) how voir dire is best conducted.

It is amazing how little is known about the amount of publicity that might be damaging. Here are some basic questions that we do not know the answer to: How much publicity does a case have to receive before an appreciable element of the jury pool has seen some of it? How much overlap is there between TV and newspaper (and radio) coverage of a trial? How much publicity does a case have to have before it begins to influence popular opinion (one way or the other) about a crime? Behavioral research and case law are equally incoherent on these questions. Loges and I (1999) took a stab at categorizing levels of coverage, and eyeballing our data we came up with categories of no coverage, 1 to 5 articles, 6 to 10 articles, and 11 or more articles. Strikingly, 62 of the federal murder or robbery cases we studied received no coverage at all, and 1 case was covered with 141 articles. Although we did find differences in outcomes between our category levels, I am still strained to believe that there is a big difference between a case that is covered in three articles and one that is covered in seven. Obviously, the trials that attain media event status—OJ Simpson, Michael Jackson, Kobe Bryant—are on a totally different scale, and lumping them in with a case covered in 11 newspaper stories is wholly inadequate. In laboratory research, the amount of coverage varies between 1 and 10 articles, but is usually shown immediately (or, at most, a couple of weeks or maybe a month) before a mock trial. Field research studies tend to focus only on those cases that are obviously high-publicity instances. No research has explored how much coverage must occur before most of the viewing public can be assumed to have seen at least some of the coverage.

Anyone seeking a more clear legal definition from the courts of when the amount of coverage becomes too onerous would find only befuddlement. The *Kelly v. Texas* (2003) court decided that 27 articles was not a lot, although it would have been one of the 11 most publicized cases in the dataset of 134 cases Loges and I compiled. In *Ohio v. Yarbrough* (2002), the court conceded that 42 of 47 potential jurors had read or heard something about the case, but decided that this was insufficient to show that publicity had "saturated the community" (p. 241). In *Ohio v. Lundgren* (1995), the court detailed that one area paper printed 227 articles, another 323, and that three area TV stations had broadcast 66, 112, and 169 stories about the case. The court then decided the case was not one of the "rare" ones where prejudice could be presumed and concluded the voir dire had been effective. What *Ohio v. Lundgren* did implicitly other courts have done explicitly, rejecting any claim of bias based on the sheer amount of coverage (e.g., *United States v. Blom*, 2001). There is neither a clear legal definition of what constitutes too much coverage, nor is there a solid empirical definition of the point at which media coverage can saturate a community, defined either as the point at which most people have heard of the case, the point at which most people have heard details of the case, or the point at which most people have prejudged the case.

Better empirical research and greater legal attention to these thresholds will improve the conduct of justice.

A second area concerns content that might be biasing. As already argued, social science findings are rather incongruent about any effect existing at all, with roughly equal numbers of studies showing an effect, showing no effect, or showing mixed results. An intuitively appealing way to resolve this seeming inconsistency is to imagine that something about the content of the coverage is crucial. The right sorts of content (perhaps front-page stories or inflammatory words) might produce an effect, whereas other content (perhaps a simple recounting of the case facts) might not. No such pattern has emerged.

It is clear, however, that coverage is almost universally antidefendant. As early as 1973, Riley concluded that the issue was settled: Media coverage was antidefendant. Referring to the hypothesis that "press coverage of crimes and pretrial proceedings is biased against the defendant" (p. 17), Riley wrote: "Content analysis studies in the area . . . have amply documented the existence and extent of potentially prejudicial information appearing in the media, and further research of this kind does not seem crucial" (pp. 17–18). Subsequent reviewers have come to identical conclusions (Carroll et al., 1986; Kramer et al., 1990; Moran & Culter, 1991; Ogloff & Vidmar, 1994). More contemporary content analyses have confirmed the antidefendant nature of coverage (Frasca, 1988; Imrich, Mullin, & Linz, 1995; Tankard, Middleton, & Rimmer, 1979). Case studies point to the same conclusion. Moran and Cutler (1991) studied a marijuana case in Illinois and a murder in Florida and reported that the extensive "coverage was universally negative" (p. 350). Nietzel and Dillehay (1983) studied five high-profile cases and found high antidefendant feelings in high-coverage areas. Similar results have been obtained in studies of the famous Hearst (Rollings & Blascovich, 1977), Joan Little (McConahay, Mullin, & Frederick, 1977), and MacDonald (Riley, 1973) trials. A study of a Canadian fraud case (Vidmar & Judson, 1981), a moderately publicized murder trial (Simon & Eimermann, 1971), and three highly publicized cases in California (Constantini & King, 1980–1981) all found coverage to be vastly slanted against the defendants.

Although coverage is antidefendant in general, research has generally failed to find that any particular type of antidefendant content is more damaging than any other. Several studies have either failed to find differences between types of pretrial publicity or found that even minimal mention of a crime is sufficient to damage defendant interests. Tans and Chaffee (1966) manipulated three types of pretrial publicity and found that the mere mention of an arrest is sufficient to produce prejudgments of guilt. Sohn (1976) found that the mention of a felony made a difference in judgments of guilt, but that no other factor had a substantial influence. Kramer and Kerr (1989) separated emotion from factual publicity, but eventually found main effects for both types of publicity on both verdicts and sentence lengths. Hoiberg and Stires (1973) similarly contrasted emotional and factual publicity and found no differences. Wilcox and McCombs (1967) varied eight types of pretrial information and concluded that respondents could not distinguish proof of guilt from mere accusations of guilt. Simon and Eimermann (1971) studied two cases involving "mild" publicity that did not violate ABA standards, and found that 65% of those who could recall the case were pro-prosecution. Tellingly, not a single respondent was prodefense. Finally, Riley's (1973) study of the MacDonald case offered a fascinating study of an instance where the coverage was not biased, but was very extensive and hardly suggested a prejudgment of guilt. Nonetheless, prejudgments of guilt were two to seven times more likely than prejudgments of innocence, and higher coverage exposure was associated with higher judgments of guilt. Persuaded largely by this and other research, commentators have concluded that even moderate exposure produces biases (Moran & Cutler, 1991), that little more is necessary to produce bias than knowledge of a crime and arrest (Carroll et al., 1986), and that the mere volume of coverage is associated with antidefendant bias irrespective of content (Ogloff & Vidmar, 1994).

A separate group of studies mitigates against these conclusions and has found that the type of pretrial publicity is important (Fein, Morgan, Norton, & Sommers, 1997; Hvistendahl, 1979; Kramer et al., 1990; Otto et al., 1994; Sue et al., 1974; Vidmar & Judson, 1981). Although these studies do present challenging information, it is difficult to discern an overall pattern suggesting that a particular type of pretrial information has an effect, whereas other types of evidence do not. Although some studies have found that prior conviction information is especially damaging (i.e., Hvistendahl, 1979; Vidmar & Judson, 1981), other studies in this group that included prior conviction did not find an effect (Otto et al., 1994). Although Otto et al. (1994) reported differences between emotional and factually biasing information, other studies have not uncovered differences between these types of information (Hoiberg & Stires, 1973; Kramer & Kerr, 1989), and in 1998 Wilson and Bornstein concluded the distinction was no longer worth pursuing.

Overall, social science research has found the content of coverage to be antidefendant, but has not uncovered a particular type of coverage more damaging than others. Relying on ABA standards of what should not be released to the press and emotional versus factual distinctions, researchers have manipulated a number of different possibilities, but none has emerged as a clear and consistent cause of juror bias. More research into the issue, perhaps with more theoretical backing than is typical to date (most studies have taken categories from the 1967 ABA standards), could improve understandings of how pretrial publicity influences jurors and give courts particular elements to look for when making rulings.

Meanwhile, courts have had an equally difficult time figuring out what content crosses the threshold of unconstitutionality. Being generally unwilling to rule that the sheer amount of coverage creates bias, many courts turn to issues of content (see *Ohio v. Yarbrough*, 2002; *Ritchie v. Rogers*, 2002; *United States v. Allee*, 2002; *United States v. Blom*, 2001; *United States v. Faul*, 1984). The *Allee* court wrote a typical conclusion: "The mere existence of press coverage, however, is not sufficient to create a presumption of inherent prejudice and thus warrant a change of venue. To create a presumption, the coverage must be inflammatory or accusatory" (p. 1000). Similarly, in denying a defendant's claim, the *Ohio v. Yarbrough* majority wrote: "Despite the appellant's allegations of 'inflammatory' media coverage, there is nothing in the record to show the *content* of the coverage" (p. 232; italics original).

Having decided to look at the content of media coverage it is not clear what the courts are seeking to find that might cause them to find the coverage too inflammatory. The *Pruett v. Norris* (1998) court described the coverage of the case this way:

> Pruett elected to make several statements to newspaper and television reporters in which he implicated himself in various crimes and boldly labeled himself a "mad-dog killer" . . . Pruett's videotaped statement that he was a "mad-dog killer" was played several times by virtually every local television station and numerous radio broadcast stations in the region . . . it became commonplace to talk about Pruett as the "self-confessed mad-dog killer." (p. 585)

Relying on Pruett's defense attorney's testimony that two other trials evidently had more damaging coverage, the court concluded the coverage was unexceptional and "perhaps even less inflammatory than publicity generated in similar cases" (p. 586). The aforementioned *Ohio v. Lundgren* case, covered in 550 newspaper and 247 TV stories, was described by the court as "massive" and "inflammatory," and the court noted that, "According to the *Plain Dealer*, the Lake County Prosecutor publicly asserted that the members of the Lundgren group were the 'most inhuman people this county has ever seen' " (p. 478). The particular case came to be known as the "Kirtland massacre." These descriptions notwithstanding, the court found that the Lundgren case was not one of the "relatively rare" cases of presumed prejudice.

One is left to wonder what would qualify. I am strained to find adjectives more inflammatory than *inhuman* and *mad-dog killer*, and those that do spring to mind are not fit to print here. Suffice it to say that the coverage in these two cases was much more inflammatory than any-thing a meek social scientist might presume to use as stimulus material, but ostensibly still not enough for courts to rule on. At any rate, courts set an especially high bar for a defendant to prove inflammatory content, and some delineation of what would satisfy that threshold would make for better case law. If social scientists are able to produce a consistent group of research findings that both define inflammatory content and es-tablish empirical relationships between particular content and juror bias, the task of the courts could be made easier.

A fourth area in need of further investigation concerns evidence. Evi-dence is a decisive and even dominant factor in determining a trial out-come (J. Freedman & Burke, 1996; Kaplan & Miller, 1978; Kramer & Kerr, 1989; Visher, 1987). Jurors, mightily motivated to reach a just verdict, will do their best to decide the case on the basis of the evidence presented. To the extent that juror bias enters a decision, it is probably because bias alters the way jurors evaluate evidence (Dexter, Cutler, & Moran, 1992; Hans & Doob, 1976; Kovera, 2002; Murray, Kaiser, & Taylor, 1997; Newman et al., 1997; Sue et al., 1974, 1975; Tanford & Penrod, 1982). This pattern of findings has convinced Loges and me (2004, chap. 5), along with Kerwin and Shaffer (1994), that pretrial publicity is likely to emerge as a factor when trial evidence is inconclu-sive. Shockingly, courts agree with us. The *United States v. Faul* (1984) dissent argued that "the evidence was not overwhelming" (p. 1230) and used that as the basis for concluding that pretrial publicity could have been decisive. Arguing the flip side of the coin, the *United States v. Bieganowski* (2002) majority reasoned that "the prosecution presented overwhelming evidence of Bieganowski's guilt at trial," and "in light of the volume of evidence against him" (p. 274), ruled against his pretrial publicity claim. Hence, if the evidence is conclusive enough, a fair trial is not all that important.

Although social science does have a number of findings suggesting that evidence is crucial, there has not been a study that has systemati-cally varied the evidence strength presented against the defendant at trial and crossed it with different levels and types of pretrial publicity. A more typical design is to measure the juror perceptions of evidence strength, which may be inadequate if publicity is shading those perceptions in the first place. A direct test would add much to our knowledge base. Mean-while, courts need to work out the tricky issue of when there is enough evidence that the pretrial publicity would not matter and whether they want to establish a rule that procedural safeguards are more important in cases where the evidence is not conclusive. On the one hand, it makes a world of intuitive sense that nonlegal factors will become more danger-ous when the evidence is less than definitive. On the other hand, it does seem to put the cart before the horse to say that we only need to apply fair standards when guilt is in doubt—a conclusion most of us believe emerges only at the end of the trial.

A fifth area of study is the question of delay. One of the better studies to date has examined the question of continuance and found that a delay failed to counteract publicity or actually exacerbated its influence (Kramer et al., 1990). The results are not entirely unequivocal; delay did eliminate the effects of factual (but not emotional) publicity, and most respondents did forget the information they encountered. Other research suggests more promise for continuance-type remedies. Mullin et al. (1996) found no effect for pretrial publicity after a delay before exposure to a trial stimulus and attributed the nonsignificant finding to the delay. Davis (1986) found that delay caused a prodefendant shift, and Kerr (1994) viewed continuance as the best available remedy to date. The most difficult reason to accept the Kramer et al. study as definitive is that it operationalized a continuance as 12 days—a much shorter period than even the normal time interval between an arrest and a trial in actual courtrooms. In *Pruett v. Norris* (1998), for example, 10 months elapsed between the spike in media coverage in the weeks following the murder and Pruett's trial. In short, social science evidence is somewhat mixed on the effectiveness of a delay, the number of studies examining the question is not large, and no study has examined delays on the scale that occurs in actual cases. Such are the classic conditions that call for more research.

Courts, meanwhile, accept both continuance and the normal delays in court proceedings as effective remedies (*United States v. Allee*, 2002; *Coble v. Texas*, 2003; *Kelly v. Texas*, 2003; *Ohio v. Nobles*, 1995; *Pruett v. Norris*, 1998). The U.S. 5th Circuit argued in *Coble v. Texas*: "The district court emphasized that all the pretrial publicity occurred more than six months before Coble's trial. . . . Although there was a fair amount of press coverage, it occurred many months before the trial" (p. 32). Such reasoning, of course, comes at tension with the right to a speedy trial. A defendant insisting on a speedy trial who was then convicted would be able to argue on appeal that, because of the short interval of time between the arrest and the trial, pretrial coverage was damaging, although it was the request of the defendant to proceed swiftly. A defendant seeking a continuance would face the unpleasant prospect of waiting in jail for a distant court date to arrive (depending, of course, on the outcome of bail hearing and the ability of the defendant to pay). There is something a little too cozy about the court's inability to swiftly move through its docket as constituting a reason that defendant rights are better protected. These legal tensions aside, the court system's reliance on the continuance remedy would be more easy to accept if a more clear body of social science evidence supported it.

Finally, the question of voir dire should be explored in more depth. On the social science front, some scholars have applauded the process for its ability to remove bias (Padawer-Singer & Barton, 1975), some scholars have reported equivocal results or admitted confusion (Carroll et al., 1986; Vidmar & Melnitzer, 1984; Zeisel & Diamond, 1978), and the strongest opinions have denounced its effectiveness (Dexter et al., 1992; Kerr, Kramer, Carroll, & Alfini, 1991; Padawer-Singer, Singer, & Singer, 1974). Despite its detractors and the mixed empirical record, jury selection obviously has some value; and at least one reading of the literature is that, although lawyers are not especially good at predicting in advance which jurors will vote for their side, the process does eliminate obviously biased or inappropriate jurors. More penetrating inquiry into the issue is warranted.

Not surprisingly, courts view the process as a crucial court function (but see the dissent in *United States v. Faul*, 1984). When they seek to review a case where juror partiality is at question, appellate courts will often empower themselves to evaluate the voir dire process. Equally unsurprisingly, the more carefully the voir dire has been conducted at the trial level, the more deference it will receive at the appellate level. In *Ohio v. Lundgren* (1995), the court upheld as sufficiently rigorous an 8-day jury selection that involved individual questioning of potential jurors. Courts seem to believe that individual voir dire (where jurors are questioned one by one about particular media exposure and other biases) is preferable, especially when there is some reason to suspect media tainting (see *United States v. Blom*, 2001). Yet group questioning (where jurors are asked a question and expected to raise their hands or indicate that they might have a bias) is typical and within the trial court's discretion (*Ohio v. Ritchie*, 1997). Defendants have no right to individual voir dire (*Ohio v. Nobles*, 1995). The state of case law suggests an urgent need for social scientists to explore in more detail the differences between individual and group jury selection, a largely unexamined area. If the former is substantially better than the latter, individual voir dire might be better used as a standard procedure rather than a matter of trial court discretion. Surely, courts with delays of 10 months or more are not significantly slowed by careful questioning of potential jurors.

THE QUESTION OF RESOURCES

Take a moment and consider the number of trials you can recall off the top of your head. We can all recite "OJ Simpson." If you are old enough or well read enough, you might conjure up Sacco and Vanzetti, the Scopes case, Hauptmann's defense in the Lindbergh prosecution, Leopold and Loeb, Alger Hiss, and even Sam Sheppard. These cases are older, and the dominant tendency was conviction. More recently, Lorena Bobbitt, the LAPD officers accused of beating Rodney King, Sean Puffy Combs (later remonikered P. Diddy), Baltimore Ravens linebacker Ray Lewis, and OJ Simpson all did something Socrates could not and beat the charges against them. Even the Menendez brothers won more legal victories than might be expected given the weight of the evidence they faced. It is a pretty good record in a system that produces convictions at an 80% to 90% clip. Why might this be?

An obvious and compelling possibility is money. Simply put, well-resourced defendants and celebrities are well defended. The best defense money can buy turns out to be a pretty good defense. Take that and add to it a presumption of innocence, and few prosecutions are so air tight that they cannot eliminate at least a few plausible alternative explanations for crucial evidence. By and large, the very rich, and those with newfound celebrity who are plausibly sympathetic (Bobbitt and the L.A.P.D. officers each had at least some moral claim), do not suffer injustice in the legal system due to a wanting of quality representation.

This is not the fate of less wealthy and unpopular defendants. The state of public defense in American is deplorable (Bright, 1997; M. Freedman, 1998; Gerber, 2001). Public defense caseloads are enormous, resources woefully inadequate, and the ability to research a case or conduct an independent investigation all but nonexistent. Compensation for court-appointed attorneys is such that "lawyers assigned cases are required to choose between working hundreds of hours without compensation or not providing competent representation" (Bright, 1997, p. 827). Consider the fate of George McFarland:

> Seated beside his client—a convicted capital murderer—defense attorney John Benn spent much of Thursday afternoon's trial in apparent deep sleep.
>
> His mouth kept falling open and his head lolled back on his shoulders, and then he awakened just long enough to catch himself and sit upright. Then it happened again. And again. And again.
>
> Every time he opened his eyes, a different prosecution witness was on the stand describing another aspect of the Nov. 19, 1991, arrest of George McFarland in the robbery-killing of grocer Kenneth Kwan.
>
> When state District Judge Doug Shaver finally called a recess, Benn was asked if he truly had fallen asleep during a capital murder trial.
>
> "It's boring," the 72-year-old longtime Houston lawyer explained. . . .
>
> Court observers said Benn seems to have slept his way through virtually the entire trial.
>
> Attorney Benn's sleeping did not offend the Sixth Amendment, the trial judge explained, because, "the Constitution doesn't say the lawyer has to be awake." (Bright, 1997, p. 829)

Neither can defendants expect appellate courts to grant new trials on the basis of this level of defense assistance. For example, the 5th Circuit in Texas has seen fit to distinguish a sleeping defense lawyer from an intoxicated one, ruling the former inadequate but the latter sufficient (*Burdine v. Johnson*, 2001; *Burnett v. Collins*, 1993). For my part, I would rather not be represented by either one. The distinction also has not helped McFarland, who has had his conviction upheld on appeal twice.

It is worth remembering, in the end, how central the question of resources is to the conduct of justice and how ephemeral questions of media often are. So long as police are undersupported and lack the resources to adequately investigate all crimes the worst elements in the force will take shortcuts or, as the Rampart experience in Los Angeles reminds, flagrantly revel in corruption. So long as the poor are represented with underpaid, underresourced, and overburdened public defenders, the courts will not do much to weed out the truly guilty from those in the wrong place at the wrong time. So long as conservative politics results in cuts to both public defense and corrections, our system will neither dispense justice nor rehabilitate the incarcerated (Gerber, 2001), nor, ironically enough, even allow us to incarcerate those convicted of multiple felonies. So long as high-profile media trials drain the system's already paltry resources and divert attention from the much more common sort of case where injustice is much more likely to occur, we are, in Biblical terms, removing splinters from some areas and ignoring planks in others. At present, we seem content to lavish procedural protections in high-profile cases while largely ignoring those that fall below the level of public attention and, therefore, public scrutiny. We should seek to understand pretrial publicity. We should seek to eliminate any unfairness it generates. Yet in this area, as with so many others, money, and not truth, seems to be the ultimate dispositor of case outcomes. When these resource inequities are erased throughout the system, alterations to the fine points of advanced jurisprudence will be less penny wise and pound foolish.

REFERENCES

Bornstein, B. H. (1999). The ecological validity of jury simulations: Is the jury still out? *Law and Human Behavior, 23,* 75–91.

Bornstein, B. H., & Rajki, M. (1994). Extra-legal factors and product liability: The influence of mock jurors' demographic characteristics and intuitions about the cause of an injury. *Behavioral Sciences and the Law, 12,* 127–147.

Bright, S. B. (1997). Neither equal nor just: The rationing and denial of legal services to the poor when life and liberty are at stake. *Annual Survey of American Law, 1997,* 783–836.

Bruschke, J., & Loges, W. E. (2004). *Free press vs. fair trials: Examining publicity's role in trial outcomes.* Mahwah, NJ: Lawrence Erlbaum Associates.

Bruschke, J. C., & Loges, W. E. (1999). The relationship between pretrial publicity and trial outcomes. *Journal of Communication, 49*(4), 104–120.

Burdine v. Johnson, 262 F.3d 336 (2001).

Burnett v. Collins, 982 F.2d 922 (1993).

Carroll, J. S., Kerr, N. L., Alfini, J. J., Weaver, F. M., MacCoun, R. J., & Feldman, V. (1986). Free press and fair trial: The role of behavioral research. *Law and Human Behavior, 100,* 187–201.

Coble v. Texas, U.S. App. Lexis 17134 (2003).

Constantini, E., & King, J. (1980–1981). The partial juror: Correlates and causes of prejudgment. *Law and Society Review, 15,* 9–40.

Davis, R. W. (1986). Pretrial publicity, the timing of the trial, and mock jurors' decision processes. *Journal of Applied Psychology, 16,* 590–607.

Demouchette v. Texas, 591 S.W.2d 488 (1979).

Dexter, H. R., Cutler, B. L., & Moran, G. (1992). A test of voir dire as a remedy for the prejudicial effects of pretrial publicity. *Journal of Applied Psychology, 22,* 819–832.

Dobbert v. Florida, 432 U.S. 282 (1977).

Fein, S., McCloskey, A. L., & Tomlinson, T. M. (1997). Can the jury disregard that information? The use of suspicion to reduce the prejudicial effects of pretrial publicity and inadmissible testimony. *Personality and Social Psychology Bulletin, 23,* 1215–1226.

Fein, S., Morgan, S. J., Norton, M. I., & Sommers, S. R. (1997). Hype and suspicion: The effects of pretrial publicity, race, and suspicion on jurors' verdicts. *Journal of Social Issues, 53,* 487–502.

Frasca, R. (1988). Estimating the occurrence of trials prejudiced by press coverage. *Judicature, 27*(3), 162–170.

Freedman, J. L., & Burke, T. M. (1996). The effect of pretrial publicity: The Bernardo case. *Canadian Journal of Criminology, 38,* 253–270.

Freedman, J. L., Martin, C. K., & Mota, V. L. (1998). Pretrial publicity: Effects of admonition and expressing pretrial opinions. *Legal and Criminological Psychology, 3,* 255–270.

Freedman, M. H. (1998). Our constitutionalized adversary system. *Chapman Law Review, 1,* 57–90.

Fulero, S. M. (1987). The role of behavioral research in the free press/fair trial controversy. *Law and Human Behavior, 11,* 259–264.

Fulero, S. M. (2002). Afterword: The past, present, and future of applied pretrial publicity research. *Law and Human Behavior, 26,* 127–133.

Gerber, R. J. (2001). Essay: On dispensing justice. *Arizona Law Review, 43,* 135–172.

Gerbner, G., Gross, L., Morgan, M., & Signorielli, N. (1986). Living with television: The dynamics of the cultivation process. In J. Bryant & D. Zillmann (Eds.), *Perspectives on media effects* (pp. 17–40). Hillsdale, NJ: Lawrence Erlbaum Associates.

Gibson, D. C., & Padilla, M. (1998, November). *Litigation public relations problems and limits.* Paper presented to the Commission on Communication & Law of the National Communication Association, New York.

Greene, E., & Loftus, E. F. (1984). What's new in the news? The influence of well-publicized news events on psychological research and courtroom trials. *Basic and Applied Social Psychology, 5,* 211–221.

Greene, E., & Wade, R. (1988). Of private talk and public print: General pre-trial publicity and juror decision-making. *Applied Cognitive Psychology, 2,* 123–135.

Hans, V. P., & Doob, A. N. (1976). Section 12 of the Canada Evidence Act and the deliberations of simulated juries. *Criminal Law Quarterly, 18,* 235–253.

Hill v. Ozmint, 339 F.3d 187 (2003).

Hoiberg, B. C., & Stires, L. K. (1973). The effect of several types of pretrial publicity on the guilt attributions of simulated jurors. *Journal of Applied Social Psychology, 3,* 267–275.

Hvistendahl, J. K. (1979). The effect of placement of biasing information. *Journalism Quarterly, 56,* 863–865.

Imrich, D. J., Mullin, C., & Linz, D. (1995). Measuring the extent of prejudicial pretrial publicity in major American newspapers: A content analysis. *Journal of Communication, 45,* 94–117.

Jones, R. M. (1991). The latest empirical studies on pretrial publicity, jury bias, and judicial remedies—not enough to overcome the first amendment right of access to pretrial hearings. *American University Law Review, 40,* 841–848.

Kaplan, M. F., & Miller, L. E. (1978). Reducing the effects of juror bias. *Journal of Personality and Social Psychology, 36,* 1443–1455.

Kelly v. Texas, 72 Fed. Appx. 67 (2003).

Kerr, N. L. (1994). The effects of pretrial publicity on jurors. *Judicature, 78,* 120–127.

Kerr, N. L., Kramer, G. P., Carroll, J. S., & Alfini, J. J. (1991). On the effectiveness of voir dire in criminal cases with prejudicial pretrial publicity: An empirical study. *The American University Law Review, 40,* 665–693.

Kerwin, J., & Shaffer, D. R. (1994). Mock jurors versus mock juries: The role of deliberations in reactions to inadmissible testimony. *Personality and Social Psychology Bulletin, 20,* 153–162.

Kovera, M. B. (2002). The effects of general pretrial publicity on juror decisions: An examination of the moderators and mediating mechanisms. *Law and Human Behavior, 26,* 43–72.

Kramer, G. P., & Kerr, N. L. (1989). Laboratory simulation and bias in the study of juror behavior: A methodological note. *Law and Human Behavior, 13,* 89–99.

Kramer, G. P., Kerr, N. L., & Carroll, J. S. (1990). Pretrial publicity, judicial remedies, and jury bias. *Law and Human Behavior, 14,* 409–437.

Kulish, M. (1998). The public's right of access to pretrial proceedings versus the accused's right to a fair trial. *Army Law, 1998,* 1–15.

Lindman, R. (1989). Sources of judicial mistrust of social science evidence: A comparison of social science and jurisprudence. *Indiana Law Journal, 64,* 755–768.

London, K., & Nunez, N. (2000). The effect of jury deliberations on jurors' propensity to disregard inadmissible evidence. *Journal of Applied Psychology, 85,* 932–939.

McConahay, J. B., Mullin, C. J., & Frederick, J. (1977). The uses of social science in trials with political and racial overtones: The trial of Joan Little. *Law and Contemporary Problems, 41,* 205–229.

Melton, G. B. (1987). Bringing psychology to the legal system: Opportunities, obstacles, and efficacy. *American Psychologist, 42,* 488–495.

Moran, G., & Cutler, B. L. (1991). The prejudicial impact of pretrial publicity. *Journal of Applied Social Psychology, 21,* 345–367.

Mullin, C., Imrich, D. J., & Linz, D. (1996). The impact of acquaintance rape stories and case-specific pretrial publicity on juror decision-making. *Communication Research, 23,* 100–135.

Murray, C. B., Kaiser, R., & Taylor, S. (1997). The OJ Simpson verdict: Predictors of beliefs about innocence or guilt. *Journal of Social Issues, 53,* 455–475.

Newman, L. S., Duff, K., Schnopp-Wyatt, N., Brock, B., & Hoffman, Y. (1997). Reactions to the O. J. Simpson verdict: "Mindless tribalism" or motivated inference processes. *Journal of Social Issues, 53,* 547–562.

Newsom, A. (2000). Pretrial publicity and individual voir dire: What has the Florida Supreme Court done to the jury selection process? *Florida Law Review, 52,* 1039–1072.

Nietzel, M. T., & Dillehay, R. C. (1983). Psychologists as consultants for changes of venue. *Law and Human Behavior, 7,* 309–335.

Ogloff, J. R. P. (2002). Two steps forward and one step backward: The law and psychology movement(s) in the 20th century. *Law and Human Behavior, 24,* 457–483.

Ogloff, J. R. P., & Vidmar, N. (1994). The impact of pretrial publicity on jurors: A study to compare the relative effects of television and print media in a child sex abuse case. *Law and Human Behavior, 18*, 507–525.

Ohio v. Lundgren, 73 Ohio St. 3d 474 (1995).

Ohio v. Nobles, 106 Ohio App. 3d 246 (1995).

Ohio v. Ritchie, Ohio App. Lexis 3421 (1997).

Ohio v. Yarbrough, 95 Ohio St. 3d 227 (2002).

Otto, A. L., Penrod, S. D., & Dexter, H. R. (1994). The biasing impact of pretrial publicity on juror judgments. *Law and Human Behavior, 18*, 453–469.

Padawer-Singer, A. M., & Barton, A. H. (1975). The impact of pretrial publicity on jurors' verdicts. In J. Simon (Ed.), *The jury system in America: A critical overview* (pp. 125–139). Beverly Hills: Sage.

Padawer-Singer, A. M., Singer, A., & Singer, R. (1974). Voir dire by two lawyers: An essential safeguard. *Judicature, 57*, 386–391.

Padawer-Singer, A. M., Singer, A. N., & Singer, R. L. J. (1977). Legal and social-psychological research in the effects of pretrial publicity on juries, numerical makeup of juries, non-unanimous verdict requirements. *Law and Psychology Review, 3*, 71–79.

Pember, D. R. (1984). Does pretrial publicity really hurt? *Columbia Journalism Review, 23*(3), 16–20.

Pember, D. R. (1990). *Mass media law.* Dubuque, IA: William C. Brown.

Pruett v. Norris, 153 F.3d 579 (1998).

Riedel, R. G. (1993). Effects of pretrial publicity on male and female jurors and judges in a mock rape trial case. *Psychological Reports, 73*, 819–832.

Riley, S. G. (1973). Pretrial publicity: A field study. *Journalism Quarterly, 50*, 17–23.

Ritchie v. Rogers, 313 F.3d 948 (2002).

Rollings, H. E., & Blascovich, J. (1977). The case of Patricia Hearst: Pretrial publicity and opinion. *Journal of Communication, 27*, 58–65.

Shaffer, R. A. (1986). Pretrial publicity: Media coverage and guilt attribution. *Communication Quarterly, 34*, 154–169.

Simon, R. J. (1966). Murder, juries, and the press. *Trans-Action, 3*(4), 40–42.

Simon, R. J. (1977). Does the Court's decision in *Nebraska Press Association* fit the research evidence on the impact on jurors of news coverage? *Stanford Law Review, 29*, 515–528.

Simon, R. J., & Eimermann, T. (1971). The jury finds not guilty: Another look at media influence on the jury. *Journalism Quarterly, 48*, 343–344.

Sohn, A. B. (1976). Determining guilt of innocence of accused from pretrial news stories. *Journalism Quarterly, 53*, 100–105.

Sommers, S. R., & Kassin, S. M. (2001). On the many impacts of inadmissible testimony: Selective compliance, need for cognition, and overcorrection bias. *Personality and Social Psychology Bulletin, 27*, 1368–1377.

Steblay, N. M., Besirevic, J., Fulero, S. M., & Jimenez-Lorente, B. (1999). The effects of pretrial publicity on juror verdicts: A meta-analytic review. *Law and Human Behavior, 23*, 219–235.

Strauss, D. A. (1998). Why it's not free speech versus fair trial. *University of Chicago Legal Forum, 1998*, 109–123.

Studebaker, C. A., & Penrod, S. D. (1997). Pretrial publicity: The media, the law, and common sense. *Psychology, Public Policy, & Law, 3*, 428–460.

Studebaker, C. A., Robbennolt, J. K., Pathak-Sharma, M. K., & Penrod, S. D. (2000). Assessing pretrial publicity effects: Integrating content analytic results. *Law and Human Behavior, 24*, 317–336.

Studebaker, C. A., Robbennolt, J. K., Penrod, S. D., Pathak-Sharma, M. K., Groscup, J. L., & Davenport, J. L. (2002). Studying pretrial publicity effects: New methods for improving ecological validity and testing external validity. *Law and Human Behavior, 26*, 19–41.

Sue, S., Smith, R. E., & Gilbert, R. (1974). Biasing effects of pretrial publicity on judicial decisions. *Journal of Criminal Justice, 2,* 163–171.

Sue, S., Smith, R. E., & Pedroza, G. (1975). Authoritarianism, pretrial publicity, and awareness of bias in simulated jurors. *Psychological Reports, 37,* 1299–1302.

Surette, R. (1992). Media trials and echo effects. In R. Surette (Ed.), *The media and criminal justice policy Recent research and social effects* (pp. 177–192). Springfield, IL: C. C. Thomas.

Tanford, S., & Penrod, S. (1982). Biases in trial involving defendants charged with multiple offenses. *Journal of Applied Social Psychology, 12,* 453–480.

Tankard, J. W., Middleton, K., & Rimmer, T. (1979). Compliance with American Bar Association fair trial-free press guidelines. *Journalism Quarterly, 56,* 464–468.

Tans, M. D., & Chaffee, S. H. (1966). Pretrial publicity and juror prejudice. *Journalism Quarterly, 43,* 647–654.

United States v. Allee, 299 F.3d 996 (2002).

United States v. Bieganowski, 313 F.3d 264 (2002).

United States v. Blom, 242 F.3d 799 (2001).

United States v. Faul, 748 F.2d 1204 (1984).

United States v. Nelson, 2003 U.S. App. Lexis 21360 (2003).

Vidmar, N. (2002). Case studies of pre- and midtrial prejudice in criminal and civil litigation. *Law and Human Behavior, 26,* 73–105.

Vidmar, N., & Judson, J. T. (1981). The use of social science data in a change of venue application: A case study. *La Revue Du Barreau Canadien, 59,* 76–102.

Vidmar, N., & Melnitzer, J. (1984). Juror prejudice: An empirical study of challenge for cause. *Osgoode Hall Law Journal, 22,* 487–511.

Visher, C. A. (1987). Juror decision making: The importance of evidence. *Law and Human Behavior, 11,* 1–17.

Walton, J. A. (1998). From O. J. to Tim McVeigh and beyond: The Supreme Court's totality of circumstances test as ringmaster in the expanding media circus. *Denver University Law Review, 75,* 549–593.

Wilcox, W., & McCombs, M. (1967). *Crime story elements and fair trial/free press.* Unpublished report, University of California at Los Angeles. Reported in Wilcox (1970).

Wilson, J. R., & Bornstein, B. H. (1998). Methodological considerations in pretrial publicity research: Is the medium the message. *Law and Human Behavior, 22,* 585.

Zeisel, H., & Diamond, S. S. (1978). The effect of peremptory challenges on jury and verdict: An experiment in a federal district court. *Stanford Law Review, 30,* 491–531.

Chapter 6

Pornographic Knowledge, the Law, and Social Science

Robert Jensen
University of Texas

The law is full of talk, of writing and speaking. Lawyers, scholars, and judges talk a lot, and they write a lot. Courtrooms and law libraries are filled with talk. Over the past five decades, there has been lots of talk about the law of obscenity, about sexually explicit material, about pornography. But there have also been many silences, from which we can learn if we choose to pay attention. Sometimes the questions not asked can tell us more than the answers to the questions that are asked.

Here is a question rarely asked about pornography: What does it feel like to be penetrated anally and vaginally at the same time? That is, if one man is thrusting his penis in your anus and another man is thrusting his penis in your vagina at the same time, how does that feel? Here is another question rarely asked: Why do men like to watch that?

Men do watch that, over and over, on pornographic videos and DVDs. It is called—in the vernacular of the pornography industry—a double penetration or a DP. Lots of pornographic films include DPs. Not just a few specialty tapes that appeal to a fringe group of consumers, but lots of tapes, right there on the mainstream shelf in your local pornographic video store. Men rent them and buy them, and they take them home and use them to masturbate to orgasm.

That is a part of the pornographic reality in the United States today. I specified two questions about that reality that seem relevant:

1. What does it feel like to be the person penetrated in a DP?

2. Why do men like to watch films with DPs?

And implied a third:

3. Why are those questions so rarely asked?

I do not know the answer to Question 1. I am not a woman. More on that later. I have ideas about the answer to Question 2. More on that later. I am pretty sure about the answer to Question 3: Fear. This culture is afraid to face what it has become. In some ways, I do not blame people for that. I have been working on the issue of pornography for 15 years, and I am afraid. I think it is sensible to be afraid. But it is not sensible to let the fear—or the law—drive us into silence.

That fear goes beyond a merely visceral reaction to the type of scene described earlier; it also takes us to a truth about systems and structures of power. A DP is the logical result of the intersection of capitalism and patriarchy. In the capitalist world in which we live, everything is a commodity, everything is in the market, everything can be bought and sold. In the patriarchal world in which we live, women exist for men. Yes, patriarchy existed before mass-mediated pornography, and, yes, capitalism buys, sells, and destroys much more than women. But in a capitalist patriarchy, DPs are, if not predictable, at least not surprising.

Welcome to the world of the DP. This is what, collectively, we have become. Not just the men who make those films or watch them, but all of us. Some celebrate it; most ignore it. Some fight against it. But we all are implicated in it.

Regardless of whether you have ever pushed play on the VCR to watch one, you live in the world of the DP. It is a world that the law has made possible. It is a world that lawyers and law scholars have helped create. By that I do not mean that all lawyers and law scholars consciously, actively work to create a pornographic world. Some small number do that, working directly for the pornographers. Of more interest, however, should be how the law in a more overarching sense helps create the world of the DP by helping create the silences that allow this particular part of the capitalist patriarchy to go largely unchallenged.

THE WORLD OF THE DP

The law is, at its core, about abstract principles. I enjoy debating abstract principles, and I think people should spend a lot of time thinking and arguing about them. But we sometimes use abstract principles to hide from what is painful in the world. The debate around pornography is one of those times. Before we wander off toward abstract principles, let us linger a bit on the shape of the world of the DP. Let us stay grounded in the pornographic world where we live.

Pornography in the post-World War II era has changed from an underground business with ties to organized crime to a flourishing industry that operates publicly and includes many small producers as well as corporations with substantial assets. In 2002, more than 11,000 new hardcore video/DVD titles were released (*Adult Video News*, 2002), and annual sales are estimated at $10 billion or higher (Lane, 2000, p. xiv).

Over 7 years, I have conducted three qualitative studies of the content of graphic, sexually explicit video pornography—what is typically called *hard core*. All the videos in these studies came from stores that rent and sell *adult product* (the industry's preferred term for pornography) in U.S. cities. All the videos were from the mainstream section of the stores, not specialty or fetish collections. None of the videos used children. In short: This is material easily and legally available in the United States, and it is representative of the standard fare the industry offers.

My work and reviews of other studies of content suggest there are a few basic themes in pornography: (a) All women at all times want sex from all men; (b) women enjoy all the sexual acts that men perform or demand, including those that are denigrating, hostile, or violent; and (c) any woman who does not at first realize this can be easily turned with a little force, although force is rarely necessary because most of the women in pornography are the imagined nymphomaniacs about whom men fantasize.

That is the general outline of contemporary pornography. Here are short descriptions of two of the six scenes from "Two in the Seat #3," a 2003 release from the Red Light District company, to provide specifics. Each scene begins with a brief interview with the woman who will be penetrated by two men.

Claire James says she is 20 years old and has been performing in pornographic films for 3 months. When asked why she is there, she says, "I'm here to get pounded" and announces that she would like to perform a double anal—being penetrated anally by two penises at the same time— that day (she does not attempt that, at least not in the video). At that point, two men enter the room. One asks, "Are you a dirty nasty girl? You must be." The other starts to handle her roughly, grabbing her face and slapping her lightly. During the initial round of oral sex, one man holds her head while the other one grabs her pigtails. "All the way down to the balls," one says. During intercourse, the men offer a steady stream of comments such as, "You're a little fucking cunt" and "You're such a little slut." At one point, Claire says, "Please put your cock in my ass." During the DP, her vocalizations sound clearly pained. The three are on the floor, with Claire braced against the couch, not moving much. The men spank her, and her buttocks are red. "Yea, I love it," she says. One man says, "I want to hear you scream."

At one point, one of the men asks, "Are you crying?"

"No, I'm enjoying it," Claire says.

"Damn, I thought you were crying. It was turning me on when I thought you were crying," he says.

"Would you like me to?" she asks.

"Yea, give me a fucking tear," he says. "Oh, there's a fucking tear."

The scene ends, as do virtually all scenes in pornography, with ejaculation on her body or in her mouth. "Feed me your cum," Claire says, displaying the first man's ejaculate in her mouth for the camera. "Swallowed," she says. After the second man ejaculates, she wipes the semen off her face with her fingers and eats it. The off-camera interviewer asks how she feels. Claire reports that her asshole feels good: "Feels great. A little raw, but that's good."

In another scene, Jessica Darlin tells the camera she has performed in 200 films and that she is submissive: "I like guys to just take over and just fuck me and have a good time with me. I'm just here for pleasure." The man who enters the room grabs her hair and tells her to beg the other man. She crawls over on her hands and knees, and he spanks her hard. When he grabs her by the throat hard, she seems surprised. The other man comes across the room and grabs her from behind, pulling her hair. During oral sex, he says, "Choke on that dick." She gags. He grabs her head and slaps her face, then forces his penis in her mouth quickly. She gags again. The other man duplicates the action, calling her a "little bitch." Jessica is drooling after gagging; she looks as if she might pass out. The men slap her breasts and then grab her by the hair and pull her up.

During intercourse, one man grabs her by the throat. At this point, Jessica is moaning/screaming. She sounds, literally, like a wounded animal. The sex continues. One man puts two fingers in her anus and then makes her suck his fingers. She says: "Fuck my ass. I'm a fucking whore. I want you to fuck my ass." The other man spits in her mouth. One man enters her anally from the rear as she is pushed up against the couch. Then the other man enters her anally while his partner puts his foot on her head. One says, "Keep your fucking ass up" when she drops too close to the floor. Finally, one grabs her hair and asks what she wants. "I want you to cum in mouth," she says. "Give me all that cum. I want to taste it."

A quick reminder of the questions:

1. What does it feel like to be the person penetrated in a DP?
2. Why do men like to watch DPs?
3. Why are those questions so rarely asked?

WHY MEN LIKE TO WATCH

The two scenes described previously are not just about sex. They are about women in pain during sex. I am not suggesting that in every scene in mainstream pornography such expressions of pain are evident. Again, I acknowledge that I cannot know exactly what the women in these films were feeling, physically or emotionally (more on that later). However, it is not necessary to reach definitive conclusions about the degree of pain women experience in such scenes to make one important observation. In these scenes, the women at some point clearly appeared to a viewer to be in pain. Their facial expressions and voices conveyed that what was being done to them was causing physical discomfort, and/or fear, and/or distress. Given the ease with which video can be edited, why did the producers not edit out those expressions? There are two possible answers. One, they may view these kinds of expressions of pain by the women as of no consequence to the viewers' interest, and hence of no consequence to the goal of maximizing sales; women's pain is neutral. The second possibility is that the producers have reason to believe that viewers like the expressions of pain; women's pain helps sales.

Given that the vast majority of those who will rent or buy these tapes are men, from that we can derive this question: Why do some men find the infliction of pain on women during sexual activity either (a) not an obstacle to their ability to achieve sexual pleasure, or (b) a factor that can enhance their sexual pleasure? Phrased differently: Why are some men so callous and cruel sexually?

By that, I do not mean to ask why men are capable of being cruel in some general sense. All humans have the capacity to be cruel toward other humans and other living things, and we have all done cruel things in our lives. Contemporary mainstream heterosexual pornography raises a more specific question: Why do some men find cruelty to women either sexually neutral or sexually pleasurable?

Feminist research into, and women's reflection on, experiences of sexual violence long ago established that rape involves the sexualization of power, the fusing in men's imaginations of sexual pleasure with domination and control. The common phrase "rape is about power, not sex" misleads; rape is about the fusion of sex and domination, about the eroticization of control. In this culture, rape is normal. That is, in a culture where the dominant definition of sex is the taking of pleasure from women by men, rape is an expression of the sexual norms of the culture, not violations of those norms. Sex is a sphere in which men are trained to see themselves as naturally dominant and women naturally passive. Rape is both nominally illegal and completely normal at the same time.

So, there is nothing surprising in the observation that some pornography includes explicit images of women in pain. From my research, both through these content analysis projects and my reading of the industry's trade magazine, it seems clear that mainstream heterosexual pornography is getting more, not less, cruel. Why?

There are only so many ways human beings can, in mechanical terms, have sex. There are a limited number of body parts and openings, a limited number of ways to create the friction that produces the stimulation and sensations, and a limited number of positions from which the friction can be produced. Sexual variation, in this sense, is finite because of these physical limits.

Sex, of course, also has an emotional component, and emotions are infinitely variable. There are only so many ways people can rub bodies together, but endless are the ways different people can feel about rubbing bodies together in different times, places, and contexts. When most non-pornographic films, such as a typical Hollywood romance, deal with sex, they draw on the emotions most commonly connected with sex—love and affection. But pornography does not because films that exist to provide sexual stimulation for men in this culture would not work if the sex were presented in the context of loving and affectionate relationships. Men typically consume pornography specifically to avoid love and affection.

That means pornography has a problem. When all emotion is drained from sex, it becomes repetitive and uninteresting, even to men who are watching primarily to facilitate masturbation. So, pornography needs an edge. Pornography has to draw on some emotion, hence the cruelty.

When the legal restrictions on pornography slowly receded through the 1970s and 1980s, and the presentation of sex on the screen was by itself no longer quite so illicit, anal sex became a standard feature. Anal sex was seen as something most women do not want; it had an edge to it. When anal sex became routine in pornography, the gonzo genre started pushing the boundaries into things like double penetrations and gag-inducing oral sex—again acts that men believe women generally will not want. The more pornography becomes normalized and mainstreamed, the more pornography has to search for that edge. That edge most commonly is cruelty, which emotionally is the easiest place to go for men, given that the dynamic of male domination and female submission is already in place in patriarchy. I think that is why men like to watch DPs.

IF YOU WANT TO TAKE
THE EASY WAY OUT—DON'T

If you want to think that the scenes described earlier are idiosyncratic, do not take easy way out #1. The contemporary video and DVD pornography market has a range of products. Some are called *features*, which typically have a minimal plot line and make attempts, no matter how badly executed, at character development. Others, like "Two in the Seat #3," are *gonzo* films that have no pretense of narrative and simply present sexual activity. The industry markets features to the so-called *couples market*. Here is a description of a scene from a feature from one of the industry's major production companies.

"Sopornos IV" is a 2003 release from VCA Pictures. The plot is a take-off on the popular HBO series about mobsters. In IV, mob boss Bobby Soporno is obsessed with the thought that everyone in his life is always having sex, including his crew and his daughter. In the final sex scene, his wife has sex with two of his men. After the standard progression through oral and vaginal sex, one of the men prepares to penetrate her anally. She tells him: "That fucking cock is so fucking huge. . . . Spread [my] fucking ass. . . . Spread it open." He penetrates her. Then she says, in a slightly lower tone, "Don't go any deeper," and she seems to be in pain. At the end of the scene, she begs for their semen ("Two cocks jacking off in my face. I want it"), opens her mouth, and the men ejaculate onto her at the same time.

"Sopornos IV" is the allegedly sophisticated, high end of the pornography market. Features are still profitable, but are being eclipsed by a gonzo market that is increasingly harsh. As Jerome Tanner put it during a pornography directors' roundtable discussion featured in *Adult Video News*, "People just want it harder, harder, and harder, because like Ron said, what are you gonna do next?" (*Adult Video News*, 2003, p. 60). Another director, Jules Jordan, was blunt about his task:

> [O]ne of the things about today's porn and the extreme market, the gonzo market, so many fans want to see so much more extreme stuff that I'm always trying to figure out ways to do something different. But it seems everybody wants to see a girl doing a d.p. now or a gangbang. For certain girls, that's great, and I like to see that for certain people, but a lot of fans are becoming a lot more demanding about wanting to see the more extreme stuff. It's definitely brought porn somewhere, but I don't know where it's headed from there. (p. 46)

Director Mitchell Spinelli, interviewed while filming the first video ("Give Me Gape") for a series for his new Acid Rain company, seemed clear where it was heading:

> "People want more. They want to know how many dicks you can shove up an ass," he says with a shrug. "It's like Fear Factor meets Jackass. Make it more hard, make it more nasty, make it more relentless. The guys make the difference. You need a good guy, who's been around and can give a good scene, fuckin' 'em hard. I did my homework. These guys are intense." (*Adult Video News*, 2004, p. 158)

Easy way out #2: A man writing about pornography cannot know how the women in these scenes feel or experience that sexual activity. I agree. I do not presume to speak for them, or for women in pornography, or for women in general. But I know that when I describe a DP to women during talks I do on pornography, the overwhelming majority of them wince—out of empathy, they tell me. They imagine the physical and emotional discomfort of such an act, and they feel. Their empathy does not seem misplaced. Here is what Belladonna, one of the women who appeared in "Two in the Seat #3," told a TV interviewer about such scenes: "You have to really prepare physically and mentally for it. I mean, I go through a process from the night before. I stop eating at 5:00. I do, you know, like two enemas. The next morning I don't eat anything. It's so draining on your body" (ABC News Primetime Live, 2003).

There is individual variation in how people experience anything, including pain. But there are also patterns to how people experience things, and to empathize with people who fit a pattern is not to ignore those who are outside it. The effect that the routine sexual activity in pornography (such as double penetrations) has on women is largely unexplored. Anecdotal evidence (Gittler, 1999), combined with extrapolations from the data available about women in prostitution (Baldwin, 1989; Farley, 2003), suggests that psychological and physical damage is common and heavy alcohol and drug use is routine. There is nothing stopping us from empathizing with those women. To empathize with them is not to argue that all women have the same experience in pornography. It is not to argue that women in pornography are dupes. The capacity for empathy is typically regarded to be a virtue.

Easy way out #3: If you want to believe that only a tiny percentage of deviant men consume such material, here is a story:

A female undergraduate student is traveling to a University of Texas football game on a bus chartered by a fraternity. During the trip, one of the men puts a hard-core pornographic video into the bus VCR. After a few minutes, the woman gathers the courage to tell the man she is sitting next to that she is uncomfortable with the video. There is some discussion among several students. Finally, the man gets up and tells his fraternity brothers that, although he enjoys watching pornography, he thinks that they should not be playing that video on the bus. The tape continues playing for a few minutes, but eventually is shut off. Three things seem worth pondering. At the (allegedly) most prestigious university in Texas:

1. A significant percentage of the men in a fraternity see nothing wrong with watching a hard-core pornographic video.
2. A significant percentage of the men in a fraternity see nothing wrong with watching a hard-core pornographic video with women present.

3. The one man, prompted by a woman, in a fraternity who dared to suggest that the video was inappropriate felt the need to preface his request with a declaration that he likes pornography, making clear he was concerned not about the action on the screen, but simply the presence of women on the bus.

Meanwhile, at Yale University, another allegedly prestigious university, students formed a "Porn 'n Chicken" club. An overwhelmingly male group (the initial story in the *Yale Herald* in 2000 reported 16 men and 1 woman present) gathered to watch hard-core pornography and eat take-out fried chicken (Ax, 2000). Media attention followed. Some of the students decided to produce their own video, about sex in the Yale Library, called "The Staxxx." The cable network Comedy Central produced a film about the group that aired in 2002 (Comedy Central, 2002).

At every talk I give on the subject, women tell me about how many men in their lives consume pornography, increasingly without any sense of embarrassment or regret. Ask a clerk at a pornography shop what kind of men patronize the business, and the answer will be, "Every kind." Who watches pornography? Who rents "Two in the Seat #3"? If you are a woman, the answer is: Your brother, your father, your uncle. If you are a heterosexual woman, the answer also is: Your boyfriend, your husband. If you are a man, you know the answer. All the easy ways out are dead ends. They lead to silences.

LAW'S QUESTIONS

There exists in the United States no law of pornography. Instead obscenity law creates a category of sexual material that the courts have deemed to be outside full protection of the First Amendment and subject to regulation by the state. *Obscene material* is defined as that which appeals to the prurient interest in sex, depicts sexual conduct in a patently offensive manner, and lacks serious literary, artistic, political, or scientific value (*Miller v. California*, 1973). *Indecency* is a term from broadcasting (over-the-air radio and TV) that defines an even broader category—language or material that, in context, depicts or describes, in terms patently offensive as measured by contemporary community broadcast standards for the broadcast medium, sexual or excretory organs or activities—that can be regulated by the federal government (Federal Communications Commission, 2004).

A separate category is child pornography—material that is either made using children or, in the digital age, made through the use of technology that makes it appear the sexual activity uses children. The former is illegal without question (*New York v. Ferber*, 1982); the status of the second remains cloudy, but, for the moment, legal (*Ashcroft v. Free Speech Coalition*, 2002). The legal status of pornography using adults depends not only on the nature of the material, but also on the community and the political climate. Much of what is sold in pornography shops in the United States potentially fits the definition of obscenity, but in most jurisdictions prosecutors choose not to initiate cases. The same obscenity laws apply to the genres of lesbian or gay pornography.

Obscenity law attempts to impose a particular moral conception of sex on an entire society. Many view obscenity law as censorship. In its existing form it is, of course, censorship: Through obscenity law, the government criminalizes certain kinds of images and words. One can argue that it is appropriate censorship, but there is no doubt it is censorship. I do not argue that obscenity law is appropriate. As the feminist antipornography movement has pointed out, obscenity law is hypocritical, stupid, and pointless. It allows a culture that is deeply conflicted over sexuality and gender to pretend to engage an issue while accomplishing nothing.

That feminist movement offered a different approach, conceptualizing the actual harm done to women in the production and use of pornography as a civil rights issue (Dworkin, 1988; MacKinnon, 1987). Rooted in the real-world experiences of women sharing experiences through a grassroots movement, the feminist critique highlighted pornography's harms to women and children: (a) used in the production of pornography; (b) who have pornography forced on them; (c) who are sexually assaulted by men who use pornography; and (d) are living in a culture in which pornography reinforces and sexualizes women's subordinate status.

The theorists and legal strategists of the movement wrote an ordinance to address those harms. That ordinance defined *pornography* as the graphic sexually explicit subordination of women and a systematic practice of exploitation and subordination based on sex, and created causes of action based on the ways in which women are (1) coerced into pornography, (2) forced to view pornography, (3) victimized by assaults caused by pornography, (4) defamed through unauthorized use of their images in pornography, and (5) subordinated through the trafficking of women in pornography (Dworkin & MacKinnon, 1988). That ordinance was tossed out by the courts on First Amendment grounds (*American Booksellers Association v. Hudnut*, 1986).

Causes of action #1, #2, and #4 raise some interesting legal questions, but are well within parameters of existing tort law. The most contentious parts of the ordinance were #3 and #5. Although I am part of the antipornography movement and support the ordinance, I do not believe that #5, the trafficking clause, can withstand constitutional scrutiny. Women are subordinated in U.S. society, and pornography plays a role in that, but that does not mean that the connection is direct enough to be addressed through the law in that fashion.

That leaves us with #3, the assault clause. Should women have a right to pursue a civil complaint seeking damages from the maker, distributor, seller, and/or exhibitor of specific pornographic material (that fits the prior definition) for a sexual assault that is "directly caused by the specific pornography" (Dworkin & MacKinnon, 1988, p. 140)? The ordinance does not assume such causal relationships exist in all potential cases, but simply creates a cause of action women could pursue in court, where they would have to establish that relationship.

This issue is typically reduced to the question, "Does pornography cause rape?" That is the wrong question. The problem is, it is not just the wrong question, but the kind of wrong question that keeps us away from the right question and an honest search for answers.

THE LAW ASKS THE WRONG QUESTIONS, SOCIAL SCIENCE HELPS TO NOT ANSWER THEM

If you want to derail serious discussion of a difficult issue, one effective way is to frame the question in a misleading way and then devise approaches to answering the question that cannot answer it, leading to a semipermanent conclusion that "we don't know enough to make a determination." That is the story of the research on the effects of pornography.

First, some fairly obvious points: If the question about the connection between pornography and sexual violence is constructed simplistically—"Does pornography cause rape?"—the answer is clearly no. Because some men who use pornography do not rape and some men who rape do not use pornography, pornography is neither a necessary nor a sufficient condition for rape. There is no way to make a convincing claim that pornography is, as the lawyers say, an "if not but for" cause—"if not but for the use of pornography, this man would not have raped."

But if we ponder the question beyond simplistic cause-and-effect models (which are not particularly useful in explaining any human behavior), we might ask, "Is pornography ever a factor that contributes to rape?" That question recognizes the limits of our ability to understand complex behavior while opening up pathways for deeper understanding within those limits.

No critic of pornography has argued that pornography is ever the sole, direct causal agent in sexual violence. No one argues that if pornography disappeared that rape would disappear. Instead, the discussion should be about the ways in which pornography might be *implicated* in sexual violence in this culture. We understand that pornography alone does not make men do it, but that pornography is part of a world in which men do it, and therefore the production, content, and use of pornography are important to understand in the quest to eliminate sexual violence.

Virtually all reviews of the literature on the potential connections between pornography and sexual violence suggest there is evidence for some limited effects on male consumers, but no way to reach definitive conclusions. If one is looking for direct causal links in a traditional science model, this is likely to be a permanent assessment; it is difficult to imagine research methods that could provide more compelling data and conclusions. However, if we expand the scope of the inquiry, other insights are possible (Boyle, 2000).

A BRIEF INTERRUPTION
FOR A DEFINITIONAL DISCUSSION

The term used most often in the public debate over sexually explicit material, as well as much of the research literature, is *pornography*, which has no commonly accepted definition. It is sometimes used as a generic term for commercially produced sexually explicit books, magazines, movies, and Internet sites, with a distinction commonly made between soft-core (nudity with limited sexual activity that does not include penetration) and hard-core (graphic images of actual, not simulated, sexual activity including penetration). In other contexts, the term is juxtaposed with *erotica*, which typically is defined as material that depicts sexual behavior in a context of mutuality and respect. In that dichotomy, pornography is defined as material depicting sex in a context of domination or degradation.

Most laboratory studies of pornography's effects, which are discussed next, typically go beyond the hard-core/soft-core and pornography/erotica distinctions, typically constructing three categories of pornography: violent, nonviolent but degrading, and sexually explicit but neither violent nor degrading. The problem with these categories is obvious: Are double penetrations or gag-inducing oral sex acts (in which men try to press their penises so far down women's throats that they gag or vomit) violent or merely degrading but nonviolent? Or are they simply sexually explicit without violence or degradation? What about a double anal? If virtually all pornography constructs women as sexual objects to be used by men, is there pornography that is not denigrating?

BACK TO THE SOCIAL SCIENTISTS

Three basic types of studies have emerged in the search for an answer to the question about the relationship between pornography and violence, two of which are within the traditional science model and of limited value. First, a few large-scale studies have investigated the correlation of the availability of pornography to rates of violence with mixed results (Jaffee & Strauss, 1987; Kutchinsky, 1991). The complexity of confounding variables and the imprecision of measures make these studies virtually useless.

Second, experimental studies in the laboratory have been constructed to investigate directly the question of causal links. A typical study might expose groups of subjects to different types or levels of sexually explicit material for comparison to a control group that views nonsexual material. Researchers look for significant differences between the groups on a measure of, for example, male attitudes toward rape. From such controlled testing—measuring the effect of an experimental stimulus (exposure to pornography) on a dependent variable (attitudes toward women or sex) in randomly selected groups—researchers make claims, usually tentative, about causal relationships.

One of the most thorough reviews of the experimental literature by leading researchers in the field concluded that "if a person has relatively aggressive sexual inclinations resulting from various personal and/or cultural factors, some pornography exposure may activate and reinforce associated coercive tendencies and behaviors" (Malamuth, Addison, & Koss, 2000, p. 81). The authors also pointed out that "high pornography use is not necessarily indicative of high risk for sexual aggression" (p. 79). Another large-scale literature review also concluded that men predisposed to violence are most likely to show effects and that men not predisposed are unlikely to show effects (Seto, Maric, & Barbaree, 2001).

Although this experimental work sometimes offers interesting hints at how pornography works in regard to men's sexual behavior, it suffers from several serious problems that limit its value. First, the definitional issues raised earlier should leave us highly skeptical about any claims to scientific precision. Beyond that, the measures of men's attitudes toward women—such as answers to questions about the appropriate punishment for rapists—do not necessarily tell us anything about men's willingness to rape. Men often do not view their sexually aggressive or violent behavior as aggression or violence; it is just sex. In other words, men who rape often condemn rape, which they see as something other men do. Also sexual behavior is a complicated mix of cognitive, emotional, and physical responses, and the answers one gives to a survey may or may not accurately reflect that mix.

Most important, these lab studies are also incapable of measuring subtle effects that develop over time. If pornography develops attitudes and shapes behavior after repeated exposure, there is no guarantee that studies exposing people to a small amount of pornography over a short time can accurately measure anything. For example, in one study, the group exposed to what the researchers called the *massive* category of pornography viewed six explicitly sexual, 8-minute films per session for six sessions, or 4 hours and 48 minutes of material (Zillmann & Bryant, 1982). Of course no lab experiment can replicate the common male practice of masturbating to pornography, which no doubt influences the way in which men interpret and are affected by pornography. Orgasm is a powerful physical and emotional experience that is central to the pornographic experience, yet there is no ethical way that lab studies can take this into account. Although most critics of the experimental research caution that such studies may overstate the effects, for these reasons it is just as likely that the research underestimates pornography's role in promoting misogynistic attitudes and behavior.

A third method of investigation—interviews with men who use pornography, especially those who are sexually aggressive, and women involved in relationships with such men—does not hold out the promise of conclusive judgments about the effects of pornography, but such work can help us achieve deeper understanding. It is especially important to include the experiences of women, the main targets of violence, who have crucial insights (Bergen & Bogle, 2000). What we learn from the testimony of women and men whose lives have been touched by pornography is how the material is implicated in violence against women and how it can perpetuate, reinforce, and be part of a wider system of woman hating. Rather than asking whether pornography causes rape, we can ask how pornography helps make rape inviting.

Based both on the lab research and such interviews, Diana Russell has argued that pornography is a causal factor in the way that it can: (a) predispose some males to desire rape or intensify this desire, (b) undermine some males' internal inhibitions against acting out rape desires, (c) undermine some males' social inhibitions against acting out rape desires, and (d) undermine some potential victims' abilities to avoid or resist rape (Russell, 1998).

Even without making claims that strong, the public testimony of women (MacKinnon & Dworkin, 1997), my interviews with pornography users and sex offenders, and various other researchers' work have led me to conclude that pornography can: (a) be an important factor in shaping a male-dominant view of sexuality, (b) be used to initiate victims and break down their resistance to sexual activity, (c) contribute to a user's difficulty in separating sexual fantasy and reality, and (d) provide a training manual for abusers (Dines & Jensen, 2004). Consider the following reports and what they tell us about the relationship between pornography and behavior:

> From a street prostitute, who reported that when one john exploded at her he said:
>
> "I know all about you bitches, you're no different; you're like all of them. I seen it in all the movies. You love being beaten. [He then began punching the victim violently.] I just seen it again in that flick. He beat the shit out of her while he raped her and she told him she loved it; you know you love it; tell me you love it." (Silbert & Pines, 1984, p. 864)

> From a woman, interviewed in a study of sexual assault:
>
> "My husband enjoys pornographic movies. He tries to get me to do things he finds exciting in movies. They include twosomes and threesomes. I always refuse. Also, I was always upset with his ideas about putting objects in my vagina, until I learned this is not as deviant as I used to think. He used to force me or put whatever he enjoyed into me." (Russell, 1980, pp. 226)

Consider the reports from three different men in my study who had been convicted of sex offenses (Dines, Jensen, & Russo, 1998):

> From a 34-year-old man who had raped women and sexually abused girls:
>
> "There was a lot of oral sex that I wanted her to perform on me. There were, like, ways that would entice it in the movies, and I tried to use that on her, and it wouldn't work. Sometimes I'd get frustrated, and that's when I started hitting her. . . . I used a lot of force, a lot of direct demands, that in the movies women would just cooperate. And I would demand stuff from her. And if she didn't, I'd start slapping her around." (p. 124)

> From a 41-year-old man who had sexually abused his stepdaughter:
>
> "In fact, when I'd be abusing my daughter, I'd be thinking about some women I saw in a video. Because if I was to open my eyes and see my stepdaughter laying there while I was abusing her, you know, that wouldn't have been very exciting for me. You know, that would bring me back to the painful reality that I'm a child molester, where I'm in this reality of I'm making love or having intercourse with this beautiful woman from the video. The video didn't even come into my mind. It was just this beautiful person who had a beautiful body, and she was willing to do anything I asked." (p. 126)

> From a 24-year-old man who had sexually abused young girls while working as a school bus driver:

"When I was masturbating to these pornography things, I would think about certain girls I had seen on the bus or ones I had sold drugs to, and I would think as I was looking at these pictures in these books, what would it be like to have this girl or whoever doing this, what I'm thinking about. . . . Just masturbating to the thought wasn't getting it for me anymore. I actually had to be a part of it, or actually had to do something about it. . . . Like sometimes after I'd see like a certain load of kids would get off the bus, I'd pick out a couple and I'd watch them or stop and look at the mirror and stare at them and stuff like that. I would think, later on in the day, I'd masturbate to some pornography, I'd just use that picture kind of as a mental, it's kind of a scenery or whatever, and I'd put in my mind I'd put myself and whoever at the time I was thinking about, in that picture." (pp. 128–129)

BACK TO THE LAW

The law is not a subtle enough instrument to address every injury in the world. Every time law is used to address an injury, one must balance the costs and benefits. Libel law, for example, allows broad protections for journalists who make unintentional errors that result in defamatory statements about a public official. That means there will be public officials who are libeled but have no recourse in law. Such a public official is asked to bear a cost (being denied a legal remedy potentially available to others who are not public officials) for the greater good (creation of a robust climate for political discourse).

One can make a plausible argument that even if injuries result from pornography, those injuries cannot be remedied by the law without creating unacceptable restrictions on freedom of expression. I can understand the argument and see the logic of it, although I think it underestimates the severity of the injuries and overestimates the value of the expression involved. Yet I have had valuable discussions with people who reach different conclusions than I.

I also have had less productive discussions with people who valorize pornography. Most of those discussions have been with men, although some have been with women. The latter tend to be more complex, and I will not speculate about them—in large part because I do not think it is my place as a man in a patriarchal society to judge the motivations of women. Yet I feel well within my rights and competence to analyze and judge the motivations of men based on a lifetime of being a man and 15 years of experience engaging men on this subject.

I think many men (a) are afraid of confronting their own use of pornography, (b) realize that because they are men living in patriarchy they can get away with that evasion, and (c) routinely use the law to do it.

They engage in what I have called the *dodges and distortions* of pornography (Dines, Jensen, & Russo, 1998), some of which I have touched on earlier, but which deserve elaboration.

DODGES

1. Definitional Dodge

If we cannot define the term with precision, some argue, then we cannot or should not try to say much of anything about pornography. As D. H. Lawrence (1955) put it, "What is pornography to one man is the laughter of genius to another" (p. 195). In other words, it is always subjective, all a matter of taste. Attempts to discuss pornography and its role in the world repeatedly are torpedoed by definitional debates. What is pornography? How is it different from erotica? Who decides which is which? All of these are relevant questions, but they become diversionary when they keep us from engaging other issues. Disputes about legal definitions, after all, need not derail a wider conversation in the culture.

Yet it is also important to remember that pornography is not necessarily more difficult to define legally than any other term. One of the jobs of the law is to define words. Legal terms do not simply drop from the sky with clear meaning, but are instead defined through application and use. The struggle over definitions is a political and legal battle—one that takes place both inside and outside the legal arena.

2. Constitutional Dodge

Because the antipornography movement came to public attention in large part through the civil rights ordinance that the federal courts ultimately rejected, it is not surprising that constitutional concerns have been prominent in discussions about the feminist critique. Yet routinely in public discussions, the First Amendment is invoked as a talisman to shut down critiques of pornography. Because the Constitution obviously prohibits legislation, some argue, there is little need for extensive analysis of how pornography works because collective action through law has been ruled out. Yet two points are important. First, interpretation of the constitutional guarantees of freedom of speech and press is but one interpretation, and interpretations change over time (Jensen, 1995). Second, even if the First Amendment, for the foreseeable future, blocks the implementation of the ordinance, society still faces the same social questions about pornography and its effects in the world. The rejection of a legislative strategy by the courts does not erase the important questions about how we as individuals and a society deal with pornography outside the legal arena. Again, a narrow focus on the legal and constitutional questions can derail important discussions.

3. Causal Dodge

Because science has not yet conclusively shown a causal link between the use of pornography and sexual violence, some pornography supporters argue, no collective action is possible. Yet as I have argued, holding out such proof as a requirement before we act is the equivalent of saying we can never act. Instead of being paralyzed by the limitations of social science, we can pay attention to testimony about the ways in which people act out pornographic sexual scenarios, which gives us some understanding of how pornography works in the world. Rather than constraining the discussion with simplistic notions about how mass communication causes specific behavior, we can think about how pornography cultivates certain views about sexuality.

DISTORTIONS

Distortion 1: Offensiveness and Oppression

Pornography supporters often frame the issue as a question of offensiveness, suggesting that the feminist antipornography critique is based on the subjective experience of feeling repulsed by pornography. This is either a fundamental misunderstanding of the critique or a deliberate attempt to distort it. The feminist critique is an analysis of power and harm that focuses on oppression, not offensiveness. As MacKinnon (1987) put it in the title of one of her essays, it is not a moral issue, meaning that the critique of pornography is not based on a judgment that depictions of sex are dirty or blasphemous. The feminist critique focuses on the role of pornography in a system of sexual subordination and the oppression of women.

A definition of *oppression* is useful in making this distinction clear. Frye (1983) defined *oppression* as "a system of interrelated barriers and forces which reduce, immobilize and mold people who belong to a certain group, and effect their subordination to another group (individually to individuals of the other group, and as a group, to that group)" (p. 33). The concept of oppression is crucial to understanding the critique of pornography, instead of simply caricaturing it as the result of some people being offended. The feminist analysis of pornography is a political critique, which of course has a connection to morality, but is not about offense to conventional sexual mores.

In a pluralistic society, I expect to be offended on a daily basis. I do not expect all people to adhere to my sense of what is beautiful, appropriate, or pleasing. However, practices that are connected to systems of oppression are the proper topic for discussion, collective judgment, and political action.

Distortion 2: Against Sex?

Antipornography feminists are often labeled *antisex* or *prudish*; critique of a sexual system of eroticized domination and submission is equated with a fear of sex. I have yet to meet anyone in the antipornography movement who fits this caricature, although I have met many people in that movement who are, as Cole (1989) put it, "against sexual pleasure as pornography and mass culture construct it" (p. 107). To work for change in an oppressive sexual system is not to work against sex, but to work for justice.

So, in one sense, the charge that antipornography feminists fear sex is simply false. In another sense, perhaps we all should fear the way in which a patriarchal culture defines and practices sex (Jensen, 1997). We live in a culture in which sexualized violence—primarily perpetrated by men against women and children—is so routine that it has to be considered normal—that is, within the norms of patriarchy. If sex in contemporary culture is fused with domination, cruelty, and violence, is not fear of that kind of sex reasonable?

I also think there is another level of fear at work in the pornography debate. It is not a fear of sexuality, but rather a more pervasive fear in the culture that if we tell the truth about just how deeply many of us have been affected by a pervasive patriarchal sexual system, we may be left for the moment with nothing to take its place. If patriarchal sex— the kind of sex that pimps and pornographers have had so much success marketing—is the sex many of us have learned, we face the challenge of reconstructing sexuality, which implies that for some time we might have to face great uncertainty about who we are as sexual beings and what kind of sex we want to have. In a hypersexualized, pornographic culture—a world in which to not have sex is a sign of deviancy—such a process can seem frightening. Yet we also could see it as an opportunity for invention. The project of unweaving "the pattern of dominance and submission which has been incarnated as sexuality in each of us" (A Southern Women's Writing Collective, 1990, p. 145) is formidable, but the rewards are likely far greater than we can know at this moment. The work of creating a world in which sex and justice are not in conflict can be a source of much passion, excitement, and hope as we move forward.

WELCOME TO THE DEAD END

In the late 1990s, I was in the audience at a symposium on computers, the Internet, and the law. At that moment in history, one of the key issues was whether laws written to restrict children's access to pornography on the Internet ran afoul of the First Amendment, as most of the people at the symposium asserted. What struck me as most important about the discussion was not the arguments against such laws, but the way in which a number of the speakers on the panel, along with people asking questions from the audience, seemed to mock parents or citizens who had concerns about Internet pornography. Implicit in many of the comments was the assumption that such people were prudes and/or rubes who did not understand computers, the Internet, the First Amendment, pornography, or human sexuality. The vast majority of these comments were made by men.

Several of them jokingly referred to their own use of pornography as children and adolescents, the implication being that boys will always seek out sexual material and, "Hey, look at me, I did it and I'm normal." That is exactly what I found so disturbing—they did seem to be relatively normal men, and they seemed to believe that contemporary pornography raises no important political or social issues. Although boys have long found ways to obtain pornography (although it is illegal to sell such material to minors), their access to hard-core pornography in the age of the VCR/DVD player and Internet has become steadily easier. While pornography has become more mainstream, it has become harsher and more overtly misogynistic. Meanwhile the mainstream media increasingly borrow themes and conventions from pornography. Hence, not only are men exposed to more and more extreme pornography at younger ages, so are girls, with effects on their conception of their own sexuality.

Shouldn't we care about that?

It is also important to recognize that pornography is but one aspect of a huge sex industry, which includes not only mass-mediated sex, but phone sex, strip clubs, massage parlors, escort services, street prostitution, and sex tourism. Sexuality—especially women's sexuality—is used in increasingly more explicit ways to sell products of all kinds in advertising and marketing. This leads to what may be the most crucial question about pornography: What kind of human feeling, empathy, and intimate connections are possible in a world in which bodies are used so routinely in the process of selling and are also for sale virtually everywhere we turn?

Shouldn't we care about that, too?

When one comes to the end of a dead end, there are two choices: Stay stuck or turn around and find another way. The law and social science helped push us down the dead end. I am not looking to either for much help in charting a new path. For me, what progress has been made in finding our way onto the path and heading in new directions has come mostly from the feminist movement—from activists, writers, and ordinary people engaged in struggle. Central to this is an expansion of our notion of the sexual and the erotic. Lorde (1984), for example, talked about the way in which women's erotic power is falsely cordoned off in the bedroom, made into "plasticized sensation" (p. 54) and confused with the pornographic. For Lorde, the erotic is a life force, a creative energy: "Those physical, emotional, and psychic expressions of what is deepest and strongest and richest within each of us, being shared: the passions of love, in its deepest meanings" (p. 56). The deepest meanings are not going to be found in a DP tape. Or the law. Or in social science.

REFERENCES

A Southern Women's Writing Collective. (1990). Sex resistance in heterosexual arrangements. In D. Leidholdt & J. G. Raymond (Eds.), *The sexual liberals and the attack on feminism* (pp. 140–147). New York: Pergamon.

ABC News Primetime Live. (2003, January). Young women, porn and profits. *Adult Video News.* (2002, December). Annual sales charts.

Adult Video News. (2003, January). AVN directors roundtable, pp. 45–68.

Adult Video News. (2004, September). Give me gape, p. 158.

American Booksellers Association v. Hudnut, ordinance judged invalid, 598 F.Supp. 1316 (S.D. Ind. 1984); judgment affirmed, 771 F.2d 323 (7th Cir. 1985); judgment affirmed, 106 S.Ct. 1172 (1986); petition for rehearing denied, 106 S.Ct. 1664 (1986). *Ashcroft v. Free Speech Coalition*, 535 U.S. 234 (2002).

Ax, J. (2000). P 'n C puts the "stick" back in "drumstick." *Yale Herald.* Retrieved from http://www.yaleherald.com/archive/xxx/2000.10.13/ae/p13pandc.html

Baldwin, M. (1989). Pornography and the traffic in women. *Yale Journal of Law and Feminism, 1*(1), 111–155.

Bergen, R. K., & Bogle, K. A. (2000). Exploring the connection between pornography and sexual violence. *Violence and Victims, 15*(3), 227–234.

Boyle, K. (2000). The pornography debates: Beyond cause and effect. *Women's Studies International Forum, 23*(2), 187–195.

Cole, S. (1989). *Pornography and the sex crisis.* Toronto: Amanita.

Comedy Central. (2002). Press release. Retrieved from http://www.comedycentral.com/press/ccseries/series.jhtml?s=ccof

Dines, G., & Jensen, R. (2004). Pornography and media: Toward a more critical analysis. In M. S. Kimmel & R. F. Plante (Eds.), *Sexualities: Identity, behavior, and society* (pp. 369–380). New York: Oxford University Press.

Dines, G., Jensen R., & Russo, A. (1998). *Pornography: The production and consumption of inequality*. New York: Routledge.

Dworkin, A. (1988). *Letters from a war zone*. London: Secker & Warburg. (Reprint edition, 1989, Dutton).

Dworkin, A., & MacKinnon, C. A. (1988). *Pornography and civil rights: A new day for women's equality*. Minneapolis: Organizing Against Pornography. Retrieved from http://www.nostatusquo.com/ACLU/dworkin/other/ordinance/newday/TOC.htm

Farley, M. (Ed.). (2003). *Prostitution, trafficking, and traumatic stress*. Binghamton, NY: Haworth.

Federal Communications Commission. (2004). Retrieved from http://www.fcc.gov/cgb/consumerfacts/obscene.html

Frye, M. (1983). *The politics of reality: Essays in feminist theory*. Freedom, CA: Crossing.

Gittler, I. (1999). *Pornstar*. New York: Simon & Schuster.

Jaffee, D., & Strauss, M. A. (1987). Sexual climate and reported rape: A state-level analysis. *Archives of Sexual Behavior, 16*, 107–123.

Jensen, R. (1995). Pornography and affirmative conceptions of freedom. *Women & Politics, 15*(1), 1–18.

Jensen, R. (1997). Patriarchal sex. *International Journal of Sociology and Social Policy, 17*, 91–115.

Kutchinsky, B. (1991). Pornography and rape: Theory and practice? *International Journal of Law and Psychiatry, 14*, 47–64.

Lane, F. S. (2000). *Obscene profits: The entrepreneurs of pornography in the cyber age*. New York: Routledge.

Lawrence, D. H. (1955). *Sex, literature and censorship: Essays by D. H. Lawrence*. Melbourne: William Heinemann.

Lorde, A. (1984). *Sister outsider*. Freedom, CA: Crossing.

MacKinnon, C. A. (1987). *Feminism unmodified: Discourses on life and law*. Cambridge, MA: Harvard University Press.

MacKinnon, C. A., & Dworkin, A. (1997). *In harm's way: The pornography civil rights hearings*. Cambridge, MA: Harvard University Press.

Malamuth, N. M., Addison, A., & Koss, M. (2000). Pornography and sexual aggression: Are there reliable effects and can we understand them? *Annual Review of Sex Research, 11*, 26–91.

Miller v. California, 413 U.S. 15 (1973).

New York v. Ferber, 458 U.S. 747 (1982).

Russell, D. E. H. (1980). Pornography and violence: What does the new research say? In L. Lederer (Ed.), *Take back the night: Women on pornography* (pp. 218–238). New York: William Morrow.

Russell, D. E. H. (1998). *Dangerous relationships: Pornography, misogyny, and rape*. Thousand Oaks, CA: Sage.

Seto, M. C., Maric, A., & Barbaree, H. E. (2001). The role of pornography in the etiology of sexual aggression. *Aggression and Violent Behavior, 6*, 35–53.

Silbert, M. H., & Pines, A. M. (1984). Pornography and sexual abuse of women. *Sex Roles, 10*, 857–869.

Zillmann, D., & Bryant, J. (1982). Pornography, sexual callousness, and the trivialization of rape. *Journal of Communication, 32*, 10–21.

Chapter 7

Creating Meaning, Creating Citizens: The U.S. Supreme Court and the Control of Meaning in the Public Sphere

David S. Allen
University of Wisconsin–Milwaukee

This chapter reflects my long interest in trying to understand the relationship between institutions of democracy, such as the U.S. Supreme Court and the press, and public life in the United States. Over the years, I have examined that relationship through the lens of critical theory and, more specifically, the work of Jürgen Habermas. As Habermas teaches us, the press is vital to the existence of an active public sphere, helping to disperse information to a wider group of citizens. The judicial system tells us how we should interact with other citizens and what the relationship is between citizens and democratic institutions. In short, these institutions can either help citizens achieve the realization of democracy or impede those efforts.

Much of my early work, arising out of critical theory, focused on critiquing press practices and court decisions that serve to limit an active public sphere. More recently, I attempted to use that critique as a way to identify ways that might serve to invigorate public life. This chapter reflects an early attempt to reformulate my understanding of speech and association rights in the United States to aid in the creation of an active public sphere. It grew out of a year-long research fellowship at the University of Wisconsin-Milwaukee's Center for 21st Century Studies during the 2002–2003 academic year. The Center brought together scholars from a number of different disciplines to conduct research on the broad theme of war. During that fellowship, I became interested in how citizens interpreted news about events in Afghanistan and Iraq. How do citizens interpret these already interpreted events? How do citizens "read" the news? How does that news come to have meaning in people's lives? Perhaps more important, I began to question what role citizens play in the construction of meaning. When the media present information, are citizens expected to be passive spectators or active interpreters?

In this chapter, I only focus on the U.S. Supreme Court and its struggle to control meaning. We can see in these decisions the difficulty justices face in trying to articulate a role for modernist legal principles in a postmodern society. Many of the justices willingly acknowledge the idea that the meaning of public expressive acts cannot be fixed, but law's need for certainty eventually overrides those views. In the end, the control of meaning becomes a way to control the public sphere—to establish boundaries and limit activism among citizens. Although that control is not absolute, it limits the public sphere by encouraging citizens to be passive spectators rather than active interpreters of public events.

The melding of critical and cultural studies is important to this study. Critical theory provides the framework for the analysis of power relationships in society and an understanding of the public sphere's importance to democratic life; cultural studies provides the important link to understanding citizens' ability to create meaning in a mediacized environment. The combination hints at new directions for us to consider if we are truly interested in activating citizens.

As this is being written, the most important question remains unanswered: What is the role of law in the public sphere if it is not to establish meaning? The final section of this chapter hints at some possible ideas. Perhaps law's role is to simply provide the institutional protection for the space citizens need to create meaning. Perhaps law should worry more about protecting the *process of meaning* creation and less about the *establishment of meaning*. Yet even I do not find this entirely satisfactory. It is finding an answer to that problem that still occupies my research.

CREATING MEANING, CREATING CITIZENS

It seems safe to say that the American legal system abhors ambiguity.[1] At least since legal formalism's attempt to turn law into a scientific endeavor (Streeter, 1995), American law has been pursuing certainty not only within the profession, but also by exporting that ideal to the general public. In other words, by turning law into a scientific enterprise that has

---

[1]As former Supreme Court Justice William Brennan (1986) once wrote, "Unlike literary critics, judges cannot merely savor the tensions or revel in the ambiguities inherent in the text—judges must decide" (p. 434).

a foundation of certainty, law has been able to increase its legitimacy in the public sphere while masking its management of the public sphere.

That is, admittedly, a broad statement. However, it is argued in this chapter that the process described earlier is demonstrated by the U.S. Supreme Court's struggle to understand meaning as it has been played out in an array of First Amendment cases since 1919. It is argued that in these cases can be seen an inherent conflict between the postmodern, polysemic quality of public expressive acts[2] and the attempt to fix the meaning of public expression to stay within the confines of an American legal system built on modernist principles such as predictability, efficiency, and control. As a result, justices find themselves trapped between two differing and, in many ways, incompatible perspectives.

Take, for example, Justice Anthony Kennedy's concurring opinion in *Texas v. Johnson* (1989), agreeing that burning the U.S. flag as an act of political protest is protected by the First Amendment. Kennedy noted that we live in an age when "absolutes are distrusted" and added, "Though symbols often are what we ourselves make of them, the flag is constant in expressing beliefs Americans share, beliefs in law and peace and that freedom which sustains the human spirit" (p. 422).

Justice Kennedy's comments reflect the tension that is the subject of this chapter. On the one hand, he admitted that the meaning of symbols is far more complex than simply what an authority says something means. The flag does not mean the same thing to all people. However, Kennedy also struggled to not let that fall into the relativism so often associated with postmodern thought. So, Justice Kennedy ended by declaring that, although the meaning of symbols is open, the flag is a unique symbol with a prescribed set of meanings. In the end, his logic fails to adequately support either claim, and it raises more questions than it answers. If the meaning of public expressive acts, such as flag burning, is open to individual interpretation, then what does that mean for our understanding of the regulation of freedom of speech and press in a democratic society? Why is a nation's flag different from other symbols in its ability to fix meaning? In many ways, this chapter examines the conflict reflected in Justice Kennedy's reasoning. It begins by looking at the question of law and the creation of meaning. It is argued in the next section that law, as a modernist enterprise, has struggled to understand the com-

---

[2]As used here, public expressive acts intends to capture a broad range of speech activities. It refers to not only what First Amendment scholars might refer to as symbolic speech—speech that has no vocal component—but also what might be termed *pure speech*, which has a strong vocal component. Public expressive acts are any speech or symbolic act that invites members of the public to wrestle with its meaning. A speech by an antiwar protester invites citizens to determine what the speaker means by her words. In that regard, a sign placed on a citizen's front lawn supporting war also invites interpretation.

plexity of meaning. This is reflected in several interpretive strategies explored by judges and scholars. The third section examines the influence of cultural studies on the understanding of the meaning of public expressive acts and what that means for the law. It is argued that the Court has ignored the insight of cultural studies that has powerfully demonstrated that public expressive acts can have a multiplicity of meanings. The fourth section illustrates how the Court has tended to see citizens more as spectators to democracy rather than active creators of meaning. This is done through an examination of cases in two areas: (a) cases related to protests against war, and (b) the public display of religious symbols. The fifth section puts forward some modest proposals for what the Court might do to empower citizens, but still retain a role for the law in a democratic society. In the end, it is argued that, by refusing to recognize the polysemic nature of meaning, the Court not only helps turn citizens into spectators, but also finds a way to manage public life. Figuring out a way to empower citizens to participate in the democratic act of meaning creation is vital to the realization of participatory democracy.

LAW AND THE CREATION OF MEANING

In some ways, the creation of meaning has been a much ignored area of study in American law. There has been much discussion about the interpretation of statutes and constitutions, but legal commentators have generally ignored the law's role in structuring the public creation of meaning. This section briefly reviews two movements in legal interpretation. Although these sketches are admittedly brief, the intent is to provide an overview of the debate about interpretation within the legal field. The argument here is not that any one perspective is dominant, but rather an attempt to demonstrate that, despite the differences, law ignores the role meaning plays in the creation of democracy. Legal theorists focus on the interpretive strategies used by judges and lawyers and are far less concerned about how those strategies might influence public life. In other words, the interpretation of meaning is seen as a legal problem, not a public problem.

Originalism

Originalism is the idea that the original meaning of the writers of statutes and constitutions can be discovered, and that once that meaning has been determined it should be controlling. Just as important, originalism does not view the meaning of texts as something that evolves over time, but rather views meaning as fixed and discoverable. U.S. Supreme Court Justice Antonin Scalia has been a vocal defender and practitioner of this methodology.

Scalia (1989) argued that, although the originalist method has never been the sole method for unpacking meaning, justices "have almost always had the decency to lie, or at least to dissemble, about what they were doing" (p. 852). Scalia, while recognizing that originalism is difficult to do and has its problems, saw it as the best option for maintaining the legitimacy of law in a democratic society. It is interesting to note that Scalia claimed that the advocates of a nonoriginalist methodology believe that "words have no meaning" (p. 856), something he refused to take seriously.[3]

For Scalia, the problems of originalism are twofold: (a) It is difficult to discover the original meaning of something, and (b) a strict originalism would be forced to support laws that have lost their public legitimacy. Scalia saw the discovery of meaning as the most difficult obstacle for originalists to overcome. Uncovering the historical documents to capture meaning is a time-consuming process, "better suited to the historian than the lawyer," and one not suited to the time pressures required of judges (Scalia, 1989, p. 857).

As for the second challenge, Scalia argued that originalism "is medicine too strong to swallow" (p. 862). To illustrate the problem, Scalia assumed that a state recently has approved a law permitting public lashing or branding of a person's hand as punishment for certain crimes. Scalia argued that no judge today would seriously argue that such legislation does not violate the Eighth Amendment to the U.S. Constitution. However, if originalist thinking is to be followed, flogging and handbranding should be allowable today as long it was not viewed as being cruel and unusual punishment in 1791. The way out of this problem for Scalia is to be a "faint-hearted originalist" who recognizes that the discovery of meaning is difficult, if not impossible, and that judges need to be cautious. As he wrote:

> Originalism does not aggravate the principal weakness of the system, for it establishes a historical criterion that is conceptually quite separate from the preferences of the judge himself. And the principal defect of that approach—that historical research is always difficult and sometimes inconclusive—will, unlike nonoriginalism, lead to a more moderate rather than a more extreme result. (p. 864)

In that same general vein, Chief Justice William Rehnquist argued for originalism not because the Founding Fathers laid out a plan that can be

---

[3]Of course Scalia overstated this criticism. No theorist would seriously argue that words are without meaning, only that the words have no fixed meaning.

expected to address every problem,[4] but rather because he does not believe that the Supreme Court should enjoy that power. He sees a move against originalism as an "end run around popular government" (Rehnquist, 1976, p. 706).

Originalist thinking is also evident in the writings of those who advocate what has come to be called *neutral principles* (Wechsler, 1961). That is, a judge should adopt neutral principles that guide decision making. As former federal Judge Robert Bork (1971) wrote, "Society consents to be ruled undemocratically within defined areas by certain enduring principles believed to be stated in, and placed beyond the reach of majorities by the Constitution" (p. 3). How does a judge go about finding those enduring principles? It is not clear in Bork's writings. He assumed that judges can pull from the Constitution—both through its text and history—principled rules that were the intent of the framers (Bork, 1971). At least when interpreting the First Amendment, however, Bork found the text and literature lacking. That lack of evidence allows the judge to use other evidence, and for Bork it is clear that the First Amendment only intended to protect a narrow range of political speech (Bork, 1971).[5]

In the end, originalists see expressive acts as having concrete meanings that can be discovered, and they see the work of judges in interpreting those words not unlike that of a social scientist engaged in an objective enterprise. To admit that expressive acts might have multiple meanings is viewed as a threat to the status quo or worse, as being a nondemocratic way of establishing meaning.

Nonoriginalism

Scalia referred to those who do not believe that judges might be able to uncover the original intent as *nonoriginalists*. Many fall into that category. Past Supreme Court justices have referred to this idea as reflecting a "living constitution"[6] to illustrate the idea that there is more to interpre-

---

[4]Rehnquist (1976) agreed with the view of Justice Holmes, adding, "scarcely anyone would disagree" (p. 694). Holmes wrote, "When we are dealing with words that also are a constituent act, like the Constitution of the United States, we must realize that they have called into life a being the development of which could not have been foreseen completely by the most gifted of its begetters. It was enough for them to realize or to hope that they had created an organism; it has taken a century and has cost their successors much sweat and blood to prove that they created a nation" (*Missouri v. Holland*, 1920, p. 433).

[5]Bork would protect only "criticisms of public officials and policies, proposals for the adoption or repeal of legislation or constitutional provisions and speech addressed to the conduct of any governmental unit in the country." However, Bork would exclude from protection speech that would advocate the forcible overthrow of the government or the violation of the law (Bork, 1971).

[6]The phrase appears to have appeared initially in a book by Howard McBain (1927), *The Living Constitution: A Consideration of the Realities and Legends of Our Fundamental Law*.

tation than the search for historical meaning. As former Justice William Brennan (1986) wrote:

> [T]he genius of the Constitution rests not in any static meaning it might have had in a world that is dead and gone, but in the adaptability of its great principles to cope with current problems and current needs. What the constitutional fundamentals meant to the wisdom of other times cannot be their measure to the vision of our time. (p. 438)

Justice Brennan publicly wrestled with the idea of the constitutional search for meaning. Brennan opposed the search for the original intent of the writers of the Constitution, labeling the search as "arrogance cloaked as humility" (p. 435). He argued instead that judges should search for the "community's interpretation" (p. 434). Although this seems to place Brennan in similar stead with modern-day literary critics such as Stanley Fish, Brennan was not advocating that there was no meaning in the constitution outside of community beliefs. Not unlike Bork, Brennan found in the Constitution certain value choices that apparently were beyond interpretation. For example, at one point, Brennan proclaimed, "It is the very purpose of our Constitution—and particularly the Bill of Rights—to declare certain values transcendent, beyond the reach of temporary political majorities" (p. 436). Brennan illustrated his interpretive strategy through the example of capital punishment. He found capital punishment to be cruel and unusual punishment, but that is not the reason it is unconstitutional in his eyes. It is unconstitutional because it is "inconsistent with the fundamental premise of the Constitution that even the most base criminal remains a human being of some potential, at least, for common human dignity" (Brennan, 1986, p. 444). In 1986, Brennan did not ignore the reality that his interpretation was not shared by the community. But it is a justice's duty to correct the community, if needed. Brennan wrote:

> Yet, again in my judgment, when a Justice perceives an interpretation of the text to have departed so far from its essential meaning that Justice is bound, by a larger constitutional duty to the community, to expose the departure and point toward a different path. On this issue, the death penalty, I hope to embody a community, although perhaps not yet arrived, striving for human dignity of all. (p. 444)

As do many nonoriginalists, Brennan struggled to deal with the polysemic nature of meaning while still maintaining some fixed point on which to build a legal system. Over the years, a number of other commentators have addressed the idea of nonoriginalism as it impacts legal interpretation, seeking answers to the same problems posed by Brennan.

Some of the ideas central to nonoriginalist thought can be traced to the legal realists, who were skeptical of the legal rules and facts that governed how judges decided cases. The realists, however, never sought a complete break from law as a scientific endeavor. As Frank (1949) noted, judges depend on the facts of the case to make decisions, but those facts are "merely a guess about the actual facts." As he wrote:

> The actual events, the real objective acts and words . . . , happened in the past. They do not walk into court. The court usually learns about those real, objective, past facts only through the oral testimony of fallible witnesses. (pp. 15–16)

Frank viewed legal decision making as a difficult art, and the job of judges was interpretation. Although the realists campaigned against rules and facts, they failed to break from the influence of the authoritarian nature of meaning. Realists recognized that meaning was difficult to determine, but that did not mean there was not a meaning to be discovered. For the realists, the problem of meaning was a methodological problem. As Boyle (1985) noted:

> The two central legal realist arguments depended upon a *critique* of essentialist rationality in linguistic interpretation and a *defense* of the essential rationality of science. Thus the judge was supposed to give up playing with words and to begin playing with policy science. (p. 707)

In recent years, the idea of nonoriginalism in legal interpretation has been picked up by a number of other writers. The works of Dworkin (1982) and Winter (1989) are used here as examples of nonoriginalist legal interpretation.

Dworkin's often-cited work on legal interpretation compares the writing of law to the writing of a chain novel. That is, that law is similar to a group of people who join together to write a novel, with each writer being responsible for a different chapter. As Dworkin wrote:

> [E]very novelist but the first has the dual responsibilities of interpreting and creating, because each must read all that has done before in order to establish, in the interpretivist sense, what the novel so far created is. (p. 541)

For Dworkin, each judge is like a novelist in that chain. His point is that legal interpretation provides judges with freedom to take the story in a new direction, but they must do so within the confines of the existing story. As such, judges enjoy freedom, but are also constrained by the institution of the law. As Dworkin (1982) wrote, "A judge's duty is to interpret the legal history he finds, not to invent a better history" (p. 544).

Dworkin's work then acknowledges that discovering the meaning of legal texts is far more complex than the originalists suggest. He acknowledged that judges do not just discover law, but also make it. However, Dworkin stopped short of endorsing the polysemic nature of meaning. Judges are confined by the parameters of the institution and a "good" interpretation that must demonstrate its political value (Dworkin, 1982). Legal interpretation, then, can accommodate both the idea of the divergent meaning of expressive acts and the legal system's need for determinacy (Tribe, 1978).

Winter (1989) offered a more complex model of the creation of meaning that is linked to the cognitive structure of communication. For Winter, meaning is largely indeterminate, but that does not mean society falls into subjectivity. Winter argued that judges, just like citizens, rely on idealized cognitive models (ICMs) to help them make sense of the world in which they live. ICMs are like "stock stories or folk theories by which humans in a given culture organize the diverse inputs of daily life into meaningful gestalts that relate that which is 'relevant' and ignore that which is not" (p. 2233). For example, Winter noted that, in the United States, discourse concerning the First Amendment often makes use of the ICM "the marketplace of ideas," a metaphor that brings with it a cultural understanding about why unpopular ideas should be tolerated.

For Winter, judges must rely on these existing narratives to ground the law in social experience. Without that grounding, the law runs the risk of being illegitimate (Winter, 1989). However, Winter argued that the recognition of the importance of these narratives does not automatically lead to determinacy in the law. As he wrote, "There is nothing that requires any storyteller to tell a particular story or to tell it in a particular manner" (p. 2271).

In important ways, both Dworkin and Winter attempted to break free of the originalist view of legal interpretation. They both tried to identify ways for alternative meanings to surface, but also found ways that law will remain firmly entrenched in its institutional and societal structure. Of course the question that arises from both is whether that mediating ground can ever be found. Dworkin put great faith in the ability of judges to take the story in new directions, yet stay within the larger confines of the law. Winter saw judges as being free to adopt a new ICM, or at the very least a different interpretation of an existing ICM, that would lead to a new understanding of the law. For the question asked in this study, both fail to provide much help. For both, an explicit mission is maintaining the legitimacy of an existing legal structure in society. Dworkin, it can be argued, sees the existing confining structure as legitimate. He refused to recognize that the chains in the storytelling process are not merely chains that control rogue judges, but also chains that prevent fundamental change. Winter, while arguing that dominant stories might be reinterpreted, still saw the primary purpose of interpretation as a legal enterprise. Both failed to recognize the importance of the creation of meaning as a way to empower the public sphere.

CULTURAL STUDIES AND PUBLIC MEANING

As described, much of the literature on legal interpretation takes a professional, institutional view of the purpose of interpretation. Missing is any attempt to recognize the democratic nature of interpretation and what role that search for meaning might play in the realization of a more participatory form of democracy. If we recognize that the courts play a fundamental role in the structure of public life, their view of the authoritarian nature of meaning becomes significant (White, 1990). Although it is true that citizens do not often engage in the business of interpreting statutes and constitutions, they do engage in the process of trying to understand the meaning of public expressive acts. As judges search for certainty on which to build law, they often close off the creation of meaning. By failing to move their study out of the institutional level, Scalia, Brennan, Dworkin, and Winter failed to recognize the democratic potential of meaning-making. This section suggests that cultural studies provides a framework for understanding the role that meaning creation plays in the realization of democracy. Rather than look at meaning as a way to create an industry (be it the law or mass communication), within cultural studies can be found a more complex understanding of the role meaning plays in the creation of active citizens.

Cultural studies has long recognized the importance of meaning to the study of public communication and has put forward a far more complex, and perhaps democratic, idea of meaning creation. Prior to the growth of the cultural studies movement, most examination of mass communication focused on what impact media had on citizens. In that regard, studies focused primarily on the media's creation of messages or what influence that message had on the people who received it. Most mass communication research focused on the individual, trying to explain differences in interpretation through social psychology or institutional influence (Delia, 1987). As Delia (1987) wrote in his history of mass communication research:

> [T]he notion of the audience as atomistic, as consisting of disparate and independent individuals, is in general harmony with the research practices of many early mass communication researchers and became progressively

more accepted with the shift to survey and marketing research methods. (p. 67)

Streeter (1989) argued that this view reflected the fears about modern society shared by the early researchers—that "the plural quality of individuals was in danger of being erased by the massifying tendencies of modern media" (p. 92). Cultural studies is an attempt to break away from the atomistic and institutional nature of understanding mass communication. Cultural studies recognizes that a more open understanding of meaning allows disempowered groups within society to have a voice (Cover, 1983; Delgado, 1989; Scheppele, 1989).

Meaning creation has long occupied a central place in cultural studies. Rather than viewing meaning as something that is transmitted from media to audience, cultural studies attempts to understand how the audience constructs the messages they receive and how they use those messages to sometimes create oppositional interpretations. As Fiske (1987) noted about TV:

> Far from being the agent of the dominant classes, it is the prime site where the dominant have to recognize the insecurity of their power, and where they have to encourage cultural difference with all the threat to their own position that this implies. (p. 326)

As such, cultural theory says much about the relationship among political power, the creation of meaning, and the role of citizens in a democratic society. The power of citizens to interpret texts to reflect their own needs and desires, even if done so within established frameworks, has been viewed by some as being empowering. Giroux (1992) noted the importance of cultural studies in the creation of "active and critical citizens capable of fighting for and reconstructing democratic public life" (p. 199). For Giroux (1992), cultural studies is important not only because it recognizes the social construction of knowledge and the role of meaning in that construction, but also because it sees culture as "contested terrain" where difference matters (p. 202). As such, Giroux called for "organizing schools and pedagogy around a sense of purpose and meaning that makes difference central to a critical notion of citizenship and democratic public life" (p. 209).

Cohen (1994) argued that, the more highly developed critical viewing skills are among TV watchers, the better able they are to participate in democratic life. Part of critical viewing is learning to acknowledge the idea that there might be multiple meanings of an expressive act. As she wrote, "The viewer who is critically empowered considers the range of subjectivities and corresponding interpretations, and is thus able to choose freely and effectively among possibilities" (Cohen, 1994, p. 107). In Cohen's eyes, although critical viewing does not automatically lead to social action, "critical viewing can provide the resources for full participation in democratic life" (p. 111). As Cohen wrote:

> A critical viewer who recognizes that their meanings were generated over time, in a social context, through symbolic choices that are often arbitrary, may have some control in the production and acquisition of knowledge by choosing among and/or creating an entire range of "possible" meanings. (p. 110)

Similar conclusions are drawn by Jenkins (1992), who found the reconstruction of TV narratives by fans to be a spark to participatory culture. Although Jenkins stopped short of saying that fandom makes all audiences active, he argued it does prove that not all audiences are passive. Critics of contemporary culture point to the manipulative forms of communication and the desire to create audiences where none exist, yet Jenkins argued that fans work to carve participatory space out of a cultural enterprise that is intended to isolate them. As such, Jenkins (1992) argued, "Fans find the ability to question and rework the ideologies that dominate the mass culture they claim as their own" (p. 284). Jenkins also wrote, "Fandom celebrates not exceptional texts but rather exceptional readings (though its interpretive practices make it impossible to maintain a clear or precise distinction between the two)" (p. 284).

The insights of cultural studies, especially the idea that public expressive acts might be open to a multiplicity of readings and how that idea might serve to activate citizens within a democratic society, has generally been ignored by the American courts. In fact, judges have been openly opposed to the idea of contested meaning. Sunder (2001) argued that law, especially reflected in freedom of association cases, has openly opposed more diverse understandings of meaning. Law protects cultural survival, but refuses to give that same level of protection to cultural dissent, Sunder (2001) claimed. As Sunder wrote:

> [L]aw legitimates exclusive rights to culture, protecting cultural borders not just against encroachment from outsiders but from members themselves. Law regressively treats cultural meanings like the private intellectual property of a culture's leadership. (p. 552)

As a result, Sunder argued that law should be required to "recognize the plurality of meanings within a culture" as a way to allow for the "proliferation of cultural meanings" (p. 557).

Calvert (1995) also noted the problematic nature of the law's search for meaning, especially in libel law. Calvert argued that meaning is a poor standard for libel law because "[t]here is no benchmark against which the defendant's alleged state of mind about meaning may be evaluated . . ." (p. 139).

Over the years, courts have sometimes adopted the rhetoric of pluralism, as reflected in Justice Kennedy's opinion at the beginning of this chapter, but they have steadfastly refused to make the structural changes needed to value and protect that pluralism. Lessig (1995) noted that First Amendment law is "obsessed" with the regulation of texts while ignoring the regulation of context. Although courts impose strict limitations on government's ability to limit what people can say or print, they turn a blind eye to government's role in the creation of social meaning. The following attempts to demonstrate how the Supreme Court has come to favor the authoritarian nature of meaning while devaluing the public creation of meaning.

THE SUPREME COURT, MEANING, AND PUBLIC EXPRESSIVE ACTS

Hall (1980) suggested that once meaning is problematized it becomes a source of social struggle. Hall's point is important for the study of the First Amendment and public expressive acts because the courts seek not to problematize meaning, but rather to establish a dominant reading. What is forgotten in the process to establish a dominant meaning is the value of the public construction of meaning to public life. The perceived judicial need to set meaning works toward an authoritarian understanding of discourse—that meaning is what someone with power and authority says it means. When the court sets meaning, therefore, a discursive moment is missed (see Glendon, 1991).

The following examines how the U.S. Supreme Court has wrestled with the concept of meaning and used it to manage the public sphere in two areas: dissent during war and the interpretation of religious symbols.

War and the Control of the Public Sphere

Over the years, issues of free speech during times of war have come to be important for understanding how the courts view public expression. During times of conflict, it is not unexpected that government would try to exert some control on dissident behavior. However, in these opinions can be seen the way the Court has tried to overtly control the public sphere through the authoritarian construction of meaning.

Early free speech cases to reach the U.S. Supreme Court centered on public criticism of the United States' involvement in World War I. These cases, usually prosecuted under the Espionage Act of 1917 and the Sedition Act of 1918, called on the courts to make interpretations about the intent of the speaker. The Court generally faced questions such as: Was it the intent of the speaker to cause insubordination in the military? Was it the intent of the speaker to obstruct recruiting and enlistment in the U.S. military?

For example, in *Schenck v. U.S.* (1919), in which the general secretary of the Socialist Party was convicted for obstructing the draft, Justice Oliver Wendell Holmes, Jr., constructed a clear model for how courts are to determine the meaning of a statement. As Holmes wrote: "If the act, (speaking, or circulating a paper,) its tendency and the intent with which it is done are the same, we perceive no ground for saying that success alone warrants making the act a crime" (*Schenck v. U.S.*, 1919, p. 52). The point here for Holmes is that public reaction to the speech is not an important part of the equation. Courts should instead focus on an evaluation of the act, make judgments about its tendency, and examine the intent of the speaker or actor. Of course judgments about the tendency of the speech might be linked to the intent of the speaker. As Holmes noted about Schenck's writing:

> Of course the documents would not have been sent unless it had been intended to have some effect, and we do not see what effect it could be expected to have upon persons subject to the draft except to influence them to obstruct the carrying of it out. The defendants do not deny that the jury might find against them on this point. (*Schenck v. U.S.*, 1919, p. 51)

Justice John Clarke followed much the same test several months later in *Abrams v. United States* (1919), where five Russian citizens living in the United States were convicted of publishing and distributing seditious material during times of war. After reviewing the leaflets distributed by Abrams and his colleagues, Clarke wrote: "The purpose of this obviously was to persuade the persons to whom it was addressed to turn a deaf ear to patriotic appeals in behalf of the Government of the United States, and to cease to render it assistance in the prosecution of the war" (*Abrams v. U.S.*, 1919, pp. 621–622). Clarke argued that people "must be held to have intended, and to be accountable for, the effects which their acts were likely to produce" (*Abrams v. U.S.*, 1919, p. 621). Such a test of meaning reinforces a notion of an inactive public. Citizens obviously play some role in the creation of meaning in that they exist to be influenced in some way by the message. Judgments about that influence, however, are made by the Court, not by the public. If the intent of the speaker is to negatively influence the audience and the speech is judged by the Court to have that tendency, the government can prohibit that speech. The public becomes the way for the Court to justify its decision—to make it legitimate—but the public plays little role in the actual creation of meaning. The Court determines meaning and then uses the phantom public to support its decision.

Holmes, in his famous dissent in *Abrams*, follows his general test for meaning, but breaks from the majority because he is far less certain that there is an intent to "cripple or hinder the United States in persecution of the war." For Holmes, it is less a question of the motives of Abrams and his friends, however, and more a question of the power of the defendants to achieve their goal. In an often quoted phrase from his dissent, "Now nobody can suppose that the surreptitious publishing of a silly leaflet by an unknown man, without more, would present any immediate danger that its opinions would hinder the success of the government arms or have any appreciable tendency to do so" (*Abrams v. U.S.*, 1919, p. 628).

Also in *Abrams*, Holmes put forward his marketplace theory: "The best test of truth is the power of the thought to get itself accepted in the competition of the market, and that truth is the only ground upon which their wishes safely can be carried out" (*Abrams v. U.S.*, 1919, p. 630). Although it has been argued that market-based tests give power to the public sphere to increase diversity and the creation of meaning, Holmes' theory of truth is less a recognition of the polysemic nature of meaning and more a statement on citizenship. It raises questions about whether citizens are capable of discovering truth. As Lustig (1992) noted, Holmes might have been "a friend of the common man, but only to the extent that such men and women would benefit by life in a society where order flowed from the needs of objective institutions rather than subjective rights" (p. 120).

The duty of the courts, then, is not to create the space to allow citizens to create meaning, but rather to search for and discover the natural meaning and tendency of an expressive act. This exists not so much in the words, but rather in the context in which the words were used (Menand, 2001). This becomes obvious in Holmes' opinion for the Court in *Debs v. U.S.* (1919), where Socialist Party leader Eugene Debs was convicted of delivering an antiwar speech that tended to disrupt military recruitment. In upholding Debs' conviction, Holmes spoke of trying to discover the "natural and intended effect" of Debs' speech (*Debs v. U.S.*, 1919, p. 215). Holmes noted of Debs' call for public opposition to the war and the jury's search for his intent:

> Evidence that the defendant accepted this view and this declaration of his duties at the time that he made his speech is evidence that if in that speech he used words tending to obstruct the recruiting service he meant that they should have that effect. The principle is too well established and too mani-

festly good sense to need citation of the books. We should add that the jury were most carefully instructed that they could not find the defendant guilty for advocacy of any of his opinions unless the words used had as their natural tendency and reasonably probable effect to obstruct the recruiting service. (*Debs v. U.S.*, 1919, p. 216)[7]

The theme of searching for the natural meaning of expressive acts carried over to *Gitlow v. New York* (1925). There the Court upheld Benjamin Gitlow's conviction for the publication of his manifesto urging the overthrow of organized government. So when Gitlow wrote, "The Communist International calls the proletariat of the world to the final struggle!", the Court, through Justice Edward Sanford, noted, "This is not the expression of philosophical abstraction, the mere prediction of future events; it is the language of direct incitement" (*Gitlow v. New York*, 1925, p. 665). Sanford wrote that Gitlow can be constitutionally punished if "the natural tendency and probable effect was to bring about the substantive evil which the legislative body might prevent" (*Gitlow v. New York*, 1925, pp. 631–632).

Holmes, joined by Justice Louis Brandeis, dissented not based on a different theory of interpretation, but rather on the question of whether Gitlow's actions had any chance of succeeding. As Holmes noted, "[W]hatever may be thought of the redundant discourse before us it had no chance of starting a present conflagration" (*Gitlow v. New York*, 1925, p. 673).

It can be argued that Holmes, in arguing to protect speech that had little chance of triggering action, was also advocating restrictions on speech that might threaten the status quo. There is no doubt that Holmes and others believed strongly that government had a right to protect itself. However, the idea of trying to anticipate public reaction as a way of deciding whether speech should be protected proves to give a great deal of power to courts. If too many people agree with speech that is "wrong" in the eyes of the Court, that speech can be prohibited because it is a threat to organized government. If a lot of people disagree with speech, it also can be used to support a justification for prohibition (see *Gilbert v. Minnesota*, 1920). Either way, dissent is limited.

The Court has continued to make judgments about the public creation of meaning involving protests against war. At times the importance of authorial intent seems so powerful in the eyes of the justices that it plays a significant role in deciding whether conduct is deserving of First Amend-

---

[7]It does not seem that Holmes believed this to mean that there was some natural meaning to words. He believed that meaning was context dependent. The meaning of language was a social good, much as Pragmatists' of the day believed. Holmes did not, however, share the Pragmatists' optimism (Menand, 2001).

ment protection. In 1974, the Court ruled that the First Amendment protected a student's right to display an American flag with a peace symbol taped on it. In a *per curiam* opinion, the Court wrote, "A flag bearing a peace symbol and displayed upside down by a student today might be interpreted as nothing more than bizarre behavior, but it would have been difficult for the great majority of citizens to miss the drift of appellant's point at the time that he made it" (*Spence v. Washington*, 1974, p. 410).

In the judgment of the Court, the intent and successful communication of the message helps move the flag from unprotected conduct to protected expression. As the Court noted, "An intent to convey a particularized message was present, and in the surrounding circumstances the likelihood was great that the message would be understood by those who viewed it" (*Spence v. Washington*, 1974, pp. 410–411). At least some of the protection provided to expression, then, is linked to the successful transmission of meaning from author to audience. Might the speech not have been protected if the message were not clear? The Court did not answer that question. The Court also does not create any space for citizens to create their own meaning or to interpret the message in a new and different way. One cannot help but come to the conclusion that if an expressive act is interpreted in a way that differs from the actor's intent, that act would not receive First Amendment protection.

It is interesting to note that the Court has not always relied on this interpretation of meaning. In 1943, the Court through Justice Robert Jackson defined meaning in a very different way. In deciding that public schools cannot force students to pledge their allegiance to the American flag, Jackson wrote, "A person gets from a symbol the meaning he puts into it, and what is one man's comfort and inspiration is another's just and scorn" (*West Virginia State Board of Education v. Barnette*, 1943, pp. 632–633). Although that definition still falls short of recognizing the discursive nature of meaning creation, it does acknowledge that meaning can and often does differ from the creator's intent. It is interesting to note that today the Court seems to have broken from Justice Jackson's idea and more firmly placed meaning in the hands of the speaker.

Over the years, the Court continues to acknowledge that the public plays some role in determining intent, but that role has never been clearly articulated. For example, in *Watts v. United States* (1969), when an 18-year-old boy was convicted of knowingly and willfully threatening the president of the United States, the Court relied on the determination of intent to overturn the conviction. During a public rally at the Washington Monument, Watts said:

They always holler at us to get an education. And now I have already received my draft classification as I-A and I have got to report for my physi-

cal this Monday coming. I am not going. If they ever make me carry a rifle
the first man I want to get in my sights is L.B.J. They are not going to
make me kill my black brothers. (*Watts v. United States*, 1969, p. 705)

The Court, through a *per curiam* opinion, ruled that Watts' speech was
a *crude* method of expressing his political opinion that, "Taken in context,
and regarding the expressly conditional nature of the statement and the
reaction of the listeners, we do not see how it could be interpreted otherwise" (*Watts v. United States*, 1969, p. 708).

The Court reiterated the importance of context in its decision in *City of
Ladue v. Gilleo* (1994). Margaret Gilleo had placed a sign on her front
lawn in 1990 expressing her opposition to the Gulf War.[8] After one sign
disappeared and a second was knocked to the ground, the City of Ladue, a
suburb of St. Louis, Missouri, informed Gilleo that her signs were prohibited by city ordinance. She then placed a sign in a second-floor window of her home stating, "For Peace in the Gulf." The city passed another
ordinance prohibiting the placement of signs other than such signs as
small residential identification signs, for sale signs, commercial signs in
commercially zoned areas, and churches, schools, or religious institutions.

Although the Court unanimously agreed that the city's ordinance un-
constitutionally restricted free speech, it took note of the important role
that the sign's location plays in the creation of public meaning. Justice
John Paul Stevens argued that signs carrying the same message can take
on different meanings in different locations.[9]

A sign advocating "Peace in the Gulf" in the front lawn of a retired general
or decorated war veteran may provoke a different reaction than the same
sign in a 10-year-old child's bedroom window or the same message on a
bumper sticker of a passing automobile. An espousal of socialism may
carry different implications when displayed on the grounds of a stately
mansion than when pasted on a factory wall or an ambulatory sandwich
board. (*City of LaDue v. Gilleo*, 1994, p. 56)

Although Stevens' argument seems to value the public creation of
meaning, it does, in the end, follow the same logic as earlier First Amendment reasoning. The public creation of meaning is valued not so much
for itself—for the public's ability to exchange views and ideas—but
rather because it is directly related to the ability of individuals to express
themselves. As Stevens noted, "The elimination of a cheap and handy me-

---

[8]The sign said, "Say No to War in the Persian Gulf, Call Congress Now."

[9]Interestingly, Justice Stevens argued that commercial signs might have lesser communicative importance (*City of LaDue v. Gilleo*, 1994, p. 56).

dium of expression is especially apt to deter *individuals* from communicating their views to the public . . ." (*City of LaDue v. Gilleo*, 1994, p. 56).

Today it seems that the Court has come to recognize the polysemic nature of public expressive acts, but it is viewing that idea through the lens of a First Amendment that values the individual rights of speakers more than the public's right to associate for the creation of meaning. The public remains important not because it is the creator of meaning, but rather because it is needed as a way to justify and legitimize existing freedoms of expression. Freedom of expression is good, in the eyes of the Court, because it allows individuals to express themselves and it aids society's need for ideas. Citizens are seen as playing little role in the creation of meaning. The public is either a group of people that might be energized by dangerous ideas or an audience for individual speech. The flow of information to the public sphere only goes one way. The public sphere is portrayed as a passive receiver of information and not an active interpreter of meaning.

The Public Meaning of Religious Symbols

The placement of religious symbols on publicly owned property has long occupied the decisions of the Court. Bringing together the speech and religion clauses of the First Amendment, the justices have tried to establish when it is acceptable for these powerful symbols to be displayed in areas such as public parks, public buildings, and on the premises of governmental buildings. Through the years, the question that has occupied the Court is whether a person who views the display will come away feeling that, because of the placement of the symbol, the government has expressly endorsed that religious view. For example, the Court has held that the placement of a Christmas tree and a menorah on the grounds of a county courthouse is acceptable, but the placement of a crèche (a representation of the nativity of Jesus) on an inside grand staircase of a county courthouse during the Christmas season is not. For at least a majority of the court, the placement of the crèche signifies official endorsement, whereas the menorah and the Christmas tree, placed side by side, signify diversity. As Justice Harry Blackmun wrote, "No viewer could reasonably think that (the crèche) occupies this location without the support and approval of the government" (*County of Allegheny v. ACLU*, 1989, pp. 600–601).

Throughout these cases, justices have struggled with how to interpret the public meaning of religious symbols. They struggle to acknowledge that not all people view these symbols through the same lens, but yet fight to establish a preferred meaning on which to set policy. The debate is highlighted by looking at *Capital Square Review and Advisory Board v.*

Pinette (1993), where various justices struggled to define the polysemic nature of public meaning.

Under Ohio law, Capital Square in Columbus, Ohio, was a forum for public discussion and activities. The Advisory Board was given authority to regulate access to the square and required users to fill out an application and meet several content-neutral criteria. In 1993, the Board rejected the application of the Ku Klux Klan to place an unattended cross on the grounds. A divided Court sided with the Klan.

Of central importance to most of the justices was how citizens might interpret the placement of the cross, its meaning, and whether its placement on the square would bring with it official governmental sanction. Justice Scalia, writing for the majority, argued that because most citizens realized that the square was open for public use, there was little if any chance that people would associate the cross' placement with government endorsement. He argued that precedent requires the Court to rely on "the community" for the dominant interpretation, although "outsiders" or uninformed members of the community might come to a different interpretation. As Scalia wrote, "Erroneous conclusions do not count" (*Capital Square Review and Advisory Board v. Pinette*, 1993, p. 765). Scalia built off of and set a dominant interpretation. If a citizen comes to the conclusion that government has endorsed the placement of the cross, Scalia labeled that an *erroneous* interpretation. Only evidence of direct government preference would raise constitutional questions. For Scalia, there was no governmental intent to endorse a particular form of religion, therefore it is unreasonable for citizens to come to such a conclusion.

Justice Sandra Day O'Connor, concurring with the decision but for different reasons, departed from Scalia's rejection of erroneous interpretation. For O'Connor, if a "reasonable observer would view a government practice as endorsing religion, I believe that it is our duty to hold the practice invalid" (*Capital Square Review and Advisory Board v. Pinette*, 1993, p. 765). She argued that her idea of a *reasonable observer* is less tied to individual interpretation and more linked to the idea of community or collective social judgment (*Capital Square Review and Advisory Board v. Pinette*, 1993, p. 780). She denied, however, that she is empowering majority views:

> There is always someone who, with a particular quantum of knowledge, reasonably might perceive a particular action as an endorsement of religion. A State has not made religion relevant to standing in the political community simply because a particular viewer of a display might feel uncomfortable. (*Capital Square Review and Advisory Board v. Pinette*, 1993, p. 780)

O'Connor agreed with the majority decision in this case, but not because of a lack of government intent. Rather, she believed that no reasonable observer can come away with an interpretation that would endorse state sanctions. She admitted she is troubled that the cross is the only display on the square, and for that reason she endorsed adding a disclaimer to the display—an action that Scalia soundly rejected.[10]

The complexity of interpreting symbols was not lost on the Court. Justice Clarence Thomas, voting with the majority, argued that the cross, as used by the Klan, was a political, racist symbol, rather than a religious symbol. He noted, "The Klan has appropriated one of the most sacred religious symbols as a symbol of hate" (*Capital Square Review and Advisory Board v. Pinette*, 1993, p. 771). However, he left little indication of how such a conclusion might influence his decision.

In dissent, Justice Stevens noted the complexity of determining the meaning of the cross. Although the meanings may vary, Stevens was willing to take a stand against any government endorsement of religion. He rejected O'Connor's argument about differing correct interpretations. Instead, he called on interpretations to be "objectively reasonable," adding, "A person who views an exotic cow at the zoo as a symbol of the Government's approval of the Hindu religion cannot survive this test" (*Capital Square Review and Advisory Board v. Pinette*, 1993, p. 800).

He went on to argue that any reasonable observer, seeing an unattended symbol in front of a capital building, would assume the government "has sponsored and facilitated its message" (*Capital Square Review and Advisory Board v. Pinette*, 1993, pp. 801–802). The placement of a United Way thermometer and the booths of artisans during a craft show carry equal governmental support, Stevens argued. It was not the cross that produced the controversy, but *where* the cross was placed. For Stevens, that demonstrates perceived government involvement, and only one meaning can be derived from the placement of the cross (*Capital Square Review and Advisory Board v. Pinette*, 1993, pp. 811–812).

The debate among the justices in this case demonstrates the increasing difficulty they have wrestling with the complexity of meaning. The majority of the Court acknowledge that there is something they need to take into account beyond the intent of the communicator, yet they recognize that, in the end, they fall back on the establishment of a dominant meaning on which to base law. Members of the Court disagree about what

---

[10]Scalia noted that, to be of much help, a sign clarifying the intent of the display would have had to be of sufficient size to make it accessible to passersby. He argued that such rules open up the possibility of allowing government to determine whether signs are large enough for citizens to see them. He noted, "Our Religion Clause jurisprudence is complex enough without the addition of this highly litigable feature" (*Capital Square Review and Advisory Board v. Pinette*, 1993, p. 769).

that meaning is and how it is established. What they refuse to accept is that the Klan's cross means different things to different people and viewpoint diversity is acceptable in a democratic society. The Court focuses on the establishment of meaning and ignores the public process of meaning creation that is vital to a participatory democracy.

MEANING, ACTIVE CITIZENSHIP, AND MANAGEMENT

The cases involving dissent during times of war and the meaning of religious symbols demonstrate not only how justices have struggled to interpret the meaning of public expressive acts, but also show how the interpretation of meaning is used to manage the public sphere. In the war cases, the court establishes a dominant meaning of an expressive act and attempts to hide that establishment behind some objective methodology. As we have seen, the Court has increasingly recognized the importance of context in the establishment of meaning, but has failed to recognize that the public plays any role other than that of a passive spectator in the establishment of that meaning. The Court fails to break free of liberal constraints, tentatively recognizing the polysemic nature of expressive acts, but turning that into a justification for greater individual freedom. In important ways, the Court adopts and adapts to the challenge put forth by cultural studies by putting forward a new understanding of meaning—one that finds a way to acknowledge the openness of meaning while still protecting the Court's institutional role in the establishment of meaning.

In First Amendment jurisprudence, intent plays a critical role in the discovery of meaning. Through the attempt to discover the original intent of a speaker, a text, or an act, law seeks to fix the meaning of public expressive acts in space and time. The search for original intent is an authoritative action that is often used to block challenges and to claim a higher status for an idea. The interpretation is no longer just the opinion of one isolated individual, but rather an agreed-on meaning that has historical and cultural power.

This becomes apparent in the writings of Justice Scalia. He recognized that the discovery of meaning is difficult, if not impossible, and that judges need to be cautious. As can be seen from Scalia's comments, if we begin from the idea that intent can be fixed in time and space, the discovery of that intent becomes a question of finding the proper methodology. More than anything else, the search for original intent makes the individual speaker or text the focus of attention, rather than the public sphere.

Recent free speech doctrine puts the control of meaning either securely in the hands of the creator or speaker (or, perhaps more accurately, in the hands of the owner). The meaning of a public event, such as a parade or public demonstration, is what the speaker or owner intends it to be. So for Scalia, a cross placed in front of a state capital can only be interpreted as state endorsement of religion through an erroneous interpretation—the state did not intend that meaning. Applied in this fashion, free speech doctrine endorses an authoritarian approach to the establishment of meaning.

Justice Scalia's opinion in *Capital Square*, as well as comments from dissenting justices, demonstrate that the intent of the speaker is far more important to the Court than how members of the public might interpret such symbols. It is entirely possible that citizens might see no connection between the placement of the cross and government endorsement of a religious view, as Scalia argued. However, Scalia had little evidence to make such a determination and, for that matter, neither do the other justices who make assumptions about what reasonable observers might think. The important point, however, is not that either view is right or wrong. Rather it is that, by making judgments about what the dominant meaning is, the Court is cutting off the discursive opportunities for the public. By building its decisions around the assumption that the establishment of a dominant meaning is necessary in order to set public policy, it limits the discursive opportunity for citizens to wrestle with what these symbols mean—to engage in what some might call *public work* (Boyte & Kari, 1996). It assumes that citizens are passive spectators to democracy, waiting for a dominant institution to tell them what a public expressive act means, how it fits into our constitutional scheme, and how they are to relate to and understand it.

The control of meaning then allows the Court to maintain its legitimacy as a major cultural force, but it also helps the Court manage public life. As we have seen, in different political periods that management allows different levels of protection for individual expression, but the Court is consistent in its refusal to recognize the value of the public creation of meaning. The Court, and liberal theorists in general, have tended to overvalue individual freedom and idealize the marketplace (Jensen, 1998). Although liberalism's ideas of individual freedom and the marketplace of ideas emerged separately, and exist in an uneasy tension, they are nonetheless influential. The merging of liberal thought and the marketplace creates an instrumental approach to freedom of expression. Liberal theory, with its connections to the marketplace metaphor, creates avenues in which individuals are to fight to achieve expressive victory. Free speech in our modern understanding of the concept deemphasizes the exchange of ideas and emphasizes individual expression and winning the debate in the marketplace of ideas. The goal is not understanding, but instead winning. The power of this instrumental understanding of free speech is illustrated in numerous writings by free speech proponents—from John Milton's (1918) famous phrase, "Who ever knew truth put to the worse in a free and open encounter?" (p. 58), to Holmes' classic articulation of the marketplace of ideas, "The best test of truth is the power of the thought to get itself accepted in the competition of the market" (*Abrams v. U.S.*, 1919, p. 22). The marketplace in liberal free speech thought is not a place where ideas are exchanged for the sake of deliberation and the creation of meaning, but a place to find a way to ensure that an idea becomes dominant.

This becomes obvious when analyzing the ideas that underlie Holmes' vision of a marketplace and its role in democratic life. Seeing combinations as a fact of modern life, he attempted to create the space for combinations (be they workers or business) to establish what would pass as truth. Holmes was content to allow the status quo to dominate and determine what was considered true. Thus, in his *Abrams* decision, he granted protection to the protesters only because there is little threat that they would achieve their objectives. In Holmes' world, the marketplace of ideas does not serve a discursive function, but rather helps establish order in the chaotic world of democratic life.

Creating an Active Public Sphere

Public meaning is discursively redeemed and does not exist solely in the creator's intent, but in complex linguistic, symbolic, and cultural relationships. The key to creating that ethical discourse is allowing all citizens who want to participate to do so. Although the purpose of this chapter is not to fully articulate a theory of the First Amendment, the cases examined here lead to some tentative ideas.

If we recognize that the creation of meaning is a process, the focus of protection changes. Protection is no longer predicated on the intentions or clarity of the individual speaker, but on the creation of meaning through the interaction of the speaker and audience. Public areas—including those that are government owned and those that are privately owned, but generally open to the public—need to be regulated to promote discursive principles. In government-owned fora, where courts have looked at the traditional use of property and/or examined the rules that have been put in place to govern speech at those locations (Kalven, 1965; Post, 1995), a more functional approach is required. Cohen (1993) suggested that free speech theory should include the "presumption that any location with dense public interaction ought to be treated as a public forum that must be kept open to the public" (p. 49). Allowing access to public facilities or facilities that have been made public does not give speakers the right to interfere with, disrupt, or block another speaker's expressive activity. To allow speakers to do so would be to allow coercion to enter the public sphere. The idea is to create opportunities for citizens to speak, not ensure effective discourse; it merely allows speakers to enter the public sphere and use it for discursive purposes and, more important, provide opportunities for citizens to be actively involved in the creation of meaning.

In addition to access issues, freedom of association is vital to the public creation of meaning. Although association is not a recognized constitutional right, the U.S. Supreme Court has been protecting associational rights for a long time. Not surprisingly, however, the Court has tended to see freedom of association through a liberal framework that is not protective of the public sphere's discursive rights. Generally speaking, there are two ways that the Supreme Court justifies freedom of association. The first is linked to the idea that freedom of association is an individual right. It allows the individual to come together with other members of society to give that citizen a stronger voice in democracy. As Justice William Brennan once wrote,

> [T]he constitutional shelter afforded such relationships reflects the realization that individuals draw much of their emotional enrichment from close ties with others. Protecting these relationships from unwarranted state interference therefore safeguards the ability independently to define one's identity that is central to any concept of liberty. (*Roberts v. United States Jaycees*, 1984, p. 619)

Brennan saw freedom of association not as an intrinsic discursive right, but an instrumental right that serves the free speech needs of individuals (*Roberts v. United States Jaycees*, 1984).

The second way the Court has justified freedom of association stems from the perceived need to protect organizational autonomy. In this line of reasoning, association is important less as a way to protect individual freedoms and more as a way to allow organizations to exist absent governmental interference. As Chief Justice William Rehnquist put it in defending the right of the Boy Scouts of America to exclude homosexuals, the right of association is "crucial in preventing the majority from imposing its views on groups that would rather express other, perhaps unpopular ideas" (*Boy Scouts of America v. Dale*, 2000, p. 647). In that view, it is not the right of individual members to express themselves that is paramount, but rather the right of the organization's official position to dominate. Today, the Court seems to have moved away from viewing freedom of association as an individual right and more toward the idea that it is an organizational right (Farber, 2001).

Both interpretations fail to aid in the formation of a discursive public because of their emphasis on autonomy, rather than the creation of community. There is no doubt that the ability to protect the right of individuals to join associations is important to democracy, as well as the right of associations to be free from government-sanctioned beliefs. It is through those associations that public life is often played out. However, too much associational freedom—either for individuals or organizations—is bad for democracy. It fragments society, creating private interest groups that often tend to speak only to themselves. Associations are not simply about communicating within groups, but rather communicating among groups. One of the dangers to public life is that as the public sphere splinters into discrete associations, it loses its vitality. Therefore, how the Supreme Court has chosen to look at associations merely reflects different sides of the same coin. Both have direct connections to liberal ideas of free speech and association. However, Justice Rehnquist's ideas seem to more directly reflect the growing expansion of corporate rights. The disagreement between Brennan and Rehnquist is not over the role that associations play in a democratic society, but rather over who gets to control the meaning of an association. Brennan would allow individuals to control the meaning, whereas Rehnquist would allow the organization to make that determination. The Court fails to recognize that the democratic value of associations is not granting freedom to simply create an association or control meaning, but rather the freedom to use the association to communicate ideas or thoughts to other members of society. The value of associations is the role they play in the creation of public meaning.

CONCLUSION

I have argued that the Court, through its construction and use of the meaning of public expressive acts, has a direct impact on limiting the role citizens play in democracy. As I have suggested, the Court needs to recognize that democratic structures should value not just the ability of citizens to speak as individuals, but also opportunities to come together and grapple with the meaning of public acts. The lack of respect for public meaning making by the Court serves not only to disempower the public sphere, but to manage public life. By limiting the ideas that are put into the public sphere, the ability of citizens to come together to discuss those ideas, and the possibility that alternative frameworks might be created from that discussion, the Court maintains the status quo. As Delgado (1989) noted, alternative interpretations of public events is one way that disempowered groups are able to promote change in a democratic society. The Court too often discourages those alternative interpretations.

Of course it can be argued that the Court's management of public life is functional for democratic society. It makes for a more efficient, orderly society, which undoubtedly is an important role for law. More important, the Court's use of meaning also supports the modern understanding of democratic life in the United States, which Bachrach (1967) referred to as the theory of democratic elitism where "the masses are inherently incompetent" and citizens are "unruly creatures possessing an insatiable proclivity to undermine both culture and society" (p. 2). Elitist theories of democracy justify the Court's need to fix meaning and control public life. Working off of a different theory of democracy—one that values citizen activism and the Court's role in promoting that activism—we can find support for valuing the formation of alternative interpretations of public expressive acts.

Does such a view of democracy require the Court to surrender all attempts at the discovery of meaning? Obviously not. Interpretation, especially of the Constitution and legislation, is an important role of the Court. That does not mean, however, that the justices cannot recognize the complexity of meaning creation and work to protect the public space that would aid citizens in the creation of meaning. As argued in this chapter, the Court has used the question of meaning as a way to maintain order and protect the individual rights of those people with whom the justices agree. One solution to the problem facing the Court is to take the process of meaning creation and alternative interpretations of expressive acts seriously. Although this chapter does not attempt to detail a new theory of the First Amendment, such a solution might take the Court in new directions. It would protect discourse in venues open to public use, value association and assembly, not allow a speaker's intent to determine meaning, and examine how people have reacted to expressive acts. Although the establishment of meaning allows the political views of justices to dominate, a focus on the process of meaning-making might encourage more diverse interpretations and empower citizens.

In these cases, the Court is called on to walk a fine line between aiding an orderly society and creating meaning in a dynamic society. Meaning has come to serve the needs of that orderly society. The Court too often uses meaning as a way to quell disagreement and dissent, failing to recognize the value of discourse about the meaning of symbols in aiding the orderly transition of society. By protecting the process, the Court might aid the transition to a more democratic society and a more active public sphere.

REFERENCES

Abrams v. U.S., 250 U.S. 616 (1919).
Bachrach, P. (1967). *The theory of democratic elitism: A critique.* Boston: Little, Brown & Co.

Bork, R. H. (1971). Neutral principles and some First Amendment problems. *Indiana Law Journal, 47,* 1–35.

Boyle, J. (1985). The politics of reason: Critical legal theory and local social thought. *University of Pennsylvania Law Review, 133,* 685–780.

Boy Scouts of America v. Dale, 530 U.S. 640 (2000).

Boyte, H. C., & Kari, N. N. (1996). *Building America: The democratic promise of public work.* Philadelphia: Temple University Press.

Brennan, W. (1986). The constitution of the United States: Contemporary ratification. *South Texas Law Review, 27,* 433–445.

Calvert, C. (1995). Awareness of meaning in libel law: An interdisciplinary communication & law critique. *The Northern Illinois University Law Review, 16,* 111–140.

Capital Square Review and Advisory Board v. Pinette, 510 U.S. 1307 (1993).

City of LaDue v. Gilleo, 512 U.S. 43 (1994).

Cohen, J. (1993). Freedom of expression. *Philosophy & Public Affairs, 22,* 207–263.

Cohen, J. R. (1994). Critical viewing and participatory democracy. *Journal of Communication, 44,* 98–113.

County of Allegheny v. ACLU, 492 U.S. 573 (1989).

Cover, R. M. (1983). Foreword: Nomos and narrative. *Harvard Law Review, 97,* 4–68.

Debs v. U.S., 249 U.S. 211 (1919).

Delgado, R. (1989). Storytelling for oppositionists and others: A plea for narrative. *Michigan Law Review, 87,* 2411–2441.

Delia, J. (1987). Communication research: A history. In C. R. Berger & S. H. Chaffee (Eds.), *Handbook of communication science* (pp. 20–98). Beverly Hills, CA: Sage.

Dworkin, R. (1982). Law as interpretation. *Texas Law Review, 60,* 527–550.

Farber, D. (2001). Speaking in the first person plural: Expressive associations and the First Amendment. *Minnesota Law Review, 85,* 1483–1513.

Fiske, J. (1987). *Television culture.* New York: Methuen.

Frank, J. (1949). *Courts on trial: Myth and reality in American justice.* Princeton, NJ: Princeton University Press.

Gilbert v. Minnesota, 254 U.S. 325 (1920).

Giroux, H. A. (1992). Resisting difference: Cultural studies and the discourse of critical pedagogy. In L. Grossberg, C. Nelson, & P. Treichler (Eds.), *Cultural studies* (pp. 199–212). New York: Routledge.

Gitlow v. New York, 268 U.S. 652 (1925).

Glendon, M. A. (1991). *Rights talk: The impoverishment of political discourse.* New York: The Free Press.

Hall, S. (1980). Encoding/decoding. In S. Hall (Ed.), *Culture, media, language: Working papers in cultural studies, 1972–79* (pp. 128–138). London: Hutchinson.

Jenkins, H. (1992). *Textual poachers: Television fans & participatory culture.* New York: Routledge.

Jensen, R. (1998). First Amendment potluck. *Communication Law & Policy, 3,* 563–588.

Kalven, Jr., H. (1965). The concept of the public forum: Cox v. Louisiana. *Supreme Court Review, 1,* 1–32.

Lessig, L. (1995). The regulation of social meaning. *University of Chicago Law Review, 62,* 943–1045.

Lustig, R. J. (1982). *Corporate liberalism: The origins of modern American political theory, 1890–1920.* Berkeley: University of California Press.

McBain, H. (1927). *The living constitution: A consideration of the realities and legends of our fundamental law.* New York: The Workers Education Bureau Press.

Menand, L. (2001). *The metaphysical club: The story of ideas in America.* New York: Farrar, Straus, and Giroux.

Milton, J. (1918). *Areopagitica.* Cambridge: Cambridge University Press.

Missouri v. Holland, 252 U.S. 416 (1920).

Post, R. C. (1995). *Constitutional domains: Democracy, community, management.* Cambridge, MA: Harvard University Press.

Rehnquist, W. (1976). Observation: The notion of a living constitution. *Texas Law Review, 54,* 693–706.

Roberts v. United States Jaycees, 468 U.S. 609 (1984).

Scalia, A. (1989). Originalism: The lesser evil. *University of Cincinnati Law Review, 57,* 849–864.

Schenck v. U.S., 249 U.S. 47 (1919).

Scheppele, K. L. (1989). Foreword: Telling stories. *Michigan Law Review, 87,* 2073–2098.

Spence v. Washington, 418 U.S. 405 (1974).

Streeter, T. (1989). Polysemy, plurality, and media studies. *The Journal of Communication Inquiry, 13,* 88–106.

Streeter, T. (1995). Some thoughts on free speech, language, and the rule of law. In D. S. Allen & R. Jensen (Eds.), *Freeing the First Amendment: Critical perspectives on freedom of expression* (pp. 31–53). New York: New York University Press.

Sunder, M. (2001). Cultural dissent. *Stanford Law Review, 54,* 495–567.

Texas v. Johnson, 491 U.S. 397 (1989).

Tribe, L. (1978). *American constitutional law.* Mineola, NY: The Foundation Press.

Watts v. United States, 394 U.S. 705 (1969).

Wechsler, H. (1961). *Principles, politics, and fundamental law.* Cambridge, MA: Harvard University Press.

West Virginia State Board of Education v. Barnette, 319 U.S. 624 (1943).

White, J. B. (1990). *Justice as translation: An essay in cultural and legal criticism.* Chicago: University of Chicago Press.

Winter, S. L. (1989). The cognitive dimension of the *agon* between legal power and narrative meaning. *Michigan Law Review, 87,* 2225–2279.

Introductory Comments to Chapter 8

Sandra Braman[1]
University of Wisconsin–Milwaukee

Every aspect of research design needs serious attention if the results are to be valid, reliable, and actually useful. Some facets of the research process, such as choosing a case or a sample, regularly receive a lot of attention, even though these familiar problems only become more complex with experience.[2] Some researchers habitually rely on analytical concepts developed by others as if the mere fact of prior use were sufficient evidence that the concepts were theoretically sound, appropriately operationalized, and valid for the problem at hand. Those with more sophistication offer full explication of key analytical concepts—a process both described and modeled by the late Steven Chaffee (1991) in his excellent—but out-of-print—book, *Explication*. Even those who explicate concepts, however, may assume that the subject matter of their research does not need the same treatment, as if it were obvious. In some cases this may be so, or becomes so following a literature review discussing the subject of the research prior to a discussion of the methods used, but in other areas it is not. The research subject of *information policy* is a premiere example of a research subject that does not have a clear identity unless the explication task is specifically taken up.

---

[1]"Information and Socioeconomic Class in U.S. Constitutional Law" originally appeared, without this introduction, in *Journal of Communication* (1989), *39*, 163-179.

[2]Charles C. Ragin and Howard S. Becker (1992) valuably edited an entire book on the problem of how to select and define a case (*What Is a Case? Exploring the Foundations of Social Inquiry*). Becker (1997) provided a service through ruminations on his research experience, revealing that any aspect of research methods that may seem obvious is not.

At the time that "Information and Socioeconomic Class in U.S. Constitutional Law" was written, in the mid-1980s, many people had recognized that existing legal and economic categories were no longer sufficient for analyzing the social change resulting from the use of digital information technologies. Scholars, theorists, and policy analysts were beginning to devote significant time and effort to thinking through what to do about that, and this journal article—which presented part of the theoretical framework for my 1988 dissertation on treatment of information policy in U.S. Supreme Court decisions (Braman, 1988)—was a contribution to that endeavor. "Information and Socioeconomic Class in U.S. Constitutional Law," the article republished here, responds to the question persistently and importantly asked by my doctoral advisor, Donald M. Gillmor, regarding what I *meant* by information policy. To answer that question, I needed to explicate the research subject itself. The result was a methodological innovation: defining the research subject of information policy as all law and regulation that pertains to the information production chain of information creation, processing, flows, and use.

I have used this approach to define information policy ever since, in studies of that realm of law and regulation as it appears in domains as diverse as international trade (Braman, 1990), arms control agreements (Braman, 1991), internet policy (Braman, 1995b), and on. Experience using this methodological innovation in research involving a wide range of policy arenas and materials deepened my understanding of the nature of the problem to be addressed and led to further refinements of the approach. Today, I view use of the information production chain as a heuristic for identifying what is information policy and what is not as the first stage in a definitional process that must suffice not only for bounding the domain, but also for guiding analysis and producing outcomes that are useful for working policymakers who still must continue to operate within the terms of what we now call *legacy law*. A full discussion of this multistage process, including examination of alternative approaches to the same problem, can be found elsewhere (Braman, 2004a, 2004b).

Besides providing an answer to my doctoral advisor, this methodological innovation has been extremely important theoretically. It brought under one analytical umbrella different versions of the same question from disparate areas of the law as traditionally categorized. The question of the privately owned interface with a public communication system, for example, has a legal history both in constitutional law (where it is raised by conflicts over the mailbox) and regulatory law (where it is raised by contention over the telephone and other "customer premises equipment" [CPE]). During the period in which the article republished here was written, there were extensive discussions of this problem in both constitutional law (including by the Supreme Court) and regulatory law (by the Federal Communications Commission [FCC]). However, because those analyses were siloed by legal category, neither conversation referenced the other. The consequence: Neither decision-making arena had access to all of the rich conceptualization and types of evidence available, and inconsistencies in the law remain. The approach to defining information policy described here cuts across preexisting categorizations of the law (and of the economy) to identify common questions for common analytical treatment irrespective of where they arise.

In "Information and Socioeconomic Class in U.S. Constitutional Law," this methodological innovation was described very briefly:

> The notion of an "information production chain" described by Machlup and Boulding can be adapted and used to define the domain as including those policies that apply to any stage of a chain that includes information creation (creation, generation, and collection), processing (algorithmic and cognitive), storage, transportation, distribution, destruction, and seeking. The all-inclusiveness of this approach permits identification of information policy irrespective of body of law as traditionally defined. This approach also permits exclusion of certain types of information, actors, or processing from some or all steps of the chain in response to cultural, aesthetic, religious, or political concerns. (Braman, 1989, p. 163)

Here I offer more detail, beginning with a look at just why the innovation was necessary in the first place.

THE DEFINITIONAL PROBLEM

When the Constitution and Bill of Rights were written, legal principles were established to ensure that citizens would be able to communicate orally and in print with each other and with their government about political matters. It was recognized that content had to be distributed as well as produced, so both the synchronous and co-present sharing of ideas through assembly and asynchronous and distributed communication through publishing and the postal system were constitutionally protected.[3] To meaningfully discuss the constitution of society, citizens need access to information and freedom to form their own opinions on

---

[3]The First Amendment protects assembly and the Postal Provision of the Constitution (Article 1, Section 8, Clause 7) established a postal service in order to provide universal access to the kind of distributed communication system considered critically necessary for the functioning of a democracy.

the basis of that information; thus, both of these were also protected.[4] The First Amendment also ensured that ideas could be shared with those in a position to make change.[5]

These were important and broad principles, but the society within which they were and are to be implemented has become ever more complicated. Technological innovation created truly mass media, expanding the set of regulatory subjects and adding issues raised by interactions among media. It was only about the time the first regulatory systems were being put in place for electronic media—in the 1920s—that the word *media* came into use (*Oxford English Dictionary*, 1989). Innovation continued to transform the fundamental nature of the technologies involved and the extent to which society is reliant on those technologies. The directly communicative functions of the media became a relatively small proportion of the overall role of information technologies in society. The distinction between public and private communicative contexts has become one of choice and will, rather than ownership, control, and history of use. Clearly both nonpolitical content and the infrastructure that carries it can have structural, or constitutive, impact.

Over time the law, too, became more highly articulated. Interpretation of constitutional law for the mediated environment identified a number of dimensions along which rights and responsibilities were differentiated: *context* (public vs. private); *content* (political vs. economic vs. cultural vs. personal); *genre* (fact vs. fiction, fact vs. opinion, news vs. history); *speakers* (public vs. private, and individual vs. corporate vs. governmental); *receivers* (voluntary vs. involuntary, adult vs. minor, and competent adult vs. incompetent adult); and *political condition* (war vs. peace, elections vs. between elections). It became deeply intertwined with—and often indistinguishable from—other policy issue areas, such as policy that dealt specifically with the development of new information and information architectures (sometimes called *information policy*), on the one hand, and *technology policy*, on the other hand. Both civil liberties and economic development were and are at stake.

All of these factors together confounded the question of just what we meant by *information policy*. A detailed look at these factors reveals that

---

[4]The principle of open government was established in a general way in the Constitution in Article 1, Section 5, which mandates that Congress report to the public on its activities through a journal, and in Article 2, Section 3, which requires the president to provide Congress with information regarding the conditions of the country. The principle that individuals and groups have the right to form their own ideas and opinions is included in the First Amendment protection of opinion and indirectly in the "mission statement" that introduces the Constitution.

[5]The right to seek change in the governance system is protected via inclusion of the right to petition the government in the First Amendment, as well as via the vote.

they fall into several classes of problems, including those raised by technologies, practices, the policymaking process, and characteristics of communication, information, and culture as a specific issue area. Many of these developments are now familiar to those who study law and regulation for information, communication, and culture, but it is worth reviewing them here from the perspective of how they affect the problem of defining the research subject.

Technology-Based Problems

The phrase "the convergence of technologies" conflates several analytical issues. New information technologies are qualitatively different from those with which communication policy has historically dealt; blur medium, genre, function and industry; are ubiquitously embedded in the objects of our material world; and replace slow-changing structuration processes with more rapid processes best described as *flexible*.

From Technology to Meta-Technology. The law has not historically distinguished among tools, technologies, and meta-technologies, although these differ along dimensions of legal importance.

1. *Tools* can be made and used by individuals working alone and make it possible to process matter or energy in single steps. The use of tools characterized the premodern era. Because communication is an inherently social act, it may only be when marks are made for the purposes of reminding oneself of something that it can be said there are communication tools.

2. *Technologies* are social in their making and use; that is, they require a number of people to work together. They make it possible to link several processing steps together in the course of transforming matter or energy, but for each technology there is only one sequence in which those steps can be taken, only one or a few types of materials that can be processed, and only one or a few types of outcomes that can be produced. The shift from tools to technologies made industrialization possible, and the use of technologies thus characterizes the modern period. The printing press and the radio are examples of communication technologies.

3. *Meta-technologies* vastly expand the degrees of freedom with which humans can act in the social and material worlds. Meta-technologies enable long processing chains, and there is great flexibility in the number of steps and the sequence with which they are undertaken. Meta-technologies can process an ever-expanding range of types of inputs and can produce an essentially infinite range of outputs. They are social, but enable solo activity within the socially produced network. Their use charac-

terizes the postmodern world. Meta-technologies are always informational, and the internet is a premiere example of a meta-technology used for communication purposes.

The shift from technologies to meta-technologies affects the scope and scale of the policy subject, as when national law must cope with global media. A vastly expanded range of alternative outcomes must be considered in the course of policy analysis; the cost of failing to do so was demonstrated by the appearance of the new vulnerabilities and liability issues referred to as the potential for information warfare, hacking, and cracking made possible as a result of government funded software research and development. Meta-technologies also involve a causal chain that is potentially much longer and more variable than those with which policy analysis has historically dealt, requiring the development of both new policy tools and new methods for policy analysis. Policymakers are most comfortable making law when they feel they understand what it is that is being regulated, but we are still just learning about the effects of the use of meta-technologies.

Convergence of Communication Styles.   Media have been distinguished from each other in the past by the number of message receivers (one, a few, or many); by the nature of interactivity, if any, between sender and receiver; and by the difference between synchronicity and asynchronicity. These dimensions together may be described as a matter of style.

In the past, specific media were characterized by a particular style of communication. Over-the-air (broadcast) TV is mass communication, from one to many; it does not permit direct interactivity between viewers and programming; and it is experienced by its entire audience at the same time, synchronously. Telephony, in contrast, is predominantly person to person (one to one), is by definition interactive, and is synchronous. Personal letter writing is one to one and interactive, but asynchronous.

The internet, however, blends communicative styles in all three dimensions. During a single session, a user may communicate with a single person, small groups, or the public en masse, often fluidly switching back and forth among the three. Similarly, one-way and interactive communications, both synchronous and asynchronous, can be mixed within single sessions of activity.

This blending of communication styles is problematic for defining the research subject because point-to-point communication with a single receiver can no longer be excluded from discussions of media law. Also, under current law, several different regulatory approaches, each with its own assignation of rights and responsibilities, can concurrently apply to a single communicative act or message. Interactivity must be included because it has been deemed constitutionally worthy of protection because of the way in which it changes a discourse and the nature of information exchanged (*Kleindienst v. Mandel*, 1972).

Blurring of Medium, Function, and Industry.   The convergence of technologies confounds any expectation that particular media, functions, and industries will map onto each other. Such expectations were always unrealistic because there has been experimental and often significant use of every medium to fill every possible type of social function. (The telephone, for example, has been used as a mass news medium and for cultural gatherings in both Europe and the United States.) In the current environment, however, shifts in the location and form of specific social functions that once unfolded across time and place now regularly take place. This confounds efforts to apply law and regulation that are industry-specific as well as efforts to use law and regulation (largely but not exclusively via antitrust law) to keep industries separate from each other. It disrupts habits of policy analysis because typically such techniques are based on assumptions about the social functions to be served by particular media industries. The economics of each of the industries involved become altered, further disturbing habitual analytical assumptions.

Ubiquitous Embedded Computing.   We are accustomed to treating the media as an identifiable set of objects in which communicative capacity can be found and which serve only communicative functions, distinct from other objects and from ourselves. Increasingly, however, information technologies are ubiquitously embedded throughout the material world in familiar objects such as cars, refrigerators, stoplights, and paper. And while, at the moment, such technologies are embedded in humans only at the margins—by scientists experimenting with connecting computer chips to neurons, artists treating their bodies as electronic art media, and penal systems taking advantage of new ways of tracking and restricting those who have broken the law—it is likely that in the future information technologies will also be ubiquitously embedded in plant, animal, and human organisms as well. This change presents a conceptual and operational challenge to those making, implementing, and interpreting media law.

The Media and Flexible Structuration.   Constitutive processes involve structuration, the interaction between structure and agency, with the latter defined as the ability to effectively act on the basis of one's own intention (Giddens, 1986). From this perspective, constitutional protections for the media are intended to ensure that individuals have the communicative agency necessary to affect governance. Of course, in the late 18th and early 19th centuries the nation–state was not the only source of structural power because religious institutions retained a great deal of power, explicitly acknowledged in the U.S. Constitution when it is relegated to the private sphere. Agency through physical power has always been available, and, as Boulding (1971) noted decades ago, social norms and perceptual frames are also important. In the terms of political science, these distinct forces are referred to as *instrumental power* (the ability to affect behavior through physical action), *structural power* (the ability to affect behavior through the design of institutions and rules), and *symbolic power* (the ability to affect behavior through shaping perceptions and modes of thought). With informational meta-technologies, a fourth form of power has become important. *Informational power* affects behavior through manipulation of the informational bases of instrumental, structural, and symbolic forms of power (Braman, 1995a).

Among the effects of informational power is a blurring of the distinction between agency and structure because informational structure itself becomes agency. Legal analysis of the effects of computer code (Lessig, 1999) and revision of the Standard Industrial Classification [SIC] codes used as the basis of economic analysis into the North American Industrial Classification System [NAICS] to take new features of the information economy into account demonstrate governmental acknowledgment of the importance of informational power. Breaking down the distinction between structure and agency makes structuration processes far more flexible; the result is that the policy subject is in a sense dissolved, and modes of causality become more complex.

Law and regulation are always based on at least implicit assumptions about causality as direct, discernible, affected by relatively few intervening variables, occurring via single or few causal steps, and effected by identifiable agents. United States communication policy of the 18th and 19th centuries constrained and used symbolic power. During the late 19th and 20th centuries, the development of antitrust law manifested the addition of structural power to the subjects of pertinent policy and the repertoire of tools used to protect individual agency in the face of the nation-state and large corporations. Today, it must adapt to the realities of informational power: There are agents that have not been recognized as such by the law, or there may be no identifiable agents at all. Causality may be indirect, indiscernible, affected by multiple intervening variables, and involve causal chains that are beyond analytical reach. These changes in the nature of agency and causality are evident in practice-based problems faced by those seeking to define the research subject when they examine issues raised by law and regulation that deal with information, communication, and culture.

Practice-Based Problems

Contemporary media practices make the problem of identifying the research subject more difficult because there is constant innovation, genres are blurred, players have multiplied, and policy subjects are now often networked rather than autonomous entities.

Constant Innovation. Information and communication products, services, and organizational forms all continue to evolve. Examples of innovation in practice include the increasingly popular habit of changing web page design in response to the number of reader hits per article and the gatekeeper-free broadcasting of news stories and documentaries by independent media groups such as IndyMedia, which are easily accessible on the web. Service innovations include individually designed content and the use of intelligent agents for information seeking and delivery. Institutional and industry innovations appear when newspapers start acting like ISPs, news-oriented organizations turn to entertainment, and firms in professional service industries such as the law start contracting out printing services. These changes problematize the definition of the research subject because historically distinct products, services, and industries were treated differentially under the law. The process of adapting statutory and regulatory law to reflect the categories of the new classification system, which came into use only at the close of the 20th century, has not yet begun.

Blurring of Genres. Genre distinctions in constitutional law—such as those fact and fiction, fact and opinion, and news and history—are fundamental to the analysis of law dealing with such matters as libel, advertising regulation, and postal rates. The blurring of genre thus adds conceptual problems to legal analysis. We continue to struggle with the application of standards of facticity that are important from the perspective of libel and fraud, docudrama, and infotainment. The long-standing distinction among history, fiction, and news based on a combination of facticity and the currency of information supported differential pricing of information distribution via the post office—but is only one of the approaches to differential pricing of web-based information, and it is being used in a *de facto* rather than a *de jure* way.

Tactical Media. *Tactical media* practitioners work with the possibilities unleashed by the interchangeability of structure and agency. Although mainstream and alternative media have historically used content to engage in political battles, the tactical media movement launched in the 1990s spurns struggles over content as a losing battle. Instead, these journalists/artists/activists take seriously Marshall McLuhan's insight that the medium *is* the message and have turned, instead, to manipulation of information production, processing, and delivery systems. The goal is to alter the semiotic and electronic realities within which media operate—an exercise of informational power. Tactical media practitioners combine news and political commentary with art. Consumption, aesthetics, and humor are viewed as opportunities to enact power, often most successful in stand-alone events rather than the persuasive campaigns to which we have become accustomed. Restricting the pertinent policy domain to law and policy focused on content are inadequate in the face of tactical media. Rather, tactical media practitioners see their work as *pre-policy*, acknowledging that what they do is stimulate legal innovation (Critical Art Ensemble, 2001).

Everyone's a Player. In the pre-digital era, most pertinent areas of law and regulation affected professional communicators almost exclusively; libel law and problems of copyright infringement are good examples. In the electronic environment, however, everyone who communicates runs the danger of bumping into the same legal and regulatory issues, even when individuals perceive themselves to be involved solely in interpersonal communication. Traditional approaches to defining the research subject that orient toward professional communications and established media organizations must be reconsidered in this context.

Antitrust in a Network Society. Antitrust law has been used heavily since the late 19th century to restrain firms in the media and telecommunications industries. Indeed, much of the current shape of the telecommunications industry still reflects antitrust decisions made in 1913 and 1956 (Kellogg, Thorne, & Huber, 1992). Intertwined ownership of the infrastructure and the multidimensional networking of firms, however, can make it difficult to treat firms as distinct and autonomous units for the purposes of antitrust law. Constant innovation, the emphasis on services rather than goods, and the interchangeability of goods and services make it difficult to conduct antitrust analysis of products; globalization makes it difficult to conduct antitrust analysis of markets.

Policy Process-Based Problems

Some of the problems in defining media policy today derive from the nature of policymaking, such as the tension between incremental and radical change, the importance of latent as well as manifest policy, invisibility, policy interdependence and precession, and relationships between public policy and other types of influential decision making.

Transition Policy.   Policy change can be radical, such as when an entire body of existing law is abandoned in favor of building anew from scratch during revolutionary periods, or incremental—in a series of small evolutionary steps. Incremental policymaking is necessary for working decision makers in both the public and private sectors who must operate within existing law under severe time and resource constraints. Too, there is always a lag between the development of new ideas about and knowledge of social circumstances and their application in arenas as detailed and complex as the law—a lag reinforced by reliance on precedent. Nor is it possible to understand all of the effects of new technologies in their entirety immediately. After all, it took about 500 years to begin to fully comprehend the effects of the printing press (Eisenstein, 1979). Those who analyze, make, and implement information policy today face the problem of trying to achieve incremental legal change during a period of revolutionary change in the policy subject.

Latent and Manifest Policy.   Not everything that falls within the domain of information policy is labeled as such. Thus, borrowing from the late Robert K. Merton (1955, 1981), it is useful to distinguish between media policy that is manifest—clearly directed at what has traditionally been understood as the mass media—and that which is latent. The general notion of latent policy first appeared in the 1920s (Cardozo, 1921) and has since gained currency in fields ranging from technology policy (Lambright, 1976) to political science (Skocpol, 1985). Latent policy includes that which is created as a side effect of decisions aimed at other subjects, such as when Securities and Exchange Commission (SEC) regulation of the financial markets mandates the distribution of particular types of information. It can develop when its subject matter is categorized under other names, as in the "confidence- and security-building measures" (CSBMs) incorporated into arms control treaties of the 1980s and 1990s that required specific types of information exchange in support of foreign policy. Latent policy can also appear synergistically when policies from a variety of decision-making arenas interact to produce something quite different in combination, as when the use of alternative dispute resolution systems to reduce the burden on the courts results in a loss of public access to the kinds of information about conflict resolution the Constitution recognized as so essential to a democracy. The effects of latent policy can be direct. Its importance adds to the definitional task by requiring inclusion within the boundaries of the field those matters that have not habitually been assumed to fall within the domain. The importance of latent forms of information policy places demands on the effort to clearly identify the research subject by requiring attention to latent as well as manifest issues, bringing the latent into visibility, and exploring relationships between those issues that are latent and those that are manifest.

Invisible Policy. Many types of information policy decisions are highly influential but little discussed, or even acknowledged. The pertinent policy world includes such things as presidential executive orders, decisions by federal and state attorneys general, and the practice of hiding statutory law directed at one issue within a piece of legislation commonly understood to deal with another matter (Braman, 2004a). The significance of invisible sources of law and regulation to media realities makes it necessary to take such decision-making venues into account in the process of defining the field. Invisible policy is formal and is developed within government, but has largely escaped attention.

Policy Interdependence. Policy made at different levels of the social structure is highly interdependent, reflecting the emergence of networked forms of organization in all aspects of life and the interpenetration of political structures. Indeed for many countries around the world, international organizations are as, or more, important than national governments in shaping their media policy pertinent to information, communication, and culture (Price & Thompson, 2002). Regional governments, too, can strongly influence national policy of this type. It was, for example, in the area of the information infrastructure that the European Economic Commission (EEC) for the first time explicitly applied Commission law to member states (Wall, 1984). Such interdependence is described as both necessary (Soma et al., 1983) and a potential "policy trap" (Pepper & Brotman, 1987). Some efforts to extend U.S. or European law outside its borders occur "naturally," through harmonization of legal systems (Bruce et al., 1986; Heisenberg & Fandel, 2004) or the movement of decision making into the realm of private contracts when there is a legal vacuum (Dezalay, 1989), rather than through the excesses of extraterritoriality (unilateral efforts by a nation-state to exert its law outside its borders). The globalization of the information infrastructure and growing appreciation of the populations in developing countries as potential markets make it more likely that developed countries will come to take the needs and concerns of developing countries into account (Renaud, 1987).

Interdependence also characterizes information policy within the United States. The need to promote the national information infrastructure has been used as an argument in support of federal preemption of state law (*Capital Cities v. Crisp*, 1984), but this runs counter to other forces urging decentralization of decision making (Noam, 1983; Teske, 1990). Influence runs from the bottom up as well as the top down because even decision making at the local level can have an influence on national policy (Lee & Sloan, 1987). Interdependence requires far more consultation, cooperation, and policy coordination to avoid intolerable disruptions of national and international economies (Spero, 1981). It complicates the problem of bounding the field of information policy for specific nation-states by adding the requirement that both supra- and infra-national laws and regulations must be taken into account.

Policy Precession.　Treatment of policy as a design problem must also take into account interactions among different laws and regulations. This is the problem of precession, the interaction of two or more systems that results in a change in a decision or event along one axis as a result of a decision or event along the axis of the other system. Application of this concept from physics to policy analysis points to the need to link analysis of several types of decisions in order to understand the implications of their interactions. The concept of path dependence suggests precession, but does not reach all of what it is involved. Path dependence does not include sensitivity to the number of precessive steps that may be linked, the degree of complexity precession adds to the analytical problem, or differences in the angles of change. When precessive links are understood by some players but not by others, it is possible to erect barriers to meaningful participation in decision making on one issue by foreclosing options through filters or actions designed by a related piece of legislation or regulation.

An example is provided by an interaction between patent and antitrust law: The ability to assert property rights in ways of doing business through patent law, combined with the trend toward asserting property rights as early as possible in a processing chain in order to claim ownership of all products of that process (Kahin, 2004), means that antitrust law may no longer be able to reach some pertinent types of anticompetitive practices. Sensitivity to precession requires a further expansion of the definition of the policy subject.

Public Policy and Other Decision Making.　Formal policy mechanisms unfold within a broader legal field as understood in the Bourdieuian sense (Dezalay, 1990). Public policy now also interacts with decisions made by private decision makers, often collaboratively through what is referred to as "policy networks" (Marsh, 1998). There are also purely private sources of decision making with constitutive impact, informal aspects of decision-making processes that are highly influential but have received relatively little analytical attention, and technological and normative trends with enormous structural force. Decisions made in all of these arenas should be included within the definition of the policy subject.

Some of these nontraditional types of information policy are relatively obscure and may require specialized knowledge to be comprehensible, such as those made by technical standards bodies. Others are easier to understand, like the role played by internet service providers (ISPs) in determining speech conditions for the internet. Although traditionally the word policy has been reserved for public sector decision making and the word strategy for private, the impact of the latter on the former today and the intermingling of the two types of decision making suggest the definition of the policy subject may also need to include both.

Issue-Based Problems

Political scientists group together issues related to the same subject into what they term "issue areas" (Potter, 1980; Rosati, 1981; Sampson, 1982). Compared to traditional issue areas such as defense, agriculture, and trade, communication policy is relatively new policy—and, for digital technologies, very new. Because policy is developed in response to perceived characteristics and effects of specific technologies, the fact that neither those characteristics nor their effects are yet fully understood complicates the already difficult definitional problem. Other unique characteristics of information policy include the multiplicity of players and decision-making arenas and the level of impact on other issue areas.

Multiplicity of Players and Decision-Making Arenas. An unusually large number of players, types of players, and decision-making venues are involved in the making of information policy. Although in other areas, such as tuna fishing, there is a natural limit to those with a legitimate involvement and few ambiguities regarding responsibilities, information technologies—and thus decision making about them—are pervasive. As a result, literally dozens of entities—governmental, quasi-nongovernmental, and private—have a history of some type of involvement and, often, a stake. Within any single branch of government, several different agencies can be involved, often in conflict with each other. In the early 1980s, one study showed that the single issue of electronic funds transfer systems was under examination by at least four different committees of the House of Representatives, none of which had enough authority to deal with all of the technological, financial, and regulatory questions raised by the prospect of such a system (Smythe, 1981), and the situation has been exacerbated since. The result is often "policy gridlock"—an inability to make policy at all. It also makes it more difficult for the United States to operate internationally because others cannot be sure with whom to work or rely on for consistency in the U.S. position. Because of this multiplicity, it is inappropriate and inadequate to use a venue-based approach (e.g., "policy made by the FCC") to defining the policy subject.

Impact on Other Policy Issue Areas. Another unique aspect of information policy is the degree to which it influences decision making in other issue areas through constraints on both decision-making processes and the lenses through which issues are viewed. This policy domain (a) creates the communicative space within which all public and decision-making discourses takes place; (b) determines the kinds of information that will be available to inform those discourses; (c) provides the stuff of the institutions within which and processes through which decision making takes place; and (d) offers many of the policy tools used to implement policy decisions directed at other types of social processes. The relative importance of information policy confounds the problem because it adds pressure to the politics of the definitional process discussed. To the degree that those involved with decision making in other issue areas understand the importance to what they do, there will be efforts to subsume communication policy within treatment of other issue areas or to define it as something other than communication altogether.

INFORMATION POLICY AND THE INFORMATION PRODUCTION CHAIN

In the face of all of these conceptual difficulties, information policy can be defined as all law and regulation that pertains to any stage of an information production chain that involves creation, processing, flows, and use. The first portion of this section looks at the history and uses of this approach, as well as its strengths and weaknesses. The section goes on to look at the specific stages involved in the information production chain.

History and Uses of the Model for Information Policy Analysis

Models of an information production chain are rife. Although they are not always explicit, such models are always at least implicit in the minds of policymakers. They are implicit in constitutional law, where they are used to distinguish among types of communicative spaces for the purposes of differential application of the First Amendment. The Office of Management and Budget (OMB) uses a model of the "information life cycle" as a frame for interventions into the statistical practices of federal agencies. Models of such a chain are myriad; the approach offered here relies on a synthesis of versions put forward by Fritz Machlup (1980) and Kenneth Boulding (1966)—two economists whose work has been of great importance to the development of economic thought required to fully address the empirical realities of the information economy. Economic and legal categories are, of course, often intimately linked. Thus, the Machlup and Boulding models are pertinent to the problem of defining the research subject in analyses of information policy not only because of the general clarity of their models, but also because their models have been used to analyze many of the same types of social phenomena and processes from an economic rather than a strictly legal perspective.

This model includes the stages of information creation (*de novo*, generation, and collection), processing (cognitive and algorithmic), storage, transportation, distribution, destruction, and seeking. Relations between stages of an information production chain change when new linkages become possible between stages of the chain, as when the web makes it possible for producers and users of information to become directly linked; when parties at a stage of the chain lose their independent functions, as when the intermediaries between producers and users are no longer necessary; or when relations among parties change in such a way that there is reason for drastic reorganization, as multiple information providers choose to pool their resources (Owen & Wildman, 1992).

Communication involves two or more stages of this chain. There are no messages to send without information creation and processing; information is often transported in the course of gathering inputs into message creation, storage may be combined with distribution (as in books or records), and, while it has received less attention than other media policy matters, destruction of the historical record created by the media is an important political issue.

One advantage of this definitional approach is that the information production chain provides a mesolevel theoretical link between the abstract and the empirical. Another advantage is that the heuristic permits exclusion of certain types of information, actors, or modes of processing from either specific or all stages of the chain, thus incorporating the sensitivities of those who resist the commoditization of all information. The model of an information production chain is useful in breaking down complex communicative processes into their elements for differential analysis and legal treatment of those elements. Thus, although interactive and noninteractive, synchronous and asynchronous, and intercast, narrowcast, and broadcast communications may all be mixed by users of the internet, the concept of an information production chain can be of value in determining just how to distinctly apply legal principles. Use of a model of an information production chain as a heuristic makes it possible to read across the categories of legacy law to determine what falls within the domain of information policy and what does not.

Of course there are also problems. Decades after such models came into explicit use, there is still no consensus on ways to distinguish among different types of information processing beyond the gross distinction suggested earlier between algorithmic and cognitive modes. Using the model emphasizes analytical complexities because many communication processes, phenomena, and products involve more than one stage of the chain.

Stages of the Information Production Chain

The phrase "information creation, processing, flows, and use" is a handy and easy way to summarize the various stages of the information production chain, but for analytical purposes it is useful to break the chain down into further discrete stages.

Information Creation. Information can be created in three ways: It can be the product of a genuinely original creative act, and thus essentially come out of nothingness (creation *de novo*).[6] It can be the outcome of systematic procedures for developing such as those referred to by the concept of facticity (e.g., the "facts" of journalism) or the methodologies of statistics (e.g., "data"). Information is also created when it is generated as a byproduct of other life activities and processes, such as when one interacts with an institution (e.g., registering for a class, getting a driver's license) or changes one's status (e.g., gets married). Media policy questions involving information creation include matters of intellectual property rights and access to both information and infrastructure.

Information Processing. Information processing can be algorithmic (undertaken through procedures describable in mathematical form and thus accomplishable by computers) or cognitive (undertaken through procedures only available to the human brain to date). Some forms of information processing may be exclusive to one or the other of these categories, whereas other forms of information processing (e.g., alphabetization) can be undertaken either way. There is a plethora of ways of more finely articulating differences among types of information processing—a task of importance across policymaking venues and issues because more subtle distinctions are critical to the interpretation and implementation of the law. The work needed to develop a set of distinctions that can achieve consensual acceptance is therefore a critical item for the research agenda. Media policy issues in this area include restrictions on information that come from defining it as not speech and therefore not

---

[6]The Electronic Privacy Information Center (EPIC), at www.epic.org, is documenting the history of debate over this issue, which has copyright implications.

covered under the First Amendment (part of the debate over encryption), or as a result of the government's claim that access to information in the public domain does not include the right to process that information (a claim made in the *U.S. v. Progressive, Inc.* case of the 1970s). Information processing also raises antitrust issues, as was seen in the legal challenge to Microsoft's treatment of the relationship between its browser and operating system (*United States v. Microsoft Corporation*, 2003).

Information Transportation. Information transportation takes place when a single message is transported (to one, a few, or many). A conversation on the street, a letter, or the production of a single documentary would be examples of information transportation. This stage of the chain involves single messages. Restrictions on content or communicative behaviors put in place by ISPs as well as in non-electronic environments, including surveillance, are examples of media policy issues that can arise here.

Information Distribution. Information distribution is distinguished from transportation because it involves regular transportation of messages over time to either narrowcast or broadcast audiences often with a commercial aspect. Rather than messages, distribution involves channels. Media policy issues at this stage of the information production chain include trying to ensure a diversity of voices in all facets of the public sphere, access to the distribution network, anonymity, and censorship via the chilling effect of surveillance.[7]

Information Storage. Information storage occurs through fixation in a medium and through archival and cultural practices. Storage is important because it enables the communication of ideas across space and time, and because it forms the basis of our social memory. From the media policy perspective, information storage and destruction issues are two sides of the same coin. Laws and regulation that mandate the creation, storage, and destruction of public records create the public memory that is so important as an input into policymaking and as a matter of identity. The reliability and security of the information infrastructure are also important.

Information Destruction. Just as information can be produced essentially *de novo*, unlike matter it can be utterly lost or destroyed as well.

---

[7]The American Library Association (ALA) is so concerned about the chilling effect of surveillance on First Amendment rights that it issued a "Policy on Governmental Intimidation" in 1973 and revised it in 1981.

The fragility of digital information, and the ease with which it can be altered, have raised the salience of issues raised by the risk of the loss of knowledge and memory as policy issues. Loss of public memory through destruction of public records is the key media policy issue at this stage of the information production chain.

Information Seeking.   Sociologists and psychologists have brought information seeking to our attention as a distinct type of cognitive and social process worthy of attention in its own right. Information seeking has also been examined from an economic perspective because its costs are of importance when considering research and development budgets, risk analysis, and a number of other arenas. Incorporating sensitivity to cultural, social, personal, and cognitive differences in modes of information seeking into laws and regulations is one possible policy response. Positive support for education in media literacy is another. Surveillance is an issue here because government knowledge of information-seeking practices can have a chilling effect.

CONCLUSIONS

"Information and Socioeconomic Class in U.S. Constitutional Law" offers the first use of a methodological innovation in defining the research subject of information policy as including any law or regulation pertaining to any stage of the information production chain. Use of this definition of the research subject makes explicit already implicit conceptual frames used in legal analysis. It joins together multiple interrelated questions raised by information, communication, and culture. It facilitates identification of common themes across historically distinct areas of the law. The period of Supreme Court decision making analyzed in this chapter covers 1980 to 1986, but the trends discussed here and elsewhere (Braman, 1990, 1991, 1995c, 2000), are still unfolding.

More broadly, this example of the need to grapple with articulation of the research subject should serve as a reminder that every stage of the research process is deserving of serious deliberation. This is particularly the case when, as today, that research subject is undergoing such significant change that the categories and approaches of legacy law no longer suffice.

REFERENCES

Becker, H. S. (1997). *Tricks of the trade: How to think about your research while you're doing it.* Chicago: University of Chicago Press.

Boulding, K. E. (1966). The economics of knowledge and the knowledge of economics. *American Economics Review, 56*(2), 1–13.

Boulding, K. E. (1971). National images and international systems. In W. F. Hanrieder (Ed.), *Comparative foreign policy: Theoretical essays* (pp. 90–107). New York: McKay.

Braman, S. (1988). *Information policy and the U.S. Supreme Court, 1980–1986.* Unpublished doctoral dissertation, University of Minnesota.

Braman, S. (1989). Information and socioeconomic class in U.S. constitutional law. *Journal of Communication, 39*(3), 163–179.

Braman, S. (1990). Trade and information policy. *Media, Culture & Society, 12,* 361–385.

Braman, S. (1991). Contradictions in Brilliant Eyes. *Gazette: The International Journal of Communication Studies, 47*(3), 177–194.

Braman, S. (1995a). Horizons of the state: Information policy and power. *Journal of Communication, 45*(4), 4–24.

Braman, S. (1995b). Policy for the net and the internet. *Annual Review of Information Science and Technology, 30,* 5–75.

Braman, S. (1995c). Trigger: Law, labeling, and the hyperreal. In D. S. Allen & R. Jensen (Eds.), *Freeing the first amendment: Critical perspectives on freedom of expression* (pp. 169–192). New York: New York University Press.

Braman, S. (2000, September). *Differential treatment by type of information processing in U.S. Supreme Court decisions of the 1990s.* Paper presented to the Telecommunications Policy Research Conference, Arlington, VA.

Braman, S. (2004a, March 15). *Turning away from the magician's hand: The "dark matter" of the law and public discourse.* Josephine Jones Lecture, Boulder, CO.

Braman, S. (2004b). Where has media policy gone? Defining the field in the twenty-first century. *Communication Law and Policy, 9*(2), 153–182.

Bruce, R. R., Cunard, J. P., & Director, M. D. (1986). *From telecommunications to electronic services: A global spectrum of definitions, boundary lines, and structures.* Boston: Butterworths.

Capital Cities v. Crisp, 467 U.S. 691 (1984).

Cardozo, B. N. (1921). *The nature of the judicial process.* New Haven, CT: Yale University Press.

Chaffee, S. (1991). *Explication.* Newbury Park, CA: Sage.

Critical Art Ensemble. (2001). *Digital resistance: Explorations in tactical media.* Brooklyn, NY: Autonomedia.

Dezalay, Y. (1989). Putting justice "into play" on the global market. *Tidschrift. für Rattssociologie, 6*(1–2), 9–67.

Dezalay, Y. (1990). The *big bang* and the law: The internationalization and restructuring of the legal field. *Theory, Culture & Society, 7,* 279–293.

Eisenstein, E. L. (1979). *The printing press as an agent of change.* Cambridge: Cambridge University Press.

Giddens, A. (1986). *The constitution of society: Outline of the theory of structure.* Berkeley, CA: University of California Press.

Heisenberg, D., & Fandel, M. H. (2004). Projecting EU regimes abroad: The EU data protection directive as global standard. In S. Braman (Ed.), *The emergent global information policy regime* (pp. 109–129). Houndsmills, UK: Palgrave Macmillan.

Kahin, B. (2004). Codification in context. In S. Braman (Ed.), *The emergent global information policy regime* (pp. 39–61). Houndsmills, UK: Palgrave Macmillan.

Kellogg, M. K., Thorne, J., & Huber, P. W. (1992). *Federal telecommunications law.* Boston, MA: Little, Brown.

Kleindienst v. Mandel, 408 U.S. 753 (1972).

Lambright, W. H. (1976). *Governing science and technology.* New York/Oxford: Oxford University Press.

Lee, A., & Sloan, T. (1987). *Competition in the local exchange telephone service market* (NTIA Report 87-210). Washington, DC: National Telecommunications & Information Administration.

Lessig, L. (1999). *Code and other laws of cyberspace.* New York: Basic Books.

Machlup, F. (1980). *Knowledge and knowledge production.* Princeton, NJ: Princeton University Press.

Marsh, D. (Ed.). (1998). *Comparing policy networks.* Buckingham, UK/Philadelphia, PA: Open University Press.

Merton, R. K. (1955). A paradigm for the study of the sociology of knowledge. In P. F. Lazarsfeld & M. Rosenberg (Eds.), *The language of social research: A reader in the methodology of social research* (pp. 498–510). Glencoe, IL: The Free Press.

Merton, R. K. (1981). Remarks on theoretical pluralism. In P. M. Blau & R. K. Merton (Eds.), *Continuities in structural inquiry* (pp. i–viii). London: Sage.

Noam, E. M. (1983). Federal and state roles in telecommunications. *Vanderbilt Law Review, 36*(4), 949–983.

Owen, B. M., & Wildman, S. S. (1992). *Video economics.* Cambridge, MA: Harvard University Press.

Oxford English Dictionary (2nd ed.). (1989). Oxford, UK: Oxford University Press.

Pepper, R., & Brotman, S. N. (1987). Restricted monopolies or regulated competitors? *Journal of Communication, 37*(1), 64–72.

Potter, W. C. (1980). Issue area and foreign policy analysis. *International Organization, 34*(4), 405–427.

Price, M., & Thompson, M. (Eds.). (2002). *Forging peace: Intervention, human rights and the management of media space.* Bloomington, IN: Indiana University Press.

Ragin, C. C., & Becker, H. S. (1992). *What is a case? Exploring the foundations of social inquiry.* Cambridge: Cambridge University Press.

Renaud, J. (1987). The ITU and development assistance. *Telecommunications Policy, 11*(2), 179–192.

Rosati, J. (1981). Developing a systematic decision making framework. *World Politics, 33*(2), 234–252.

Sampson, M. (1982). Policy coordination and issue type. *Issues in international policy coordination* (pp. 83–101). Denver, CO: University of Denver Monograph Series.

Skocpol, T. (1985). Bringing the state back in. In P. Evans, D. Rueschemeyer, & T. Skocpol (Eds.), *Bringing the state back in* (pp. 3–37). Cambridge: Cambridge University Press.

Smythe, D. W. (1981). *Dependency road: Communications, capitalism, consciousness and Canada.* Norwood, NJ: Ablex.

Soma, J. T., Peterson, R. D., Alexander, G., & Petty, C. W. (1983). The communications regulatory environment in the 1980s. *Computer Law Journal, 4*, 1–54.

Spero, J. (1981). *The politics of international economic relations.* Belmont, CA: Thomson/Wadsworth.

Teske, P. (1990). *After divestiture: The political economy of state telecommunications regulation.* Albany, NY: State University of New York Press.

United States v. Microsoft Corporation, No. 98-1232 U.S. D.D.C. (2003).

United States v. Progressive, Inc., 467 F.Supp. 990 (W.D. Wis. 1979).

Wall, S. (1984). The British telecommunications decision. *Harvard International Law Journal, 24*(2), 299–328.

Information and Socioeconomic Class in U.S. Constitutional Law

Sandra Braman

The Supreme Court's information policy decisions support socioeconomic class divisions "by providing relatively few protections for media available to those at the bottom of the socioeconomic scale, directly limiting spending in some cases, deferring to labor law, and defining informational rights and responsibilities by profession."

Predictions about how new information technologies will affect different socio-economic classes range from suggestions that class lines will be abolished to warnings of a greater knowledge gap. People see different futures not only because they may be looking at different realities, but because they have different ideas about how a variety of social forces affect the shape and direction of technological development and distribution. Political will, availability and distribution of resources, cultural norms, and legal residue and innovation all influence which, how, and how fast technologies will develop, to whom they become available, under what constraints, and to whose advantage.

One factor determining the actual impact of the new technologies on specific classes is information policy. Although information policy as a distinct and coherent body exists in few nation-states, in the United States (as elsewhere) a corpus of rules, drawn from constitutional, statutory, common, and regulatory law, can be identified that functions as an information policy and can be analyzed as such.

Two heuristics help us identify laws, regulations, and decisions that fall within the information policy domain. The notion of an "information production chain" described by Machlup (5) and Boulding (1) can be adapted and used to define the domain as including those policies that apply to any stage of a chain that includes information creation (creation, generation, and collection), processing (algorithmic and cognitive), storage, transportation, distribution, destruction, and seeking. The all-inclusiveness of this approach permits identification of information policy irrespective of body of law as traditionally defined. This approach also permits exclusion of certain types of information, actors, or processing from some or all steps of the chain in response to cultural, aesthetic, religious, or political concerns.

The second heuristic is the notion of latent, as well as manifest, information policy. Manifest policy, such as traditional First Amendment law or law of intellectual property, directly and explicitly deals with information creation, processing, flows, and use. Latent policy indirectly or implicitly shapes information and its flows. Latent policy develops as a side effect of decisions made in other areas, synergistically when policies made in different areas combine with often unintended effects, and when information policy is subsumed under other labels. Trade law, securities regulation, and zoning decisions are among the sources of latent information policy.

These conceptual tools can be used to identify the information policy of any decision-making arena or governmental unit. The information policy of the United States Supreme Court is of particular interest at this historical conjuncture.

First, though there are a number of different ways of defining information, the broadest and most significant treat information as a constitutive force in society (2). From this perspective, which should provide the first and final analyses during the policy-making process, decisions about information policy are decisions about the way society will be structured—how socioeconomic classes will be formed and how people can act within and between them. Thus, the decisions of the Supreme Court, the governmental institution assigned the task of making judgments in light of their constitutive impact on society, are of particular interest in the information policy realm.

Second, during the formative phase of a policy-making process, constitutional bases for policy making are of particular importance. Identification of information policy as a distinct realm for policy making is recent, and the analytical tools are still being developed. Thus there is great need for understanding of constitutional principles and modes of thinking.

U.S. Supreme Court information policy decisions of the 1980s were examined here for their impact on the relationship between information and socio-economic class. By the 1980s, a sufficiently high level of technological change had permeated society for a long enough period of time to permit new types of problems to rise to the Supreme Court level. The decade also saw the beginnings of a shift in the nature of the Supreme Court into its fourth historical period of relative conservatism. While it is true that changes in the makeup of the Court—and in the minds of justices who continue to sit—mean one can never predict the outcome of future cases, certain trends are nonetheless clearly identifiable.

An examination of these decisions reveals a constitutional information policy that has the effect of producing and reproducing socioeconomic class lines by (a) acknowledging the relationship between informational class and socioeconomic class, (b) upholding labor-management lines developed to reify a specific type of industrial organization, (c) assigning differential informational rights and responsibilities by profession, and (d) distinguishing among the informational rights available to different economic groups.

The Supreme Court is explicitly aware of the relationship between socioeconomic and informational class and has addressed it directly in several cases. Some of these cases dealt with access to training in the creation, processing, storage, and use of information— that is, with education. In other cases, the Court explored problems* of people who are informationally or socioeconomically disadvantaged.

Brennan articulated the Court's general philosophy in *Plyler v. Doe* (457 U.S. 202 [1981]), in which it was declared unconstitutional to deny children of illegal aliens access to the free Texas public educational system:

> [E]ducation has a fundamental role in maintaining the fabric of our society. We cannot ignore the significant social costs borne by our Nation when select groups are denied the means to absorb the values and skills upon which our social order rests. . . . Illiteracy is an enduring disability. The inability to read and write will handicap the individual deprived of a basic education each and every day of his life. The inestimable toll of that deprivation on the social, economic, intellectual, and psychological well-being of the individual, and the obstacle it poses to individual achievement, make it most difficult to reconcile the cost or the principle of a status-based denial of basic education with the framework of equality embodied in the Equal Protection Clause (pp. 221–222).

Brennan directly questions the value of creating and perpetuating a "subclass of illiterates," as do Powell in a concurrence and Burger in a dissent. Denial of the right to education is understood to be particularly unfair in this case because it would result from (in Brennan's biblical terms) visiting the sins of the parents upon the children.

The Court here widens the notion of cost from the short-term efficiency concerns of the school system to the long-term cost concerns of society. On the one hand, it is argued, the savings that would result from excluding those children had not been demonstrated to have a significant educational benefit. On the other hand, the cost to society of a subclass of illiterates is demonstrably high in terms of crime, unemployment, etc. Brennan notes that concern for protecting resources is not sufficient to justify the use of a particular classification system for allocating those resources.

Brennan stops just short of calling education a fundamental right, but Blackmun, in a concurrence, equates it with the right to vote. Blackmun does, however, question the ability of the judiciary to adequately assess the effects of complex social policies, while Burger dissents because he feels that the Court does not have jurisdiction to address the problem of illegal immigration. Marshall, in a concurrence, reinforces the link between education and basic constitutional values.

Although in *Plyler* the Court would not permit a line to be drawn between children of illegal aliens and others, in *Martinez v. Bynum* (461 U.S. 321 [1982]) the Court was willing to exclude Mexican children living with relatives in Texas from the state's free public schools. The Court, through Powell, this time accepted the school system's argument that a residence requirement is justified in order to protect system efficiency. Provision of primary and secondary education is again stressed as one of the most important functions of local government. Marshall notes in dissent, however, that the relationship between exclusion of students and system efficiency again had not been proven.

The Court has been ambivalent about whether institutions should be able to use handicapped status to draw class lines. In one education case, the Court was willing to support some specialized services, though not all those requested. In another case, however, it supported the decision of the Federal Communications Commission not to require signing for the deaf on publicly funded television.

The decision in *Board of Education, Hendrick Hudson Central School District v. Rowley* (458 U.S. 176 [1981]) came in response to a request by parents of a deaf child to trade some elements of her specialized educational program for a sign-language interpreter. The student in this case was able to catch less than half of what was said in the classroom under her present program (though, even so, she consistently achieved above-average grades). In terms that will penetrate other discussions of access, Rehnquist's opinion noted the complexities of defining equal access under the Education of the Handicapped Act:

> [F]urnishing handicapped children with only such services as are available to non-handicapped children would in all probability fall short of the statutory requirement of "free appropriate public education"; to require, on the other hand, the furnishing of every special service necessary to maximize each handicapped child's potential is, we think, further than Congress intended to go. Thus to

speak in terms of "equal" services in one instance gives less than what is required by the Act and in another instance more. The theme of the Act is "free appropriate public education," a phrase which is too complex to be captured by the word "equal" whether one is speaking of opportunities or services . . . The right of access to free public education . . . is significantly different from any notion of absolute equality of opportunity regardless of capacity (pp. 198–199).

Rehnquist specifically mentions that the amount of financial resources spent per child does not have to be equal.

The Court in *Rowley* ultimately defined a basic floor of opportunity that included access to specialized instruction and related services individually designed to provide educational benefit to the child; operationalization of the standard was left to the states, and parents were assigned the role of protecting children from state and local decisions. White's dissent in this case accused Rehnquist and the Court of backing down from constitutional policy-making responsibilities. In his eyes, the Court *is* competent to decide that a child who is hearing less than half of what is said does not have equal access to the classroom.

In another decision dealing with the handicapped, the Court upheld the FCC's decision that public television stations do not need to be accessible to the deaf, despite requirements of the Rehabilitation Act of 1973. Pressed by a citizens' group that sought denial of a license renewal because signing was not offered, in *Community Television of Southern California v. Gottfried* (459 U.S. 498 [1982]) the Court denied the importance of the Rehabilitation Act as information policy and accepted die FCC's exclusion of the deaf from participation in public television.

Burger's opinion in *Bethel* v. *Fraser* (478 U.S. 92 L. Ed.2d 529 [1986]), a case dealing with punishment for sexual speech in a high school, addressed the school function of ensuring that every individual finds a place within the social order. The school is described as a direct instrument of the state-, the objective of public education is to inculcate the fundamental values required for maintaining a democratic system. Expelling a student for sexual innuendoes in a student assembly speech is justified because behavior as well as curriculum is to "teach by example the shared values of a civilized social order" (*Bethel*, p. 448).

The Court also addressed problems generated by today's underclass. In *Boag* v. *MacDougall* (454 U.S. 364 [1980]), a District Court had rejected as frivolous a prisoner's complaint about solitary confinement because the complaint was illiterate. In a *per curiam* (brief and unanimous) decision the Supreme Court reversed the District Court, insisting that unartful pleadings must be construed liberally. The Court focused on ensuring that lack of skill in information creation does not hamper an individual's efforts to articulate his or her rights within the legal system or to receive appropriate protections.

Atkins v. *Parker* (472 U.S. 115 [1984p involved the question of whether notice of a change in the Food Stamp Act—with consequences that vary in significant detail from person to person—must be individualized. It was argued that only with specific data can people know how to plan their household budgets. Such information is also required in order to decide whether to appeal the agency's decision to change the amount assigned; in this case, the agency knew that miscalculations had been made for a large class of recipients. The Court held that individualized notice was not required because, in Stevens's words, "The entire structure of our democratic government rests on the premise that the individual citizen is capable of informing himself about the particular policies that affect his destiny" (p. 131).

Marshall's dissent evolved from the fact that most unsophisticated recipients were unable to translate the general notice into terms meaningful to themselves. Brennan argued that logic, history, and function require individualized information about a change in food stamp laws. His dissent points to what may be a key area of information policy in the future: the relationship between statutory entitlements—the "new" property interests of the underclass—and information issues. Since statutory property rights like food stamps or Medicaid exist only to the degree determined under law, questions about decision-making techniques and mandated information flows affect the creation and protection of these new types of property rights.

In sum, the Court is sensitive to the relationship between information and socioeconomic class. It is in general opposed to die idea of using information policy decisions to create socioeconomic class lines and tries to diminish the impact for today's subclass. The arguments offered stress the value to both the individual and to society, emphasizing harmonization of society as a goal.

The fact that efficiency is so often used as a counterargument points to the importance of how a system itself is defined. Something that is inefficient in the short term for a local system (such as a school) may be efficient in the long term for the broader system of society in general. Disagreements in this area are often simply over where to draw the system boundaries. The value of harmonization of the social system seems at this point to dominate over notions of civil liberties or social equity.

Despite a general position to the contrary, in specific areas, such as labor relations, the Court is willing to uphold class stratifications. In *Ellis* v. *Brotherhood of Railway, Airline & Steamship Clerks* (466 U.S. 435 [1983]), the Court made explicit its understanding that labor laws abridge First Amendment rights. In *United Steelworkers of America w. Sadlowski* (457 U.S. 102 [1981]), it made clear that speech rights granted union members are not coextensive with First Amendment rights.

In *National Labor Relations Board (NLRB)* v. *Hendricks County Rural Electric Membership Corp.* (454 U.S. 170 [1980]), class membership was actually determined by the type of information to which an employee had access. The Court held that it was legitimate to keep employees with a labor nexus, i.e., access to management information concerning labor matters, out of the bargaining unit. Employees with access to other confidential information, such as that regarding sales contracts or government relations, however, must be permitted to enter the union.

Brennan's opinion emphasizes that it was precisely to control information flows at the corporate decision-making level that the labor/management line was drawn in the first place; he suggests that this is a service for labor as well as management. At issue in this case was whether class lines should be drawn by function (access to confidential information) or by role ("secretary" was not specifically mentioned in the law). The Court felt that the informational function was more important than role in determining legal status. Powell, however, felt that the Court still went too far by permitting *some* employees with access to confidential information into the bargaining unit. Explaining his view of congressional intent, he describes in detail how a secretary could pass critical information to union members during a strike.

Decision making internal to a union was at issue in two cases. Business agents fired by a new union president (*Finnegan* v. *Leu*, 456 U.S. 431 [1981]) and union members who didn't want dues spent on non-union political activities (*Ellis* v. *Brotherhood*) complained that their First Amendment rights had been abridged. The Court in both cases upheld the right of union management to make its own decisions, justifying this position—as well as their intrusion into internal union decision making in general—as necessary to protect union democracy.

Non-union workers' access to decision-making processes of the government as an employer was the issue in *Minnesota State Board for Community Colleges* v. *Knight* (465 U.S. 271 [1983]). Non-union members of the state college faculty claimed a right to have their views heard by government officials who made policy affecting the college, a right denied by the Court in O'Connor's quite clear language: "Appellees have no constitutional right to force the government to listen to their views. They have no such right as members of the public, as government employees, or as instructors in an institution of higher education" (p. 283). In this opinion O'Connor also explicitly denies constitutional status for academic freedom.

Marshall's concurrence in this case suggests a more subtle approach, determining the authority of a decision-maker to choose information sources according to the nature of the decision at issue and the institutional environment in which it must be made. Stevens dissents because he feels that it is unacceptable to make the union the only authorized spokesperson for all employees on political as well as contractual matters. He is outraged that the Court should suggest a state interest in fostering any private monopoly on information flows.

Union members were favored over non-union members in a different way in *United Brotherhood of Carpenters & Joiners of America v. Scott* (463 U.S. 825 [1982]). Here, non-union workers who were beaten and had their work destroyed by union members alleged a conspiracy to deprive workers of their First Amendment rights of association. The Court chose to interpret conspiracy law as narrowly as possible and found no First Amendment violation because there was no state action.

A law against permitting non-union members to influence union elections through financial support beyond a specified limit was upheld in *United Steelworkers of America v. Sadlowski*. Again, the Court relied on the notion of protecting union democracy. White dissented, emphasizing that to restrict funds spent on speech is to restrict speech itself.

In *National Association for the Advancement of Colored People (NAACP) v. Claiborne Hardware Co.* (458 U.S. 886 [1981]), the Court came down on the side of a union boycott, even though some members of the group involved engaged in behavior not protected by law. Stevens's opinion noted that speech does not lose its protection just because it encourages others to act; nor do the actions of some cause an entire group to lose protection for their speech activities. In two cases, *International Longshoremen's Association, AFL-CIO v. Allied International* (456 U.S. 212 [1981]) and *DeBartolo Corp. v. NLRB* (463 US. 147 [1982]), the Court refused to protect picketing of companies related to the target (secondary picketing), based on distinctions among stages of production.

In the area of labor relations, then, the Court is quite willing to use information policy decisions to reinforce socioeconomic divisions, even using access to information itself as a demarker of class lines. Union members in general are favored over non-union, and union management over rank and file. We are reminded of the tenuousness of academic freedom.

The Court acknowledges that the free speech rights of unions are not coextensive with those of the First Amendment, for unions are not facets of the state in the sense required for state action under the First Amendment. What is more interesting, however, are the arguments made by the government for intruding into nongovernmental speech activities in the first place. During a time when greater amounts of a wider variety of types of power are being ceded from the public to the private sector, the question of information policy *internal to* organizations such as unions (or corporations), as well as the "foreign policy" of organizations as they interact across institutional boundaries, becomes of key importance.

The Court also linked socioeconomic and informational class by defining informational rights, limits, and responsibilities according to profession. During the period under study, the Court ruled on the informational practices of attorneys, physicians, law enforcement professionals, stock market tippees, and investment counselors.[1]

FBI v. Abramson (456 U.S. 615 [1981]) explored the informational rights and responsibilities of law enforcement officials as it unraveled a Freedom of Information Act (FOIA) case dealing with work papers. At stake were investigatory records that had been subsequently incorporated into records compiled for other purposes, and the question was whether an FOIA exemption still applied once the information had been processed again. The Court said yes: Once information has been processed for law enforcement purposes, it is always protected, regardless of subsequent further processing, transportation, or exchange. Blackmun, dissenting, is uncomfortable with the trend toward treating information differently for legal purposes depending on its source and argues that information shouldn't have to be "parsed" for its sources in order to determine legal treatment.

In a rare unanimous opinion, *US v. Arthur Young* (465 U.S. 805 [1983]), the Court stressed the importance of information collection—and therefore accountants—to the functioning of the tax system as a whole. In this case, a corporation tried to withhold documents from the Internal Revenue Service (IRS) by calling them work products. Accountants here were distinguished from attorneys in terms of the nature of their public service. Accountants are responsible to the entire society; thus, the public interest demands that communications between accountants and those whom they are auditing be accessible to governmental inspection. Attorneys, on the other hand, are understood to serve private clients, not the public, making privileged communications between attorney and client acceptable.

Federal Trade Commission (FTC) v. Grolier (462 U.S. 19 [1982]) specifically explored the question of whether the status of protection of attorneys' work products changes with the stage of the litigation process. The Court held such papers to be protected irrespective of the status of the litigation for which the information had been prepared. There was concern that without such protection, much of what is now written down while preparing a case would no longer be recorded for fear of disclosing working methods to current or potential opponents.

The Court concluded in *Upjohn v. US* (449 U.S. 383 [1980]) that the work products doctrine also applies to attorneys working within the corporate context Thus, attorneys' questionnaires to corporate employees

---

[1]Journalistic practices have been explored by the judiciary in the past (3,4).

regarding bribes to foreign governments were protected from collection by the IRS. The Court stressed the need to be able to predict when one will have privileged communication.

In *In re RMJ* (455 U.S. 191 [1981]), the Court held unconstitutional a lower court ruling that listed categories of information and language which attorneys were forbidden to use in advertising. Although these specifics were rejected, Powell's opinion drew attention to the assumption underlying controls on attorney advertising: it is easier to deceive people when information is complex, sophisticated, and unfamiliar. There was also fear that uncontrolled advertising would be degrading to the profession.

Limits on the informational activities of physicians were also discussed during this period. In *Akron v. Akron Center for Reproductive Health* (462 U.S. 416 [1982]), a municipal ordinance that delineated just what and how information about abortions was to be transmitted by doctors to patients was held to be unconstitutional by a Court that believed such regulation intruded on the professionalism of physicians. In this case, the information specified went against previous Court thinking by espousing one specific theory of when human life begins. It was feared that the persuasive effect of the information, combined with the time and money required to conduct such conversations, might reduce the number of those choosing abortions.

The Court did support, however, compelling a physician to notify the parents of a minor who seeks an abortion in *H. L. v. Matheson* (450 U.S. 398 [1980]). Burger here distinguished between knowledge and decision-making power, stating for the Court the view that informing the minor's parents confers the former but not the latter.

The informational rights and responsibilities of the "profession" of tippee in the stock market were explored in two cases during this period that defined a specific role for tippees in the "harmonized marketplace" often mentioned by the Court as an ultimate goal. In *Dirks v. Securities and Exchange Commission (SEC)* (463 U.S. 646 [1982]), the Court found no breach of SEC rules when a tippee broker passed on fraudulent information to clients before the public. The Court based its argument on the fact that the tippee's duty derives from that of the insider and is inherited with the transfer of information. Without an insider, reasoned the Court, there is no tippee responsibility under SEC rules.

In *Bateman Eichler, Hill Richards, Inc. v. Berner* (472 U.S. 299 [1984]), an insider provided false and incomplete information that was then passed on by a tippee. When sued by the tippee for fraud, the insider claimed that the tippee shared culpability. The Court found that the culpability of the two parties differed, with the tippee not as culpable as the tipper whose breach of duty gave rise to the tippee's liability in the first place. Brennan's opinion for the Court argues that denying the defense of shared responsibility best protects the investing public and promotes the national economy by allowing defrauded tippees to bring suit against defrauding insiders, deterring insider trading. He also notes that the *in pari delicto* ("at equal fault") defense is no good when there is an inequality of information.

The profession of investment advisor is distinguished from that of publisher in *Lowe* v. *SEC* (472 U.S. 181 [1984]). Stevens argues for the Court that the danger of fraud and deception is higher in personalized communications than in publications sold on the open market. Providing factual information about past transactions and market trends, and publishing newsletters on general market conditions, are protected as press activities.

Again, the nature of the service to the public is the criterion. Publishers serve the public interest by passing along information of value to the masses in an anonymous relationship; investment advisers develop person-to-person fiduciary relationships characterized by individualized advice. White's concurrence, however, notes that Congress does not have an untrammeled right to restrict speech by defining fiduciary relationships.

Definition of the informational rights and limits of various professions is based on two notions. First, the criterion used for determining those rights and limits is the nature of the relationship between professional and client and, in turn, between the client or "client" population and the general public; are they one and the same, overlapping, or in opposition? These features appear to define the public interest for the Court.

Second, there is a sense that all types of information are *not* equal in the eyes of the public in terms of ability to deceive. Cases discussed earlier, such as *Atkins* v. *Parker*, as well as those touched on here, refer to three sources of variance. There can be differences in the motivations and abilities of the sender of the message, in the level of difficulty or complexity of the message itself, or in the ability of the receiver to handle the message on several levels. The regulatory consequence is to regulate more tightly those professions, such as law, that are thought to handle the more difficult, and therefore potentially deceptive, information.

Another consequence of constraints and protections on information activities of various professions is the establishment of property rights in information resources and the value added through processing. The tippee's rights over the property of information are increased as his or her liability for fraudulent information received from an insider decreases, for example, and police ownership of information processed for their purposes continues even when that information is reprocessed for other purposes.

In cases exploring the economics of information processing, the Court has treated differently media available at different levels of the socioeconomic scale, limited some expenditures, and moved toward the position that information services and resources should be available only for a fee. Some time was spent by the Court exploring the general relationship between money and speech. In *Citizens against Rent Control/Coalition for Fair Housing* v. *Berkeley* (454 U.S. 290 [1980]), a municipal ordinance prohibiting political associations from accepting over $250 per contribution was found unconstitutional. Here Burger stressed the importance of association in amplifying speech, ensuring that through collective effort people can make their voices heard when individually they might be lost.

Blackmun's concurrence distinguishes the ability of funds to corrupt in the electing of a representative and in voting on ballot measures, where the people themselves render the ultimate political decision. Dissenting, White suggests that individuals find different types of speech activities interchangeable. Thus, assuming a user will easily and happily turn from one medium to another, for White denial of access to a particular medium is of no great concern.

The issue of limits on spending for speech was poignantly distilled in *Walters* v. *National Association of Radiation Survivors* (473 U.S. 305 [1984]). This case was brought by an organization of veterans who were victims of atomic bomb testing and of the use of Agent Orange in Vietnam. In seeking help from the government in coping with the effects of their service-induced injuries, individual veterans had found their attempts limited by a Civil War statute restricting to $10 the amount that a veteran can pay an attorney for representation when petitioning the government. (The fee was the Civil War equivalent of $580 in today's market.) This, claimed veterans of the 1980s, was an abridgment of First Amendment rights, since it was impossible to find adequate representation for such a fee.

The Court, through Rehnquist, here deferred to Congress and, stressing the age of the law, upheld it. Stevens, in disgust, dissented bitterly and starkly: "The Court does not appreciate the value of individual liberty" (p. 358). He points out that the right to have legal help when petitioning the government has never before been questioned and rejects the Court's reliance on administrative arguments. Stevens notes that the importance of adequate representation in dealing with the Veterans' Administration had been made vivid by evidence that showed routine examples of cases denied because of poor preparation. In his eyes, this matter is not trivial: "If the Government, in the guise of a paternalistic interest in protecting the citizen from his own improvidence, can deny him access to independent counsel of his choice, it can change the character of our free society" (p. 370).

Cost barriers to access to the national information distribution system were at issue in *U.S. Postal Service* v. *Greenburgh Civic Association* (453 U.S. 114 [1980]). The association sought the right to use the mails without paying access fees (that is, buying stamps). Their First Amendment argument was that their small budget should not prevent them from being able to use the postal system. Rehnquist's opinion denying that claim was based on the historical relationship between the postal service and sovereignty itself, saying, "Government without communication is impossible" (p. 121). Administrative arguments such as protecting mail revenues and facilitating efficient and secure delivery of mails were accepted, with an emphasis on the quid pro quo: when privately owned mailboxes become a part of the nationwide system, their owners agree to abide by system rules; in exchange, owners receive not only the services provided by the post office, but also the protection of the mails.

White's concurrence saw the postal system as a public forum, but one whose use can be legitimately restricted to those who will pay the fee. For Brennan, the issue is free speech. His concurrence firmly upholds the importance of access to the mails, quoting Justice Holmes: "[T]he use of the mails is almost as much a part of free speech as the right to use our tongues" (Holmes in dissent, in *U.S. ex rel. Milwaukee Social Democratic Publishing Company* v. *Burleson*, 255 U.S. 407 [1921], p. 437). Postal regulations are acceptable, Brennan believes, because they are reasonable regulations of "time, place, and manner."[2]

Marshall dissented, arguing that the point of the Postal Provision of the Constitution was to place "the powers of the Federal Government behind a national communication service" (p. 142). While acknowledging the need to protect the economic viability of that service, he claims that the regulation in this case is inconsistent with that purpose. More important, he notes that the decision goes against the Court's previous stance that efficiency and economy must yield before speech as a value. He points to the District Court determination that

> only by placing their circulars in the letterboxes may appellees be certain that their messages will be secure from wind, rain, or snow, and at the same time will alert the attention of the residents without notifying would-be burglars that no one has returned home to remove items from doorways or stoops. The court concluded that the costs and delays of mail service put the mails out of appellees'

---

[2]"Time, place and manner" regulation of First Amendment activities is permitted when there are no alternative regulatory mechanisms available, the regulation is drawn as narrowly as possible, and there are alternative channels of communication left open. Thus, for example, it is an acceptable time, place and manner regulation that forbids making loud noise in a hospital zone, since alternative venues for speech are left open and there is no other way to serve the legitimate social goal of aiding the sick.

reach, and that other alternatives such as placing their circulars in doorways are "much less satisfactory" (p. 144).

Marshall also distinguished the Postal Service from other public forums such as mass transportation because the very purpose of the Postal Service is to facilitate communication. He stressed the right of box owners to receive information as part of their First Amendment rights. And he notes the creeping spread of Post Office "property" rights:

> *I remain troubled by the Court's effort to transform the letterboxes entirely into components of the governmental enterprise despite their private ownership. Under the Court's reasoning the Postal Service could decline to deliver mail unless the recipients agreed to open their doors to the letter carrier—and then the doorway, or even the room inside could fall within Postal Service control (p. 151).*

Stevens's dissent also supports a right to receive information. On another front, he challenges the assumption that the mails must be a subsidized public monopoly and claims that the public interest may be better served by privatizing some portions of the system. He still challenges the dominance of efficiency as a value in the decision-making process:

> *Conceivably, the invalidation of this law would unleash a flow of communication that would sink the mail service in a sea of paper. But were that to happen, it would merely demonstrate that this law is a much greater impediment to the free flow of communication than is presently assumed. To the extent that the law prevents mailbox clutter, it also impedes the delivery of written messages that would otherwise take place (p. 155).*

The Court defended subsidized public television in *FCC v. League of Women Voters of California* (468 U.S. 365 [1983]), declaring unconstitutional the Public Broadcast Act rule against editorializing by public stations. There was strong dissent in this case, however. Rehnquist argued that the government has the right to decide where it will spend its money and need not do so to support particular political positions or candidates through public television editorials. Stevens dissented from a radically different perspective. Recalling Hitler's use of radio, Stevens fears government propaganda and suggests that the difference between legislators and judges on this point may come from where they sit:

> *Members of Congress, not members of the Judiciary, live in the world of politics. When they conclude that there is a real danger of political considerations influencing the dispensing of this money and that this provision is necessary to insulate grantees from political pressures in addition to the other safeguards, that judgment is entitled to our respect (p. 416).*

Restrictions on low-cost forms of speech were the subject of several other cases. *Clark* v. *Community for Creative Non-Violence* (468 U.S. 288 [1983]) dealt with the cheapest form of speech of all—sleep, available even to the homeless who wanted to demonstrate by sleeping in a park across from the White House. The group claimed abridgment of their First Amendment rights when they were denied a Park Service sleeping permit, arguing that without it the size and duration of the demonstration would decrease. (Many of the homeless were not as likely to participate without a place to sleep or without hot food.) The Court upheld the permit denial as a reasonable restriction of time, place, and manner, since other elements of the demonstration had been left in place, including a symbolic city, signs, and a day–night vigil; the group was not denied access to the media or to the public for their intended message.

Marshall dissented because he believes that the argument of efficiency again used here is not appropriate as a governing principle in information policy matters. He claims that its use leads to constitutionally insensitive decisions; his suspicions come from experience with problems that he believes are endemic to bureaucracies:

> What the Court fails to recognize is that public officials have strong incentives to over-regulate even in the absence of an intent to censor particular views. This incentive stems from the fact that of the two groups whose interests officials must accommodate—on the one hand, the interests of the general public and, on the other, the interests of those who seek to use a particular forum for First Amendment activity—the political power of the former is likely to be far greater than that of the latter . . .
>
> [G]overnment agencies by their very nature are driven to over-regulate public forums to the detriment of First Amendment rights (pp. 315–316).

Marshall argues emphatically that content neutrality does not necessarily mean that the weight of a regulation will fall equally upon members of all classes:

> A content-neutral regulation that restricts an inexpensive mode of communication will fall most heavily upon relatively poor speakers and the points of view that such speakers typically espouse. This sort of latent inequality is very much in evidence in this case for respondents lack the financial means necessary to buy access to more conventional modes of persuasion.
>
> A disquieting feature about the disposition of this case is that it lends credence to the charge that judicial administration of the First Amendment, in conjunction with a social order marked by large disparities in wealth and other sources of power, tends systematically to discriminate against efforts by the relatively disadvantaged to convey their political ideas (pp. 313–314, n. 14).

Billboards, another relatively low-cost mass medium, were at issue in *Metromedia* v. *San Diego* (453 U.S. 490 [1981]). A city ordinance discriminating between billboards that advertised goods and services sold where they were being advertised, and those sold off-site, permitting the former and prohibiting the latter, was declared an unconstitutional content distinction on its face. Although the city claimed traffic safety and aesthetic concerns, several justices in this case emphasized what they saw as the unique characteristics of billboards. Brennan's concurrence in particular stressed their importance for certain purposes and speakers because of their relative inexpensiveness.

Los Angeles v. *Taxpayers for Vincent* (466 U.S. 788 [1983]) discussed other inexpensive media—handbills and signs on public property, such as utility poles. The Court upheld the constitutionality of a municipal ordinance that restricted their use on aesthetic grounds, though both Blackmun and Brennan specifically rejected this argument because they saw no evidence of a comprehensive aesthetic program. Although it is acknowledged that the decision will reduce the total amount of communication in the city and prohibits people from communicating in a certain manner, Stevens defends the Court's position:

> A distributor of leaflets has no right simply to scatter his pamphlets in the air— or to toss large quantities of paper from the window of a tall building or a low flying airplane. Characterizing such an activity as a separate means of communication does not diminish the State's power to condemn it as a public nuisance (p. 809).

Further, while government property such as lampposts may be used for signs, "the mere fact that government property can be used as a vehicle for communication does not mean that the Constitution requires such uses to be permitted" (p. 814).

Brennan, dissenting again, defended the use of inexpensive media such as signs as distinct and critically important, particularly for the "little people." He stressed many of the characteristics that also contribute to the attraction of billboards as a distinct medium:

> Use of this medium of communication is particularly valuable in part because it entails a relatively small expense in reaching a wide audience, allows flexibility in accommodating various formats, typographies, and graphics, and conveys its message in a manner that is easily read and understood by its reader or viewer. There may be alternative channels of communication, but the prevalence of a large number of signs in Los Angeles is a strong indication that, for many speakers, those alternatives are far less satisfactory (p. 819).

Clearly, the Court understands that access to funds greatly facilitates the exercise of First Amendment rights, including the right to petition the government and the right to association, as well as speech and press rights. In *USPS* v. *Greenburgh Association*, as well as in other cases, the Court begins to restrict information goods and services to those who can pay, raising a cost barrier to access.

Media available to those at the bottom of the socioeconomic scale are the least protected. Thus, the cycle of the mutually reinforcing link between socioeconomic and informational class is completed: socioeconomic deprivation directly translates into an informational handicap that has, in turn, a potential socioeconomic consequence.

Harmonization—of the social system, of the marketplace—has come to replace the free flow of information as the metaphor that dominates Court thinking. It appears in discussions about matters as far-ranging as education and the stock market. Even explorations of the nature of the public interest responsibilities of various professions hinge on an at least implied notion of how each profession fits into a harmonized marketplace or society.

Efficiency, as a result, has risen to the top of the value hierarchy used to justify Supreme Court decisions. The appropriateness of cost-benefit analysis in constitutional decision making has been questioned elsewhere in Court decisions. Constitutional scholar Lawrence Tribe (6) opposes using any type of mathematical calculation as the basis for decision-making in the constitutional realm, where, he claims, one should not be just allocating resources among existing categories in a predetermined manner but rather redefining the categories themselves and relationships within and among them.

In the cases discussed here, various justices argued the pros and cons of efficiency as a constitutional value, and decisions came down on both sides. It is clear, however, that the impact of "efficient" (bureaucratic) administration of justice is felt most heavily by those who are already the most disadvantaged. Content neutrality is another regulatory technique that has come to be questioned.

The Court has displayed a tendency often found in public opinion on First Amendment matters: it will stand on principle when principle is cast in general terms, but will change position when faced with a specific question. Thus, while in general the Court opposes the production or reproduction of socioeconomic class lines through its information policy decisions, in particular instances it is quite willing to uphold the constitutionality of a system that blocks information flow from non-union members to their government employers. It is willing to subject its own soldiers—largely from the lower socioeconomic ranks—to nuclear fallout and Agent Orange, and then deny them the right to hire the necessary representation to petition the government for help in coping with their injuries.

In general, the Court does support socioeconomic class divisions through its information policy decisions by providing relatively few protections for media available to those at the bottom of the socioeconomic scale, directly limiting spending in some cases, deferring to labor law, and defining informational rights and responsibilities by profession. The Court also brings to our attention ways in which information policy decisions actually create or destroy property rights.

Information policy stands between the development of new information technologies and their actual impact on various classes. Future decision making could be guided by more comprehensive thinking and research about the effects of existing policy as well as exploration of the normative issues involved.

REFERENCES

1. Boulding, K. "The Economics of Knowledge and the Knowledge of Economics," *American Economic Review* 56 (2), 1966, pp. 1–13.
2. Braman, S. "Defining Information: An Approach for Policy Makers." *Telecommunications Policy* 13 (3), 1989, pp. 233–242.
3. Glasser, T. L. "Newsworthy Accusations and the Privilege of Neutral Reportage." *Communication Quarterly* 28, 1980, pp. 49–56.
4. Hart, J. R. "The Right of Neutral Reportage." *Journalism Quarterly* 56, 1979, pp. 234–243.
5. Machlup, F. *Knowledge and Knowledge Production.* Princeton, N.J.: Princeton University Press. 1980.
6. Tribe, L. H. "Constitutional Calculus: Equal Justice or Economic Efficiency?" *Harvard Law Review* 98, 1984, pp. 592–621.

Part II

MULTIDISCIPLINARY METHODOLOGICAL APPROACHES

Introductory Comments to Chapter 9

Bill F. Chamberlin
University of Florida

The chapter that follows has been nearly 40 years in the making. It started in the 1970s with the efforts of John B. Adams and Sharon Iorio to develop a research tool for comparing state open meetings laws. I had long wanted to develop a more sophisticated research tool if possible, and I received encouragement for my interest in state access laws when I was hired in 1987 to focus on freedom of information law at the University of Florida as the Joseph L. Brechner Eminent Scholar of Mass Communications. Brechner, a long-time Orlando, Florida, TV station owner, and Ralph Lowenstein, the dean of the College of Journalism and Communication at the time, wanted to fund a scholar who would study state access laws, promote open government through the newly established Brechner Center for Freedom of Information, and develop a graduate program in media law.

Beginning in the 1990s, I encouraged graduate students to study state access laws—particularly 50-state studies of specific provisions of state open meetings and open records laws. My students looked at—among other things—enforcement provisions of open meetings laws, the fee structure of public records laws, and whether states changed their laws to respond to the computerization of government records.

In 1998, Brechner's widow, Marion, president of the Brechner Management Company, agreed to provide funding for a research project leading to the rating of the 50 state access laws. The proposal—developed with the help of my colleague Sandra Chance—was endorsed by FOI activists, and Marion Brechner established a $600,000 endowment for the project in 1999. The state of Florida provided $420,000 in matching funds, and the John S. and James L. Knight Foundation awarded a supplemental grant of about $275,000 to jump-start the project.

The goals for the ambitious multiyear Marion Brechner Citizen Access Project were to:

- provide a research tool that would allow scholars to examine state open meetings and public records laws more intensively than ever before;
- encourage state access law research that seemed to be at least in part frustrated by the massive effort required, therefore limiting the abilities of students to take on comparative studies in classes and theses;
- provide public policymakers with better tools for developing public access laws;
- provide citizens with a better understanding of how other states were addressing the same public access questions they faced;
- give educators more tools to teach access law; and
- give journalists newsworthy data that would be reported so that the public in general could better understand access issues.

While developing the project's research methodology, I sought the help of social scientists, including Michael F. Weigold, an associate professor of advertising at the University of Florida. Although Weigold's research interests often focus on science and health communication and persuasion, he was particularly interested in applying social science techniques to law in a way that could impact public policy.

I developed the research reported in this chapter with PhD students in mass communications law, including Amanda Reid and Nissa Laughner, both funded by the Marion Brechner Citizen Access Project. Both also earned JD degrees. Another University of Florida PhD student, Cristina Popescu, first drafted the manuscript. Popescu, specializing in public relations, has shown an interest in combining social science methods with the study of legal aspects of mass communications. A University of Florida 2002/2003 Advising/Mentoring award that I received for my work with doctoral students funded her work on this project.

Chapter 9

Merging Legal Research and the Practices of Social Science: Comparing State Access Laws

Bill F. Chamberlin
Cristina Popescu
Michael F. Weigold

THE BEGINNING: USING SOCIAL SCIENCE TOOLS

Freedom of information advocates, mass communication scholars, journalists, and public policymakers have often asked the personnel at the Brechner Center for Freedom of Information at the University of Florida to tell them which public access laws are "the best in the country." The Brechner Center and other FOI organizations have had to say that no one has conducted an effective study, and therefore "no one knows." Although not yet complete, the Marion Brechner Citizen Access Project provides a clearer look at how state public records and open meetings laws rate. The project combines extensive legal research with a research design guided by fundamental social science research principles to evaluate statutes, court decisions, and constitutional provisions.

Mass communication scholars Cohen and Gleason (1990) said, "Legal scholars have been interested in social research for nearly a century" (p. 16). For example, law professor Blasi (1971) used a survey to study journalists' use of confidential sources. Stanford law professor Franklin (1980) used a content analysis of libel cases to find out the nature of the words that led to libel suits. Likewise, law practitioners at times have relied on scientific research to provide evidence for or strengthen their legal arguments. Louis Brandeis, former U.S. Supreme Court Justice, is the first known to use social, economic, and public health research in a legal brief to provide factual evidence (*Muller v. Oregon*, 1908). Later justices deciding two other landmark cases used the same approach: *Brown v. Board of Edu-*

cation (1954) and *Chandler v. Florida* (1981). In *Brown*, social research findings were used to demonstrate that separating Black and White children in school led to learning inequity for the former. In *Chandler*, the Court considered research showing the psychological effects of using cameras in the courtroom. A 1980 study of U.S. Supreme Court decisions reported that in about one third of 601 cases analyzed, justices "resorted to identifiable social science materials, although these were not necessarily crucial to the ratio decidendi in a case" (Abraham, 1980, p. 248).

An early attempt to combine legal and social science research to explore the issue of access to meetings was the work of Adams (1974) at the University of North Carolina. He wanted to analyze state laws and whether they facilitated or restricted public access to official information with the presumption that "all meetings of all bodies at all levels of government should be conducted before citizen or media spectators" (Adams, 1974, p. 1). Adams used a two-step method to evaluate open meeting laws in all 50 states. First, he used content analysis to survey the then current, as well as pending, laws on open meetings on the basis of presence or absence of elements that he believed would make an "ideal" law.[1] For each criterion met by a state law, Adams assigned one point to a state. Thus, a state with "an ideal law" could score as many as 11 points and a state with no law would score 0 (Adams, 1974). Adams did not explain how he arrived at his list of 11 criteria for "maximum openness."

Adams' quantitative content analysis of state open meetings laws revealed that one state, Tennessee, met all 11 criteria. Arizona, Kentucky, and Colorado received 10 points. At the other end of the scale, Mississippi, West Virginia, and New York had no provisions at all regarding open meetings, and the states of Maryland and Rhode Island met only one of the criteria. The mean rating was 6.7. Adams made no effort to weight his criteria, but acknowledged that "Substantial differences might exist between two states with the same score since some characteristics have more value for openness than others" (Adams, 1974, p. 5).

The second step of Adams' research involved a survey in which editors of newspapers in the capital cities of the 50 states were asked to evaluate the effectiveness of open meetings laws in general. Thirty-three editors sent their answers in—for a response rate of 66%. The majority of editors

---

[1]Adams' criteria used to evaluate the openness of state laws were to: (a) include a statement of public policy in support of openness; (b) provide for an open legislature; (c) provide for open legislative committees; (d) provide for open meetings of state agencies of bodies; (e) provide for open meetings of agencies and bodies of the political subdivisions of the state; (f) provide for open county boards; (g) provide for open city councils (or their equivalent); (h) forbid closed executive sessions; (i) provide legal recourse to halt secrecy; (j) declare actions taken in meetings which violate the law to be null and void; and (k) provide for penalties for those who violate the law.

wrote in favor of open meetings laws with or without restrictions. According to Adams, two editors said that "laws create loopholes and things are therefore better without law" (p. 18). Another two editors, although in favor of open meetings legislation, did not know that their respective states had such provisions.

A second comparative analysis of state open meetings laws, conducted by Iorio in 1984, updated the Adams (1974) study. Iorio first compared the 1974 and 1984 open meetings statutes using Adams' criteria and categories with one addition: "to clarify the nature of the executive session and provide a more realistic perspective of current law" (p. 743). She found that by 1984, all 50 states had adopted laws requiring open meetings, compared with only 47 states in 1974. The mean score in 1984 across all the 11 categories was 8 (or 73.8% compliance), whereas in the previous study the mean was 6.7. "Compared to legislation in 1974 [and accounting for the additional category], 36 state scores increased, the scores of seven states remained the same, and the scores of seven states decreased" (Iorio, 1984, p. 745). As in the earlier study, only Tennessee scored a perfect 11. Eight states scored 10, whereas Alabama, Minnesota, and South Dakota scored the lowest with a 5.

The second part of Iorio's (1984) research rated open meetings laws in four additional categories "developed to judge the laws in terms of precise delineation for their operation" (p. 742) and "based on provisions included in the federal law and in model legislation and suggestions from law review articles" (p. 743).[2] Thirty-four state laws met the four additional criteria (86.5% compliance). Overall, across all 15 categories in both parts of the study, Iorio found that one state, Tennessee, scored a perfect 15. Another eight states scored 14. At the other end of the scale, Alabama scored the lowest with 5.

In another comparative study, Cleveland (1985) measured the range of openness across all 50 states of open meetings statutes and higher education. Twenty-five criteria of openness were identified, "not determined by any scientific method but by personal response to the laws" (p. 33), and no attempt was made to weight the importance of the categories.[3] Tennessee met the most criteria with 22, followed by Florida with 21. At the

---

[2]In addition to Adams' 11 criteria, Iorio used the following categories: (a) definition—sets parameters for operation of the law by providing accurate explanation of terms such as public body, agency meeting, and so on; (b) minutes—establishes a permanent record open to public review; (c) prior notice of meetings—provides information concerning time and place of meetings; and (d) rules for the conduct of executive sessions—sets safeguards against abuse of executive session privilege.

[3]The criteria used were: policy statement, no bodies explicitly exempted, all final action in open meeting, discussion in open meeting, gathering information in open meeting, committee meetings open, advisory boards open, informal meetings open, quasi-judicial meetings open, meetings of local entities open, meetings of less than quorum covered, involved

other end of the scale, the least open states were Mississippi, South Dakota, and Wyoming with a score of eight and Pennsylvania with a score of five (Cleveland, 1985).

In 2002, the Chicago-based Better Government Association (BGA) conducted a fourth study analyzing FOI laws in each of the 50 states and the District of Columbia (Better Government Association, 2002). The organization looked at the text of each open record statute, but decided not to use case law or attorney general opinions "to keep the analysis as objective as possible" (Better Government Association, 2002). Each state was rated against a "gold standard" of five criteria—three procedural criteria and two penalty criteria—that "were chosen as an effort to conduct the most objective analysis of the law in each state."[4] Compliance with each of the five criteria was measured on a 5-point scale, with 0 the lowest and 5 the highest possible score. The resulting score was then converted to a 4-point scale (multiplying by .80) and given an academic grade point average (GPA; i.e., A = 4.0, B = 3.0, etc.). The scores for the five criteria were added, and the states were ranked according to their overall GPA (Better Government Association, 2002). The BGA study reported that Nebraska had the highest score, with a 3.3 GPA—equivalent to (and therefore) a B. New Jersey followed closely with a 3.1. At the low end of the scale, Alabama and South Dakota did not meet any of the five criteria, and were thus given an F grade and a 0.0 GPA.

The Reporters Committee for Freedom of the Press (2001) published a guide to open government law somewhat similar to the work of the Marion Brechner Citizen Access Project (MBCAP). *Tapping Officials' Secrets*, currently in its fourth edition, provides summaries of law regarding access to public records and official meetings for each of the 50 states and the District of Columbia. The legal outlines are prepared by attorneys expert in open government issues. The outlines begin "by describing the general structure of the state law, then provide detailed topical listings explaining access policies for specific kinds of records or meetings" (Reporters Committee for Freedom of the Press, 2001). The Internet version of the publica-

---

parties may request openness, substantial minutes of closed meetings required, remedial action (voiding or equitable relief), criminal penalty may be levied, exemptions exclusive, personal character or reputation, employment, property, other financial matters, legal, labor strategy, labor negotiations, enforcement agency, and security.

[4]The procedural criteria were: (a) the amount of time a public agency or department has to respond to a citizen's request for a public document; (b) the process a citizen must go through to appeal the decision of an agency to deny the request for the public record; and (c) whether an appeal is expedited when it reaches the court system. The penalty criteria were: (a) whether the complaining party, upon receiving a favorable judgment in court, is awarded attorney fees and costs; and (b) whether the agency that has wrongfully withheld a record is subject to any civil or criminal punishment. The BGA study is available online at www.ire.org/foi/bga/index.html.

tion is fully searchable, allowing for comparisons of a few states at a time for one category or for complete legal summaries by individual states. The project, however, does not have a page to allow looking at all states at once and does not evaluate access laws in terms of their degree of openness; nor does it look at laws other than statutes. MBCAP will.

THE MARION BRECHNER
CITIZEN ACCESS PROJECT[5]

In contrast to Adams' research, conducted with significantly fewer resources, the Marion Brechner Citizen Access Project (MBCAP) focuses exclusively on summarizing and rating access laws. Project researchers did not arbitrarily select categories to rate, but used a research method called *grounded theory*, allowing the laws to "speak for themselves." MBCAP includes state constitutions and court opinions, as well as statutes. The project's director, Bill F. Chamberlin, knew from his previous research that mapping all state laws, including constitutional provisions and court opinions, affecting access to government records would be an immense project taking several years. Given the complexity of the project, the research so far has focused on statutes and constitutional provisions for public records. Eventually, the court opinions for public records and the statutes, court proceedings, and constitutional provisions for open meeting laws will be rated as well.

MBCAP attempts to quantify a state comparison of access laws and provide information that will help Web site users understand the laws. The project does not try to evaluate laws as "good" or "bad." A "good" law depends as much on an individual's perspective as it does on the characteristics of the law. For example, a state access law involving privacy rated *mostly open* by MBCAP may be good for journalists, but less adequate for people who are afraid their personal information will become public.

---

[5]The researchers working for the MBCAP under project director Bill Chamberlin are students in either the College of Journalism and Communications (CJC) or the College of Law at the University of Florida, or both. All of the students doing legal research have had at least one course in legal research methods, and most have had more. Most of them are doctoral or master's students specializing in media law or working toward a joint communications/law degree (MA/JD or PhD/JD). A few undergraduate students assist in nonlegal research aspects of the project. A number of faculty members from the CJC, as well as other universities around the country, have worked closely with the project director, providing methodological and technical expertise. Chamberlin particularly appreciates the work of Michael Weigold, Debbie Treise, Melinda McAdams, David Carlson, and Craig Lee of the CJC; Shannon Martin of the University of Maine; and Robert Stevenson of the University of North Carolina at Chapel Hill.

The openness of government records and meetings can be a critical component of a democratic republic, allowing citizens to take a more active role in governing (Blasi, 1977). However, few citizens or public officials doubt the need for some closure of information that would damage national security or subject a crime victim to additional threats. In an effort to help scholars, public officials, and citizens better understand the public policy choices of disclosure and nondisclosure, MBCAP uses the tools content analysis and quantitative ratings for the purpose of providing users of the MBCAP Web site with a systematic "landscape," including comparisons, of access laws across all 50 states.

The data, including the ratings and summaries of laws, can be accessed on MBCAP's Web site (www.citizenaccess.org), along with direct links to all state access laws and FOI compliance audits of public officials. The Web site also provides substantial and frequently updated lists of books, booklets, and articles written about the individual state access laws, and contact information for all of the organizations known to be actively involved in education or public interest advocacy related to access to government meetings and records.

Early in the project, the project director established an advisory board as the primary tool to evaluate the state access laws. The criteria for selecting members included their familiarity with access laws, familiarity with the legal system, commitment to open government, personal reputation and visibility within the field, and willingness to spend the time it would take to participate in the project. Members were chosen to represent different regions of the country, different professional backgrounds, and different organizations to obtain as representative a rating among those with an expertise in access laws as possible. Currently, the board has 11 active members and 3 associate members who may replace active members who cannot be available when statements of law are being reviewed.[6]

---

[6]The 2004 Sunshine Advisory Board included: Rebecca Daugherty (JD), director of the FOI Service Center, a project of the Reporters Committee for Freedom of the Press; Sandra Davidson (JD), who teaches media law in the School of Journalism at the University of Missouri; Robert Freeman (JD), executive director of the New York Committee on Open Government; Kevin Goldberg (JD), an associate at Cohn and Marks LLP, specializing in First Amendment and media law issues; Harry Hammitt (JD), editor and publisher of *Access Reports*, a biweekly newsletter on the Freedom of Information Act (FOIA) and other open government laws and policies; Forrest (Frosty) Landon, former president of the National Freedom of Information Coalition and executive director of the Virginia Coalition for Open Government; Linda Lightfoot, executive editor of the Baton Rouge *Advocate*; Ian Marquand, a broadcast journalist for KPAX-TV of Missoula, Montana, and a recent co-chair of the FOI Committee for the Society of Professional Journalists; Charles Tobin (JD), a litigation and media law attorney with Holland & Knight in Washington, DC, and a former journalist; Patrice McDermott, assistant director in the Office of Government Relations of the American Library Association; and Eric Turner (JD), an attorney and director of public education for the Connecticut FOI Commission.

Creating Summaries of Law

Because the MBCAP Web site is intended to offer information about access laws to any individual with an understanding of how to use the Internet, regardless of whether he or she is familiar with legal terms, the first step in the research project was to create summaries of law, or capsules, without the jargon and complex sentences often found in statutes and court opinions.

Previous research (Adams, 1974; Better Government Association, 2002; Iorio, 1984) conducted systematic content analyses using preestablished criteria to measure access laws. In MBCAP, the research did not start with a priori categories, but with categories and subcategories based only on the text of statutes, constitutions, court opinions, and perhaps eventually administrative law. The MBCAP team, using a research method called *grounded theory* (meaning that the research frame is dependent on what is found in the laws as they are reviewed, rather than forcing the law's language into preconceived categories), reads all statutory language related to access to see what issues states include in their laws (Strauss & Corbin, 1991). Although Chamberlin necessarily established a set of major research categories that allows researchers to focus on one issue at a time, the categories and subcategories are regularly adjusted as the project director and the researchers see what is actually in the laws.

Instead of starting the research with a particular set of criteria as previous scholars have done, Chamberlin initiates a particular search by asking a researcher to examine the provisions across the 50 states in one of six major categories. Chamberlin's "starter list," based on his previous reading and research and on what he has learned in the project so far, includes the definition of a public record, fees for copying records, procedures involved in requesting records, the public and private bodies covered under the states' records laws, the subject matter included and exempted from records laws, and the laws providing for appeals, remedies, and punishments in records cases. Categories, such as computer records and constitutional protection for records, allowing for user search capabilities are also used, but those categories will eventually be subsumed into the six major categories for the purpose of creating one overall rating. The six major categories, unless they are adjusted, act as an umbrella over all possible public records law provisions. As subcategories of the major categories—and of the subcategories—are discovered in the research, Chamberlin tries to organize the data to minimize the number of times one aspect of a law is rated.

Once research assistants are given a specific category to research, such as provisions regulating which government bodies are subject to the law, they conduct keyword searches using comprehensive legal databases. They look for any aspect of every state law that mentions that the government agencies are required to disclose public records. The researchers do not limit their searches to public records laws—related laws can be found under the statutes describing the law controlling school boards or the duties of county clerks, for example. So far, for each category, researchers have examined state constitutions, state statutes, and a few state appellate court decisions. In addition to keyword searches, the researchers also use the citations and references from those searches to find other statutes, court opinions, and constitutional provisions.[7]

In addition, project researchers have examined the pertinent literature, including law reviews and periodicals. They look for items related to the project in online news databases and clip files. The MBCAP office maintains a library of books about state media law as well as newsletters distributed by state access groups.

Once researchers have identified relevant legal statements, they summarize them in full citation form for the database following a rigorous set of guidelines. The project director reviews all legal summaries, called *capsules*, in their final form. The process of preparing the summaries and fitting them into categories usually involves both the researcher and Chamberlin looking at the proposed capsules several times.[8]

After writing the full legal summary, researchers create a duplicate of the summary that minimizes words and terms that might help members of the advisory board identify the state from which the law comes. In other words, citations, state names, and perhaps names of agencies peculiar to individual states are eliminated. MBCAP staff want to avoid the recognition by advisory board members of the state laws they are reviewing or the legal source of those statements to protect as much as possible against bias when rating legal statements. The versions of the legal capsules without identification, called *neutral statements*, are given unique numbers that allow the project staff to link each of them to the

---

[7]Chamberlin hopes to eventually rate all state and federal appellate court opinions, state administrative bodies with legal authority, and state attorney general opinions.

[8]For example, although Chamberlin might start a MBCAP staff member with a broad category such as "Fees," that category is broken down into subcategories as Chamberlin and the student determine the different ways that states decide to charge fees for copying records. For the sake of both the board members and the Web page users, the categories are broken down until subcategories focus on only one issue of the larger category "Fees." Subsequently, the advisory board member is not asked to rate more than one issue at one time. From "Fees," the MBCAP team subdivides that category into several subcategories such as "Fees, Fixed Fees," "Fees, Distribution of Records," and "Fees, Cost of Production." In addition, the category of "Fees, Cost of Production" is broken down into subcategories of laws that, for example, account for the cost of personnel time, cost of duplication, and cost of record medium such as paper or computer disks.

full version that will be posted on the project's Web site. All legal statements for one category or subcategory are sent to the advisory board at the same time whenever possible. When updates are necessary, previously rated summaries are provided to the review board, along with the updates, for comparison. The review board members usually receive 75 to 150 summaries every 3 to 4 weeks.

Because context is important when the advisory board members are rating a law, specific categories are carefully defined. For example, the degree to which state records are open to any person or U.S. or state citizen, the advisory board is sent the entire sentence, which might say, "Any person can inspect a nonexempt public record without revealing the purpose of the request." Advisory board members are instructed to rate only the category of the kinds of people allowed to see public records. The issues of exemptions and the "Purpose of the Request" are rated independently. The project tries to preserve advantages of context while being sure all board members are reviewing one subject at a time.

In addition, advisory board members are reminded with every set of legal summaries that they are to evaluate the statements only for whether the law facilitates or limits access to government information. The ratings are "not intended to reflect the quality of the language of a law, nor the value or morality of a law. We are only rating the degree to [which] government records are open or closed to the public, and we are rating only the law in effect" at the time of the rating.[9]

In one batch of legal summaries for one category, advisory board members may be reviewing two or three legal summaries from one state. Every constitutional provision, statute, and appellate court opinion for each category is rated and posted on the Web site separately, and the project rates all legal statements for each category at the same time if possible. When it comes to developing the rating for a major category such as "Fees," the rating of the component parts is calculated first. If one of the component parts, such as "Fees, Cost of Production," has its own component parts, such as "Fees, Cost of Labor," the latter will be rated before the former. As a matter of fact, the average rating of the component parts becomes the rating for "Fees, Cost of Production." The average rating for categories immediately below "Fees" becomes the rating for "Fees."

Rating Procedure

Advisory board members have 2 to 3 weeks from the day they receive the legal statements to complete the rating. Because the project director requires at least an 80% response rate from the small advisory board, a

---

[9]Bill Chamberlin, e-mail communication, April 1, 2001.

minimum of 9 of the 11 members must send in their ratings for one category before the data can be tabulated and entered into the database. In special circumstances, when one board member knows in advance that it will be difficult or impossible to meet the ratings deadline, the project director asks one of the associate board members to complete the task.

Before beginning to rate legal statements, the board agreed to rate them on a 7-point semantic differential scale, with 7 indicating that the law allows for maximum *openness* to government records and meetings, and 1 meaning the law facilitates the most *closure*. Although scholars have created and used semantic differential scales with 5, 9, and 11 points, traditionally it has been held that 7-point scales provide the most valid results. In this particular case, the legal research team decided the 7-point scale was best to keep the scaling as simple as possible while allowing the board members to rate subtle differences in legal language.

The advisory board members are told to rate the legal statements without discussions with other board members. For each legal statement, board members are given the numerical scale of 1 to 7 and asked to circle the number that best fits the *openness* of the legal statement. Once MBCAP staff members receive the members' ratings, they average them to obtain the mean raw rating for each legal statement—a raw score between 1 and 7.

However, this result does not represent the rating that appears on the project's Web site. The board members agreed at the beginning of the project that the ratings should reflect a fundamental principle of law—that legal institutions constitute a hierarchy. The legal authority at the top of the hierarchy, the constitutions and the highest court for each state legal system, can trump the decisions of legal institutions lower in the hierarchy, such as trial courts and administrative bodies or individuals. The legal statements made by institutions at the top of the hierarchy have more precedential value for future legal decisions.

To recognize the importance of the different legal authorities, in the early stages of the project, Chamberlin provided the Sunshine Advisory Board members the opportunity to vote independently to arrive at a weighting scale, as well as determine the weight appropriate for each legal source. The project director and consultants decided on a 10-point weighting scale after tabulating the advisory board ballots. The 10-point scale was used to allow for a fairly large range of values and avoid possible ties when averaging the weights. The mean weights for the legal authorities after the voting were: state constitution—9.6; state supreme court—8.84; state statute—7.62; federal appellate court—7.28; state appellate court—6.5; federal trial court—5.38; state administrative body with legal authority—5.28; and state attorney general—4.08. A reliability analysis of judges' weight ratings was conducted. The resulting Cronbach's alpha was .9675 and the standardized alpha coefficient was .9692, indicating an almost perfect agreement among review board members at the time. Six of the 11 board members taking part had formal legal training. The remaining five members had extensive exposure to the legal system.

The MBCAP Web site has rated not only statutes, constitutions, and court opinions, but also has tried to indicate which of the documents best represents the current state of the law by providing a rating for the "most recent statement of law." Chamberlin developed the "most recent statement of law" because he wanted Web site users to be able to tell how the overall law of the state—the combination of statutes, constitutional provisions, and court decisions—would rate. However, the weighting of the legal authorities made that difficult. Each category potentially had three different scores even if they received the same rating because each kind of document was weighted differently based on its legal precedential authority. After the project research team decided that a sum or multiple of the three scores would be meaningless, it tried to establish a mathematical process that would best represent each state's overall rating. With reliability concerns in mind, the project director compiled nine possible solutions and sent a ballot out to board members. The advisory board selected the "most recent statement of law," meaning that the most recent court opinion, statute, or constitutional provision would represent the state's law for that category.[10] Once the project started using the designation, however, Chamberlin discovered that "the most recent statement" was often a law that spoke to only part and not the complete category. As a result, he is working on a new solution to the problem of an overall rating for the state to present to the board. Meanwhile, the "most recent statement of law" rating remains for some categories.

Data Manipulation

Chamberlin and the other scholars working on the project faced another potential methodological problem. Because access laws originate from legal authorities with different weights, the research team worried that a neutral statement rated low on *openness* but coming from a high legal authority (thus carrying more weight) would be given a higher overall rating than a better law from a lower source. Once a 7-point scale had been

---

[10]Marion Brechner Citizen Access Project, methodology file, ballot options—second methods mailing (April 4, 2001).

decided on as the measuring tool for the ratings, the scholars wanted a standard 1 to 7 scale for the ease of understanding by both advisory board members and the users of the MBCAP Web site. To overcome the potential mathematical problem and account for the positive and negative valence of the ratings (i.e., open vs. closed laws), the research team decided to convert the average ratings received from the review board to a bipolar scale: the 1 to 7 scale becomes –3 to 3 before the weighting process begins.

This method has been used by Ajzen (1991) to explicate his theory of planned behavior. According to Ajzen, the transformation makes intuitive sense because evaluations (such as open–closed) form a bipolar continuum—negative at one end of the scale and positive at the other end. Arithmetically, the conversion represents a linear transformation in which a constant (four in this case) is subtracted from the original scale values—a process that does not alter its properties.[11]

Therefore, once the original ratings (the 1 to 7 scale) are received from the board members, MBCAP research assistants convert them to the bipolar scale by subtracting 4. The mean raw score is then calculated, and the weight corresponding to that respective legal authority is applied. Finally, the result is converted back to a 1 to 7 scale by adding the constant 4 subtracted previously.

State ratings are posted on the project's Web site as raw numbers and corresponding openness icons. The value 7 corresponds to a *sunny* icon (or completely open); 6 is *mostly sunny*; 5 is *sunny with clouds*; 4 means *partly cloudy* (neither more open nor more closed); 3 represents *cloudy*; 2 means *almost dark*; and 1 is *dark* (or completely closed).

Results

The enormity of the project means that the project's interactive Web site contains far more results than could be discussed in a book chapter. It also means that the MBCAP staff still has a lot of work to do. Although many of the major categories for public records were substantially done as the book deadline approached, only the statutes categories of "Definition of Records" and "Requesting Records" had been completed. In "Definitions of Records," for example, the Sunshine Advisory Board gave the state of Louisiana the highest rating overall—a 5 or *somewhat open*. A more favorable overall rating would have been difficult given that 9 sub-

---

[11]To assess which of the two types of scales yielded better results, Ajzen correlated two independent variables from his planned behavior model, first using a unipolar scale (1 to 7) and then a bipolar one (–3 to 3). He found that the bipolar scale led to substantially stronger correlations than the unipolar scale.

categories were examined; no state was likely to have a perfectly open law on all nine criteria.[12] Louisiana's definition, certainly one of the most comprehensive, as summarized by the MBCAP staff, was:

> The Louisiana public records law provides that all books, records, writings, accounts, letters and letter books, maps, drawings, photographs, cards, tapes, recordings, memoranda, and papers, and all copies, duplicates, photographs, including microfilm, or other reproductions thereof, or any other documentary materials, regardless of physical form or characteristics, including information contained in electronic data processing equipment, having been used, being in use, or prepared, possessed, or retained for use in the conduct, transaction, or performance of any business, transaction, work, duty, or function which was conducted, transacted, or performed by or under the authority of the constitution or laws of this state, or by or under the authority of any ordinance, regulation, mandate, or order of any public body or concerning the receipt or payment of any money received or paid by or under the authority of the constitution or the laws of this state, are "public records," except as otherwise provided by the public records act or the Constitution of Louisiana. (*Louisiana Revised Statutes*, 44:1 (1)(A)(2), 2001)

Other states with high "Definition" ratings were New Mexico, Connecticut, and Minnesota. The advisory board gave those states a rating of 4, *partly cloudy—neither more open nor more closed*. The only state with no apparent explicit or implicit definition of a record was North Dakota, which received a rating of 2, or *nearly dark*, by the advisory board. Three other states were rated at 2. These three states only suggested what might be the definition of a record. For example, the law in South Dakota stated,

> . . . the statute does provide that if the keeping of a record is required of an officer or public servant under any statute of this state, the officer or public servant shall keep the record, document, or other instrument available and open to inspection by any person during normal business hours. (*South Dakota Codified Laws*, § 1-27-1, 2001)

One of the most timely categories of legal statements created by the MBCAP researchers is "Security and Safety," a subcategory of the major

---

[12]The MBCAP team measured states' definitions of public records by whether a state required ownership of a record; required the record to be in a particular physical format, including a separate category for computer records; required that a record be related to government activities; required that a record be authorized by law; required only for a state to maintain a record; required that a record be made or received by an agency; required that a record have a relationship to state funds; and a miscellaneous category of criteria not reflected in most state laws.

category, "Subjects Open/Closed." Although the researchers started looking for laws with the word *terrorism* included, they found few mentions of the word. However, MBCAP researchers did find that states were largely adopting laws to protect against terrorism by using the words *security* and *safety*. According to the definition created by MBCAP and available on the project's Web site, the topic of security and safety represents "information related to security of government, government officials, government facilities or government meetings." Most of the laws have been passed since September 11, 2001. As the researchers continued to explore the topic, they could sort the related laws into the categories of "Plans and Procedures," "National Security," "Facilities," "Federal Law," "Investigations," "Medical Records and Drugs," and "Personal Information."

When the overall category of access to "Safety and Security" records was rated across all 50 states by statutes, the states scored between 3 and 5, between *somewhat closed* and *somewhat open*. The board rated no state at the extremes—*dark* (1) or *sunny* (7). Tennessee rated the lowest, at 3, *somewhat cloudy* or *somewhat closed*. The Tennessee Open Records Act exempts all records created to respond to, or prepare for, "any violent incident," such as a "terrorist incident" (*Tennessee Code Annotated*, § 10-7-503(2) (e), 2001). The Tennessee law also exempts contingency plans of a government entity created in response to or to prepare for "any violent incident, bomb threat, or ongoing act of violence at a school or business, ongoing act of violence at a place of public gathering, threat involving a weapon of mass destruction, or terrorism incident" (*Tennessee Code Annotated*, § 10-7-504(20) (a) (ii), 2002).

In contrast, Nebraska received a relatively high rating for openness, with a score of 5 and a law that easily can be compared to Tennessee's. Nebraska's statute reads:

> In a section of the state statutes dealing with state officers, Nebraska allows a custodian to withhold information developed or received by any public bodies "charged with duties of investigation or examination," that is "a part of the examination, investigation, intelligence information, citizen complaint or inquiries, informant identification, or strategic or tactical information used in law enforcement training." If, however, this information has been previously and publicly disclosed in an open court, administrative proceeding, or meeting "by a public entity pursuant to its duties," the information is subject to the state's public records law. (*Nebraska Revised Statutes Annotated*, § 84–712.05 (5), 2002)

Tennessee's law uses vague terms that can be read expansively. Nebraska's law is directed toward more specific activity. Nebraska also has a provision designed to minimize unnecessary closure, whereas Tennessee does not.

Also rated a 5, or *somewhat open*, Minnesota had no law that restricted access to terrorism information. The absence of any restrictions on access to official documents appears to have led the advisory board to rate this state higher than a state that explicitly denied access to similar records. When a state has no law, the project director has told advisory board members to rate the fact that there is no law rather than provide review members with a set value for "no law" for all categories. The reason for this is that "no law" for "Safety and Security" might mean more openness, but "no law" for redaction of nonconfidential material from confidential material, for example, would rate at the other end of the scale—this was given a 1 by the board.

CONCLUSION AND LIMITATIONS

MBCAP Director Chamberlin and MBCAP Sunshine Advisory Board member Rebecca Daugherty have often said that deciding which state supposedly has the best public records or open meetings laws would not necessarily be useful information. The laws have too many dimensions, the two have contended, for every state to be best at everything. Chamberlin and Daugherty suggested that a more important contribution to the understanding of access laws comes with a clearer understanding of which individual statutory provisions maximize openness.

The MBCAP project allows anyone with access to the Internet to see a summary of more than 150 legal categories for each of the 50 states and the District of Columbia. The project posts more summaries and ratings every month. Users of the project Web site can, for the first time, obtain an easy-to-understand overview of all state laws in one category, organized by which states maximize and minimize access to government information. The project provides raw data for public policymakers, public access advocates, academic researchers, and journalists.

The project provides some interesting insights into records laws as well. For example:

- The state of Florida has by far the most comprehensive constitutional provision protecting access to government information and it is rated highly. Most states offer limited constitutional protection for access.
- In general, states that FOI activists would predict to have the most progressive access laws—states such as Florida, North Carolina, and Virginia—so far rate highly in many categories, including access to computer records.

- One state with a national reputation for providing poorly for public access to records—Pennsylvania—rates toward the bottom of many categories. Others often near the closed end of the scale include North and South Dakota, Wyoming, and Nevada.
- The MBCAP advisory board said that a definition of a public record that includes "used for public business," a phrase that may sound attractive, limits public access to more records than a definition that emphasizes any record a public agency creates, receives, holds, and maintains.
- In only one category so far, laws controlling inspection of public records, did all states receive a rating better than 3, *cloudy* and *somewhat closed*.
- More than 40 states allow repayment of attorney fees to individuals who have sued to obtain closed documents. FOI advocates support the repayment of attorney fees to people denied access to records as a way to encourage citizens to risk paying the money it costs to go to court to retrieve records from officials.

In addition to providing a better long-term or overall understanding of public records laws, the project also tries to provide timely information for the public. The project regularly updates its database on state laws governing access to information about issues related to terrorism, for example. Within days of the U.S. Supreme Court's consideration of state laws providing information about sex offenders to the public, MBCAP's summary and ratings of those laws appeared in more than two dozen newspapers.

Of course many limitations make the project's ranking of access laws imperfect. Probably foremost is the research time involved—although trends can be detected with an incomplete database, an overall rating of all access provisions is not available for a long while. A second limitation of the project is that the measurement tool is the analysis of the laws by about a dozen individuals, who, although experts in the field, can never provide the perfect analysis. When advisory board members see 50 state laws, it is difficult to make sure that the same rating is given to similar laws.

A third limitation of the study is that no project can effectively measure the similarities and differences in state laws because of the legal language involved. In this project, subcategories of major categories are given the same weight, although some clearly are more important than others. For example, overall, the fees for the cost of the production of records are much more important for most people than fees for overhead costs or fee waivers, if only because of the comparatively few states that have laws for the latter two categories. However, all three categories are treated as equals because of the project methodology. Yet to try to weigh subcategories adds to the complexity of the project without telling us much more. Any weighting is largely subjective.

A fourth limitation is that even an accurate rating of the laws as well as court decisions would not tell anyone whether the laws were enforced or whether requestors usually gained access to the records they sought. Testing the effectiveness of laws by seeing whether public officials provide public records when asked gives us a better understanding of behavior than any study of the laws. Therefore, links to citizen efforts to document compliance and noncompliance with their state laws are listed on the MBCAP site.

Even with the project's limitations, the positives outweigh the negatives. Added information about public access laws will help policymakers, educators, and journalists better examine and understand the statutes and court decisions. An overview of laws will make them easier to study and compare. By increasing access to information about public records and open meetings laws, the project highlights the importance of government information to the democratic process. It showcases the states that comparatively make public access a priority and provides an impetus to other states to improve.

MBCAP could help provoke public conversation about access to government information in a way similar to what the environmental groups did for issues of water and air pollution, neglected by the public and press until the 1960s and 1970s. A better discussion and understanding of access laws can lead to a more thorough consideration and less polemic when issues such as the need to have access to information held by the government and the necessity of protecting individual privacy collide.

At a broader level, the project helps both legal and social science scholars to better understand how the two research methodologies can be blended for an improved understanding of other areas of law, particularly the cross-state examinations of media law. Smaller projects than this one certainly are within the range of a single scholar or a small group of scholars.

MBCAP's data have been visible in a number of places. Chamberlin has been asked to participate in the debate over providing more access to information in numerous states, including California, Florida, and New Jersey. He regularly talks to reporters about access issues, and the project's work has been the focus of numerous newspaper and magazine articles. Project data are reported to FOI activists trying to improve access. Chamberlin has received one award for the project and two others in part based on the project. Most important, more information about state access laws is more readily available and understandable than ever before.

The MBCAP illustrates that the combination of legal research and social science methodology can better help us understand and use law.

REFERENCES

Abraham, H. J. (1980). *The judicial process: An introductory analysis of the courts of the United States, England, and France* (4th ed.). New York: Oxford University Press.

Adams, J. B. (1974). *State open meetings laws: An overview.* Columbia, MO: Freedom of Information Foundation.

Ajzen, I. (1991). The theory of planned behavior. *Organizational Behavior and Human Decision Processes, 50,* 179–211.

Better Government Association. (2002). *Freedom of information in the USA: Part One.* Chicago, IL. Retrieved June 8, 2003 from http://www.ire.org/foi/bga/index.html.

Blasi, V. (1971). The newsman's privilege: An empirical study. *Michigan Law Review, 70,* 229–284.

Blasi, V. (1977). The checking value in First Amendment theory. *American Bar Foundation Research Journal, 2*(3), 521–649.

Brown v. Board of Education, 347 U.S. 483 (1954).

Chandler v. Florida, 449 U.S. 560 (1981).

Cleveland, H. (1985). *The costs and benefits of openness: Sunshine laws and higher education.* Washington, DC: Association of Governing Boards of Universities and Colleges.

Cohen, J., & Gleason, T. (1990). *Social research in communication and law.* Newbury Park, CA: Sage.

Franklin, M. (1980). Winners and losers and why: A study of defamation litigation. *American Bar Foundation Research Journal, 5*(3), 455–500.

Iorio, S. H. (1984). How state open meeting laws now compare with those of 1974. *Journalism Quarterly, 62,* 741–749.

Louisiana Revised Statutes. (2001).

Muller v. Oregon, 208 U.S. 412 (1908).

Nebraska Revised Statutes Annotated. (2002).

Reporters Committee for Freedom of the Press. (2001). *Tapping officials' secrets.* Arlington, VA. Last examined July 29, 2005 at http://www.rcfp.org/cgi-local/tapping/index.cgi?key=users.

South Dakota Codified Laws. (2001).

Strauss, A., & Corbin, J. (1991). *Basics of qualitative research: Grounded theory procedures and techniques.* Newbury Park, CA: Sage.

Tennessee Code Annotated. (2002).

Introductory Comments to Chapter 10

Robert M. Entman[1]
George Washington University

This research started as an effort to understand the political content and effects of local TV news, the top news source for the plurality of Americans. After viewing many hours of tapes from 36 different cities, two things became apparent: The most popular topic was crime, and the subtext of crime news was race. Whatever its intentions, the credo of "If it bleeds, it leads" seemed likely to raise the salience and seeming threat of street crime—drugs, gangs, robberies, and murders (Romer et al., 2003). Because a disproportionate share of easily covered defendants and victims in most cities is African American, the heightened salience and threat seemed likely to have racial meanings for White Americans. It further struck me that the racial messages of local news were remarkably congruent with the theory of modern racism advanced by David Sears and others. Sears argued that although overt beliefs in Blacks' racial inferiority may have faded, they have been replaced by negative emotions such as fear and resentment as core themes of racial animosity among Whites, as well as by denial that racism remains a problem. Local news seemed tailor-made to stoke precisely those sentiments.

[1]"Blacks in the News: Television, Modern Racism, and Cultural Change" originally appeared, without this introduction, in *Journalism Quarterly* (1992), 69, 341–362. In the original article, the author noted, "This research was supported by the Markle Foundation, the Gannett Urban Journalism Center at Northwestern and the Chicago Community Trust Human Relations Foundation. The author would like to thank these people for help: Andrea Durbin, Natalie Bullock, Steve Simon, and Leah Smith."

On the basis of these hunches, I fashioned a detailed content analysis protocol that was unique at the time in three ways: It was rooted in theory (modern racism), it compared portrayals of Blacks and Whites in similar stories, and it probed both the visual and verbal dimensions of TV news in close enough detail to illuminate potential impacts on Whites' racial perceptions and responses. Since the original publication of a small study (Entman, 1990) that served as the pilot for the paper reprinted here, other scholars have found similar patterns in local news of other cities. Research has also revealed highly significant impacts of racial images on race-related opinions. Of particular relevance in the current context, studies have shown that even a brief exposure to Blacks accused of crime in a TV news story is sufficient to cause experimental subjects to develop more fear of crime and more punitive attitudes toward criminal defendants (see e.g., Gilliam & Iyengar, 2000; Gilliam et al., 2002; Kang, 2005; Peffley et al., 1996; Romer et al., 1998).

The implication of the local news study reprinted here and of the other studies cited earlier should be clear: Most White jurors in most urban areas will have seen years or decades of images that cultivate negative stereotypes and emotions about Blacks—and, ironically, also reinforce ignorance about the very fact that such sentiments persist in affecting the lives of African Americans. The same holds for White judges, prosecutors, witnesses, and police. These experiences in turn are likely to have heightened conscious and unconscious tendencies to presume Black defendants guilty and to favor harsher treatment for them.

On the basis of these findings, what started as a book on local TV news turned into a book on media and race that also covered network news, prime time entertainment and advertising, and Hollywood film (Entman & Rojecki, 2000). This larger study suggests more subtle impacts of mainstream media on Whites' attitudes toward Blacks and therefore on the functioning of the legal system. In briefest compass, the research suggests that media images of Blacks and of Black–White interactions systematically discourage Whites from empathizing with Blacks. At the same time, what the media convey and what they leave out encourages Whites to regard Blacks as out of place—as not truly fitting into the American community. That community, the unconscious definition and idealized image of America, is White. As one simple illustration, the book discusses how whenever *Time* or *Newsweek* have a cover story with a theme depicting humans or Americans in general, the individual on the cover is White. For example, the covers of "How Your Love Life Keeps You Healthy" (*Time*, January 19, 2004) and "Are Too Many Jobs Going Abroad?" (*Time*, March 1, 2004) depict Whites. The reasons include not just racial bias at the magazines, but commercial incentives—putting a Black on the cover tends to reduce sales. Thus, the roots of the problematic media contributions to race relations are deep; they cannot be remedied merely by putting more minority members in the newsroom.

I believe the research in this area justifies the following policy proposal: require judges to instruct juries that scientific studies reveal how unconscious racial biases distort individual decision making and group deliberations in America. Jurors should be admonished to monitor themselves for unconscious thoughts and emotions that may push them toward disregarding the exculpatory information and overweighing the incriminating information when evaluating ethnicities other than their own. This instruction might reduce the tendencies for unconscious fears and assumptions to color decisions among the racially ambivalent majority of Whites who are not outright racists. With more self-consciousness, too, it would become easier for Blacks and others to challenge those White jurors who are racist when they veil their prejudice by using oblique, racially coded, but ostensibly neutral language. In addition, the admonition could diminish other ethnic prejudices (Blacks judging Asians, Korean Americans judging Latinos, etc.) that may undermine the fairness of the legal system in our increasingly multi-ethnic society.

REFERENCES

Entman, R. M. (1990). Modern racism and the images of Blacks in local television news. *Critical Studies in Mass Communication, 7,* 332–345.

Entman, R. M., & Rojecki, A. (2000). *The black image in the white mind: Media and race in America.* Chicago: University of Chicago Press.

Gilliam, F. D., Jr., & Iyengar, S. (2000). Prime suspects: The influence of local television news on the viewing public. *American Journal of Political Science, 44,* 560–573.

Gilliam, F. D., Jr., Valentino, N. A., & Beckmann, M. N. (2002). Where you live and what you watch: The impact of racial proximity and local television news on attitudes about race and crime. *Political Research Quarterly, 55,* 755–770.

Kang, J. (2005). Trojan horses of race. *Harvard Law Review, 118*(5), 1489–1593.

Peffley, M., Shields, T., & Williams, B. (1996). The intersection of race and crime in television news stories: An experimental study. *Political Communication, 13,* 309–327.

Romer, D., Jamieson, K. H., & Aday, S. (2003). TV news and the cultivation of fear of crime. *Journal of Communication, 53,* 88–104.

Romer, D., Jamieson, K. H., & deCoteau, N. J. (1998). The treatment of persons of color in local television news. *Communication Research, 25,* 286–305.

Blacks in the News: Television, Modern Racism, and Cultural Change

Robert M. Entman

Local news may be one vehicle through which television helps, inadvertently, both to preserve and to transform cultural values. Content analysis on the evening news on four Chicago television stations over a lengthy period suggests local television responds to viewing tastes of black audiences. However, data on these Chicago television news programs suggest racism still may be indirectly encouraged by normal crime and political coverage that depict blacks, in crime, as more physically threatening and, in politics, as more demanding than comparable white activists or leaders. Ironically, widespread employment of black television journalists suggests to viewers that racial discrimination is no longer a significant social problem. The mix of these two views of blacks encourages modern white racism—hostility, rejection and denial toward black aspirations—the study argues.

This study explores the possible impact of local television news on whites' attitudes toward blacks. Content analysis of local news in Chicago suggests that, on balance, the medium may help to discourage and delegitimize traditional racist attitudes among white audiences. Yet the data also support the hypothesis that local news contributes to the phenomenon social scientists have labeled "modern racism."

Modern racism is a compound of hostility, rejection and denial on the part of whites toward the activities and aspirations of black people. In part, local television's inadvertent contribution to this phenomenon may arise from its coverage of blacks involved in crime and in politics. And in part, paradoxically, it may arise from the very responsiveness of local news to black audiences. In this way television news appears to be helping to change the shape of whites' racial attitudes to fit the system's current political practices and social realities.

MEDIA AND RACISM

The change from traditional to modern racism is subtle, but critical to an understanding of mass media's influence on racial attitudes, Traditional racism comprises negative "beliefs about black intelligence, ambition, honesty and other stereotyped characteristics, as well as support for segregation and support for acts of open discrimination."[1] Traditional racism is thus *open* bigotry that endorses "restrictions on interracial social contact . . . and opposition to equal access or equal opportunity. . . ."[2] Only in the past 25 years or so have expressions of such traditional racist sentiments nearly disappeared from the media and from public discourse generally. Surveys now show only declining number of whites endorsing such traditional racist sentiments as "Black people are generally not as smart as whites" or "It is a bad idea for blacks and whites to marry one another."[3]

According to social scientists, this reduction in measured racism has two basic causes. First, traditional racist sentiment has actually declined, perhaps in part because of changes in law and public policy.[4] Second, white Americans now realize that it is frowned upon to assert that blacks are inherently inferior, socially undesirable and therefore deserving of legally-enforced segregation.[5]

In response to the measurement difficulties and the manifest continued significance of race to American society,[6] social scientists developed the concept of "modern" (or "symbolic") racism. According to Sears, modern racism centrally involves "anti-black affect" combined with attachment to "traditional [American] values."[7] This orientation leads modern racists

---

[1]John McConahay, "Modern Racism, Ambivalence, and the Modern Racism Scale," in John Dovidio and Samuel Gaertner, eds., *Prejudice, Discrimination, and Racism: Theory and Research* (New York: Academic Press, 1986), p. 93.

[2]David Sears, "Symbolic Racism," in Phyllis Katz and Dalmas Taylor, eds., *Eliminating Racism* (New York: Plenum Press, 1988), p. 55.

[3]See McConahay, *op. cit.*, p. 108.

[4]Sears, *op. cit.*

[5]The standard items used to measure racism became "reactive in that most white Americans knew the socially desired answers. . . ." McConahay, *op. cit.*, p. 93.

[6]As McConahay, *op. cit.*, pp. 92–93 points out.

[7]Sears, *op. cit.*, p. 56.

to express "antagonism toward blacks' 'pushing too hard' and moving too fast . . . resentment toward . . . racial quotas in jobs or education, excessive access to welfare, [or] special treatment by government, . . . [and] denial of continuing discrimination."[8] Whites who have modern racist sentiments do not necessarily believe that blacks are inherently inferior or that discrimination should be legal. What many whites with modern racist tendencies do consciously feel is some amalgam of negative affect (especially fear and resentment), rejection of the political agenda commonly endorsed by black leaders, and denial that racism is still a problem.

Modern racist attitudes are measurable, since most whites do not know about the theory of modern racism and do not find the pertinent items in surveys socially undesirable. Whites frequently endorse such survey items as: "Blacks are getting too demanding in their push for equal rights" (Agree is the modern racist answer); "It is easy to understand the anger of black people in America" (Disagree); and "Over the past few years, the government and news media have shown more respect to blacks than they deserve" (Agree).[9] Studies have shown that such items compose a psychometrically valid attitude scale and that scores predict policy attitudes and voting behavior. Many whites who fail to endorse traditional racist attitudes do score high on modern racism and consistently oppose pro-black policies and vote against black or pro-black politicians.[10]

Despite empirical support, some scholars attack the concept of modern racism. Some assert that the real explanation for whites' hostility to blacks' striving is group-based conflict over scarce resources;[11] others argue that whites may oppose government intervention favoring blacks on conservative ideological grounds having nothing to do with racial animosity.[12] Each explanation may apply to some individuals who score high on instruments measuring modern racism, but the validity of the concept itself appears well-supported. The most convincing evidence is

---

[8]Sears, *op. cit.,* p. 56.

[9]Taken from the literature review in Sears, *op. cit.,* p. 57.

[10]See McConahay, *op. cit.,* and Sears, *op. cit.* Whites may support candidates who oppose pro-black policies because of the politicians' stands on unrelated issues, such as agriculture policy or inflation. The explanation of candidate choice is an enormously complicated task well beyond the scope of this paper, but the literature already cited shows the independent effect of modern racism on voting, controlling for other variables.

[11]Lawrence Bobo, "Group Conflict, Prejudice, and the Paradox of Contemporary Racial Attitudes," in Katz and Taylor, *op. cit.*

[12]Byron M. Roth, "Social Psychology's Racism," *The Public Interest* No. 98: 26–36 (Winter 1990); and cf. Paul M. Sniderman, Thomas Piazza, Philip E. Tetlock and Ann Kendrick, "The New Racism," *American Journal of Political Science* 35 (May 1991): 423–447.

that scores on modern racism scales predict behavior. Measures of individuals' attachment to group interests do not, and, for reasons of social desirability, measures of old-fashioned racist views cannot.[13]

There has also been some discussion of whether the term "racism" should be avoided. A less pejorative description such as "racial conservatism" could be substituted, but that usage obscures the concept's connection with old-fashioned racism as it dishonors conservatism. For now, following the typical usage of scholars studying race relations, "modern racism" seems most appropriate.[14]

BLACK PORTRAYAL IN THE PRESS

The previous literature on the portrayals of blacks in U.S. news media has focused mostly on visibility in print. Sentman found relatively low visibility for blacks in *Life* magazine for the period 1937–72, but extending the time period and media sampled, Lester and Smith discovered a pattern of rising coverage, as did Martindale.[15]

Since data on local TV news suggest that blacks have now achieved high visibility, the more relevant research concerns the portrayals of the blacks who are visible. Hartmann and Husband[16] found that British news tends to portray many general social problems as dilemmas involving or caused by blacks, thus promoting an image of blacks as sources of threats and burdens to society. Hall and his colleagues in Britain and Van Dijk's cross-cultural research came to similar conclusions.[17] Finally, Gray argued that U.S. news traces failure among the black "underclass" to individual shortcomings. Thus, he concluded, television perpetuates the notion that "racism is no longer a significant factor. . . ."[18] All these

---

[13]See Sears, *op. cit.*, and the many studies cited there.

[14]See Phyllis Katz and Dalmas Taylor, "Introduction," in Katz and Taylor, *op. cit.*, p. 7.

[15]Mary Alice Sentman, "Black and White Disparity in Coverage by *Life* Magazine from 1937 to 1972," *Journalism Quarterly* 60: 501–508 (Autumn, 1983); Paul Lester and Ron Smith, "African-American Photo Coverage in *Life, Newsweek* and *Time,* 1937–88," *Journalism Quarterly* 67: 128-136 (Spring, 1990); Carolyn Martindale, *The White Press and Black America* (New York: Greenwood Press, 1986).

[16]Paul Hartmann and Charles Husband, *Racism and the Mass Media* (London: Davis-Poynter, 1974).

[17]Stuart Hall, Chas Critcher, Tony Jefferson, John Clarke and Brian Roberts, *Policing the Crisis: Mugging, the State, and Law and Order* (London: The Macmillan Press, 1978), Teun van Dijk, *Communicating Racism: Ethnic Prejudice in Thought and Talk* (Newbury Park, Calif.: Sage, 1987). Also see John Downing, *The Media Machine* (London: Pluto Press, 1980).

[18]Herman Gray, "Television, Black Americans, and the American Dream," *Critical Studies in Mass Communication* 6 (December 1989), p. 384. Gray does not analyze regular TV news programs, relying instead upon a 90-minute CBS News documentary by Bill Moyers.

works lend convergent validity to the findings reported here, but none connect the theory of modern racism to TV news and American political culture.[19]

METHODS AND THEORY

Based on a pilot study,[20] two elements of the stories were chosen for close analysis: the visual portrayals of the accused and the allocation of "sound bites," that is, quotes of various actors in their own voices. The specific message dimensions chosen grew out of the research not just on modern racism but on racial prejudice generally. To summarize an enormous literature,[21] the basic understanding of prejudiced thinking is that individuals from the disliked outgroup (here, blacks) are homogenized and assimilated to a negative stereotype by the ingroup (whites), whereas those in the ingroup see themselves as individuated members of a diverse group impossible to stereotype. The key to anti-black racism, then, is whites' tendency to lump all or most blacks together into categories with negative characteristics.

Human information processing appears to operate by using stored categories called schemas, which are themselves similar to stereotypes; thus it is easy for people to fall into stereotyped thinking.[22] For audiences and journalists alike, this inherent bias of information processing combines with existing social structures and political processes to promote the stereotyping of the black outgroup.

Because old-fashioned racist images are socially undesirable, stereotypes are now more subtle, and stereotyped thinking is reinforced at levels likely to remain below conscious awareness. Rather than the grossly demeaning distortions of yesterday, stereotyping of blacks now allows abstraction from and denial of the racial component. Examples of stereo-

---

[19]There is a larger literature on portrayals of blacks in American fictional television. The data suggest that blacks now fill more diverse and less stereotypical roles than they once did, although certain racial biases persist. See, e.g., Carolyn Stroman, Bishetta Merritt, and Paula Matabane, "Twenty Years After Kerner: The Portrayal of African Americans on Prime-Time Television," *The Howard Journal of Communications* 2: 44–56 (Winter 1989–90); cf. J. Fred MacDonald, *Blacks and White TV: Afro Americans in Television since 1948* (Chicago: Nelson-Hall Publishers, 1983).

[20]See Robert Entman, "Modern Racism and the Images of Blacks in Local TV News," *Critical Studies in Mass Communication* 7:332–345 (December 1990).

[21]See David Hamilton and Tina Trolier, "Stereotypes and Stereotyping: An Overview of the Cognitive Approach," in Dovidio and Gaertner, *op. cit.*; Patricia Linville, Peter Salovey and Gregory Fischer, "Stereotyping and Perceived Distributions of Social Characteristics: An Application to Ingroup-Outgroup Perception," in *ibid*.

[22]Hamilton and Trolier, *ibid*.

typed news subjects that might trigger stored information processing categories and associated negative affective responses would be "threatening young black male" or "demanding black activist"; the (unjustified) threat and the (unfair) demand would be the conscious stimuli of the negative affect rather than the racial identity.

Journalists who repeatedly transmit these images may not themselves support modern racism. News personnel shape reports in accordance with professional norms and conventions. When confronted with events or issues that the social structure and political process routinely produce, these journalistic practices yield visuals and sound bites that fit audience stereotypes. Thus, to take one example, when journalists select sound bites for a story about black political activity, they will often choose those that convey drama and conflict. Black leaders produce an ample supply of such quotes because the structures of social and political power often marginalize them, inducing them to employ demanding and emotional rhetoric.[23] Those quotes are not the only things the blacks say, but they are the ones that make "good television"—they convey drama and induce emotion, they provide aural variation in what might otherwise be a dull talking head story. Since similar sound bites have been conveyed frequently over the years, the audience may come to expect them in narratives of black political activity. News personnel know this and, following professional norms, attempt to fulfill audiences' expectations. What reinforces stereotypes from the perspective of the communication theorist is simply following news conventions and audience expectations to the journalist.

To find the ways that mass cultural institutions may promote negative stereotypes that are congruent with modern racism, one must now analyze subtle distinctions between visual and verbal representations of blacks and whites. These implicit comparisons of blacks and whites may deny individuation and associate blacks with negative traits, while implicitly individuating and associating whites with more positive qualities. It is in this way that TV can—without manifestly derogating blacks—encourage modern racism.

To test its hypotheses, this paper relies exclusively upon media content. Therefore, like all studies based purely on content analysis, it can only provide inferential evidence as to the effects of the messages it documents; the discussions of how the different images of blacks and whites affect attitudes is inevitably speculative. As always, media images are polysemic, and audience responses may be diverse; it is possible that con-

---

[23]Blacks also seem to use emotional communication differently from whites, which may cause whites to feel threatened. See Thomas Kochman, *Black and White Styles in Conflict* (Chicago: University of Chicago Press, 1981); cf. Entman, "Images of Blacks," *op. cit.*

tinuing exposure to local news has no effect on racial attitudes. Based upon current understanding of racist thinking and the content analysis, the paper merely attempts to build a *plausible* case that local news may stimulate and reinforce modern racism, at least among those whites most likely to find that orientation appealing. A definitive case awaits future research.[24]

HYPOTHESES

Modern racism is operationalized as having three major components paralleling the dimensions of survey instruments used to measure the concept: general affective hostility toward black persons; rejection of blacks' political aspirations;[25] and denial that discrimination continues to be a problem for blacks. This breakdown yields three specific hypotheses about how the typical images of blacks on local TV news may reinforce stereotyping that feeds modern racism.

H1. There Are Consistent Differences in Portrayals of Blacks and Whites in Crime Stories That May Stimulate the Hostility Component of Modern Racism.
Lewis and Salem write that: "[A]ttitudes of citizens regarding crime are less affected by their past victimization than by their ideas about what is going on in their community—fears about a weakening of social controls on which they feel their safety and the broader fabric of social life is ultimately dependent."[26] Such fears may be compounded and focused on blacks by the reporting practices of local TV news. Local news in Chicago and elsewhere appears to grant high priority to crime stories.[27] It is thus no surprise that a large proportion of the local TV news featuring black persons focused on crime, most of it violent.

Statistics indicate that young black males are "in fact" involved with Chicago's criminal justice system far more than young whites. In 1989, a study found, 29% of black males between the ages of 20 and 29 spent

---

[24]The author is collecting large-scale sample survey data to test the impact of exposure to local TV news on racial attitudes.

[25]Readers should not infer that all blacks agree on the public policies government pursue; however, blacks are significantly more "liberal" and vote much more heavily for the (more liberal) Democratic Party than whites. See Barry Sussman, *What Americans Really Think* (New York: Pantheon, 1988).

[26]Daniel Lewis and G. Salem, *Fear of Crime: Incivility and the Production of a Social Problem* (New Brunswick, N.J.: Transaction Books, 1986), p. 9.

[27]For evidence from a 36-market study of local TV news, see Robert Entman, *Democracy Without Citizens: Media and the Decay of American Politics* (New York: Oxford University Press, 1989), pp. 110–113.

time in Cook County jail, versus 4% of young whites.[28] But there is no inherent definition of news that says crime *must* comprise a major proportion of local television news programming. Nonetheless, TV stations seem to believe audiences for local news want a lot of crime coverage, and judging by the ratings success of the programs, perhaps they do. Thus do news norms, audience expectations, and social structure interact to produce stereotypes that may feed modern racism.

H2. There Are Consistent Differences in Portrayals of Blacks and Whites in Political Coverage That May Arouse the Second Component of Modern Racism, Resistance to Blacks' Political Demands.

A major source of modern racist sentiments is attachment to traditional American individualist values, including suspicion of government intervention in the free market. If local news portrays blacks in politics as more strident and demanding of government favoritism than whites, it may generate or reinforce resistance among those in the majority group who oppose government intercession in the workings of America's meritocracy. So the second hypothesis is that local television's political coverage reinforces a second dimension of modern racism by encouraging a negative stereotype of blacks' political activities.

H3. The High Visibility of Authoritative Black Journalists Communicates Messages Likely to Support the Third Element of Modern Racism, Denial of Racial Discrimination.

The third hypothesis concerns the paradoxical function of stations' responsiveness to the interests of the black community. The stations' most visible response is employing African-American anchors and reporters. The hypothesis is that these journalists stand as symbolic affirmations that discrimination no longer impedes African-Americans, thereby contributing to a stereotyped understanding of black progress that undergirds the third component of modern racism. But the prominent black presence in local news may also undermine traditional racist stereotypes.

Findings

The study is based on content analysis of approximately 55 days of local television news in Chicago as broadcast by WBBM (CBS affiliate), WGN

---

[28]"29% of young black men jailed in '89 study says," Chicago *Tribune* (September 23, 1990), pp. 1, 18. Note that the study does not appear to establish that all of those black males jailed were residents of Cook County or that individuals did not give different names when arrested repeatedly. The data are thus of uncertain reliability. However the *Tribune* reports a similar study in Los Angeles County that also found a figure of 29% there.

(Independent), WMAQ (NBC) and WLS (ABC), sampled from the period of December 1, 1989 through May 10, 1990.[29] The program was the 10 p.m. news for the three network affiliates and the 9 p.m. news for independent WGN. Analyzing data limited to one city allowed intensive exploration of the connections between modern racism and television news in a concrete context for one of America's largest urban areas. Whether the findings can be generalized to other metropolitan areas can only be determined by future research, although there is no reason not to think local news programming is similar from city to city.[30]

Local television appears to be a particularly important news medium in Chicago. Half the TV households in the Chicago area watch the late local news (at 9 or 10 p.m.) on the average night. This compares with an average combined rating of 26 for the three network evening news shows (shown at 5:30 or 6:00 p.m.).[31] Adding impetus to this study, most local news reports originate close to home. The images in all likelihood help to shape the audience's emotional and cognitive responses to community conditions in a way that national news cannot.

---

[29]The data are from video recordings of the local news broadcast by WBBM, WGN, WLS, and WMAQ for selected periods from December 1989 through May 1990. The period December 1–7, 1989, was originally the pilot study week (WGN was not included in the pilot). These programs are included in the analysis along with a sample of programming from the next five months. In each month after December, two five day periods were chosen. In an attempt to cover every day of the month, dates were staggered purposively but randomly to cover 10 days from each month: January 10–14 and 21–25; February 6–10 and 16–20; March 1–5 and 26–30; April 21–30; and May 1–10. The word "approximately" is used in the text because of preemptions of the news (usually by sports events) and equipment malfunctions (bad reception or faulty timer settings); some programs in the sample periods were not recorded. The total number of programs included in the sample is 207. The total number of possible programs, had there been no preemptions, would have been 221. With some preemptions, the actual potential number of news shows was about 215. The possibility that the absence of these few programs from the sample introduces any biases in the results is remote; the 207 programs analyzed comprise a large and representative sample of the late evening, local television news in Chicago. Coding was done by the author and by students trained and supervised by the author. Reliability was checked by the author's recoding of 15% of the material. Average reliability was .94 for the crime material and .86 for the political.

[30]Stephen Hess, "Washington as Seen on Local TV Newscasts," paper presented at the 1990 Annual Meeting of the American Political Science Association, San Francisco, August 30–September 2, 1990; Raymond Carroll, "Market Size and TV News Values," *Journalism Quarterly* 66: 49–56 (Spring 1989); Robert Entman, "Super Tuesday and the Future of Local News," in Philip Cook, Douglas Gomery and Lawrency Lichty, eds., *The Future of News* (Baltimore: Johns Hopkins University Press, 1992).

[31]See A. C. Neilsen Company, *Neilsen Station Index* (Chicago Metered Market Service for February 1989) (New York: Neilsen Media Research, 1989). Some households may watch both WGN at 9 and another station at 10, so that the actual percentage of households watching the late news may be slightly under 50%.

As a proportion of the total news time analyzed, approximately 37% featured blacks[32] more than incidentally.[33] From this figure it is clear that local television news does not neglect black persons or the black community. Politics comprised the largest single category of stories involving blacks, followed by crime. Together, these two categories accounted for 49.8% of all stories in which blacks appeared. Thus, images of blacks as either acting in politics or as involved somehow in crime dominated local news portrayals of African-Americans. These two areas of news turn out to be critical to the hypothesized role of local TV news in fostering modern racism.

White Hostility and Black Crime News

The first hypothesis is that crime coverage, a primary topic for local news, produces different images of blacks and whites, differences likely to stimulate negative affect among whites toward blacks. In testing this hypothesis, the unit of analysis is the story. During the study period, a total of 429 stories about the breaking of law appeared in which *a person was accused by name*. These were selected for close analysis because they were the stories most likely to provide information on the race of the accused, usually via a photograph or motion video footage of the person(s). The analysis focuses on 321 stories in which the race of the accused was actually conveyed and was either white or black. Of these, 231 or about 72% of the accused named were white, and 90 or 28% were black.[34]

Because the type of crime rather than the race of the accused could affect differences in coverage, the stories were divided into two categories, those dealing with violent and drug-related crime, including murder, rape, robbery and drug dealing,[35] and those about non-violent crime, including fraud and political corruption. All analyses were conducted separately for the two categories to prevent the confounding of racial differences in reporting with differences related to the nature of the crime.

However, even if the explanation for any racial differences is that blacks and whites tend to commit different types of newsworthy crimes, the most salient point for public opinion is that the media convey a diver-

[32]The period analyzed included a total of approximately 2,484 minutes of news. This figure was arrived at by taking the total number of programs analyzed, 207, and multiplying by an average 12 minute news hole in each broadcast. The remainder of the 30-minute news show is taken up by weather, sports, banter among anchors, program credits and introductions, and commercials.

[33]An example of an incidental appearance would be a black person walking by a news scene on the street.

[34]For 22 stories, the accused was of another race.

[35]Drugs were considered a violent crime because drug dealing is so closely associated with violence, even if a particular story only mentioned the sale or abuse of drugs.

TABLE 10.1
Percentage of Blacks and Whites Accused of Crimes
in Selected Visual Depictions for all Crimes

	Blacks	Whites	χ^2
A. Accused named in still photo	48.9	65.3	2.8
Accused not named in still photo	51.1	34.7	
N	(45)	(98)	
B. Accused shown in motion	52.3	66.3	4.3*
Accused not shown in motion	47.7	33.7	
N	(86)	(187)	
C. Accused well-dressed	45.6	69.4	9.2**
Accused poorly dressed	54.4	30.6	
N	(57)	(160)	
D. Accused physically held	37.8	17.6	7.0**
Accused not physically held	62.2	82.4	
N	(45)	(153)	

*p < .05
**p < .01

gent pattern of racial images. Therefore, data are presented first for all stories together without controlling for type of crime.

Visual and aural messages were coded. Visual analysis tested whether blacks accused of crimes were depicted in ways that might tend to make them look more threatening and less individualized than whites, thereby reinforcing negative stereotypes. The visual attributes of still photographs of the accused included a label giving the person's name; whether the accused was shown in motion and whether, if so, the accused was being held physically by a police officer; and how the accused was dressed. The analysis revealed that on these dimensions there were differences in visual treatment that may tend to reinforce whites' fears. In other instances the visual analysis revealed no significant racial differences. These included whether the still photo was black and white or color, whether it was framed in color, whether the accused was handcuffed and the locations in which the accused was shown.[36]

Table 10.1 shows the racial breakdown of still photos with and without names for those accused of violent crimes. Blacks were named less frequently: 49% of blacks but 65% of whites were shown with names. Statistical significance (by the chi square test) is at the .09 probability

---

[36]In analyzing visual elements of the coverage, we enter upon largely uncharted territory in social science. Communications scholars are only beginning to recognize and measure the impact of visual images upon audiences (see Doris Graber, "Seeing is Remembering: How Visuals Contribute to Learning from Television News," *Journal of Communication* 40: 134–156 (Summer 1990)), so there is no avoiding the speculative component of the discussion that follows.

level, short of the standard .05 cutoff, but better than the .10 sometimes used in social research. This is the first of a series of differences that all point toward negative stereotyping; the others are significant below .05 (by chi square), suggesting that this finding is not due to chance. But more research is needed to confirm significance.

At a symbolic level, the absence of naming could be significant. Prejudice is fed by a tendency to homogenize, to assume there are no significant differences among individual members of the outgroup.[37] When blacks are not given a name in a picture, it suggests the visual representation can be assimilated to a larger, undifferentiated group, in this case the stereotype of a dangerous black male. The anonymous individual portrait exemplifies the stereotype; the name is not important since the individual simply stands for a familiar category of persons outside the whites' own group.[38]

This interpretation should not be pushed too far. Large numbers of black stills did contain a name label, and many white stills did not, but the results could suggest an unconscious tendency for those who put together local news shows to disregard the individuality of black accused lawmakers more than white, in part perhaps because they assume the white majority cares little about the identity of blacks accused. When combined with the other content features documented here, and when exposure is repeated over a long time, this practice could help reinforce stereotyping among white audiences.[39]

Another element of the visual treatment that may be related to individualization and humanization of the accused subject is whether the person is shown in motion video. To show a person moving is to symbolize that person as a human being, to disclose something about his size, facial expressions, and other elements of his individuality. Table 10.1 reveals that blacks were significantly less likely to be shown in motion than whites: 52% versus 66%.[40]

Table 10.1 also displays data on how the accused shown in motion video was dressed. Well-dressed means the accused had on a coat and tie or casual sportswear; poorly dressed means the accused wore street clothes (jeans and T-shirts and the like) or jail clothing. The blacks were significantly more likely to be shown in street or jail clothing. This is not surprising, given the apparent differences in social class of the blacks and

---

[37]See essays in Katz and Taylor, 1988 *op. cit.*; Linville, *op. cit.*

[38]Every still picture of a black violent criminal was of a male.

[39]Although possible impacts on black audience members, or on those of other racial backgrounds are significant, they are beyond the scope of the research here.

[40]Meanings of visual images are not always straightforward. Thus blacks shown in motion but being held by a police officer, may stimulate more negative affect than blacks shown only in an anonymous still photo. Classing motion video as humanizing may be inaccurate in some cases. Such complexities await further research.

whites accused in the news (more on this below). Still, the depictions may contribute to whites experiencing greater threat from the more shabby-clad blacks than from whites who are accused.

A similar pattern emerges in Table 10.1-D, which reveals whether the motion video of black and white defendants showed them being physically grasped by police. Symbolically, being held suggests that the person in custody—and perhaps the racial category of persons to which he belongs—is dangerous. If blacks are significantly more likely to be shown in this manner, the message could be conveyed over repeated exposures that they are more menacing than whites. As the table shows, blacks were indeed much more likely to be portrayed in the grip of a restraining officer than whites (38% vs. 18%). This finding may be traceable in part to class differences correlated with race, and here again we see the traces of social structure interacting with news choice: white criminals were more likely to be middle or upper class. With access to bail money, whites were less likely to be shown in the physical grip of the police; being free from jail and having money, whites on average could also dress better than blacks.

The visual analysis was extended to the aural dimension with a probe of how "sound bites" were distributed. Stories were coded to determine how much attention was given pro-prosecution and pro-defense speakers, if any; what actor was quoted first in the story; whether the accused himself spoke on screen; and the race of any police officers quoted. There was no statistically significant pattern in quotes given pro-prosecution sources, whether the accused spoke,[41] or in type of source quoted first.

But there were two significant findings, displayed in Table 10.2. Table 10.2 shows that 11% of stories about blacks compared with 29% of those about whites included quotes from pro-defense actors. The data suggest that stories about black persons accused of crimes were substantially less likely to allow them or their defenders to present information in their own voices. Not only does this suggest that whites were less likely to be subjected to the general pro-prosecution slant that pervades crime news,[42] on a symbolic level it suggests, once again, less humanized, less individualized treatment of the black accused. If the audience hears directly from the alleged lawbreaker or someone speaking for him, they may be more likely to see the accused as a human being with his own individual story and perspective rather than as part of an undifferentiated mass of miscreants.

---

[41]While for both races the vast majority of accused were not heard speaking, blacks were less likely to speak than whites. About 6% of the black accused and 14% of the whites spoke. The significance level of the difference was .08.

[42]Cf. Celeste Condit and J. A. Seizer, "The Rhetoric of Objectivity in the Newspaper Coverage of a Murder Trial," *Critical Studies in Mass Communication* 2: 197–216 (September 1985).

TABLE 10.2
Percentage of Blacks and Whites Accused of Crimes
in Selected Aural Depictions for All Crimes

	Blacks	Whites	χ^2
A. Number pro-defense sound bites			
None	88.8	70.6	11.7**
One	9.0	18.6	
Two or more	2.2	10.8	
N	(89)	(194)	
B. Race of police speaking on screen			
Black police official	32.3	4.0	30.9***
White police official	48.4	94.7	
Both black & white police official	19.4	1.3	
	(31)	(75)	

**p < .01
***p < .001

Table 10.2 also shows the race of political officials quoted on screen about the accused. The table reveals that blacks accused of crimes were frequently discussed by white police officers or by both black and white police officers in the same story. On the other hand, whites accused of crimes were almost always discussed *only* by white police. There is a kind of symbolic segregation of police authority. Blacks are framed frequently by the words of white police, but not vice versa. Symbolically this could suggest to white audiences that blacks are not trusted (and perhaps cannot be trusted) to exert police authority over white persons. This finding probably reflects the residential segregation of Chicago and the practices of the police force in assigning officers of different races to specific neighborhoods. But whatever the underlying social structures, the pattern of images absorbed by the white audience may over time affect their racial attitudes.

One complication in this analysis is the presence of a prominent, continuing story during the period studied. This was the Dowaliby murder trial, involving a white couple charged with killing their own child. The Dowaliby crime received more attention than any other violent crime during the period (41 stories). Much of this coverage was sympathetic to the defendants.[43] Therefore, including it could bias the results. However, for the data in Tables 10.1 and 10.2, excluding Dowaliby stories only slightly reduced statistical significance levels; all findings remained significant beyond .05.

---

[43]As suggested by findings reported below, which show that removing Dowaliby coverage reduces the racial disproportion in pro-defense sound bites.

Blacks and Crime

The data point to the following conclusion. Leaving aside type of crime—grouping violent and non-violent crime stories together, as the news programs themselves do—the images of blacks accused of crimes appear to be different from those of whites. Although on some dimensions there were no racial differences (data not shown), every case of difference appeared likely to stimulate negative emotions toward blacks among white audiences.

Separating out news of the non-violent crimes, Tables 10.3 and 10.4 present the data for violent crimes only. In each case, the relatively negative imagery of blacks holds. That is, even when we look only at reporting of violent crime, the blacks accused appear to be treated in a less favorable manner than allegedly violent whites. The statistical significance of the findings changes, however.

For violent crime, Table 10.3 shows that blacks were less often named than whites; though the finding was not quite significant at the .05 probability level, if we exclude Dowaliby stories (data not shown), the relationship actually does become statistically significant (at p=.036); with the Dowaliby's excluded, 43% of the blacks versus 67% of the whites accused of violence have name labels on their still photos.

Table 10.3 shows blacks accused on violence receiving significantly less favorable visual treatment than whites on the other three dimensions. However, excluding the Dowaliby stories from these latter three erases the statistical significance of the results (data not shown). For this particular period, the news conveyed an important lesson about white

TABLE 10.3
Percentage of Blacks and Whites Accused of Crimes
in Selected Visual Depictions for Violent Crimes Only

	Blacks	*Whites*	χ^2
A. Accused named in still photo	42.9	62.2	
Accused not named in still photo	57.1	37.8	3.1
N	(35)	(90)	
B. Accused shown in motion	52.2	67.7	
Accused not shown in motion	47.8	32.3	4.3*
N	(69)	(155)	
C. Accused well-dressed	37.5	59.6	
Accused poorly-dressed	62.5	40.4	5.8*
N	(48)	(114)	
D. Accused physically held	47.2	24.3	
Accused not physically held	52.8	75.7	5.6*
N	(36)	(103)	

*p < .05

TABLE 10.4
Percentage of Blacks and Whites Accused of Crimes
in Selected Aural Depictions for Violent Crimes Only

	Blacks	Whites	χ^2
A. Number pro-defense sound bites			
None	88.9	66.0	
One	8.3	18.5	
Two or more	2.8	15.4	13.8***
N	(72)	(162)	
B. Race of police speaking on screen			
Black	34.5	3.2	
White	44.8	95.2	
Black and white	20.7	1.6	30.3***
N	(29)	(62)	

***p < .001

criminal defendants that was significantly less likely to be aired about blacks: they are human beings, individuals who might even be innocent. But in another time period, one without such an extraordinary case, the racial disparity might not have emerged.

Table 10.4 displays the sound bite data for allegedly violent blacks and whites. The blacks received much less opportunity to convey their perspectives in their own voices and were much more likely than whites to be discussed by a police official not of their race. On this aural dimension, excluding the Dowaliby defendants did not eliminate the statistical significance of the differences.

Finally, separating stories covering violent crimes from those about non-violent offenses suggests that a major reason for the comparatively negative imagery of blacks is that they are reported more frequently in connection with violence. For non-violent crimes alone, most racial differences diminished to beneath statistical significance or disappeared altogether.[44] Of the black alleged offenders in this study, 84% were assertedly involved in violent crimes, compared with 71% of whites (a difference significant by chi square at p=.03). Local television's emphasis on violent crime may mean that disproportionately more imagery of blacks will be threatening.

---

[44]Most notable are the aural differences in non-violent crime stories: 7% of stories about blacks, compared with 33% of stories about whites, contained one or more sound bites from a defense-oriented actor. Although this finding is not statistically significant, the difference is large and the reason for the lack of significance may be the small number of stories. The result was similar (though also not statistically significant) for the quotation of police officials. Only one white accused of a non-violent crime was spoken about by a black police official; all the rest of the whites (12) were discussed by white police.

White Rejection of Black Politics

Beyond the emotional hostility that may be bolstered by crime reporting, a second component of modern racism is rejection of political actions or proposals that advance the interests of the black community.[45] With this in mind, the study looked at stories of blacks and whites participating in politics. The analysis revealed that black activists often appeared pleading the interests of the black community, while white leaders were much more frequently depicted as representing the entire community. News about blacks who acted politically conveyed the notion that they spoke and behaved more than whites to advance "special interests" against the public interest.

In testing the second hypothesis, the unit of analysis is the directly quoted assertion (sound bite) about public policy; the analysis coded every sound bite in every story. Members of both racial groups were heard frequently talking about government and policy issues. Blacks spoke about government policy in 146 stories and made a total of 200 coded assertions; whites spoke in 339 stories, a total of 523 times. Individuals or spokespersons for groups representing other ethnic or interest groups, or for groups representing a mixture of ethnics, made most of the rest of the 862 total assertions relevant to policy issues.[46]

The analysis coded assertions attributed to all those (individuals or groups) criticizing, defending, or making recommendations for action by government or public officials. (Stories about politicians that focused only on campaign details or events were excluded.) The analysis determined the *basis* for each utterance; each explicit or implicit claim that the government was *violating or should be serving an interest* was noted as a basis. The four possible bases were: public interest (452 assertions were based on this appeal); ethnic self-interest (180 assertions); interest in corruption-free government (181 assertions); and special interests not identified with race, such as gays and lesbians (49 assertions).[47]

Among the ethnic interests asserted, *black* interests were defended 115 times, *white ethnic* interests 43 times, and *other ethnic group* interests 22

---

[45]The black community is diverse and may have no single interest any more than does the white community. What the theory of modern racism assumes, however, is that the majority of blacks do have interests in electing African-American office holders and in public policies that redress the results of discrimination.

[46]For some assertions, race could not be ascertained.

[47]For example: a claim was coded as "public interest" if the person endorsed a policy on the grounds it would "serve the people of Chicago." An ethnic self-interest claim would be something like "It is time Mayor Daley stopped cutting aid to hospitals serving the black community." A corruption-related claim would be "The city's restaurant inspectors frequently solicit bribes." And other special interests might be endorsed by a person who said "The city government is ignoring the needs of the gay community."

times. Thus Chicago local news frequently transmits claims that government is violating, or should be serving, blacks' interests: 64% of all ethnic interests defended in the news study were blacks' interests. It seems likely that exposure to such a pattern would over time feed some whites' resentment of blacks' seemingly demanding stance relative to other groups in society.

Black individuals or spokespersons for black groups themselves made 66 of those 115 assertions seeking government responsiveness specifically to black interests; as a proportion of the 200 total assertions uttered by blacks, this came to about 33%. Thus, fully one-third of the time audiences heard blacks endorsing or criticizing a government action, the blacks were pleading the specific ethnic interests of the black community. In contrast, white spokespersons made 28 pro-white assertions (the other 15 pro-white claims were not made by individuals or groups identifiably white); as a proportion of the 523 assertions by whites, these 28 utterances came to about five percent. Whites appeared much less prone to promoting ethnic self-interest than blacks. This implicit comparison of black and white political actors may further stimulate resistance especially among whites most wedded to the traditional American ideology of self-help and limited government intervention.

Possibly compounding this feeling is that white political actors were shown endorsing government service of blacks' interests 38 times. This means that whites in politics were shown explicitly defending blacks' interests more often than overtly defending whites' own interests (which, again, they did 28 times). On the other hand, black actors explicitly defended the notion that government should serve whites' interests only one time. White audiences could infer that blacks demand a lot from government and receive quite a bit of support from whites in that quest, but then fail to endorse government action that favors whites. This impression may be accurate; it may be that black activists and elites treat Chicago politics as a zero sum game in which any gain for whites is a loss for blacks. The accuracy of these images is beyond the scope of this study.

The other side of this finding is that black political actors appeared disproportionately unmoved by the *public* interest. Most of the time whites spoke about government action, they defended it in terms of the public or larger community interest. The ratio of public interest to ethnic self-interest assertions for whites looks like this: 278 to 28 or a 10 to 1 balance favoring the public interest. In comparison, for blacks the ratio was 64 to 66 or 1 to 1. For every public interest claim, blacks uttered a self-interested demand.

Note that all of these data tap *rhetoric*, not politicians' or political actors' actual goals or thoughts. Political actors frequently rationalize selfish demands in terms of the public interest. The assumption here, though, is that the overt assertions, not the hidden agendas of quoted

speakers, shape audiences' perceptions. In this realm of image and rhetoric, blacks were portrayed in ways that may well foster whites' resistance to and rejection of blacks' political goals.

Perhaps most of the time black political leaders do speak up only for
black interests; many theories of representation would endorse just such
behavior. However, it seems highly unlikely that white political actors
are as purely civic-minded as depicted in the implicit comparison constructed by the news. But, the whites' halo does reflect genuine structural conditions. To protect white privileges, white politicians need only
defend the status quo in general terms (e.g., by invoking "the public interest") or in terms of non-racial values such as meritocracy or low taxes.
They do not need to use an overt rhetoric of white power; they need not
mention power at all.

The Alleged Disappearance of Racism

Beyond the threatening criminals and demanding political activists, more
benign blacks appeared in local news, usually occupying roles of respected authority. They included most importantly the many black
anchorpersons and reporters. Authorities that for all practical purposes
might as well have been white, their behavior and words on screen were
not linked in any way to their racial identities, and indeed denied black
identity as it was constructed by crime and politics news. Such images
could buttress perceptions that racism is no longer a problem for black
persons, and in this way contribute to the third component of modern
racism, the belief that blacks no longer suffer from discrimination. In this
section, only qualitative data are available; the discussion will be based on
these observations.

Unlike criminals and political actors, blacks occupying the role of authoritative spokesperson did not appear threatening, did not talk in angry
or demanding tones. They were unemotional, friendly but businesslike.
They followed middle class, white patterns of conversational communication.[48] Black anchors spoke from the same perspective as white anchors; there was no difference between their reporting, which of course is
what their job descriptions demanded. Voicing a black perspective would
have meant defining the problems covered in the news—such as violent
crime—in ways that might be endorsed by a majority of blacks.[49]

---

[48]See Kochman, *op. cit.*

[49]Blacks may fear crime as much as whites, but their interpretations of crime's causes
and cures are, on average, different from those of whites, and those differences could in theory construct a different narrative perspective on crime involving blacks. For example, poll
evidence suggests blacks are significantly more likely to see discrimination as a major continuing problem than whites. See Barry Sussman, *op. cit.*, p. 110.

Black anchors may be particularly significant to the formation of whites' impressions. A separate study revealed that fully 11 of 13 stations in 13 of the nation's 25 largest markets employed at least one black in a co-anchor role.[50] The Chicago stations frequently place blacks at the anchor chair. These anchors may provide the images of authoritative blacks most frequently encountered by many white Chicagoans, who typically live in segregated neighborhoods and work for white bosses.

It thus appears reasonable to hypothesize that the positive images of black authority in local news may unwittingly have two simultaneous effects: on one level, black anchors demonstrate that blacks are capable of behaving according to and reporting from the perspective of dominant white values. But on another level, the innocuous black anchors may also reinforce whites' impatience with the poor or demanding blacks who appear so frequently as news subjects. The anchors' very presence suggests that if blacks just keep quiet and work hard, the system will indeed allow them to make progress and even earn more money than most whites.[51] Showing attractive, articulate blacks in such a prestigious public role implies that blacks are not inherently inferior or socially undesirable—and that racism is no longer a serious impediment to black progress. The image that undermines old-fashioned racism may promote modern racism. Ironically, local stations' responsiveness to the interests of black audiences in seeing black role models may produce imagery that bolsters modern racism, even if it also helps diminish traditional racism.

Beyond this, viewing local news featuring a black anchor can symbolically affirm for white viewers that they are not racist.[52] Modern racists may even feel an unconscious attraction to local news because its content helps confirm their sentiments, while its presentation allows them to deny they are racists. The presentation is made in part by blacks, and the racial messages are subtle. Watching the news may thus protect frequently-ambivalent modern racists from confronting their own racial anxieties, stimulating anti-black feelings that remain unacknowledged and thus unthreatening to a non-racist self-image.[53]

---

[50]Entman, "Super Tuesday," *op. cit.*

[51]For evidence that blacks with college degrees earn much less than whites and that the relative position of middle class blacks actually deteriorated in the 1980s, see Bennett Harrison, *Los Angeles Times*, September 2, 1990, p. M4.

[52]See Gaertner and Dovidio, "The Aversive Form of Racism," in Dovidio and Gaertner, *op. cit.*

[53]For many of those with moderate to high modern racism scores, research suggests ambivalence toward blacks rather than outright negativity may be operating (see McConahay, *op. cit.*, and Gaertner and Dovidio, "The Aversive Form of Racism," in Dovidio and Gaertner, *op. cit.*) The racially ambivalent whites recognize that it is undesirable to be a racist and when made consciously aware of their anti-black sentiments attempt to convince

Compounding the possible impacts, black anchors and reporters frequently cover crime and political stories that may reinforce modern racism in ways described earlier. That blacks frame the stories may embolden and authorize whites to voice modern racist sentiments without considering them racially charged—after all, blacks themselves provided the information. Legitimizing modern racism as something other than anti-black prejudice may have great political significance because the benign guise makes whites more willing to voice those sentiments in personal conversation. Hearing modern racist ideas openly expressed further legitimizes and spreads the notions, in a kind of reversal of Noelle-Neumann's "spiral of silence."[54]

It would be absurd to suggest that these potential impacts make it undesirable for stations to employ black journalists in positions of visible authority. The point here, as throughout the paper, is that actions which stations undertake for commercial or even public-spirited reasons, such as hiring blacks and covering their political activities, may inadvertently contribute to modern racism.

Conclusions

These findings should not be misconstrued. The strength of the relationships is mixed, and more research is needed. Every dimension of the news message was not slanted against blacks. In some dimensions, the content analysis turned up no difference between images of blacks and whites. Even on the dimensions of the news that showed statistically significant differences in the *average* treatment of blacks and whites, there were many instances in which news treated blacks and whites similarly. However, where there were significant differences, they were always in the same direction, with blacks covered in ways likely to support negative stereotypes. Hence the data do suggest that exposure over time to local TV news presents viewers with an accumulation of images that make blacks appear consistently threatening, demanding and undeserving of accommodation by government. Again, these are only inferences from news content; empirical confirmation of the effects on racial attitudes awaits future research.[55]

---

themselves that these are not manifestations of racism. Depending on the circumstances, such persons may respond in ways that appear prejudiced toward blacks, or in ways that suggest tolerance (McConahay, *op. cit.*, pp. 99–101).

[54]Elisabeth Noelle-Neumann, *Public Opinion—Our Social Skin* (Chicago: University of Chicago Press, 1984); cf. van Dijk, *op. cit.*

[55]Hartmann and Husband, *op. cit.*, empirically demonstrate effects of media portrayals on racial attitudes in Britain.

If the hypotheses do prove valid, they would suggest some insights into television's role as a "cultural forum."[56] While some believe audience members actively mull contesting ideological readings of society's conflicts, the data indicate that cultural self-examination, tension and change can be played out in television quite unconsciously. Neither the producers nor the viewers of local television news are likely to be conscious of the patterns described here. What follows is a tentative outline of the way that television may come to its role of changing yet preserving racism as a component of American culture. In this view, the key to television's involvement in culture change would be the interaction of elite discourse with the underlying structural realities of American society as reflected in television news.

Traditional American racism identified blacks as inferior and undesirable. But this strand of culture is no longer socially acceptable. Elite rhetoric no longer validates old-fashioned racism. And elites came to a consensus against legally enforced discrimination and segregation. To some degree, the beliefs of the mass public have changed accordingly. Old-fashioned racism is no longer a central tenet of the American culture, and this alteration in culture is reflected in the content and the hiring practices of local television news programs. No longer are blacks invisible as subjects or purveyors of news, no longer are old-fashioned racist assertions and stereotypes frequently displayed and thereby validated.

Yet we have seen that the news appears congruent with racism in its updated variant. Television news, especially local television, is defined largely in emotional terms: it alerts audiences to threats and provides reassurance.[57] Black crime and black politics are considered newsworthy because they alert black and white audiences (in somewhat different ways) to possible dangers and sources of succor. And these are not fictions: reflecting the legacy of discrimination, there really are high crime rates among poor blacks and high levels of demand for government services.[58]

But reality alone does not explain the news' constructions of reality; they are framed by elite discourse.[59] Having outlawed discrimination, white elites have not come to a consensus on who is responsible for nega-

---

[56]Horace Newcomb and Paul Hirsch, "Television as Cultural Forum: Implications for Research," in Horace Newcomb, ed., *Television: The Critical View* 4th ed. (New York: Oxford University Press, 1987).

[57]David Paletz and Robert Entman, *Media Power Politics* (New York: Free Press, 1981).

[58]The racial distribution of government services is a more complicated matter than it appears. To take just one example, the ability to deduct mortgage interest from income taxes provides a large subsidy for middle and upper class housing that probably benefits whites disproportionately.

[59]Cf. van Dijk, *op. cit.*, pp. 360–370.

tive conditions in the black community. With the dominant white elites continuing to argue about blacks, there is in essence no settled element of "culture" that directly addresses and replaces the traditional racist view of black-white relations. Other elements of traditional American ideology that white elites do generally agree upon (or at least endorse rhetorically) and that persist within the culture will more consistently shape the news, and audiences' processing of it. These components of culture include distrust of big government and, especially, the assumption that individuals are responsible for their own fate. Such affirmations help to produce modern racism by denying the history of discrimination whose residue—high crime, high and impatient demand for services—local television so graphically emphasizes. Material sympathetic to blacks and contradictory to modern racism does appear, reflecting some elites' emphases on other American values, such as egalitarianism. Thus the movement of American culture from its dominant strain of traditional racism to its current ambivalent compound of hostility, sympathy and indecision reproduces itself in individuals, in part through television's images.

Introductory Comments
to Chapter 11

Glenn Leshner
University of Missouri

This research project began as a discussion of the depictions that Entman (1990, 1992, 1994a, 1994b) measured in local and network TV news. Entman's substantial body of work in the area of how minorities are portrayed in TV news is important in any discussion of race and media. His content analyses of how race is portrayed in TV news suggested to us a research project that would test the effects of these depictions on viewers. Much of media effects research tests the possible effects of media content that has already been established by prior research. After all, if no measurable effect of the content could be detected, then perhaps the negative portrayals of African-American males in TV news might be much ado about nothing.

However, our hunch was that these images do have measurable effects, and that it would be worthwhile to try to detect what some of those effects might be. Our first attempt, not reported here, was to test the depiction styles using the Modern Racism Scale (MRS) as the possible effect. We did not find much probably because the scale, although it represented a more subtle form of racial attitudes than traditional measures, still caused reactance among our participants. Examples of items in the MRS include, "It is easy to understand the anger of Black people in America," and "Blacks are getting too demanding in their push for equal rights" (McConahay, 1986). Given the attention that universities typically pay to diversity issues and multicultural aspects of our curriculum, it is likely that our students, who served as participants in our study, were sensitized to the MRS items.

We then decided to adopt a more implicit measure of viewers' judgments and opted for a response latency measure often used in cognitive and social psychology research. The latency measure is purported to measure construct (stereotype) activation; that is, how accessible a mental construct is. Faster response latencies were taken as indicative of stereotype activation. The quicker the activation of a stereotype, the higher the likelihood that the construct would influence subsequent judgments and evaluations. Such a measure is designed to be less reactive than more obvious questions about racial attitudes.

Our results indicate that the depiction style does matter, and that, for African-American males suspected of committing a crime in a TV news story, the dehumanizing depictions resulted in faster responses to negative adjective traits than for nondehumanized depictions. This particular pattern held when African-American suspects were shown in an unnamed mug shot and in still motion. When the suspect was shown restrained by authorities, responses to negative adjective traits were quicker for both White and African-American suspects. These findings corroborate Entman's suspicions—that dehumanizing depictions of African-American males in TV news crime stories encourage stereotyping in judgments about those suspects. However, we also found that perceived credibility of the stories was enhanced with stereotypic depictions.

Can TV journalists incorporate the results of this study, and others like it, in how they develop their TV news stories? I have some graduate students who are seasoned journalists. Some argue that they are provided more opportunities to record the "perp walk," a common way for authorities to parade their suspects in front of news media, when the suspect is African American than when the suspect is White, hence, placing the responsibility for such depictions on the authorities. Others argue that, because journalists have a great deal of discretion over how to present the visual material in TV news stories, the data in our study and others like them would be helpful to reduce the stereotyping effects of their stories. It seems that those journalists who take more responsibility for their product are more likely to adjust their coverage to reduce unintended negative outcomes than those who take less, provided that they are doing so based on credible data.

Certainly, this study represents a modest advancement in our understanding of how media portrayals of race influence viewers' cognitions. Further research, which is currently be taken on by proficient scholars in mass communication and allied fields, will likely generate important data that can inform journalists and media consumers alike.

REFERENCES

Entman, R. M. (1990). Modern racism and the images of blacks in local television news. *Critical Studies in Mass Communication, 7,* 332–345.

Entman, R. M. (1992). Blacks in the news: Television, modern racism, and cultural change. *Journalism Quarterly, 69,* 341–361.

Entman, R. M. (1994a). African Americans according to TV news. *Media Studies Journal, 8,* 28–38.

Entman, R. M. (1994b). Representation and reality in the portrayal of blacks on network television news. *Journalism Quarterly, 71,* 509–520.

McConahay, J. B. (1986). Modern racism, ambivalence, and the Modern Racism Scale. In J. Dovidio & S. Gaertner (Eds.), *Prejudice, discrimination, and racism: Theory and research* (pp. 91–125). New York: Academic Press.

The Effects of Dehumanizing Depictions of Race in TV News Stories

Glenn Leshner[1]

The daily parade of shackled Black prisoners on TV news paints a picture of Blacks as violent and threatening toward Whites, self-interested and demanding toward the body politic—continually causing problems for the law-abiding, tax-paying majority. A number of studies support the notion that TV crime news often includes racial images (Campbell, 1995; Entman, 1990, 1992; Entman et al., 1998; Gilliam & Iyengar, 2000; Hurwitz & Peffley, 1997; Peffley, Shields, & Williams, 1996; Romer, Jamieson, & de Coteau, 1998). By their professional judgments, the gatekeepers of news project how consequential minorities are to American society and determine the ways in which minorities are portrayed to the majority audience (Wilson & Gutierrez, 1985).

When covering stories about Black individuals, journalists may not merely be representing a single newsworthy event in which a Black person happens to be involved. Journalists may also be selecting exemplars that can represent the category of "Black Americans" and subsequently be compared to Whites' images of themselves. Research on African Americans and TV clearly shows that minorities are represented in a limited number of roles and by a preponderance of negative images (Campbell,

[1]This research was supported in part by a Summer Research Fellowship granted by the Office of Research at the University of Missouri. The author would like to acknowledge Lillian Dunlap, Maria Len-Rios, Jaeyung Park, and Ryan Marshall for their contributions on this research project.

233

1995; Gandy, 1994; Gandy & Baron, 1998; Gilens, 1996; Gilliam, Iyengar, Simon, & Wright, 1996; Roberts, 1975; U.S. Commission on Civil Rights, 1977). Further, studies that examine local nightly newscasts continuously find that news disproportionately focuses on violent crime and non-White criminals, racially linking the criminal to the crime type, as well as depicting minority suspects in such stories in dehumanizing ways (Entman, 1990, 1992, 1994a, 1994b; Gilliam, Iyengar, Simon, & Wright, 1996; Iyengar, 1991).

Although the interaction of depictions, style, and race in TV news has obvious import, no conclusions can be drawn about the possible effects these depictions have on viewers based simply on their documentation of occurrence in TV news programs. Greenberg and Brand (1994) lamented the dearth of studies that attempt to see whether such content has any measurable effects, although recent research has begun to address this issue (Barnett, 2003; Domke, McCoy, & Torres, 1999; Gilliam & Iyengar, 2000; Oliver, 1999; Peffley, Shields, & Williams, 1996). The primary question the current study addresses concerns the effects of the interaction between the race of a target suspect in a crime TV news story and dehumanizing depictions. Do viewers respond to White and Black suspects differently depending on how these suspects are depicted? A key purpose of this study is to test the functions of dehumanizing visual depictions Entman (1992) found common in local news stories by experimentally testing the notion that these depictions and the race of the suspect might elicit stereotypic responses from viewers. This study is meant to forge the link between content and effects by assessing the relationship among types of depictions of alleged criminals (Black and White) in TV news stories and subsequent social judgments of the target suspects. The pattern of responses might be informative to journalists as they explore ways to better cover both racial and crime stories in their communities.

STEREOTYPING

The theoretical framework that informs the current study is the relationship between stereotyping and ingroup–outgroup biases, which is well documented in the social cognition literature. The tendency to distinguish between social ingroups and social outgroups based on categories such as age, gender, race, nationality, or university is a fundamental aspect of social perception (Linville & Fischer, 1993). Despite their general ability to detect group variability, people's perceptions of variability are biased. One type of biased perception toward another group is the outgroup homogeneity effect—the tendency to see outgroup members as more similar to each other in their traits and behavior than ingroup members (Thompson, Kohles, Otsuki, & Kent, 1997).

Linville and Fischer (1993) proposed that second-hand exemplars, which one would develop through either media or oral descriptions by friends and family members, frequently represent widely shared homogeneity about groups. However, they say first-hand exemplars encountered in direct observation or interaction with group members more truly reflect the diversity within social groups. Their argument is that second-hand exemplars, such as those in TV news, are a relatively greater source of people's knowledge of outgroups, so people tend to perceive less variability among outgroup members.

The outgroup homogeneity effect appears to be quite robust across a variety of natural groups, including profession, nationality, race, religion, age, college major, and sorority–fraternity affiliation (Linville & Fischer, 1998). The perception of ingroup heterogeneity and outgroup homogeneity allows people to feel individualized and unique from others and, thus, encourage "we" versus "they" judgments, attitudes, and perceptions.

This tendency may occur when people view crime suspects in TV news stories. As mentioned earlier, naturally occurring groups such as Whites and Blacks have been traditionally used to identify ingroup and outgroup distinctions. A person's race is indeed an obvious cue, and therefore biased perceptions of race are more likely to be mentally activated within the explosive context of violent crime (Peffley, Shields, & Williams, 1996). Thus, White viewers may view Black crime suspects as members of an undifferentiated outgroup.

This mechanism may also work when outgroup members are depicted in an unusual (e.g., dehumanizing) way. Dehumanizing depictions may enhance the rating of extremity effect over the effect one might expect for the outgroup in general. In his study of local TV news, Entman (1992) found the news media have a tendency to more frequently portray accused minorities in a dehumanizing way by means of nameless photos, still pictures (i.e., without motion), and authority restraint. Entman suggested that anonymous individual portraits may cause viewers' to perceive that because the name is not important, the individual merely stands for a familiar category of the outgroup. He made a similar argument for the depiction of a crime suspect in a still picture rather than in full motion. Showing a person in a still photo tends to discourage viewers from individuating that person presumably because such a depiction carries fewer elements of human characteristics. Finally, showing crime suspects physically restrained by the police also dehumanizes those suspects by taking away freedom of movement, and may suggest to the audience that the suspects are more dangerous and menacing than their counterpart group.

Entman's (1992) study implies that viewers may categorize crime suspects on the basis of such dehumanizing available cues commonly found in TV news stories. This negative feeling may be enhanced when the race of a crime suspect interacts with dehumanizing depictions. That is, people may rate outgroup members depicted in a dehumanizing way more negatively than those outgroup members depicted in a non-dehumanizing way.

CULTURAL STEREOTYPES

Cultural stereotypes are comprised of a well-defined set of characteristics for a social group and are thought to be widely learned within a culture. Devine (1989) and others (Brigham, 1972; Ehrlich, 1973; Katz, 1976) argued that, because of common socialization experiences, people are equally knowledgeable of the culture stereotype of African Americans regardless of their level of expressed prejudice (Devine, Monteith, Zuwerink, & Elliot, 1991).

Devine (1989) showed that stereotypes and personal beliefs about groups are conceptually distinct cognitive structures. Although stereotypes and personal beliefs about a particular social group contribute to one's entire knowledge base, beliefs can differ from one's knowledge about the group. This dissociation, she argued, is the result of automatic and controlled processing (e.g., Bargh & Chartrand, 1999; Schneider & Shiffrin, 1977). Devine (1989) and others argued that everyone knows what the cultural stereotypes are, but their outward expression is mediated by the particular beliefs an individual holds. That is, prejudice is the product of an individual's controlled thinking and represents the expression of beliefs about stereotypes. Stereotypes are represented in knowledge structures that can be automatically activated regardless of an individual's desire to express them.

Automatic processes involve the unintentional or spontaneous activation of cognitive structures in memory that have been developed through repeated activation. A key feature of automatic processes is their inevitability. They occur despite deliberate attempts to bypass or ignore them. Controlled processes, however, are intentional and require the active attention of the individual. Although limited by mental capacity, controlled processes are more flexible, which makes them useful in decision making, problem solving, and the initiation of intentional behaviors.[2]

---

[2]The conceptual distinction between automatic and controlled processes has been the source of considerable contention in the recent social cognition literature. The dual-process conceptualization turns out to be more complicated than originally expressed. Research

Devine (1989) asserted that racial stereotypes are part of the American knowledge structure and that, on viewing a person of a stereotyped racial group, the stereotype is automatically activated. She found that high- and low-prejudice persons were equally knowledgeable of the cultural stereotype. When participants' ability to consciously monitor stereotype activation was precluded, both high- and low-prejudice participants produced stereotype-congruent evaluations. When participants were directed to consciously list thoughts about a target person, only low-prejudice participants inhibited the automatically activated stereotype-congruent thoughts and replaced them with thoughts reflecting the suppression of the stereotype.

RESPONSE LATENCY AND STEREOTYPING

Because stereotypes are thought to be automatically activated (Bargh & Chartrand, 1999), researchers have reasoned that the time which elapses between the activation of the stereotype and an individual's response represents the degree to which the stereotype was accessed. Essentially, faster response times to a prime represent the stronger activation of a stereotype. For example, Fazio, Jackson, Dunton, and Williams (1995) verified the use of response latencies to visual primes in measuring automatic activation of attitudes. The authors presented digitized photographs as primes of the race of subject (White or Black) on a TV screen and then presented the participants with positive or negative words. The subjects were told to react as quickly as possible to the words, rating the words as *good* or *bad*. Latencies of responses were used to measure stereotype activation. Slower response latencies for positive words and faster response latencies for negative words were taken as indicative of stereotype activation. This measurement technique is thought to be less reactive than other response measures of stereotyping, such as the Modern Racism Scale (MRS). Dovidio, Evans, and Tyler (1986) found that when White subjects were primed with Black or White primes, subjects responded faster to negative words when primed with a Black target than to a White target, indicating that the White subjects held negative stereotypes of Blacks and the stereotypes could be automatically activated. Bargh and Chartrand (1999) indicated that this technique has been used successfully in studies to measure automatic evaluations, judgments,

---

suggests that there are a number of contingent conditions on stereotype activation and that it is not unconditionally automatic (Devine & Monteith, 1999). However, Bargh (1999) argued that stereotypes are likely activated automatically and persist even if a person is motivated to engage in egalitarian behavior. For the purposes of this study, it is useful to distinguish between automatic and controlled processing, and it is evident in the discussion of results.

and behavior in the case of stereotype priming. This study experimentally tested the effects of the interactions between race of target suspects in TV news stories and how they are depicted. The effects examined in this study include the activation of stereotypes, indexed by latencies of target suspect evaluation, and perceptions of guilt.

HYPOTHESES

The automatic activation of stereotypes should be most pronounced, and therefore produce the quickest response latencies, to dehumanized Black suspects. For negative evaluative words, the following interaction is predicted:

> H1: Participants will respond quickest to dehumanized Black suspects than to nondehumanized Black suspects and White suspects, both dehumanized and nondehumanized.

This study also tested the effects of three of the dehumanizing depictions Entman (1992) reported. Therefore, each of these depiction types and their influence on response latencies is asked, both as main effects and as interactions with suspect race.

> RQ1: Which of the depiction types (mug, action, custody) most influences response latencies?

> RQ2: Do the individual depiction types interact with suspect race on response latencies?

Barnett (2003) reported that participants who saw a visually dehumanizing portrayal of a crime suspect in a TV news story rated the suspect as more guilty than when portrayed in a nondehumanizing way. Although the restraint depiction was confounded with showing suspects in prison jumpsuits, we can expect that dehumanized depictions encourage evaluations of guilt.

> H2: Respondents will rate dehumanized Black suspects more guilty than nondehumanized Black suspects and White suspects, both dehumanized and nondehumanized.

Story credibility is a concern for journalists (e.g., Meyer, 1988). If the way journalists depict subjects in their stories affects viewers' credibility perceptions, then journalists would need to know how. As a professional concern, story credibility is an important measure added to this study.

RQ2: How will race and depiction influence ratings of story credibility?

METHOD

Design and Independent Variables

The current study was a 2 (race of target: Black/White) × 2 (depiction: dehumanized/nondehumanized) × 3 (shot type: mug shot, action, custody) within-subject, partially crossed design. Race and depiction were message variables in that participants saw only one of two possible combinations. Half the participants saw the combination of White suspect/dehumanized and Black suspect/nondehumanized, whereas the other half saw the combination of White suspect/nondehumanized and Black suspect/dehumanized. The experiment was run in a research laboratory at the University of Missouri over a 6-week period. Students participated in the experiment one at a time, and the entire procedure lasted approximately 45 minutes.

Dependent Variables

There were two sets of dependent variables. The first was the response latency for positive and negative attributes. The attribute words were chosen by first asking 56 people to rate each of 72 words, on a 7-point scale, how relevant they thought each word was to a typical criminal that they were instructed to bring to mind (1 = *not at all relevant*, 7 = *very relevant*). The 72 words were chosen from three studies (Fujioka, 1999; Krueger, 1996; Levine, Carmines, & Sniderman, 1999). The 10 words with the highest means (i.e., relevant to a typical criminal) were chosen as the target words—that is, words that participants would think were good descriptors of the target suspects. The 10 words with the lowest means (i.e., not relevant to a typical criminal) were chosen as foils for the response latency task.

The second set of dependent variables was evaluations of the suspect (guilt) and the news stories (credibility), which participants recorded via pencil-and-paper questionnaire. Guilt was assessed by asking participants to respond on a 7-point scale how guilty they thought the suspect was. Credibility was measured by an index of three variables—fair, informative, balanced—each measured on a 7-point scale ($\alpha = .85$).

Participants

Forty-one graduate and undergraduate students from various majors at the University of Missouri were recruited to participate in the study. Participants were paid with a coupon for a free slice of pizza and a soft drink at a popular restaurant adjacent to the university.

Stimulus Materials

Thirty-six news stories were selected from a video archive of the Radio and Television News Directors Association's award submissions. Twelve stories represented all possible combinations of the experimental manipulations of race, depiction, and shot type, with three stories for each level of each independent variable ($N = 36$). Stories were edited and postproduced at a local TV station so that they would reflect one of the race by depiction by shot type categories.

Each story visually presented a suspect of a serious felony (rape, assault, murder, etc.). Six videotapes were edited so that six stories appeared on each. Each participant watched six stories, which represented 6 of the 12 possible combinations of the independent variables, with the constraint that each saw three stories with a Black target and three with a White target, three stories with dehumanized depictions and three with nondehumanized depictions. Also each participant saw all three possible shot types (mug, action, custody). The six videotapes represented six different story orders.

The response latency task took place on a Macintosh G3 computer. Each participant was primed with a still picture of the suspect in the story just seen. After the picture was presented, 20 words appeared individually on the computer screen and stayed on the screen until one of the buttons was pressed on the response box. The computer displayed the 20 words at random without replacement.

Procedures

The procedures for the experiment were modeled after Dovidio, Evans, and Tyler (1986), but involved some methodological changes. Dovidio et al. asked their participants to judge whether an adjective trait (e.g., *ambitious*) could ever be true of a category (e.g., White people) or must always be false, whereas we asked participants to decide whether the adjective was a good way to describe the suspect in the story. The task was developed so the stereotypic response to all crime suspect relevant (negative) person-descriptive adjectives ($N = 10$) following the target suspect prime was yes. Crime suspect irrelevant (positive) person-descriptive adjective words ($N = 10$) were included as foils so that participants had real decisions to make, enhancing the meaningfulness of the response latencies.

The response keys (yes/no) were rotated on the response box between participants to control for handedness. Participants were given a practice trial to acquaint themselves with the apparatus. First, a 30-second real estate description was presented on the TV set. Then the participant turned to the computer for the response latency task. After the researcher read the instructions to the participant, the task began. A still picture of the house that was the topic of the video presentation just seen appeared on the computer screen for 1,500 milliseconds (msec). Then a series of words appeared individually on the screen, some of which described the house depicted (e.g., *white, wood, traditional*) and some of which did not (e.g., *red, brick, contemporary*). Following the practice trial, participants were asked whether they understood the procedure. In addition to verbal instructions, additional instructions appeared on the computer screen to help guide the participant through the study.

After watching each news story, participants completed a brief questionnaire that contained the questions about perceived guilt and story credibility and then completed the response latency task, judging positive and negative words in response to the picture of the suspect in the story just watched. This continued until all six stories were seen and six latency tasks were completed.

Apparatus

The words to which participants responded were displayed and their responses were compiled by Psyscope (Cohen, MacWhinney, Flatt, & Provost, 1993), a psychological software program. A Macintosh G3 computer was used to display the suspect picture and the person description adjectives. Psyscope collected participants' responses, accurate to $+/- 1$ msec, and stored the data in a data file, which was later converted to SPSS for analysis. Participants registered their responses (yes/no) on a response box connected to the Macintosh G3.

RESULTS

Data Examination

Three participants were eliminated from the response latency analysis. One participant was "wrong" 90% of the time, meaning that he pressed the "no" button for the negative words and the "yes" button for the positive words. Another participant pressed the same button repeatedly regardless of the word that appeared on the screen, 119 out of 120 times. A third participant was eliminated because he simply pressed alternating buttons throughout the entire response latency task. Thus, the overall N for the latency analyses is 4,560 (38 participants × 120 responses).

For two evaluation-dependent variables, perceived guilt and credibility, one participant was eliminated because he did not answer the questions. Thus, the N for these analyses was 37.

Prior to conducting the primary analyses of interest in this study, distributions of the response latencies were examined. The response latency data distribution revealed the usual set of outliers, either extremely fast or extremely slow responses. These outlying responses typically indicate either anticipations (responses occurring prior to stimulus perception) or momentary inattention (or attention to something other than the task at hand). The solution was to recode response latencies to 300 msec for those latencies shorter than 300 msec or to 3,000 msec for those latencies longer than 3,000 msec (Greenwald, McGhee, & Schwartz, 1998). With this data-trimming procedure, 97.7% of the response latencies remained intact. Response latencies were then standardized, but are reported here in original units (msec) to facilitate interpretation.

A diagnostic was computed to test for the effect of trial on latencies. A significant finding for trial would suggest a systematic change in response speed over the course of the 20 person-descriptive adjectives across six stories. An analysis of variance (ANOVA) was computed across trials for all the latencies, but was not statistically significant ($F_{(119, 4440)} = 1.09$, $p =$ n.s.).

Another diagnostic was computed to test for the effect of word valence (positive/negative) on response latencies. A 2 (suspect race) × 2 (depiction) × 2 (valence) ANOVA was computed with response latency as the unit of analysis. There was no significant main effect for valence ($F_{(1, 4552)} = 1.92$, $p =$ n.s.), meaning that participants did not respond slower or faster for positive words than for negative words. Because there was no effect for valence, it was dropped from further analysis. The following analysis reports results only for the negative words, which were intended to evaluate stereotypic responses of crime suspects.

Tests of Hypotheses and Research Questions

If participants stereotyped Black male crime suspects based, in part, on their dehumanizing depiction, we would expect response latencies to be quicker for dehumanized depictions of Black suspects than for both White dehumanized and nondehumanized depictions and for Black non-dehumanized depictions. Further, subject race was included in the model, although there were only eight African-American participants. Cultural stereotyping would predict that participants would not vary in their responses based on their own race. Clearly, this is not a fair test of the cultural stereotyping theory given such a small sample of African-American participants, but the analytic model should account for any effect for participant race on latencies especially because we want to examine the effects of depiction type on responses and its interaction with suspect race. Therefore, a 2 (suspect race) × 2 (subject race) × 2 (depiction) ANOVA was computed for response latency to test H1. There were no significant main effects for suspect race ($F_{(1, 2272)} = 3.24, p =$ n.s.), subject race ($F_{(1, 2272)} = 0.90, p =$ n.s.), or depiction ($F_{(1, 2272)} = 0.98, p =$ n.s.). Because there was no effect of subject race on latencies, this factor was dropped from further analyses.

However, there was a significant interaction ($F_{(1, 2272)} = 65.08, p <$ .001, partial eta squared = .028) between suspect race and depiction, as shown in Fig. 11.1. The pattern of the interaction supports H1. Respondents were quickest to judge White suspects who were nondehumanized ($M = 994.56$) and slowest to judge Blacks who were nondehumanized ($M = 1127.65$). Most important, responses to dehumanized Black suspects ($M = 1027.13$) were quicker than responses to nondehumanized Black suspects. The reverse was true for White suspects. This suggests that the combination of dehumanized depictions and Black suspects encouraged stereotyping. However, the same combination for White suspects did not.

To address both RQ1 and RQ2, and to further investigate the relationship between suspect race and depiction type, the next set of analyses ex-

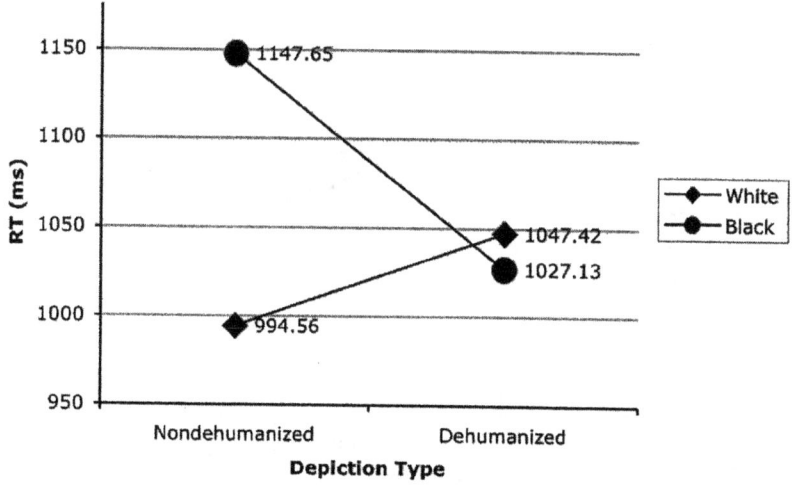

FIG. 11.1.   Response latency for suspect race and depiction.

amined each depiction type individually. A 2 (suspect race) × 2 (depiction) ANOVA was computed for only those stories in which a mug shot was used. As with the depiction type analysis earlier, Fig. 11.2 shows the significant interaction between suspect race and mug shot ($F_{(1, 756)} = 8.51$, $p < .01$; partial eta squared = .011), such that when Black suspects were shown in mug shots without their name (dehumanized), response latencies were quicker ($M = 1064.38$) than when they were shown with their name ($M = 1157.25$). However, the reverse was the case for White suspects. Respondents were quicker to respond when White suspects were named ($M = 914.46$) than when they were unnamed ($M = 1035.55$). Therefore, Black suspects encouraged quicker latencies when they were dehumanized in a mug shot, whereas White suspects encouraged quicker latencies when they were not dehumanized in a mug shot.

The action depiction type was the next to be examined. A similar analysis as before was conducted with similar results. As shown in Fig. 11.3, the interaction between suspect race and action was significant ($F_{(1, 756)} = 6.12$, $p < .05$, partial eta squared = .008), such that when Black suspects were shown in a freeze frame (dehumanized), response latencies were quicker ($M = 1070.07$) than when they were shown in full motion ($M = 1168.39$). Again the reverse was the case for White suspects. Respondents were quicker to respond when White suspects were shown in full motion ($M = 979.58$) than when they were shown in freeze frame ($M = 1081.39$). As with the mug shot analysis, Black suspects elicited quicker

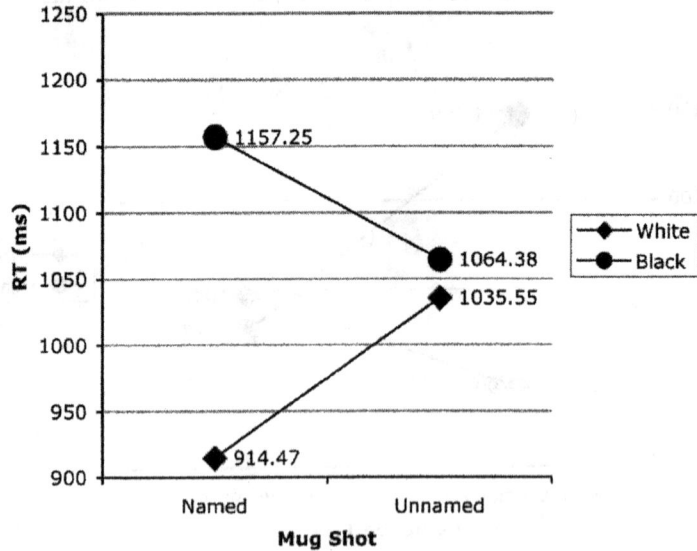

FIG. 11.2. Response latency for suspect race and mug shot depiction.

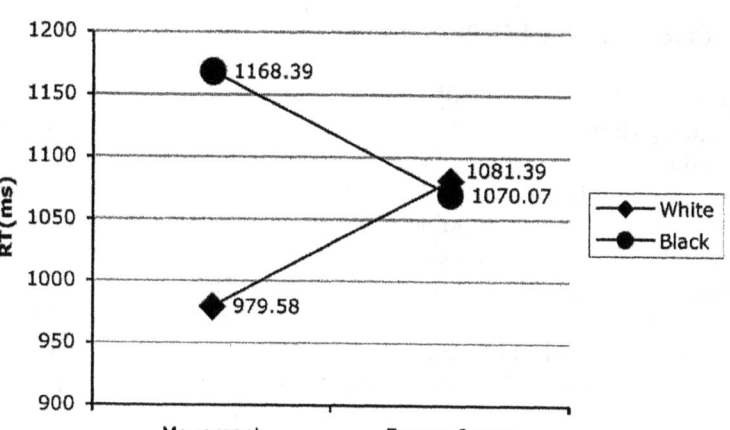

FIG. 11.3. Response latency for suspect race and action.

latencies when they were shown dehumanized, whereas White suspects elicited quicker latencies when they were shown nondehumanized.

A similar analysis was performed for custody (unrestrained vs. restrained). There was a significant main effect for custody ($F_{(1, 756)}$ = 8.87, $p < .01$, partial eta squared = .012) on response latencies. However, there was no significant interaction between suspect race and custody ($F_{(1, 756)}$ = 1.81, p = n.s.). The custody analysis shows a different pattern than the two other depiction types, but that difference was for White suspects only. In this case, both White and Black suspects elicited quicker response latencies when they were shown restrained by authorities (M = 982.00) than when they were not (M = 1102.02).

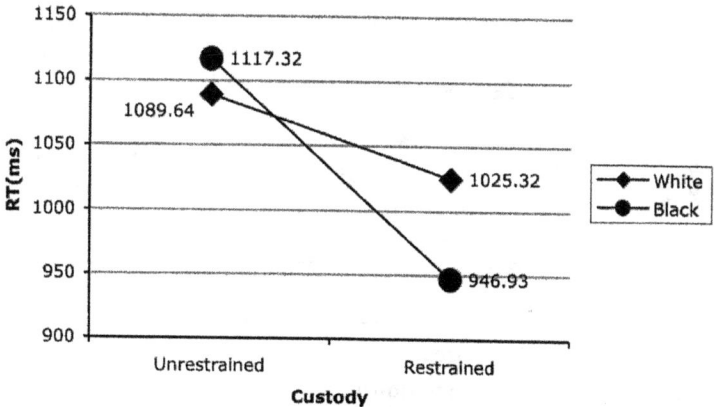

FIG. 11.4. Response latency for suspect race and custody.

Results for Perceived Guilt and Credibility

H2 predicted that respondents would rate dehumanized Black suspects more guilty than nondehumanized Black and White suspects, both dehumanized and nondehumanized. To test for the effect of suspect race and depiction on guilty ratings, a 2 × 2 mixed ANOVA was computed, with suspect race as the within-subjects factor and a message variable (which represented the combination of suspect race and depiction type) as the between-subjects factor. Only suspect race affected guilty ratings ($F_{(1, 35)}$ = 9.11, $p < .01$, partial eta squared = .206). H2 predicted that Black suspects would be rated as more guilty than White suspects, but the participants in this study rated the White suspects as more guilty than the Black suspects (M_{white} = 5.78, M_{black} = 5.32). Neither the main effect for depiction ($F_{(1, 35)}$ = 2.73, p = n.s.) nor the interaction between suspect race and depiction ($F_{(1, 35)}$ = 0.12, p = n.s.) was significant.

The final analysis tests RQ2—whether suspect race and depiction influenced participants' ratings of story credibility. Similar to the prior analysis for guilty ratings, story credibility was tested with a 2 × 2 mixed ANOVA, with suspect race as the within-subjects factor and the message variable as the between-subjects factor. Figure 11.5 shows these results.

The interaction between depiction and suspect race approached significance ($F_{(1, 35)}$ = 3.79, p = .059). When the suspects were depicted in dehumanizing ways, participants did not differentiate story credibility between nondehumanized and dehumanized depictions ($M_{nondehumanized}$ = 4.00, $M_{dehumanized}$ = 4.04). Yet when the race of the suspect was included, Black nondehumanized stories were rated less credible (M = 3.65) than the Black dehumanized stories, and the White nondehumanized stories

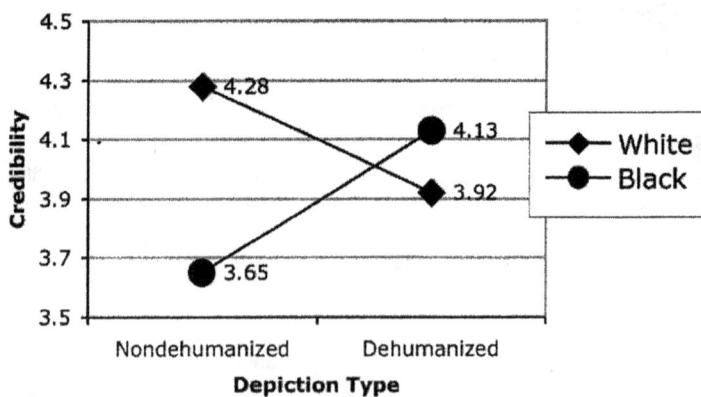

FIG. 11.5. Credibility ratings for suspect race and depiction.

were rated the most credible ($M = 4.25$). The main effect for race was not significant ($F_{(1, 35)} = 2.72$, p = n.s.).

DISCUSSION

The purpose of this study was to test the effects of Entman's (1992) findings that dehumanizing portrayals of Black crime suspects affect the way viewers perceive them. For the most part, the findings in this study corroborate Entman's predictions. Participants in this study negatively evaluated Black suspects quicker when they were shown in dehumanizing ways than when they were shown in nondehumanizing ways. This pattern held for all three depiction types tested in this study: mug shot, action, and custody. Faced with a Black male suspected of a serious crime in a TV news story, participants were quicker to evaluate him when he was shown in a dehumanizing way—unnamed mug shot, freeze frame, or restrained by authorities. These results suggest that the dehumanizing depiction encouraged participants to rely more on cultural stereotypes when making target evaluations than the nondehumanizing depictions. Yet when the suspect was White, participants were quicker to negatively evaluate him when he was shown in a nondehumanizing way for mug and action depictions. The interaction between depiction type and race of the suspect promoted stereotypical evaluations when the suspect was Black in all dehumanizing depictions.

The interaction effect between race and depiction type was not observed when the suspect was shown either restrained or unrestrained by authorities. However, the pattern for Black suspects was the same as for the other depiction types. When any suspect (Black or White) was shown restrained by authorities, participants were quicker to negatively evaluate him.

The pattern for perceptions of guilt did not conform to the stereotyping expectations. Prior literature suggests that Black suspects shown in a dehumanizing way would be perceived as more guilty than when they are shown in a nondehumanizing way (Barnett, 2003). In this study, depiction type had no effect on guilt perceptions. Further, participants rated White suspects as more guilty than Black suspects. There are two possible explanations for this finding. The first is that the participants were aware of the race manipulation and, to respond in a socially desirable way, decided to compensate for any possible bias they might report by overreporting guilt for White suspects. After the study, participants were asked what they thought the study was about. All of them reported they thought the study was about how the race of a crime suspect in TV news affected their evaluations of the suspect. No one detected the depiction (mug, action, custody), nor did anyone detect the depiction types (dehumanizing, nondehumanizing). Another possibility is that the White suspects shown in these stories were suspected of more violent crimes than the Black suspects. An analysis of the distributions of crimes between races suggests this explanation is less likely. There were 18 stories selected for this study. Nine were stories where the suspect was suspected of a single murder (4 White, 5 Black). Five stories detailed suspects of multiple murders (3 White, 2 Black). Two stories dealt with assault (1 White, 1 Black). There was one story about rape (White) and one about illegal drug and weapon possession (Black). On its surface, it appears that the nature of the crime was distributed evenly across race.

Another finding that did not square with prior literature was that, on average, participants were quicker to evaluate Whites than Blacks. Nearly all previous studies indicate that participants would be quicker to judge Black suspects in the context of crime. It is possible that participants slowed their judgments to Black suspects (albeit an imperceptible average of 60 msec) to appear less prejudiced. An examination of the error rates of responses (responding "yes" to positive words and "no" to negative words) supports this notion. If participants were not trying to differentially give socially desirable responses, one would predict the error rates to be the same regardless of the suspect race. However, this was not the case. For negative words, respondents were more likely to say "no" for Black suspects (30.6%) than they were for White suspects (17.8%; $\chi^2(1) = 51.72, p < .001$). A similar pattern was found for positive words, although not to the same extent. For positive words, respondents were more likely to say "yes" for Black suspects (8.2%) than they were for White suspects (4.3%; $\chi^2(1) = 14.54, p < .001$). This suggests that participants were monitoring their responses to race, but it says nothing about participants monitoring their responses to depiction types.

Story credibility evaluations also reflected the interaction between race and depiction. The least credible stories were the nondehumanized Black stories, whereas the most credible were the nondehumanized White stories.

Dehumanizing depictions tended to equate the story credibility across races, but nondehumanizing stories exacerbated the difference. Showing a Black suspect in a nondehumanized way was rated less credible than showing a Black suspect in a dehumanized way. For Whites, the pattern was reversed: Showing a White suspect in a nondehumanized way was rated more credible than showing a White suspect in a dehumanized way. This suggests an indirect effect of the interaction between race and depiction. Evaluative differences applied not just to the target suspects, but extended to perceptions about the stories.

This study examined only three depictions—mug, action, custody—and only one style of news. Certainly, other types of news stories—political, economic, social—can be examined using the methods described in this and other studies. Future research should examine the effects of race/depiction combinations on other kinds of news stories. Perhaps this research could contribute to the development of a typology of news story effects based on the interaction between race and the various ways that TV journalists depict the subjects of their stories.

Additional research should focus on African-American audience responses to dehumanizing depictions. The automatic activation of cultural stereotypes suggests that audiences would respond in a similar fashion as the participants in this study, to the extent that the audience members had established knowledge of the cultural stereotypes and the extent to which those stereotypes are automatically activated.

Overall, the response latency findings here suggest that the dehumanizing depictions detected by Entman (1992) produced more stereotypic responses from participants when the suspect was Black. The symbolism conveyed by such pictures is notable, Entman argued, rather than the frequency of restrained Blacks in the real world.

> . . . even if the explanation for any racial differences is that blacks and whites tend to commit different types of newsworthy crimes, the most salient point for public opinion is that the media convey a divergent pattern of racial images. (Entman, 1992, p. 349)

Journalists may suggest that they have little control over certain depiction styles—for example, whether to show the suspect restrained by authorities. If one assumes that TV journalists have some level of control over the content of their pictures, even whether to show a suspect in handcuffs and grasped by authorities, the findings reported here should be at least part of the newsgathering and editing process. Journalists may find it efficient to videotape the "perp walk," in which a criminal suspect is paraded in front of video camera, rather than to obtain other, less antagonizing supporting video materials. Yet given that TV news has been found to rely more on such depictions for Black suspects than for Whites, and given that such depictions tend to encourage viewers to stereotype Blacks, it seems incumbent on TV news professionals to consider the possible effects of these depictions.

Conversely, story credibility aligned with stereotypic portrayals presents a dilemma for journalists. The findings here suggest that story credibility is enhanced with stereotypic images, yet opting for less stereotypic images decreases it. Perhaps journalists can view their role, in part, as deconditioning cultural stereotypes available in media by presenting less inflammatory images in their newscasts, even at the risk of losing credibility.

REFERENCES

Bargh, J. A. (1999). The cognitive monster: The case against the controllability of automatic stereotype effects. In S. Chaiken & Y. Trope (Eds.), *Dual-process theories in social psychology* (pp. 361–382). New York: Guilford.

Bargh, J. A., & Chartrand, T. L. (1999). The unbearable automaticity of being. *American Psychologist, 54*(7), 462–479.

Barnett, B. (2003). Guilty and threatening: Visual bias in television news crime stories. *Journalism & Communication Monographs, 5*(3), 105–155.

Brigham, J. C. (1972). Racial stereotypes: Measurement variables and the stereotype-attitude relationship. *Journal of Applied Social Psychology, 2*, 63–76.

Campbell, C. (1995). *Race, myth and the news.* Thousand Oaks, CA: Sage.

Cohen, J. D., MacWhinney, B., Flatt, M., & Provost, J. (1993). PsyScope: A new graphic interactive environment for designing psychology experiments. *Behavioral Research Methods, Instruments & Computers, 25*(2), 257–271.

Devine, P. G. (1989). Stereotypes and prejudice: Their automatic and controlled components. *Journal of Personality and Social Psychology, 56*, 5–18.

Devine, P. G., & Monteith, M. J. (1999). Automaticity and control in stereotyping. In S. Chaiken & Y. Trope (Eds.), *Dual-process theories in social psychology* (pp. 339–360). New York: Guilford.

Devine, P. G., Monteith, M. J., Zuwerink, J. R., & Elliot, A. J. (1991). Prejudice with and without compunction. *Journal of Personality and Social Psychology, 60*, 817–830.

Domke, D., McCoy, K., & Torres, M. (1999). News media, racial perceptions and political cognition. *Communication Research, 26*, 570–607.

Dovidio, J. F., Evans, N., & Tyler, R. B. (1986). Racial stereotypes: The contents of their cognitive representations. *Journal of Experimental Social Psychology, 22*, 22–37.

Ehrlich, H. J. (1973). *The social psychology of prejudice.* New York: Wiley.

Entman, R. M. (1990). Modern racism and the images of blacks in local television news. *Critical Studies in Mass Communication, 7*, 332–345.

Entman, R. M. (1992). Blacks in the news: Television, modern racism, and cultural change. *Journalism Quarterly, 69*, 341–361.

Entman, R. M. (1994a). African Americans according to TV news. *Media Studies Journal, 8*, 28–38.

Entman, R. M. (1994b). Representation and reality in the portrayal of blacks on network television news. *Journalism Quarterly, 71*, 509–520.

Entman, R. M., Langford, R. H., Burns-Melican, D., Munoz, I., Boayue, S., Croce, C., Raman, A., Kenner, B., & Merrit, C. (1998). *Mass media and reconciliation.* Cambridge: John F. Kennedy School of Government.

Fazio, R. H., Jackson, J. R., Dunton, B. C., & Williams, C. J. (1995). Variability in automatic activation as an unobstrusive measure of racial attitudes: A bona fide pipeline? *Journal of Personality and Social Psychology, 69*, 1013–1027.

Fujioka, Y. (1999). Television portrayals and African-American stereotypes: Examination of television effects when direct contact is lacking. *Journalism & Mass Communication Quarterly, 76*(1), 52–75.

Gandy, O. H. (1994). From bad to worse: The media's framing of race and risk. *Media Studies Journal, 8*, 39–48.

Gandy, O. H., & Baron, J. (1998). Inequality: It's all in the way you look at it. *Communication Research, 25*, 505–527.

Gilens, M. (1996). Race and poverty in America: Public perceptions and the American news media. *Public Opinion Quarterly, 60,* 515–541.

Gilliam, F. D., Jr., & Iyengar, S. (2000). Prime suspects: The influence of local television news on the viewing public. *American Journal of Political Science, 44*(3), 560–573.

Gilliam, F. D., Jr., Iyengar, S., Simon, A., & Wright, O. (1996). Crime in black and white: The violent, scary world of local news. *Harvard International Journal of Press/Politics, 1*(3), 6–23.

Greenberg, B. S., & Brand, J. E. (1994). Minorities and the mass media: 1970s to 1990s. In J. Bryant & D. Zillmann (Eds.), *Media effects: Advances in theory and research* (pp. 273–314). Hillsdale, NJ: Lawrence Erlbaum Associates.

Greenwald, A. G., McGhee, D. E., & Schwartz, J. L. K. (1998). Measuring individual differences in implicit cognition: The implicit association test. *Journal of Personality and Social Psychology, 74*(6), 1464–1480.

Hurwitz, J., & Peffley, M. (1997). Public perceptions of crime and race: The role of racial stereotypes. *American Journal of Political Science, 41,* 375–401.

Iyengar, S. (1991). *Is anyone responsible?* Chicago: University of Chicago Press.

Katz, P. A. (1976). The acquisition of racial attitudes in children. In P. A. Katz (Ed.), *Toward the elimination of racism* (pp. 125–154). New York: Pergamon.

Krueger, J. (1996). Personal beliefs and cultural stereotypes about racial characteristics. *Journal of Personality & Social Psychology, 71*(3), 536–548.

Levine, J., Carmines, E. G., & Sniderman, P. M. (1999). The empirical dimensionality of racial stereotypes. *Public Opinion Quarterly, 63,* 371–384.

Linville, P. W. (1982). The complexity-extremity effect and age-based stereotyping. *Journal of Personality and Social Psychology, 42,* 193–211.

Linville, P. W., & Fischer, G. W. (1993). Exemplar and abstraction models of perceived group variability and stereotypicality. *Social Cognition, 11,* 92–125.

Linville, P. W., & Fischer, G. W. (1998). Group variability and covariation: Effects on intergroup judgment and behavior. In C. Sedikides, J. Schopler, & C. A. Insko (Eds.), *Intergroup cognition and intergroup behavior.* Mahwah, NJ: Lawrence Erlbaum Associates.

Meyer, P. (1988). Defining and measuring credibility of newspapers: Developing an index. *Journalism Quarterly, 65*(3), 567–588.

Oliver, M. B. (1999). Caucasian viewers' memory of black and white criminal suspects in the news. *Journal of Communication, 49*(3), 46–60.

Peffley, M., Shields, T., & Williams, B. (1996). The intersection of race and crime in television news stories: An experimental study. *Political Communication, 13,* 309–327.

Roberts, C. (1970). The portrayal of blacks on network television. *Journal of Broadcasting, 15*(1), 45–51.

Roberts, C. (1975). The presentation of blacks in television network newscasts. *Journalism Quarterly, 52*(1), 50–55.

Romer, D., Jamieson, K. H., & de Coteau, J. J. (1998). The treatment of persons of color in local television news—Ethnic blame discourse or realistic group conflict? *Communication Research, 25,* 286–305.

Schneider, W., & Shiffrin, R. M. (1977). Controlled and automatic human information processing: I. Detection, search, and attention. *Psychological Review, 84,* 1–66.

Thompson, S. C., Kohles, J. C., Otsuki, T. A., & Kent, D. R. (1997). Perceptions of attitudinal similarity in ethnic groups in the US: Ingroup and outgroup homogeneity effects. *European Journal of Social Psychology, 27*(2), 209–220.

U.S. Commission on Civil Rights. (1977, August). *Window dressing on the set: Women and minorities in television.* Washington, DC: Government Printing Office.

Wilson, C. C., II, & Gutierrez, F. (1985). *Minorities and media.* Newbury Park, CA: Sage.

Introductory Comments to Chapter 12

Robert Drechsel[1]
University of Wisconsin–Madison

Tom Grimes
Kansas State University

The First Amendment notwithstanding, communication is the basis for a great deal of legal liability. Miscommunication, false communication, and failure to communicate all may cause problems that end up in litigation. Yet the very law that permits liability and establishes its conditions is often based on assumptions about communication and its impact, which have long been taken for granted although they could be tested.

The possibility of testing such assumptions—combined with the inherent multidisciplinary nature of the field of mass communication—is precisely what led to the following study. One of the authors, Drechsel, has long been intrigued by the law of torts, of which libel is a part. He was aware of libel cases in which a central question was whether plaintiffs had been defamed by communication, which could be argued to have linked them to defamatory information although it did not explicitly say anything bad about them.

The other author, Grimes, became intrigued by the TV messages that viewers take from a newscast, which are often not the messages their producers intended to convey. Grimes' 15 years as a TV news director,

[1]"Word-Picture Juxtaposition, Schemata, and Defamation in Television News" originally appeared, without the authors' introduction, in *Journalism & Mass Communication Quarterly* (1996), *73*, 169–190. In the original, the authors noted that they "contributed equally to writing this article. The authors wish to acknowledge the assistance of Professor Jeanne Meadowcroft and Sarah Johnson, an outstanding undergraduate student at the University of Wisconsin."

reporter, and news anchor yielded multiple instances in which stories that were intended by their producers to convey one particular message ended up conveying to viewers something entirely different.

One such example is the juxtaposition of voice and video, each innocuous in itself, but which occasionally combine to create libel. Both Drechsel and Grimes drew from case law to re-create the circumstances that produced the libel. In so doing, it was their aim to understand why defamation would result from the way the video and audio relate to one another. The re-created voice-over discussed a neighborhood prostitution problem while video showed a clearly identifiable woman who, in fact, had nothing to do with prostitution. Although not explicitly linked to prostitution by either the voice or video, should the woman be able to bring a libel action? Would the voice-video juxtaposition actually communicate to viewers that the woman is a prostitute? What variables might play a role in whether viewers would take such meaning from the broadcast?

The answers to such questions can be of both theoretical and practical interest. Thus began a conversation between the two authors—one (Drechsel) whose interests came from the legal perspective and the other (Grimes) whose interests were in the psychological processes that might play a role in the construction of meaning by viewers of the allegedly defamatory broadcast. Further discussion began to tease out the relevance of schema theory, which in turn suggested race and gender as possible variables worth close examination in the creation of meaning. In the prostitution scenario, for example, would viewers be more likely to conclude that the plaintiff is a prostitute if her race coincides with viewer racial schemata that suggest as much?

Such questions evolved into testable hypotheses and an experimental design. Meanwhile, stimulated by another actual libel case, the authors began to discuss the possible relevance of gender as well as racial schemata. The result was a second experiment in which Drechsel and Grimes attempted to evoke subjects' gender schemata in the context of an allegedly libelous story about medical malpractice. More specifically, they wondered whether a doctor would be more or less likely to be linked with malpractice in viewers' minds depending on the doctor's gender.

The results of the experiments—which did find that race and gender schemata appear to make a significant difference—continue to intrigue the authors. Preliminary indications are that there are other legal contexts involving communication in which race, gender, or other variables evoking reader or viewer schemata might have a significant impact on the strength or validity of a legal argument because of their role in creating meaning (Gibbons, Vogl, & Grimes, 2003; Gibbons, Traxel, Vogl, & Grimes, 2002). If this is the case, do judicial decisions track with what we learn about schemata and creation of meaning? Should they? If we can establish that schema are at work in other legal contexts, what more can be done to mitigate their impact? The authors hope others will explore these and other questions, and hope to do so in the future themselves.

REFERENCES

Gibbons, J., Vogl, R., & Grimes, T. (2003). Source confusion for characters in a TV news story. *Journal of Broadcasting & Electronic Media, 47,* 99–112.

Gibbons, J. A., Traxel, N. M., Vogl, R. J., & Grimes, T. (2002). The effects of story affect and story role on participants' memory for character gender in news stories. *The International Journal of Cognitive Technology, 7,* 23–32.

Word-Picture Juxtaposition, Schemata, and Defamation in Television News

Tom Grimes
Robert Drechsel

Defamation allegedly caused by misleading word-picture combinations has frequently led to libel actions, but the communication assumptions underlying such actions have rarely been examined empirically. Television news, with its combination of voice-over and video, is particularly vulnerable to claims that juxtaposition has created unintended defamatory meaning. This study finds that viewers' gender and race schemata can be used to help determine whether would-be libel plaintiffs can plausibly claim to have been identified and harmed by audio-video juxtaposition, even though nothing defamatory may have been communicated literally.

Potential misunderstanding resulting from the juxtaposition of pictures and words has often bred libel litigation. Most commonly, a photograph, not defamatory in itself, connects those it portrays with defamatory references contained in accompanying text.[1] In television news, the accompanying "text" generally takes the form of a reporter's voice-over. Thus, for example, libel suits have arisen where juxtaposition of video and voice-over has allegedly linked passers-by with venereal disease, an innocent neighborhood resident with prostitution, a property owner with slum-like conditions, an airline with CIA activity, a dairy store with price-fixing, and innocent third parties with accused criminals or criminal activity.[2]

The audio-visual juxtaposition problem therefore directly involves one of the essential requirements of any libel suit—that the alleged libel or distortion be "of and concerning" the plaintiff.[3] What matters is who the recipients of a message may reasonably believe was the subject of the defamation, regardless of the communicator's intent.[4]

Further compounding the issue is the fact that, in a television context where the aural and visual are combined, the message news story viewers actually recall can differ significantly from what was literally communicated.[5] Thus, there would appear to be heightened risk of unintentionally creating defamatory meaning in television news, regardless of journalists' benign intentions.

Judges' and juries' determination of whether particular word-picture juxtapositions create misunderstanding sufficient to defame people has tended to be more a judgment based on common sense, plausibility, and anecdotal testimony than on systematic evidence. As Cohen and Gleason have noted, scholarly research has only recently begun to apply communication theory to libel law.[6]

Just how plausible are plaintiffs' claims that the juxtaposition of otherwise harmless aural and visual messages defame them? By what cognitive process might such defamation be created? This experimental study is a first effort to wrestle with such questions. Its goal is to submit libel plaintiffs' assumptions about communication to empirical test.

To do so, the study draws on two actual libel cases involving broadcast news, and applies what would appear to be a particularly relevant branch of communication theory—schema theory—in an effort to assess the plausibility of plaintiffs' claims. The study invokes schemata regarding race and gender, and examines their impact on the creation of false, defamatory meaning "of and concerning" libel plaintiffs.

THEORY AND HYPOTHESES

Schema theory posits that individuals' perceptions are guided, in part, by cognitive structures—called schemata—that help individuals construct meaning out of the otherwise overwhelming number of external stimuli to which they are exposed. When schemata are invoked, they help classify, label, and identify incoming information. Much of this classification is based on one's previous experience and expectations.[7] The more unclear or ambiguous the message, the greater the role recipients' schemata may play in giving meaning to the message.[8]

Schema theory finds some of its strongest support in the context of race and gender expectations. In more than a dozen experiments, race and gender schemata have been hypothesized and supported empirically.[9] As Levy and Carter have observed, gender typing is attributable to "readiness on the part of individuals to encode and organize information along the lines of what is considered appropriate or typical for males and females."[10] Apparently, gender schemata form at an early age. For example, Liben and Signorella showed children photographs depicting people performing various jobs, some of which were consistent with traditional gender roles—a woman as a secretary, for example—and some of which were not. Later, the children more accurately recalled the photos depicting people in traditional gender roles than in nontraditional roles.[11]

Similarly, Boon and Davies showed subjects some photos depicting blacks as victims of a robbery with a white perpetrator and other photos with whites as victims. They used race schemata to explain why subjects incorrectly remembered the blacks as perpetrators significantly more often than as victims.[12] Likewise, a classic study by Allport and Postman showed that when a black person is portrayed as the victim of a crime perpetrated by a white person, the black person is most often remembered as the perpetrator instead of as the victim, particularly by whites.[13]

Misattributions consistent with gender and race schemata have led to libel litigation. For example, a Chicago gynecologist, Dr. Victoria Maclin, sued WMAQ television for libel after the station broadcast a story about a newly-filed medical negligence suit and used file footage showing her performing a gynecological procedure. The negligence suit, however, did not involve Dr. Maclin. Rather, it had been brought against a hospital where personnel allegedly treated a patient with a cotton swab that had previously been used on a patient with AIDS. Maclin's suit alleged that the voice-video juxtaposition essentially identified her as a physician guilty of malpractice.[14]

Similarly, a Detroit resident, Ruby Clark, sued ABC News alleging that a story on prostitution left viewers with the false impression that she was a prostitute rather than an innocent resident of a neighborhood that had become the locus of serious prostitution problems. She argued—and an appellate court agreed—that video showing her walking down the street of her neighborhood immediately after prostitutes were mentioned in voice-over could have caused viewers to think she was a prostitute, even though the audio track accompanying the video identified her as a neighborhood resident.[15]

Situations such as those in the Maclin and Clark cases suggest an obvious application of race and gender schema theory. Maclin's claim rests in part on an assumption that viewers would mistake her for a physician who has been accused of malpractice. But gender schemata would seem to work against her claim, given that women are not generally expected to be physicians. Clark's legal argument that she would be mistaken for a prostitute seems more plausible given race schemata that African-Americans are more likely to be criminals than victims.

To test this type of reasoning, two experiments were constructed with stimulus material patterned roughly after the Maclin and Clark scenarios. We used actors, shot the video, and employed a professional narrator to do the reporter's voice-over, then placed the stories in a realistic newscast format.

Since gender schemata affect the way viewers might be expected to perceive women's occupations, we created several versions of a fictional news story about an androgynously-named "Dr. Pat Jones." The voice-over identified Jones as a plastic surgeon who has been sued for malpractice. The video showed Dr. Jones examining patient records while the reporter described the malpractice charges. Next, the video showed another physician, a colleague of Dr. Jones, examining patient records while the narrator reported that this colleague had criticized Dr Jones' treatment of patients. In one version of our story, Dr. Jones was a male and the colleague was a female; in a second, Dr. Jones was a female and the colleague was male. Nothing else was changed.

As noted above, the gender schematic expectation is that women are unlikely to be highly trained professionals. Therefore, we expected that the innocent colleague would more often be taken for an alleged malpractitioner when Dr. Jones was a woman and the colleague was a man, because viewers will expect an androgynously named plastic surgeon to be a man. Thus:

> HI: When Dr. Pat Jones is portrayed as a woman, viewers are more likely to confuse the colleague with the malpractitioner than when Dr. Jones is portrayed as a man.

We also created a story about prostitution becoming a serious problem in a particular neighborhood. The video at one point showed an individual who was clearly identified by voice-over as a prostitute. Then the video showed another woman, who lived in the neighborhood, walking down a street while the narrator explained that neighborhood residents were becoming extremely frustrated. In one version of the story, the prostitute was black and the resident white; in the other version the prostitute was white and the resident black. The stories were identical in every other respect.

Here one would predict race schemata to lead viewers to expect blacks to be perpetrators, not victims, of crime, and therefore we anticipated that:

> H2: When the neighborhood resident is portrayed as black, viewers are more likely to confuse her with the prostitute than when the neighborhood resident is portrayed as white.

The literature on schema theory also indicates that time enhances schemata's effect.[16] Schema-inconsistent material is less accurately recalled as time passes. Therefore, as television viewers forget the particulars of the story, they should increasingly rely on schemata to reconstruct the story line. We would thus expect that:

H3: A 72-hour delay between viewing and testing of viewers' recall will increase the magnitude of the effect described in hypotheses 1 and 2.

Finally, defamation suits are based not only on mistaken identification, but also on the reputational harm the plaintiff claims to have suffered as a result. General principles of libel law hold that, to be considered legally defamatory, a communication must tend to prejudice a person "in the eyes of a substantial and respectable minority" of the community.[17] If viewers share widely held schemata related to race and gender—and those expectations lead them to misunderstand what they have seen and heard in a news story—an innocent bystander may be falsely defamed in the minds of a "substantial and respectable minority of the community."

Knowing a viewer's attitude toward a character portrayed in a TV news story can help predict that viewer's future evaluations of the credibility and trustworthiness of the character.[18] That is precisely the concern of the typical libel plaintiff—that the plaintiff's false, defamatory portrayal in a news story will leave him or her with a besmirched reputation. We expect viewers' confusion of blameless and blameworthy individuals to be greatest in the schema-inconsistent stories where Dr. Jones is a woman and the neighborhood resident is black. Therefore, we predict:

H4: Subjects will more negatively evaluate the critical colleague and neighborhood resident when they appear in schema-inconsistent stories than when they appear in schema-consistent stories.

METHOD

To test these hypotheses, we conducted a pretest and two experiments. Directly asking questions to ascertain subjects' gender and race schemata presented a substantial risk of unmasking our purpose. Therefore, we showed a pretest group of 30 undergraduate white males and females[19] still frames of the actors we used in the malpractice and prostitution stories. The frames were taken directly from the stimulus materials. The subjects were asked to identify a nurse, a physician, a resident of a neighborhood, and a prostitute. Without exception, they identified our actors as the schema literature predicts—men as physicians, women as nurses, blacks as criminals, whites as victims.[20] These results made us reasonably confident that the gender and race schemata we intended to invoke would be invoked.

For the first experiment, 100 undergraduates were recruited from an introduction to mass communication course and given extra course credit for participating. All subjects were white and native to the United States. No African-American students were available. Forty-eight subjects were male and 52 were female. Once subjects were recruited, we employed a 2 (Time of Test) × 2 (Version of Story) factorial design.

Four experimental stories—two versions of the malpractice story and two versions of the prostitution story—were prepared. One version was always "schema-consistent"—depicting Dr. Pat Jones in the malpractice story as a man, or the neighborhood resident in the prostitution story as white. The other version was "schema-inconsistent"—depicting Dr. Jones as a woman, or the neighborhood resident as black. The experimental stories were produced with broadcast-grade video equipment. Camera angles, lighting, the visual background, and the clothing of actors were controlled in order to guarantee that the only variation between versions was in either gender or race. The distractor stories were taken from a genuine newscast.

Four versions of a newscast were thus created. Each consisted of one version of the malpractice story, one version of the prostitution story, and the two distractor stories. The newscasts themselves were prepared by the ABC News affiliate in a midwestern city. They began with the station's usual opening theme, introduction of the news anchor, the anchor's "good evening," and then the four stories presented in varying order. Over the four newscasts, each experimental story appeared in all possible positions within the four-story array. Experimental stories were always separated by a distractor story.

Subjects were told they were participating in a TV newscast study and were going to be asked what they remembered seeing and hearing. They were shown the newscasts in groups ranging in size from 9 to 14. After viewing, half of the subjects remained for immediate testing, and the other half were dismissed, then recalled for testing 72 hours later.[21]

For the second experiment, 65 more undergraduates were recruited from an introduction to mass communication course and given extra credit. The procedure and variables were identical to those in the first experiment. However, this time we created two new versions of the prostitution and malpractice stories. In version one of the prostitution story, all actresses were black. In version one of the malpractice story, all actors were male. In version two, the prostitution story featured all white actresses, and the malpractice story featured all females. Thus the second experiment erased the gender and race differences among actresses and actors.

The data from these subjects were merged with the data from the subjects in Experiment 1 so that we could compare all possible versions of the stories.

In a free recall test, all subjects were asked to describe in detail as many of the physical characteristics they could recall for the prostitute, the neighborhood resident, Dr.Pat Jones, and Dr. Jones' critical colleague. The expectation was that subjects might mention race or gender in their descriptions.[22]

The responses were analyzed by 3 coders who gave subjects a 1 for each answer in which race or gender was accurately recalled for the prostitute, the resident, Dr.Pat Jones, and the critical colleague. A 0 was assigned for incorrect recall of gender or race. Therefore, any given subject's total score could vary from 0 to 4.[23]

In a cued recall test, all subjects were given two multiple-choice questions about Dr. Pat Jones, the critical colleague, the prostitute, and the neighborhood resident. One question referred to the race of the characters in the prostitution story, the other to the gender of the characters in the malpractice story. The respondent had to select the answer that correctly described the actors with respect to gender or race. A fifth choice, "don't know," was also provided. Subjects received a score of 1 for each correct answer and a 0 for each answer in which they made a mistake as hypothesized.[24]

Finally, subjects were shown still frames of each of the actors who appeared in the prostitution and malpractice stories. The attitudinal measurement instrument consisted of a Likert scale on which subjects were asked to rate each person in the still frames on 29 paired adjectival opposites. The paired adjectives were placed at opposite ends of a 10-point scale. A score toward 1 meant that a subject viewed the person in the still frame more favorably. A score toward 10 meant that a subject viewed the person in the still frame more unfavorably.

Factor analysis revealed that the prostitution and malpractice stories not only shared one factor, but also the same six items in that factor. This "reputational" factor consisted of adjectival opposites of like/dislike, worthy/unworthy, high/low, praiseworthy/worth condemning, nice/vicious, and admire /detest. It accounted for half the variance in both stories, and thus we used it as an index of subjects' attitudes toward the actors in both the prostitution and malpractice stories.[25]

RESULTS

The first hypothesis predicted that when the alleged malpractitioner, Dr. Pat Jones, was a woman, viewers would be more likely to associate her male colleague with malpractice than when Dr. Pat Jones was a male. H2 predicted that when the neighborhood resident was black, viewers would be more likely to identify her as a prostitute than when the neighborhood resident was white. The cued recall data provided support for these hypotheses, but the free recall data did not.

When the cued recall data from the two stories were combined, subjects who viewed the schema-consistent versions—male Dr. Pat Jones/ white neighborhood resident—were significantly more likely to accurately recall the gender and race of our actors than subjects who saw the schema-inconsistent versions (F(l,91)=19.346, p<.01). Subjects who saw schema-consistent stories (mean=.887, n=48) got the race and gender designations correct more often than subjects who saw schema-inconsistent stories (mean=.613, n=47). Responses of male and female subjects did not differ.

When the stories were considered individually, the prostitution story yielded a significant difference in the predicted direction (t(42)=8.052, p<.01). Subjects who saw schema-consistent stories (mean=.999, n=25) correctly recalled the race and gender of the characters more often than subjects who saw schema-inconsistent stories (mean=.342, n=19). For the malpractice story, the means were in the hypothesized direction, but the difference was not significant at the .05-level. Male and female subjects did not differ.

One significant difference did emerge in the malpractice story when the free recall data were analyzed (F(l,37)=4.258, p<.05), but in precisely the opposite direction from what the hypothesis predicted. Women who viewed the schema-inconsistent version of the story were actually less likely to confuse the gender of the malpractitioner and the critical colleague (mean=.652, n=23) than female subjects who viewed the schema-consistent version (mean=.306, n=18). Only the female subjects—not the males—consistently and correctly distinguished the woman as the malpractitioner and the male as the critical colleague in the free recall test.

H3 predicted, in essence, that memories of schema-inconsistent stories would become more schema-consistent with the passage of time. The free recall data supported this hypothesis, but the cued recall data did not.

Subjects given the free recall test 72 hours after viewing remembered the race and gender of the actors less accurately than subjects who were tested immediately (F(l,75)=19.041, p<.01). When only the schema-inconsistent version was considered, subjects tested after seventy-two hours more often incorrectly recalled the male as the malpractitioner and the neighborhood resident as a prostitute (mean=.423, n=26) than subjects who were tested immediately after stimulus exposure (mean =.688, n=28) (p<.05). The responses of male and female subjects did not differ.

There was also a difference in free recall scores between subjects in the schema-consistent condition who were tested immediately and those who were tested seventy-two hours later ($F(1,35)=13.941$, p<.01). Subjects tested after seventy-two hours more often correctly recalled Jones as male and the neighborhood resident as a prostitute (mean=.824, n=18) than subjects who were tested immediately after stimulus exposure (mean=.423, *n=19*) (p<.01). This suggests that when a message is consistent with viewers' schemata, the passage of time actually reinforces viewers' memory of the schema-consistent events portrayed in the news story. But when those roles are not schema-consistent, the passage of time appears to alter memory so that the roles are "remembered" consistent with viewers' expectations.

H4 predicted that viewers would more negatively evaluate the critical colleague and neighborhood resident when they appeared in schema-inconsistent stories than when they appeared in schema-consistent stories.

As expected, there was a significant difference between the two story versions ($F(1,95)=18.563$, p<.01). Subjects in the schema-inconsistent versions (mean=4.221, n=48) liked both the black resident and the male colleague less than subjects in the schema-consistent versions (mean=3.229, n=51) where the resident was white and the alleged malpractitioner was a woman. Subjects who saw the schema-inconsistent version of the malpractice story liked the male colleague significantly less (mean=4.040, n=48) than subjects who saw the schema-consistent version of the story where the critical colleague was a woman (mean=3.031, n=51) ($F(1,95)=11.014$, p<.01). Likewise, subjects who saw the schema-inconsistent version of the prostitution story liked the black neighborhood resident significantly less (mean=4.408, n=48) than subjects who saw the schema-consistent version with a white resident (mean=3.458, n=51) ($F(1,95)=10.737$, p<.01).

Further, with the data from all subjects combined, there was a significant correlation between the affective ratings and the cued recall scores. More specifically, where the resident and critical colleague were confused with the prostitute and Dr. Pat Jones, their reputational ratings were more negative than when they were not confused ($r=-.246$, r-square=.06, p<.01, n=98).

Nevertheless, irrespective of the experimental manipulation, subjects may simply have liked the white female neighborhood resident and the female medical colleague better than the black neighborhood resident and male colleague. Or subjects might have formed their reputational judgments when they were tested, not when they actually viewed the stories.

To address these possibilities, the second experiment was conducted. The goal was to suppress the invocation of gender and race schemata by not permitting race and gender to vary. The results suggest that schemata do play a role in the reputational ratings in the malpractice scenario, but perhaps not in the prostitution scenario.

The male who played the critical colleague in the schema–inconsistent version was evaluated significantly less favorably (mean=4.331, n=28) than he was in the all male version (mean=3.220, n=28) (p<.04). But there was no corresponding difference among reputational evaluations in the prostitution story. Subjects' evaluation of the black actress who portrayed the neighborhood resident was essentially the same in both the schema–inconsistent version (mean=4.914, n=28) and the all black version (mean=4.208, n=27).

The data were examined further by comparing the reputational ratings subjects gave our all-black team of actresses with our all-white team of actresses. The white woman who played the neighborhood resident was evaluated more favorably (mean=3.333, n=55) than the black actress who played the neighborhood resident (mean=5.045, n=55) (F(3,106)=30.325, p<.01). Thus it is possible that subjects simply did not like the particular black actress who played the resident, or even that subjects generally disliked blacks.

DISCUSSION

Because the only elements that varied between story versions were the gender and race of the principal characters, differences in subjects' memories are consistent with the idea that viewer expectations—what we have called race and gender schemata—can influence how people remember news stories that are likely to have invoked those schemata. The results also offer a plausible explanation for how defamatory misunderstanding can result from picture-word juxtaposition.

Subjects' memory errors occur in a way that leads them to attribute negative characteristics to "innocent" people who appeared in the stories. Further, it appears that the passage of time can enhance the likelihood that gender and race schemata will shape viewers' recollection of what they saw and heard. Such findings are consistent with previous research on the existence and operation of gender and race schemata, and with schema theory generally.

But there are also seeming anomalies in the findings. Why, for example, were the results not consistent between the free recall and cued recall data, and can these inconsistencies be reconciled? Why did female subjects more accurately remember schema-inconsistent information in the malpractice story when given the free recall test? And why did subjects so consistently dislike the black neighborhood resident in the prostitution story?

Differences between free and cued recall may be related to the way subjects encode messages in long-term memory. Cued recall and recognition responses appear to bring with them memory for specifics not central to the overarching message, a process Smith and Graesser have called "data-driven processing."[26] Subjects tested immediately after viewing may not have responded as hypothesized on free recall measures because they did not regard race and gender data as central characteristics. Thus, they tended not to mention race and gender in their narratives.

The fact that the cued recall differences were not magnified by the passage of time may be attributable to the test itself. Perhaps in the immediate test condition, subjects were aided by the cues sufficiently to erase any difference that might be obtained between subjects in the delayed test condition.

If the free recall and cued recall results differed because subjects did not regard gender and race as sufficiently salient to encode into long-term memory, the potential for libelous misunderstanding might be partially mitigated. Many viewers might not clearly recall a damaging message, and harm to reputation might be minimized.

On the other hand, and perhaps more plausibly, viewers might be likely to erroneously recall a false, damaging message just when it can do the most harm. Suppose a viewer later requires plastic surgery and happens to be referred to the innocent colleague. The viewer/patient might then "remember" the malpractice story but misattribute the allegation to the innocent colleague, and thus refuse his services. In effect, the need for surgery might cue memory of the malpractice story and with it resurrect the error. And if, with the passage of time, more and more viewers erroneously identify a libelous message with an innocent party, obviously the potential for harm is multiplied. From the standpoint of both libel victims and the media, such a possibility emphasizes the importance of immediate, prominent, and absolutely clear corrections or clarifications.

The fact that more female than male subjects, when presented with a female version of Dr. Pat Jones, recalled Jones as being female actually may offer additional support for the notion that gender-based schemata were driving our subjects' memories for the malpractice story. At least this is the case if we assume that women are less likely than men to hold the "women-are-not-professionals" schema. However there is little specific support in the literature for such a generalization, and our own pretest indicated that gender schemata did not vary among males and females.

Racial schemata did appear to be a factor in misidentification of an innocent neighborhood resident with prostitution. But we are left with the disquieting possibility that our subjects' dislike for the black neighborhood resident in the prostitution story was a function not of schemata per se, but of prejudice and dislike for blacks in general. Of course, such prejudice itself might be viewed as a form of schemata. Unfortunately, we were unable to obtain a racially or ethnically diverse subject pool. More messages, of different kinds, using different racial and ethnic subject pools ought to be manipulated in further research.

Nevertheless, the overall findings suggest that in contexts where race and gender can play a role in audience members' construction of meaning, the conditions may be conducive to the creation of libel. In both experimental scenarios, nothing literally defamatory was communicated—nothing was said to explicitly link the innocent physician to malpractice or the neighborhood resident to prostitution while either of their images was on screen. Yet many of our subjects made just such linkages, both immediately and three days later. And not surprisingly, such erroneous linkages translated into reputational harm, at least in the malpractice scenario.

The common sensical judgment that juxtaposition of otherwise innocuous audio and video can cause defamatory misunderstanding "of and concerning" an innocent party thus finds support in these experiments. Ruby Clark, on whose case our prostitution story was patterned, may indeed have been libeled by the television story of which she complained. It is highly plausible that significant numbers of viewers—at least white viewers—confused her with the prostitutes mentioned elsewhere in that story.

But the process can cut both ways. As our malpractice story illustrates, in some situations gender schemata may actually make it more difficult for women than for men to argue that they have been defamed. When our hypothetical critical colleague was a man, viewers were more likely to incorrectly associate malpractice with him than when our critical colleague was a woman. This is not to say that it is impossible for a woman in a schema-inconsistent role situation to meet the "of and concerning" requirement. Libel law does not require statistically significant evidence. But knowledge that gender schemata can work this way may be of use to defendants.

Finally, the experiments confirm the value of applying communication theory to legal issues. Race and gender schemata may not be applicable in the majority of libel suits, but other schemata—if not other theoretical models—may be. Schema theory may also be useful in better understanding and assessing claims for false light invasion of privacy where juxtaposition is commonly alleged to have caused offensive distortion. Television news, with its constant combination of visual and auditory messages, may offer a particularly fruitful environment for further work. But schema theory may also be helpful in situations involving juxtaposition of still photos and text, and in entertainment as well as news contexts.[27] Clearly, it is time for more intense study of what libel really is: a communication problem.

NOTES

1. See, e.g., Robert D. Sack and Sandra S. Baron, *Libel, Slander, and Related Problems*, 2d ed. (NY: Practising Law Institute, 1994), 101–4; Marc A. Franklin and David A. Anderson, *Mass Media Law*, 4th ed. (Westbury, NY: Foundation, 1990), 244–45; Kent R. Middleton and Bill F. Chamberlin, *The Law of Public Communication*, 3d ed. (NY: Longman, 1994), 86.

2. *Duncan v. WJLA-TV*, 10 Media L. Rep. 1395 (D.D.C., 1984); *Clark v. American Broadcasting Companies, Inc.*, 684 F.2d 1208 (6th Cir., 1982), cert. denied, 460 U.S. 1040 (1983); *Lal v. CBS, Inc.*, 551 F.Supp. 356 (E.D. Pa. 1982); *Southern Air Transport v. ABC*, 877 F.2d 1010 (D.C. Cir. 1989); *Dairy Barn Stores v. ABC*, 15 Media L. Rep. 1239 (Sup. Ct. N.Y. 1988); *Hartman v. Meredith Corporation*, 638 F. Supp. 1015 (D. Kan. 1986); *Wilhoit v. WCSC, Inc.*, 358 S.E.2d 397 (Ct. App. S.C. 1987); *Puckett v. American Broadcasting Companies*, 18 Media L. Rep. 1429, 1990 US App. LEXIS 19761 (6th Cir. 1990). The Duncan, Clark, Hartman and Puckett cases included additional claims based on the closely related theory of false light invasion of privacy—claims that word-picture juxtaposition created a distorted meaning regarding the plaintiff. False light differs from libel in that false light plaintiffs need not establish defamation, but must demonstrate that the communication in question is offensive. Further, the harm addressed in a false light action is plaintiffs' hurt feelings, not harm to reputation. Sack and Baron, *Libel, Slander, and Related Problems*, 563–69; Restatement (Second) of Torts §652E (1977). Not all jurisdictions recognize false light as a theory of liability, and in most cases of piggybacked claims, it is the libel claim that is central.

3. Sack and Baron, *Libel, Slander, and Related Problems*, 149–65. False light invasion of privacy also requires plaintiffs to prove that the alleged distortion of which they complain is actually "of and concerning" them. Sack and Baron, *Libel, Slander, and Related Problems*, 563–64.

4. Sack and Baron, *Libel, Slander, and Related Problems*, 149–50; Restatement (Second) of Torts §564 (1977).

5. See, e.g., Tom Grimes, "Encoding TV News Messages into Memory," *Journalism Quarterly* 67 (winter 1990): 757–66; P.W. Thorndyke and F.R. Yekovich, *A Critique of Schemata as a Theory of Human Story Memory*, Report No. P–630 (Santa Monica, CA: The Rand Corporation, 1979).

6. Jeremy Cohen and Timothy Gleason, *Social Research in Communication and Law* (Newbury Park, CA: Sage, 1990), 91. Examples of such work include Jeremy Cohen and Albert C. Gunther, "Libel As A Communication Phenomenon," *Communication and the Law* 9 (October 1987): 9–30; Jeremy Cohen, Diana Mutz, Vincent Price, and Albert Gunther, "Perceived Impact of Defamation: An Experiment on Third-Person Effects," *Public Opinion Quarterly* 52 (summer 1988): 161–73; Jeremy Cohen, Diana Mutz, Clifford Nass, and Laurie Mason, "Testing Some Notions of the Fact/Opinion Distinction in Libel," *Journalism Quarterly* 66 (spring 1989): 11–17, 247; Jeremy Cohen and Sara Spears, "Newtonian Communication: Shaking the Libel Tree for Empirical Damages," *Journalism Quarterly* 67 (spring 1990): 51–59; Albert Gunther, "What We Think Oth-

ers Think: Cause and Consequence in Third-Person Effect," *Communication Research* 18 (1991): 355–72.

7. Thorndyke and Yekovich, *A Critique of Schemata*.

8. U. Neisser and R. Becklen, "Selective looking: Attending to Visually Specified Events," *Cognitive Psychology* 7 (1975): 480–94; Charles N. Cofer, Donna L. Chmielewski, and John P. Brockway, "Constructive Processes and the Structure of Human Memory," in *The Structure of Human Memory*, ed. Charles N. Cofer (San Francisco: Freeman, 1976), 190–203.

9. M. Lavallee and R. Pelletier, "Ecological Value of Bem's Gender Schema Theory Explored Through Females' Traditional and Non-Traditional Occupational Contexts," *Psychological Reports* 70 (1992): 79–82; P.W. Linville and E.E. Jones, "Polarized Appraisals of Out-Group Members," *Journal of Personality and Social Psychology* 38 (1980): 689–703; A.G. Goldstein and J.E. Chance, "Memory for Faces and Schema Theory," *Journal of Psychology* 105 (1980): 47–59; S. L. Bem, "Gender Schema Theory: A Cognitive Account of Sex Typing," *Psychological Review* 88 (1981): 354–64; J.E. Chance, E.L. Turner, and A.G. Goldstein, "Development of Differential Recognition for Own- and Other-Race Faces," *Journal of Psychology* 112 (1982): 29–37; R.J. Larsen and E. Seidman, "Gender Schema Theory and Sex Role Inventories: Some Conceptual and Psychometric Considerations," *Journal of Personality and Social Psychology* 50 (1986): 205–11; D.E.S. Frable and S.L. Bem, "If You Are Gender Schematic, All Members of the Opposite Sex Look Alike," *Journal of Personality and Social Psychology* 49 (1985): 459–68; C.L. Martin and C.F. Halverson, "A Schematic Processing Model of Sex Typing and Stereotyping in Children," *Child Development* 52 (1981): 1119–1134; C.J. Mills and D.J. Tyrell, "Sex-Stereotypic Encoding and Release from Proactive Interference," *Journal of Personality and Social Psychology* 45 (1983): 772–81; J.C.W. Boon and G.M. Davies, "Rumours Greatly Exaggerated: Allport and Postman's Apocryphal Study," *Canadian Journal of Behavioral Science* 19 (1987): 431–40.

10. Gary D. Levy and D. Bruce Carter, "Gender Schema, Gender Consistency, and Gender-Role Knowledge: The Roles of Cognitive Factors in Preschoolers' Gender-Role Stereotype Attributions," *Developmental Psychology* 25 (1989): 444.

11. L.S. Liben and M.L. Signorella, "Gender Related Schemata and Constructive Memory in Children," *Child Development* 51 (1980): 11–18.

12. Boon and Davies, "Rumours Greatly Exaggerated," 431–40.

13. Gordon W. Allport and Lee J. Postman, "The Basic Psychology of Rumor," in *Readings in Social Psychology*, ed. E.E. Macoby, T.M. Newcomb, and E.L. Hartley (NY: Holt, Rinehart and Winston, 1958), 54–65.

14. Liza Schoenfein, "WMAQ-TV Suit Stirs Debate on File Footage," *Electronic Media*, 10 June 1991, 8; James Warren, "Channel 5's Apology for Use of Tape Doesn't Stop Doctor's Lawsuit," *Chicago Tribune*, 3 June 1991, Chicagoland section, p. 2 (north sports final edition). No final disposition has been reported.

15. *Clark v. American Broadcasting Companies, Inc.*, 684 F.2d 1208 (6th Cir. 1982). Clark also sued for false light invasion of privacy.

16. F.C. Bartlett, *Remembering: A Study in Experimental and Social Psychology* (London: Cambridge University Press, 1932); D.A. Smith and A.C. Graesser, "Memory for Actions in Scripted Activities as a Function of Typicality, Retention Interval and Retrieval Task," *Memory & Cognition* 9 (1981): 550–59; S.E. Taylor and J. Crocker, "Schematic Bases of Social Information Processing," in *Social Cognition: The Ontario Symposium on Personality and Social Psychology*, vol 1, eds. E.T. Higgins, C.A. Herman, and M.P. Zanna (Hillsdale, N.J.: Lawrence Erlbaum Associates, 1981), 89–134; Cofer, Chmielewski, and Brockway, "Constructive Processes."

17. Restatement, §559, Comment e.

18. D.R. Roskos-Ewoldsen and R.H. Fazio, "The Accessibility of Source Likeability as a Determinant of Persuasion," *Personality and Social Psychology Bulletin* 18 (1992): 19–25.

19. No black subjects were available to us.

20. In addition, a small number of subjects was randomly assigned to conditions and pretested with the full experimental protocol, with 5 subjects per condition. Cross tabulations and mean frequency counts showed that all subjects were performing on the dependent measures as predicted. No changes were made in the material or measures.

21. Seventy-two hours was chosen because previous experiments using 48-hour lags suggested that increased delay might enhance subjects' reliance on schemata. Grimes, "Encoding TV News."

22. Out of 100 available subjects, responses from 87 were used. Thirteen subjects did not mention information from which coders could infer race or gender, and were thus deleted from the analysis of the free recall data.

23. Scott's pi reliability coefficient for the average of the three coders over all subjects was .98.

24. Out of 100 available subjects, responses from 96 were used. Four subjects did not properly fill out the test form and were deleted from the analysis of the cued recall test.

25. When the factor was taken from the prostitution story, it had a Cronbach's alpha reliability score of .955 (eigenvalue of 6.685) and accounted for 50% of the variance. When it was derived from the malpractice story, it had a reliability rating of .961 (eigenvalue of 7.449) and accounted for 49% of the variance. Principal-components factor analysis with varimax rotation was used.

26. Smith and Graesser, "Memory for Actions," 552. However, teasing out the encoding strategies of subjects was not central to this study.

27. Among the examples are *Parnell v. Booth Newspapers, Inc.*, 572 F.Supp. 909 (W.D. Mich. 1983) (allegation that still photos illustrating story on prostitution left erroneous impression that plaintiff was a prostitute); *Cibenko v. Worth Publishers*, 510 F.Supp. 761 (D.N.J. 1981) (allegation that juxtaposition of text and photo in textbook showing white police officer prodding black man created impression of racist behavior by officer); and *Geary v. Goldstein*, 831 F.Supp. 269 (S.D.N.Y. 1993) (allegation that juxtaposing actual video from commercial with explicit sexual depiction left erroneous impression that actress was involved with pornography).

Introductory Comments to Chapter 13

Brooke Barnett
Elon University

Several years ago as a doctoral student, I took a privacy law class at the Indiana University law school. Privacy law was then, and still is, quite a hot legal topic. After taking the class, I decided I wanted to do some type of research in the area. At the time, every state had either passed or proposed some sort of privacy legislation. One piece of legislation in particular—the federal Driver's Privacy Protection Act—appeared to have some serious implications for journalists. Many journalists and lawyers had written about the potentially damaging effects of this Act, but none had taken a social science approach to look at what might be lost if driver's license records were closed off from the public and the media. The legal question at hand was, "How does limiting previously public record information in databases affect the way journalists do their jobs?"

At the time, a social science approach made sense simply because I was a graduate student also studying social science methodologies. On reflection, I realize this is not the best reason to choose a social science method, but in this case, it turned out to be a good methodological choice despite my reasoning at the time. Specifically for this project, I was able to provide some numbers to the generalizations that many people were making about the impact of the Act.

I decided to take a quantitative approach, looking at a national sample of journalists, so that I could generalize to the profession on a national level. But I worried that this might not tell the complete story of the impact that closing off databases might have on the media. The survey would tell how often the databases were being used, but it might not give a clear indication of the types of stories created by database use or the reasons that database use might be limited. I thought that having this kind of information would make the study more interesting because of the compelling nature of people's personal stories of success and frustration and because it could provide examples of stories that had been generated from database searches. Because of this, the qualitative, in-depth interviews were added to complement the quantitative survey.

Because I had not personally used the databases in question, I started the research with visits to several newsrooms and news libraries. I conducted in-depth interviews on how the databases were used and asked for anecdotes about the types of stories uncovered. I used this information to construct the survey. I also included an open-ended section to the survey where the journalists could explain their answers and provide further comments. The open-ended comments and in-depth interviews were used to flesh out the quantitative data. For example, the survey data showed the percentage of database stories that were enterprised—that came completely from the database search, not from a lead that led to the search—but the open-ended comments offered examples of those stories.

I wrote two versions of this piece before submitting it for publication. I worked with advisors in the journalism school and the law school on this research, and their suggestions made it quite clear that the methodological approaches of the two were quite different. The law journal version of this study required more emphasis on the case law, less emphasis on the methodology, and a clear normative argument about the privacy legislation. That version of this piece was previously published in the *Federal Communications Law Journal* (Barnett, 2001).

The social science version is published here. It has a more detached tone, a longer description of the methodology, and detailed statistical information. The same data set was used for each version of this study. The sections from the *FCLJ* piece are included with permission.

REFERENCES

Barnett, B. (2001). Use of public record databases in newspaper and television newsrooms. *Federal Communications Law Journal, 53*(3), 557–572.

Chapter 13

The Stories They Couldn't Tell: How Journalists Use Public Record Databases

Brooke Barnett

The right of access to public record information can be found explicitly in statements of the country's founders, as well as in state and federal statutes, and implicitly in the decisions of the Supreme Court. However, a trend toward privacy protection manifested, for example, in the federal Driver's Privacy Protection Act poses a serious threat to First Amendment interests and threatens to substantially harm American journalists. This study systematically investigates journalists' use of public record databases. The study is set up with a traditional legal literature review looking at the rights of access historically and currently. Then to ascertain the possible effect of current access laws, the study combines in-depth interviews and survey research to offer a more complete view of how these databases are being used in TV or newspaper stories and what is at stake if access to public record databases is eliminated.

A TRADITION OF ACCESS TO PUBLIC RECORDS

Open government records are a linchpin in the democratic process. An informed citizenry is crucial to a functioning democratic government, and access to information about the workings of the government is key to that process. The founding fathers noted this right, and it was perhaps most concisely stated by James Madison when he wrote: "Knowledge will forever govern ignorance: And people who mean to be their own

Governors, must arm themselves with the power which knowledge gives" (Hunt, 1910, p. 103). First Amendment theorists Meiklejohn (1948), Emerson (1970), and Blasi (1977) discussed access to free flowing information as central to the American system of free expression.

Although a historical precedent exists, the U.S. Supreme Court has not been explicit in recognizing this First Amendment right to obtain government information. However, judicial statements have hinted at this right. Justice Potter Stewart said that the Constitution is "neither a Freedom of Information Act nor an Official Secrets Act" (Potter, 1976). Justice White wrote in *Branzburg v. Hayes* (1972) that "without some protection for seeking out the news, freedom of the press could be eviscerated." However, the court has implicitly recognized this right of access when dealing with the public's right to attend trials or receive other information (*Richmond Newspapers v. Virginia*, 1980; *Red Lion Broadcasting Co. v. FCC*, 1969). The right of access to information is firmly grounded in federal and state statutory law in the United States.

Federal access laws developed after World War II, beginning with the Administrative Procedures Act of 1946, which was amended in 1966 to include the Freedom of Information Act (FOIA). The FOIA mandates that all government information must be disclosed except for material fitting within nine specific exemptions—for example, matters of national security, law enforcement, or personal privacy. However, the exemptions are still framed in favor of disclosure, whereas nondisclosure is permissive, not mandatory; it remains at the discretion of the agency based on its assessment of the privacy risk. The September 11 terrorist attacks on the United States have hampered that access. On October 12, 2001, the Attorney General issued a new statement of administration policy regarding the Freedom of Information Act. In that statement, Attorney General John Ashcroft (2001) asked executive branch agencies to employ a new standard in deciding whether to release information to the public or the media. The new standard is much more protective of government information than the previous one ordered by former attorney general Janet Reno in 1993.

State access laws came about more slowly. Prior to 1940, only 12 states had substantial public access laws, but by 1992, all states and the District of Columbia recognized this right. Although all states have some type of law, these state statutes vary greatly in definitions of *public record* and *openness*.

It seems that the Supreme Court never had to develop a constitutional right to access because statutes have been so generous with it. However, this appears to be changing. Because access rights are statutory, legislatures are often amending the laws, sometimes to benefit certain interest groups or to protect privacy interests. Numerous state bills that would limit access to parts of the public record are proposed every year.[1]

An example of legislative tampering with access to information at the federal level is the Driver's Privacy Protection Act (DPPA), enacted in 1994. The law bars states and their employees from releasing information from motor vehicle records including names, addresses, photographs, and telephone and social security numbers. Senator Barbara Boxer of California introduced the Act as an amendment to the Violent Crime Control Act of 1994 after the shooting death of actress Rebecca Schaeffer. A stalker murdered Schaeffer at her California apartment after acquiring her home address through a private detective who found the information in state motor vehicle records (Watkins, 1998). Ironically, the law as enacted would not have prevented the death that instigated it; the current law carves out an exemption for private investigators along with law enforcement officials, courts, and government agencies. Yet there is no exemption for the news media, which many contend is a clear violation of the First Amendment's free press guarantee.

Only one senator discussed the First Amendment ramifications of this Act. Senator Orin Hatch stated that a potential harm of the DPPA would be restricting access to information used for newsgathering. Hatch read a letter from the Utah branch of the Society of Professional Journalists on the senate floor. This letter outlined important journalistic uses of such information (Letter from the Society of Professional Journalists, 1993). The organization cited several examples of important stories that came about after searching driver's license records. For example, journalists used a computerized list of driving records from the Department of Motor Vehicles (DMV) to document current school bus drivers with dangerous driving records. Another story uncovered Minnesota airline pilots who had lost driving privileges because of alcohol-related offenses, but were still flying planes (Millhollon, 1995).

Testimony and editorials from journalists also indicated the wealth of stories that have come from searching these records. *The Miami Herald* used DMV records to document nearly 500 drivers who each had six or more DUI convictions, but were still licensed to drive. *The Orlando Sentinel* used driver records to locate home addresses for Kennedy Space Center

---

[1]For example, the following is a list of proposed or pending state legislation in the year 2000: AK HB 324/ SB 232; AZ SB 1212; AZ HB 2676; CA AB 2799; CA SB 1409; CA SB 99999; CO HB 1110; FL HB 1967; ID SB 1409; ID SB 1435; IL SB 1357; KS BILLS; KY HB 822; MI HB1357; MI HB 5227; MI HB 5230; MI HB 5270; MN HF 2481; MN SF 2237; MN SF 2992; MO SB 538; MO HB 1079; MO HB 1693; MS HB 354; NH HB 1612; NY AG bill; TX HB 99999; UT HB 70; UT SB 174; VA HB 777; VA HB 1085; VA HB 1493; WI AB 22; WI AB 315; WI SB 260.

workers who, when interviewed at home and away from watchful eyes, discussed government mistakes that led to the Challenger explosion. WCCO-TV uncovered a ring of automobile title laundering where unsuspecting car buyers purchased cars that had been totaled and rebuilt (Dalglish, 2000).

Despite concerns from First Amendment advocates and professional journalists groups, Congress passed the DPPA and President Clinton signed it into law. Meanwhile, media advocacy and professional journalism groups have continued to speak out against the DPPA (Callahan, 1995; Millhollon, 1995; Sullivan & Goldberg, 1997) as well as its recently passed amendment, which eliminates highway funds for states that release any personal information from drivers' records without the consent of the licensee (Department of Transportation and Related Agencies Appropriations Act, 1999).

The final blow to media advocates came when, after a series of legal challenges and two lower courts ruling the DPPA unconstitutional, the Act was upheld in a unanimous *Reno v. Condon* (2000) Supreme Court ruling. The discussion was narrowly confined to issues of federalism. The court did not address the privacy concerns at hand, nor the implications to the public and press of limiting information that has traditionally been available to the public.[2]

However, the legislative history proves that privacy was a motivation for the legislation and many fear the start of more privacy-inspired legislation. Media advocate Lucy Dalglish (2000) wrote: "The bottom line is that a valuable source of public information has been shut down, and privacy advocates are setting their sights next on voter registration, property tax and land transaction records" (p. 2). Dalglish expected legislative and congressional efforts fueled by the privacy wave to keep wiping out access to these records.

PRIVACY AND THE MEDIA

The conflict between the press and privacy advocates stems from opposing social values of individual privacy and the public's right to know. Privacy concerns have often come on the heels of new technological developments. The advent of the printing press spawned the first concerns about privacy when mass-produced works threatened to turn private affairs into public fare. The benchmark Warren and Brandeis (1890) law review

---

[2]The court has ruled against access in several other key cases. See also *United Reporting Publishing Corp. v. Los Angeles Police Department*, 146 F.3d 1133 (9th Cir., 1998); *U.S. Department of Justice v. Reporter's Committee for Freedom of the Press*, 489 U.S. 749 (1989).

article attempting to establish the right of privacy was prompted by yet another new technology: photography. These early concerns surrounded public figures and were not much of a threat to the average person. This is changing.

Today's concerns about privacy stem from the use of data and computer technologies that affect the general population. Federal aid, credit and banking card transactions, insurance forms, and other agreements all leave a paper and now an electronic trail of personal data. Marketers have realized the value of this information, and the subsequent onslaught of telemarketing and mass mailing may have prompted the public outcry to be left alone.

These are issues of great concern to journalists. Sometimes journalists are the specific targets of privacy groups, particularly in today's climate when many think the media are afforded too much latitude. This was true in the first Freedom Forum (2002) State of the First Amendment survey conducted after the September 11 terrorist attacks, when nearly half of those surveyed said that the First Amendment goes too far.

The 2003 survey showed that support for the First Amendment had returned to pre–9/11 levels, with only about 34% indicating the First Amendment goes too far (Freedom Forum, 2003). Sixty-five percent favored the policy to embed journalists in military combat units, but two out of three surveyed said the government should be able to review in advance those reports from combat zones.

Ninety-five percent of people surveyed think that people should have the right to express unpopular opinions. But that support waned as specific activities were outlined. A little less than half (49%) think that people should be able to say things in public that are offensive to religious groups, and 38% think that people should be able to say things in public that are offensive to racial groups.

The public also has mixed opinions about the use of public records in general and by journalists specifically. A 1998 survey showed that more than half of people surveyed thought that driving records should be available to anyone (Driscoll, Splichal, Salwen, & Garrison, 1999). More than 80% think that making government records available serves as a check on government, but half feel that this also threatens individual privacy. It seems that opinions about access also vary according to who is accessing the information. A majority (85%) thinks that law enforcement agencies should have access to do their jobs, but less than half (49%) think that journalists need access to do their jobs—just slightly more than banks considering a loan (47%).

Once again, advancing technology has fueled privacy concerns. Some seem to think that computers have made it too easy to find information. It appears that the judiciary also leans toward a different standard for public record databases as opposed to individual public records. The court has distinguished between compilations of data and single sources, even when all the information is in the public record (*U.S. Department of Justice v. Reporter's Committee for Freedom of the Press*, 1989). This could be a sign of the way courts plan to deal with access to databases of computer compilations of information in the future.

As a result, commercial database vendors, possibly anticipating government intervention, have developed industry regulations. To appease privacy advocate groups and ward off potential legislation, personal information such as social security numbers has been deleted from the databases.[3] This has been a hindrance to journalists and could make news less accurate because social security numbers are often used to verify information or confirm the identity of a person.

To better understand the potential effect of regulation, we need to understand how these public records and particularly databases are being used. Despite intense lobbying and discussion about the use of public record databases, no survey research gives a clear picture of how these records are being used. This study combines survey research with in-depth interviews to show how often public record databases are being used, for what stories, and by what organizations. It also provides a clearer picture of the types of stories that might not be reported if public record databases are restricted further.

RESEARCH QUESTIONS

Because so little research is available about the impact of public record databases on reporters, this study poses research questions rather than hypotheses. They are:

R1: What are the demographics of journalists who are searching databases and those who are not?

Journalists were asked a series of questions about gender, age, education, organization size, and position at organization. This offers a composite of those who do the most searching.

R2: What kind of information are they searching and for what types of stories?

A series of open-ended questions were asked about specific types of information sought and then coded into categories. Subjects were also asked to name how often they used databases for certain types of stories, such as investigative stories or features.

---

[3]Individual Reference Service Group Principles were adopted in December 1997.

They responded with "All of the time," "Most of the time," "Sometimes," and "Rarely."

R3: What are the predictors for whether journalists search databases?

Independent variables include size of organization, gender, familiarity with the computer, education level, and journalistic training, and these were placed in a logistic regression model.

R4: For those who do not search databases, what are their reasons and do they differ based on the medium, TV or newspapers?

Journalists were given a list of reasons that they might not search databases. They were asked to respond how much these were factors on a 10-point Likert scale. Reasons include accuracy, cost, time, and lack of computer skills.

R5: For those who do search databases, what prevents them from searching databases as much as they would like, and do these reasons differ based on the medium, TV or newspapers?

These reasons model the reasons stated for those who do not search, such as accuracy, cost, time, and lack of computer skills.

R6: How are journalists searching for public records, and how does this differ based on organization?

This section of questions lists a variety of ways to search public records and asks how often each is used. One section deals with records on the computer, and the other deals with more traditional ways of seeking records such as requests by mail or in person.

R7: How many organizations are using vendor databases, and why are they choosing them?

This section asks about the use of commercial databases, which are those services that charge for time spent searching. The survey asked those journalists using these services to give reasons that they choose vendor services and to rate the accuracy of specific services used.

METHOD

The Survey

A national sample of daily newspapers and TV stations with news departments was compiled. The newspaper sample was drawn from a list of all 1,486 daily newspapers named by *Editor & Publisher* (1999). A stratified probability sample of 250 daily newspapers was constructed based on circulation size. Indiana University's survey center completed interviews with 23.6% of newspapers in the largest circulation category (newspapers with a circulation of more than 100,000) and approximately 14% of newspapers in all other circulation categories.

The TV sample was selected from stations listed in *The Broadcasting and Cable Yearbook* (1999). Every third station listed was selected, resulting in 435 stations selected from 1,305 stations. Digital stations and noncommercial stations were excluded from the sample. After calling began, stations that were not currently broadcasting, did not have a news department, or were satellite providers were excluded.

The newspaper group was pretested on November 23, 1999, and production began on December 14, 1999. Minor changes for clarity were made to the questionnaire after the pretest. We pretested the TV group on January 3, 2000, and began production on the same day. The average interview length was 13.2 minutes for both groups.

Data were collected by telephone using the University of California Computer-Assisted Survey Methods software (CASES). The data collection staff included two supervisors, one supervisor's assistant, and three senior interviewers. All interviewers received at least 15 hours of training in interviewing techniques before production interviewing and 1 hour of training specific to the study. Interviewers were instructed to read questions and response categories at a slower-than-typical conversational pace, to use neutral probes, and to give neutral feedback phrases.

Interviewers first asked to speak to the person at the organization who does the most database research to ensure that the most knowledgeable person on the topic completed the survey. After reaching that person, callers again confirmed that this person was actually the one doing the searching. Then a series of questions were asked about frequency and type of databases searched, how they were used, and reasons for not using more, as well as a series of demographic questions.

If no one at the organization did database searching, the interviewer asked to speak to someone who searched public records and could address why databases were not used. This person was then given a list of reasons that they do not use databases and asked to rate how important a reason this was for not using. They were also asked a series of demographic questions.

The Interviews

In-depth interviews were conducted with newspaper librarians, reporters, editors, and TV producers before the survey questionnaire was developed to ensure clarity of the survey instrument and provide examples of innovative uses of database records. Information from these interviews as well as comments offered and transcribed during the phone interviews were used to flesh out the close-ended responses in the survey.

RESULTS

R1: What are the demographics of journalists who are searching databases and those who are not?

Of the people searching databases for public records, most are young, educated, male managers with journalism degrees. They have used databases an average of 47 times in the last year. More men (66.6%) than women (31.6%) are using databases. The majority is 45 years old or younger (69.3%), and 86% have at least a college degree, with almost half (47%) having majored in journalism. The majority (75.6 %) is in management or editing positions, 20% are reporters or producers, and 3.5% are in research or librarian positions.[4]

No statistical differences were found for the size of newspaper organizations among those who used databases and those who did not. However, the larger TV stations are doing more database searching than the smaller ones. More than a fourth (28.2%) of stations that are using databases are in the largest 50 markets, compared with 16% of stations that do not. This is most likely attributed to larger staffs and budgets at the larger stations, which in turn mean more money and time to spend on database searches.

R2: What kind of information are they searching and for what types of stories?

When asked what type of information they are seeking, journalists say they are using criminal and court records the most (33.5%), followed by personal background information such as names and addresses (18.4%). Voter information and campaign expense and donation records make up 16.9% of the most searched records. Property, financial, or business information (13.2%) are also hot areas.

The types of information sought seem logical when considering how the information is used. As Table 13.1 shows, employees at TV stations and newspapers search public record databases most often for investigative stories, followed by crime stories, city-state stories, and political

---

[4]A profile is only useful for those journalists who use databases. Interviewers asked to speak to the person at the organization who does the most database searching because this person would most likely be the most knowledgeable about the topic. For those who do not use databases, interviewers talked to the person who searches public record, but does not use databases, or in some cases the person who answered the phone and agreed to speak for the organization. Therefore, the individual characteristics of those who do not use databases are neither meaningful nor generalizable.

TABLE 13.1
Types of Stories That Use Public Records From Databases

In the past year, how often, if at all, did you search public records for stories?

Type of Story	Most of the Time	Often	Sometimes	Rarely	Never
Investigative	32.5%	23.4%	29.0%	12.7%	2.4%
Feature	1.2%	8.0%	36.1%	43.8%	10.8%
Sports	2.1%	5.4%	20.5%	46.9%	25.1%
City or state	17.1%	39.4%	35.1%	7.6%	0.8%
Political campaign	14.3%	32.7%	29.5%	16.3%	7.2%
Crime	25.6%	38.4%	28.0%	5.6%	2.4%

$N = 252.$

campaign stories. Databases are not used that often for features or sports stories. Thus, the databases are used most often for what are considered to be the most important stories covered by the media: investigative, crime, and political stories. Because journalists rely so heavily on databases to cover these topics, these stories may not be reported at all with database regulation.

It seems that TV stations are using public records slightly more often than newspapers for all types of stories. As Table 13.2 shows, TV stations featured information from public record databases significantly more often than newspapers in features, sports, city/state, and political campaign stories.

Perhaps the most interesting finding is that, on average, 11.3 stories a year from each organization developed from searching the public records. These are instances when reporters are not looking for specific informa-

TABLE 13.2
Differences Between TV and Newspapers in Terms of Types of Stories That Use Public Records From Databases

In the past year, how often, if at all, did you search public records for stories?

Type of Story	t	df	Newspaper M	TV M
Investigative	− .841	250	2.24	2.36
Feature	−4.294*	250	3.36	3.80
Sports	−3.016*	250	3.72	4.08
City or state	−2.295*	250	2.24	2.50
Political campaign	−2.422*	250	2.55	2.89
Crime	− .466	250	2.18	2.24

$N = 252.$
*$p \leq .05.$

tion, but rather cross-matching information from two databases, such as when looking for voter fraud by cross-referencing voter rolls and recent deaths. Follow-up interviews with journalists showed that these are the types of stories that would be virtually impossible to identify without database usage. The time it would take to match paper records in this manner makes it prohibitive. Also many connections would not be obvious without compilations of data. The databases are useful because they are quick, provide a depth of information difficult to compile with paper resources, and are available on the weekends and at night. Databases allow the researcher to combine resources in ways that may not be obvious or even possible with paper copies.

Research Librarian Barbara Oliver of the *St. Petersburg Times* said that they use public record databases to uncover stories of "people behaving badly." This can range from minor civil and criminal infractions to major crimes. Nora Paul of the Poynter Institute says that public record databases are good for filling in information holes that a source is not going to give you, checking source information, making a connection between people who do not want to seem connected, and uncovering stories through routine checks.

One fruitful use of the public records has been routine background checks (e.g., checks on people in or running for public office or people running organizations). A striking example comes from the *St. Petersburg Times*, where the story about Baptist Church leader Henry Lyons' alleged embezzlement broke. This story came about after routine database checking of property records showed that Lyons owned a million dollar second home. A reporter then started looking further into Lyons' personal and organization finances.

Routine checks of public records by researchers at the *St. Petersburg Times* have also uncovered many instances of fraud or misleading conduct. For example, searches of financial records uncovered that a man running for the office of treasurer had filed for personal bankruptcy three times and corporate bankruptcy twice, and that the new director of a large arts organization that solicited donations had been charged with fraud in his home state. Another routine check of professional licenses found that a new school director of psychology who introduced himself as "Dr." had no degree in psychology.

Most of the people interviewed at the larger papers agreed that if it became more difficult to use the databases or if the vendors decided to delete more information from them, then routine checks such as these would no longer be useful. For example, a routine run of license plate numbers on cars parked at a council member's house that showed an illegal meeting in violation of the sunshine laws was taking place would not have been possible. Barbara Oliver fears that the DPPA will allow such illegal meetings to go unnoticed.

In-depth interviews indicate that TV stations use the databases more deliberately, often for investigative pieces after receiving a tip. Producer Roscoe Glisson of Tampa's News Channel 8 said, "Television has a short attention span, so we only use public records on pieces we work on for a long time." Glisson said that reporters in ambush-style situations often use the records when they confront subjects with evidence of wrongdoing. Mapping—using the database to plot a graphic representation—is often used because it provides a visual element for a story. One example comes from Tampa's News Channel 8, where public records combined with mapping showed how at least two bodies were buried in each plot of the local cemetery. This story emerged because a viewer called the station after he went to visit a deceased relative but could not find his gravestone. Tampa's News Channel 8 also used public record databases to map out the area where the most purse snatching occurs in Hillsboro County, to uncover abuses in day-care subsidies for meals, and to expose a narcotics ring across the street from an elementary school.

R3: What are the predictors for whether journalists search databases?

Multiple regression was used to see whether age, organization size, and journalistic training were predictors of database use. Because this is an exploratory study, there was no theoretical basis that would suggest an order to enter these variables; therefore, hierarchical regression was not used. Instead the variables were entered as one block.

As Table 13.3 shows, when looking at the TV sample, a model including TV market size,[5] age, and journalistic training of the journalists accounts for 10% of the variance. However, TV market size, when controlling for the other two variables, is the only significant predictor. It appears that as TV station size increases, so does searching for public records. In other words, journalists from the larger TV stations are doing more searching.

As Table 13.4 shows, for the newspaper sample, a model including newspaper circulation, age, and journalistic training of the journalists accounts for 20% of the variance. However, newspaper circulation size, when controlling for the other two variables, is the only significant pre-

---

[5]The TV market size was recoded so that it would intuitively make more sense because smaller market numbers actually mean bigger stations.

TABLE 13.3
Multiple Regression for TV Sample Based
on Circulation Size, Age, and Journalistic Training

Variables	Regression Coefficients	Standard Error of Coefficient	Beta Weight
Year of birth	.303	.440	.067
Journalistic training	−3.274	2.735	−.116
Market size	.227	.078	.279*

R = .441, R- square = .194.
N = 103.
*p ≤ .05.

TABLE 13.4
Multiple Regression for the Newspaper Sample Based
on Circulation Size, Age, and Journalistic Training

Variables	Regression Coefficients	Standard Error of Coefficient	Beta Weight
Year of birth	−254	674.814	−.057
Journalistic training	−.645	1.858	−.027
Newspaper circulation	2.018E-04	.000	.436*

R- square = .194.
N = 103.
*p ≤ .05.

dictor. As with the TV stations, journalists from the larger organizations are doing more public record database searching.[6]

Because much of the variance is unaccounted for in both the newspaper and TV models, clearly other factors are at work here. It could be that budget or staff issues of the organization or other characteristics of the journalists are factors. Follow-up interviews show that time is probably a factor for whether databases are searched. However, this concept is difficult to measure in a quantitative survey.

---

[6]There are some problems with using a multiple regression for both of these dependent variables because they violate some of the assumptions needed for proper use of the multiple regression statistic. Although the tolerance and VIF show there is no collinearity problem, the histogram shows that the dependent variable is not normally distributed, but is rather a bimodal distribution. The scatter plot shows a definite pattern, and the P-plot does not follow the expected pattern. With these clear model assumptions, it might be best not to parse out the effects of particular predictor variables, but to rather only look at the variance accounted for as a block.

R4: For those who do not search databases, what are the reasons and do they differ based on the medium, TV or newspapers?

As Table 13.5 shows, the main reason for not using databases is lack of time, followed by cost, complicated computer technology, concerns about accuracy, and difficulty navigating the Web. There were no statistically significant differences between TV and newspaper in reasons for not using databases.

Survey subjects were given the chance to add comments to the closed-ended questions. One TV news director from a mid-size market summed up many of the sentiments by saying they do not search because there are "not enough people, not enough time, not enough money."

Others commented on the lack of local records online, specifically local government records. Many commented on how they would like to use the resources more often: "It's 100% a cost issue. Also, we have only ten reporters and unless you have an investigative unit, it's not cost effective. Although I think it is the most valuable tool to journalists, and it's a shame we don't use it." Others expressed a general lack of audience interest in stories that use these resources as exemplified by this statement from a small market news director: "We don't believe in covering that way. We prefer to stay locally. Studies have shown that people really don't care about numbers and public records."

R5: For those who do search databases, what prevents them from searching databases as much as they would like, and do these reasons differ based on the medium, TV or newspapers?

Those who used databases were asked to rank from 0 to 10 the reasons that prevent them from using as frequently as they want. As Table 13.6 shows, the expense of databases and the amount of information available prevent journalists from using databases as much as they would like. Ac-

TABLE 13.5
Main Reasons for not Using Databases

Reason	M
They cost too much money	4.43
There was not enough time	5.08
Computer technology is too complicated	3.20
Information may not be accurate	2.38
Navigating the Web is too difficult	1.74

Means from a scale of 0 to 10, with 0 meaning *not at all important* and 10 meaning *very important*.
$N = 92$.

TABLE 13.6
Reasons That Prevent Those Who Use Databases
From Using Them as Much as They Would Like

How much does _____ *prevent you from using databases as much as you would like?*

Reason	A Lot	Somewhat	A Little	Not at All
Subscription rates	48.0%	27.0%	10.3%	13.9%
Concerns about accuracy	8.3%	32.1%	38.5%	19.8%
Lack of computer knowledge	7.9%	19.8%	23.0%	49.2%
Lack of information available	6.0%	32.5%	26.2%	34.9%
Difficulty with using databases	5.6%	32.1%	29.0%	32.5%
Lack of knowledge about Web	2.4%	13.1%	17.5%	67.1%

N = 252.

curacy, computer skills, and Web knowledge are not major concerns. Almost half (48.4 %) of those journalists who use databases say high subscription rates prevent them from using databases as much as they would like. More than a third (38.7%) say that the lack of information available prevents them *a lot* or *somewhat* from using databases as much as they would like. Accuracy is less of a concern, with only 8.3% saying that it prevents them *a lot* from using, and more than half (58.3%) saying that concerns of accuracy have nothing to do with how often they use. A majority say neither lack of knowledge about the Web (67.1%) nor computers (50%) affect how much databases searching they do.

T tests showed no statistically significant difference between newspapers and TV in terms of what prevents those who use databases from using them as much as they would like. Again comments added to the closed-ended survey questions provide further insight into what prevents journalists from using these databases more often. One local TV producer said that the TV news' local emphasis prevents use of databases:

> Our primary function is local news. We don't do many stories about statewide or national trends, so the type of information available over the Internet or CD—that's not what we do. We do local, that is still available through the courthouse. If they put it on the Internet, we'll look at it over the Internet. That is the primary limiting factor. The databases that concern us are not available over the computer.

One TV journalist said that journalists are often not aware of the options for online searching: "Perhaps if these search groups or databases made themselves more available to the media and let us know who they are and what they do we might use them more often." A newspaper journalists expressed a similar sentiment:

> My biggest problem is finding the database source to go to. I usually use more time finding the particular database than actually doing the searching. It is lack of knowledge that prevents me from actually getting to where I want to go.

Although many journalists discussed personal reasons, such as time and difficulty with searches, some journalists touched on the ways that difficulty with government agencies, violation of the FOIA, and privacy concerns are stymieing reporters. These journalists said that government agencies are less cooperative about providing records in electronic formats. One newspaper editor said there is an

> artificial barrier erected by bureaucrats. People that have the data in their files construe it to be too difficult to share or too expensive or don't have the knowledge or don't like what we're going to do with it. I would say that when they provide on paper rather than in electronic form that's an artificial barrier.

Others touched on the information removed from databases because of privacy concerns. One newspaper reporter said that this is a major reason he does not do more searching:

> Databases are unavailable, for instance, if an investigation is in progress; certain information is cut off from the public. So information is blocked and it is unavailable to use and becoming more and more so. There are legal and privacy concerns that stop us from accessing a lot.

Based on the open-ended comments, it appears that these journalists are already feeling the effects of regulation.

> R6: How are journalists searching for public records and how does this differ based on organization?

When looking for public records in the last month, journalists made more requests in person ($m = 17.8$) than on the computer ($m = 8.23$) or by mail ($m = 2.38$). A t test showed that people at newspapers are more likely to make requests in person ($t = 4.67, p \leq .05$)—an average of 24 times in a month at newspapers compared with just under 10 times a month at TV stations. This again may be attributed to staff or budget concerns or simply to location of the organization.

Interviews confirmed that location of the organization affected how records are obtained. Many newspapers are in the heart of the community and thus closer to courthouse and government agencies. Television stations are often on the outskirts of town, where requests in person may be more cumbersome. Some journalists noted that it is easier for them to find what they need when dealing with people familiar with the records. Such comments have particular resonance when compared to comments that unfamiliarity with databases hinders their work and makes such searches too time consuming. However, others complained that face-to-face dealings can inhibit the process and the anonymity of computer requests is also preferable, particularly in smaller towns.

When journalists are using the computer to find public records, free Web sites are used *most of the time* by 32%, commercial vendors *most of the time* by 8.3%, and government purchased databases *most of the time* by 4.4%. No statistically significant difference was found between newspapers and TV in terms of where they are searching public records on the computer.

R7: How many organizations are using vendor databases and why are they choosing them?

Many journalists are not using commercial databases that charge for time spent searching. A majority (74.6%) says it *rarely* or *never* uses these services; only about 8% use them *most of the time*. Of that small percentage who say that they use commercial databases, almost half (47%) choose them because they have more information and are easier to use than free Web sites or finding the records in person. Thirty-seven percent say they choose vendor databases because they are more accurate, and only 12.2% say they use vendor databases because they are cheaper.

Again the in-depth interviews touched on the cost factor of using these databases, particularly among those interviewed from smaller newspapers and TV stations. Budgets simply do not allow for vendor fees. However, regular users of the vendor services that charge for search time say that skilled searchers can find the necessary information so quickly that cost becomes less of an issue. In-depth interviews with those who rely on vendor services show that vendor databases are seen as easier ways to find information.

DISCUSSION

It seems that TV and newspaper journalists are using public record databases in similar ways: to report on and develop socially significant stories. These databases are used most often for what are considered the most important stories covered by the media: investigative, crime, and political stories. In-depth interviews with journalists have indicated that if databases were limited, some of these stories would still be reported or developed in other ways, but that stories which come about from routine searching, so-called *enterprise stories*, would not be. This is particularly troubling considering the frequency with which some journalists are enterprising stories from database searches. Further, a qualitative look at the caliber of stories enterprised shows that the public would be missing out on stories of government abuse and safety violations. Some would argue that these kinds of stories are the most important stories that the media can report, fulfilling its role as a watchdog press.

Another main advantage of databases may be the time they can save. Although information can often be found in other ways, time and cost factors actually render other ways of gaining records impractical and, in some noted cases of data matching, impossible. Paper requests would be particularly cost-prohibitive for stories that involve research in different states, which require sending someone to look at the records or paying someone from another state to find records. In terms of time, it may take 8 minutes to find a document with an online vendor that could take a full day if a person had to obtain the paper version.

Cost is cited as the main reason for not using general databases and vendor services in particular. Government regulation of these vendor services could in turn drive costs up further and could also affect accuracy in reporting. A common complaint of the current industry regulation is it can make it more difficult to verify information because social security numbers are no longer available for cross-checking to see whether records are referring to the same person. Further regulation would inhibit the ability to verify information.

This chapter shows that public record databases are a necessity for journalists to uncover wrongdoing and effectively cover crime, political stories, and investigative pieces. Some of these stories would not be uncovered without the use of public record databases. Industry or government regulation would simply remove verification options for those researching stories, and increased rates would prohibit vendor use for many organizations. This could greatly hinder the journalistic mission of informing the public.

REFERENCES

Ashcroft, J. (2001, October 12). *Memorandum for heads of all federal departments and agencies.* Retrieved from www.usdoj.gov/oip/foiapost/2001foiapost19.htm

Barnett, B. (2001). Use of public record databases in newspaper and television newsrooms. *Federal Communications Law Journal, 53*(3), 557–572.

Blasi, V. (1977). The checking value in First Amendment Theory. *American Bar Foundation Research Journal, 3*, 521–649.

Branzburg v. Hayes, 408 U.S. 665 (1972).

Broadcasting and Cable Yearbook. (1999). New Providence, NJ: R. Bowker.

Callahan, C. (1995, November). License revoked. *American Journalism Review, 17*, 40–44.

Dalglish, L. (2000). Coming soon: More closure. *News Media & the Law, 24*(1), 2.

Department of Transportation and Related Agencies Appropriations Act. (1999). Public Law No. 69.

Driscoll, P. D., Splichal, S. L., Salwen, M. B., & Garrison, B. (1999). *Public support for access to government records: A national survey.* Paper presented in the law division at the Association for Education in Journalism and Mass Communication annual meeting, New Orleans, LA.

Editor and Publisher Yearbook. (1999). Retrieved from http://www.editorandpublisher.com/eandp/resources/yearbook/jsp

Emerson, T. I. (1970). *The system of freedom of expression.* New York: Vintage Books.

Freedom Forum. (2002). State of the First Amendment survey. Retrieved from http://www.firstamendmentcenter.org/about.aspx?id-2185

Freedom Forum. (2003). State of the First Amendment survey. Retrieved from http://www.firstamendmentcenter.org/about.aspx?item=state_of_First_Amendment_2003

Hunt, G. (Ed.). (1910). *The writings of James Madison.* New York: G. P. Putnam.

Letter from the Society of Professional Journalists, Utah headliners chapter. (1993). Congressional Record 139, S15, 763.

Meiklejohn, A. (1948). *Free speech and its relation to self-government.* New York: Kennikat.

Millhollon, M. (1995, October). Countdown to closure: Don't let the door hit you on your way out of the DMV office. *Quill, 83*, 26–27.

Potter, S. (1976). Or of the press. *Hastings Law Review, 26*, 631–636.

Red Lion Broadcasting Co. v. FCC, 395 U.S. 367 (1969).

Reno v. Condon, 528 U.S. 141 (2000).

Richmond Newspapers v. Virginia, 448 U.S. 555 (1980).

Sullivan, D., & Goldberg, H. (1997, September). Public speaking out on privacy concerns. *Quill, 85*, 17–19.

United Reporting Corp. v. Los Angeles Police Department, 146 F.3d 1133 (9th Cir., 1998).

U.S. Department of Justice v. Reporter's Committee for Freedom of the Press, 489 U.S. 749 (1989).

Warren, S. D., & Brandeis, L. D. (1890). The right to privacy. *Harvard Law Review, 4*(5), 193.

Watkins, W. J., Jr. (1998). The Driver's Privacy Protection Act: Congress makes a wrong turn. *South Carolina Law Review, 49*, 983–984.

Introductory Comments to Chapter 14

Amy Reynolds[1]
Indiana University

Historian Howard Zinn has said that it is easy to protect free speech and expand public discourse about significant political issues when the stakes are small. Yet when the issues are life or death, America's democratic government has a history of choking the debate (Zinn, 1990).

Zinn based this assessment on history. When I first came across Zinn's writings about the First Amendment, I was far from an expert on First Amendment history. In 1996, when as a doctoral student I took a First Amendment history course with David Rabban at the University of Texas Law School, I started to understand why I did not know much beyond a few common historical highlights.

Rabban introduced his course by talking about what he calls the three eras of First Amendment history—the framing of the Constitution and the passage of (and prosecutions from) the Alien and Sedition Actions of 1798; the 19th century and its lack of First Amendment Supreme Court cases and a perceived lack of general free speech activity (with a few exceptions); and the post-World War I era, which begins with the Espionage Act cases and the infamous Holmes and Brandeis dissent and ends

---

[1] "The Impact of *Walker's Appeal* on Northern and Southern Conceptions of Free Speech in the Nineteenth Century" originally appeared, without the author's introduction, in *Communication Law & Policy* (2004), 9, 73-100.

with modern-day Supreme Court First Amendment interpretations (Rabban, 1997).[2]

Legal historians and scholars generally interested in the First Amendment have largely explored this last era. Much of their work supports what Zinn has noted—that during times of war or in situations that involve national security or personal safety, the First Amendment often takes a back seat. Much First Amendment case law clearly demonstrates this. What about before the 20th century? How did free speech function in America before the Civil War? After the ratification of the First Amendment in 1791? How did people think about free speech during these times? Did people even claim a First Amendment right to speak, write, or assemble more than 150 years ago? What limits did the government and/or the public place on the right to free speech or press? The second era—the era that Rabban characterized as largely neglected due to limited Supreme Court case law to study, really appealed to me.

I had too many questions to answer, of course. I needed to focus my research, and I needed exposure to what had already been discovered. Scholars such as Tim Gleason, Margaret Blanchard, John Nerone, Michael Kent Curtis, William Lee Miller, Rabban, and a few others had begun to explore this fascinating period of history through a First Amendment lens. I looked to their work to find unanswered questions that I could explore, and I found myself continually returning to one question—How did people conceptualize the right to expression, particularly regarding controversial issues, at a time when it was not clear how the Supreme Court defined the First Amendment and its limits?

I decided the best way to address this issue was to focus on controversial figures who were exercising their rights to speak and were often challenged for doing so, whether by the public or the government. William Lloyd Garrison was the first person who popped into my mind.

Why?

One of the central questions in American politics in the mid- to late 1830s involved the degree to which the government would try to stop the abolitionists from criticizing the legal institution of slavery in the South. Because the scope of the First Amendment was limited to federal action prior to the ratification of the Fourteenth Amendment in 1868, many of the debates of the early 1800s focused on the states' ability to suppress abolitionist speech (Curtis, 1995).

Abolitionist speech was considered either incendiary or seditious by virtually all of the slaveholding states in the South in the late 1820s. Al-

[2]The Espionage Act cases are *Schenck v. United States* (1919), *Frohwerk v. United States* (1919), *Debs v. United States* (1919), and *Abrams v. United States* (1919), in which justices Holmes and Brandeis offered a powerful dissent that promoted the value of free speech in a democracy.

though events of the late 1830s—such as the censorship of the mail and the directed free speech attacks by the Southern states on the abolitionists' incendiary publications—significantly identified free expression issues that were centered on the abolitionists, the roots of these issues started to grow much earlier. Garrison was often at the heart of these debates (Reynolds, 2001).

Studying Garrison and his abolitionist newspaper, *The Liberator,* led me to David Walker and his *Appeal,* the focus of the article reprinted here. I had never heard of David Walker's *Appeal* until I read about it in *The Liberator.* Once I discovered Walker and began to sense the free speech issues that his abolitionist writings raised, I knew that studying Walker could help us better understand more broadly the limits to free speech in the early 1830s—limits in terms of public perception of what speech was permissible and legally protected, and limits in terms of how state governments interpreted the idea of free speech in the specific context of speech about slavery.

The legal historical research reprinted here does not employ traditional legal research methods. Rather, it looks mostly to nonlegal sources and uses historical methods with sensitivity to the fact that free speech is an idea—one that means something different today than it did in the 19th century. Many scholars have attempted to trace the history of an idea or concept and have noted the inherent challenge to this. Rabban (1997), in commenting on the problem of studying a concept whose meaning evolves over time, noted that,

> A sensitive historian can be open to the possibility of difference in the past. Such a historian should be able to avoid reducing the unfamiliar past to the categories of the familiar present. Historical exploration may disclose meaningful origins and illustrations of a current conception of an idea, but it may also uncover lost versions that are better as well as different. (p. 13)

My goal with this research was to avoid searching for a conception of free speech that only fits contemporary notions or my own notions about what free speech means. Rather, I relied on a variety of historical sources to reconstruct the ways in which people understood the concept of free speech in the early 19th century, specific to the controversy about *Walker's Appeal.* Newspapers, pamphlets, diaries, personal letters, and other articles found in manuscript collections, as well as additional printed documents such as old state statute books (a traditional legal historical source) and minutes from meetings and conventions are the primary sources used in this research.

Newspapers were perhaps the most valuable of these primary sources because the newspapers at the time provided clear insights into the views of both publishers/writers as well as subscribers/readers who would send contributions and letters. Of course newspapers do not provide a perfect reflection of the views of all people, but they do allow historians the opportunity to uncover the general sentiments of many segments of a geographic population. In support of the use of newspapers as primary sources in this specific context, historian Mary Ryan (1997) noted that,

> As the primary nexus of an extended, multivoiced conversation the newspaper may be as close as historians can get to the voice of the public. This is not to say that these published records speak of the people any more accurately and authentically than does any other species of historical document. At the same time, newspapers and published records supply an admirably complete empirical record . . . the historian becomes witness to the oral, the imagined, the distorted, the living public. (p. 13)

Historians caution researchers about relying too heavily on newspapers because of concerns for accuracy, missed information because of deadlines, and, in the case of using 170-year-old publications, the potential tendency to take information or opinions out of context (Davidson & Lytle, 1992; Kyvig & Marty, 1982). Still, to help establish Northern and Southern public sentiment and reaction to *Walker's Appeal*, newspapers were a valuable source for this research.

Beyond making a contribution to historical understanding, why care about the struggles of the David Walkers of the world? Why care what people thought about an abstract idea more than 150 years ago? I think it is because Howard Zinn is right. It is in times of crisis and when the stakes are high that *all* voices must be heard. The First Amendment requires it. Yet history shows us that in such times the government as well as the public tends to shrink rather than expand debate. The power of free speech and the First Amendment is seen in the stories of the David Walkers of the world. History can help us not only learn from our mistakes, but also help us embrace the significance of a Constitutional guarantee to free expression in times of peace and prosperity as well as in times of crisis.

REFERENCES

Abrams v. United States, 250 U.S. 616 (1919).

Curtis, M. K. (1995). The curious history of attempts to suppress antislavery speech, press and petition in 1835–1837. *Northwestern University Law Review, 89*(3), 785–870.

Davidson, J. W., & Lytle, M. H. (1992). *After the fact: The art of historical detection.* New York: McGraw-Hill.

Debs v. United States, 249 U.S. 211 (1919).

Frohwerk v. United States, 249 U.S. 204 (1919).

Kyvig, D. E., & Marty, M. A. (1982). *Nearby history, exploring the past around you*. Walnut Creek, CA: AltaMira.

Rabban, D. M. (1997). *Free speech in its forgotten years*. Cambridge, England: Cambridge University Press.

Reynolds, A. (2001). William Lloyd Garrison, Benjamin Lundy and criminal libel: The abolitionists' plea for press freedom. *Communication Law and Policy, 6*, 577–607.

Ryan, M. P. (1997). *Civic wars: Democracy and public life in the American city during the nineteenth century*. Berkeley: University of California Press.

Schenk v. United States, 249 U.S. 47 (1919).

Zinn, H. (1990). *Declarations of independence: Cross-examining American ideology*. New York: Harper Perennial.

The Impact of *Walker's Appeal* on Northern and Southern Conceptions of Free Speech in the Nineteenth Century

Amy Reynolds

The antislavery pamphlet Walker's Appeal *helped shape the debates about limits on free speech more than three decades before the Civil War and the subsequent ratification of the Fourteenth Amendment. The pamphlet, by David Walker, influenced discussions about incendiary writing and expression and more general discussions about the value of free speech in the nineteenth century. This article explores the tension between political speech and perceived threats of violence against both citizens and the state in the context of* Walker's Appeal. *The experiences of abolitionist writers like Walker show that in the late 1820s and early 1830s the power to suppress speech still clearly remained with the states. But this article suggests that at the time public opinion was ahead of the law. A broad support of the value of free speech in the North helped protect abolitionists from Northern state suppression of their speech.*

When Supreme Court Justice Oliver Wendell Holmes dissented in *Abrams v. United States*[1] he put forth what many legal scholars today hold to be a guiding principle of the First Amendment: "[T]hat we should be eternally vigilant against attempts to check the expression of opinions that we loathe and believe to be fraught with death unless they so imminently threaten immediate interference with the lawful and pressing purposes of the law that an immediate check is required to save the country."[2] Many prominent legal scholars, whether conservative, libertarian or critical,

---

[1] *Abrams v. United States*, 250 U.S. 616 (1919).
[2] *Id.* at 630 (Holmes, J., dissenting).

agree that at the heart of the First Amendment is the most stringent protection for political speech.[3]

But what happens when political speech is considered to imminently threaten harm to either citizens or the national security of the government? This question has resurfaced since the September 11, 2001, terrorist attacks, but it is not unique. History shows that both popular opinion and the Supreme Court of the United States are willing to place limits on political expression if the right conditions exist.[4] This article explores the tension between political speech and perceived threats of violence against both citizen and state in the context of an antislavery pamphlet called *Walker's Appeal* that circulated in the late 1820s and early 1830s. *Walker's Appeal* helped shape the debates about limits on free speech more than three decades before the Civil War and the subsequent ratification of the Fourteenth Amendment. David Walker, the free black man who wrote *Walker's Appeal*, and his influence on discussions about incendiary writing and expression as well as more general discussions about the value of free speech in the nineteenth century is not addressed in the scholarly work about this period, yet *Walker's Appeal* is often cited in the newspapers of the time as the sole reason for the enactment of many Southern suppression laws.[5]

The nineteenth century provides a useful context in which to study free speech and its value to a democracy since it comes prior to both *Gitlow v. New York*,[6] in which the Supreme Court explicitly addressed the application of the First Amendment to the states for the first time, and to

---

[3]*See* OWEN M. FISS, THE IRONY OF FREE SPEECH 2 (1996); HARRY KALVEN, A WORTHY TRADITION: FREEDOM OF SPEECH IN AMERICA 119-149 (1988); ALEXANDER MEIKLEJOHN, FREE SPEECH AND ITS RELATION TO SELF-GOVERNMENT (1948); Robert H. Bork, *Neutral Principles and Some First Amendment Problems*, 47 IND. L.J. 1-35 (1971).

[4]For one example, see the series of Supreme Court cases generally called the Espionage Act cases: Abrams v. United States, 250 U.S. 616 (1919); Debs. v. United States, 249 U.S. 211 (1919); Frohwerk v. United States, 249 U.S. 204 (1919); Schenck v. United States, 249 U.S. 47 (1919). For a look at free speech implications of government regulations after Sept. 11,2001, *see* Amy Reynolds & Brooke Barnett, *Free Speech in the Wake of September 11*, in STUDIES IN TERRORISM: MEDIA SCHOLARSHIP AND THE ENIGMA OF TERROR 129-146 (Naren Chitty, Ramona R. Rush & Mehdi Semati eds., 2003).

[5]*See* HERBERT APTHEKER, ONE CONTINUAL CRY: DAVID WALKER'S APPEAL TO THE COLORED CITIZENS OF THE WORLD (1829-1830), ITS SETTING AND ITS MEANING 46-48 (1965); HENRY HIGHLAND GARNET, WALKER'S APPEAL WITH A BRIEF SKETCH OF HIS LIFE 1 (1848); PETER P. HINKS, TO AWAKEN MY AFFLICTED BRETHREN: DAVID WALKER AND THE PROBLEM OF ANTEBELLUM SLAVE RESISTANCE 196-236 (1997); ROY F. JOHNSON, THE NAT TURNER SLAVE INSURRECTION 160-161 (1966); ALICE FELT TYLER, FREEDOM'S FERMENT 485 (1944); Amy Reynolds, *William Lloyd Garrison, Benjamin Lundy and Criminal Libel: The Abolitionists' Plea for Press Freedom*, 6 COMM. L. & POL'Y 577 (2001).

[6]268 U.S. 652 (1925).

Near v. Minnesota, which established that the First Amendment prohibits prior restraint with only three exceptions.[7]

Because the First Amendment prohibited only the federal government from passing laws that would abridge the freedom of expression, the nineteenth century has become a fruitful area for the study of free speech—some of the mass communication and legal scholars who have turned their attention to this time period have helped establish the climate toward free expression both before and after the Civil War.[8] For example, Timothy Gleason's study of nineteenth century state libel cases shows that English common law prevailed when lawyers, judges and litigants tried to define freedom of the press.[9] Gleason writes, "Judges recognized constitutional protections, but looked to English common law to determine the meaning and extent of the protection provided under the Constitution."[10] Margaret Blanchard notes that through nineteenth century state court decisions, "The basic assumptions upon which Supreme Court decisions were constructed are found. . . . [T]he state courts played an important role in laying the foundations for a modern-day understanding of freedom of speech and of the press."[11]

Given the importance of state government and state courts in interpreting the law during this period, the abolitionists are a significant group to study. A central question in American politics in the mid- to late–1830s involved the degree to which the federal government would try to stop the abolitionists from criticizing the legal institution of slavery in the South.[12] At the time the First Amendment was believed to only prohibit the federal government from passing laws that would abridge the freedom of expression, so free speech debates centered on the individual states' ability to suppress abolitionist speech. Although events of the

---

[7]283 U.S. 697, 716 (1931) (obscenity, threats to national security and incitement to violence).

[8]*See* MICHAEL KENT CURTIS, FREE SPEECH, "THE PEOPLE'S DARLING PRIVILEGE," STRUGGLES FOR FREEDOM OF EXPRESSION IN AMERICAN HISTORY 117-241 (2000); DONNA L. DICKERSON, THE COURSE OF TOLERANCE: FREEDOM OF THE PRESS IN NINETEENTH CENTURY AMERICA 81-221 (1990); TIMOTHY W. GLEASON, THE WATCHDOG CONCEPT: THE PRESS AND THE COURTS IN NINETEENTH CENTURY AMERICA 39-99 (1990); DAVID RABBAN, FREE SPEECH IN ITS FORGOTTEN YEARS 1-21 (1997); Margaret A. Blanchard, *Filling in the Void: Speech and Press in State Courts Prior to Gitlow*, in THE FIRST AMENDMENT RECONSIDERED: NEW PERSPECTIVES ON THE MEANING OF FREEDOM OF SPEECH AND PRESS 14-43 (Charlene J. Brown & Bill F. Chamberlin eds., 1982); Michael Kent Curtis, *The Curious History of Attempts to Suppress Anti-Slavery Speech, Press, and Petition in 1835-37*, 89 NW. U.L. REV. 785 (1995); Reynolds, *supra* note 5, at 577-607.

[9]GLEASON, *supra* note 8, at 39.

[10]*Id.* at 42.

[11]Blanchard, *supra* note 8, at 43.

[12]*See* Curtis, *supra* note 8, at 785.

late 1830s (censorship of the mails and the directed free speech attacks by the Southern states on the abolitionists' incendiary publications, for example) significantly identified free expression issues focused on the abolitionists, the roots of these issues started to grow a decade earlier largely due to the writings of Walker, William Lloyd Garrison, Benjamin Lundy and other abolitionists.[13] As both common sense and general history would suggest, the North and the South disagreed about the extent of guaranteed protections for abolitionist speech. Some of this disagreement hinged on whether abolitionist speech would cause slaves to revolt, leading to an imminent threat against both a state and its citizens.

THE ABOLITIONISTS AND FREE SPEECH

In 1855, Frederick Douglass spoke to the Rochester Ladies Anti-Slavery Society and noted that by 1830, "Speaking and writing on the subject of slavery became dangerous," and that "like true apostles, as they were, [the abolitionists'] faith in their principles knew no wavering."[14] Noted early nineteenth century abolitionist writers and publishers like Benjamin Lundy and William Lloyd Garrison encountered difficulty in expressing their opinions even prior to 1830,[15] but widespread attempts to suppress abolitionist speech did not really occur until after 1830.[16] Suppression efforts were greatest in the South, where fear of slave insurrection ran high, especially after the Nat Turner uprising in Virginia in 1831.[17] But expressing anti-slavery sentiments could also be dangerous in the North—mob violence was one way disgruntled Northerners attempted to suppress abolitionist speech.[18] Despite a general dislike of abo-

---

[13]*See* Reynolds, *supra* note 5, at 577.

[14]FREDERICK DOUGLASS, THE ANTI-SLAVERY MOVEMENT: A LECTURE BY FREDERICK DOUGLASS BEFORE THE ROCHESTER LADIES ANTI-SLAVERY SOCIETY 20 (1855).

[15]For a detailed account of Lundy and Garrison's free speech struggles, *see* Reynolds, *supra* note 5, at 590-607.

[16]*See* Curtis, *supra* note 8, at 785.

[17]*See* JOHNSON, *supra* note 5, at 160.

[18]Historian Thomas C. Leonard has attempted to explain the reasons for Northern dislike of abolitionist speech. He concludes that the people who lived in the North were frightened by abolitionist speech because it threatened to change the nature of political communication by circumventing established newspapers to spread abolitionist messages and by undermining the authority of community leaders through self-organized rallies and meetings. In a broader sense, many historians have suggested that some individuals in the North reacted so strongly to the abolitionists in the 1830s because they had gained significant power and through that power might actually cause the dissolution of the union. For a detailed account of these arguments and other possible reasons for the North's general antagonistic reaction to the abolitionists, *see* THOMAS C. LEONARD, NEWS FOR ALL: AMERICA'S COMING OF AGE WITH THE PRESS 69-73 (1995); LEONARD L. RICHARDS, "GENTLEMEN OF PROPERTY AND STANDING": ANTI-ABOLITION MOBS IN JACKSONIAN AMERICA 20-82 (1970).

litionist rhetoric, freedom to criticize slavery in the North was seen by many as "inherent in free speech, free press and popular sovereignty."[19] This belief was especially embraced by Northern legislatures and public officials who continually denied requests by Southern officials to suppress abolitionist writings, despite their personal feelings about the offensive nature of some anti-slavery speech.[20]

In the South, however, criticism of slavery was widely seen as unacceptable. Southerners who advocated suppression in the form of laws, argued that the abolitionists threatened to ignite slave rebellion and that the threat of rebellion actually threatened the survival of the union. These sentiments are clearly seen in the two words Southerners used most often when denouncing abolitionist writings—"incendiary" and "seditious."[21] A clear distinction regarding which abolitionist writings the Southerners considered incendiary and which they considered seditious does not emerge from an examination of the printed documents (newspapers, letters, diaries and laws) of the period. Both words are frequently encountered, but no explicit distinction between the two is made or implied.[22] Most likely, Southerners saw the two concepts as directly linked—incendiary publications could lead to sedition and seditious publications by their very nature were also incendiary. The almost synonymous use of these words is intriguing, but it cannot be explained in the context of the writings and events examined here.

Closely tied to the Southern concerns of sedition and incitement was "a view of the constitutional compact that made abolitionism illegitimate."[23] By attempting to spread their message in the South, the abolitionists, many people believed, were violating or circumventing valid state laws. So the question about the suppression of abolitionist speech was a complex one, largely because the North and South "had separate systems with different assumptions and needs."[24]

---

[19]Curtis, *supra* note 8, at 814.

[20]Southern attempts to suppress abolitionist writing by requesting support from public officials and legislatures in the North was common in 1829-30. *See* APTHEKER, *supra* note 5, at 46-48; JOHNSON, *supra* note 5, at 160-161; TYLER, *supra* note 5, at 485.

[21]These two terms were often used synonymously. In general, the word "incendiary" referred to stirring up agitation or violence or creating sedition; something was considered "seditious" if it challenged the authority of the state or could potentially cause rebellion against the state. *See* Amy Reynolds, Emancipation and Expression: How Abolitionists Helped Define Free Speech in the Early Nineteenth Century 1-15, 170 (1998) (unpublished Ph.D. dissertation, University of Texas at Austin, 1998) (on file with the University of Texas Library).

[22]*See id.*

[23]Curtis, *supra* note 8, at 802.

[24]*Id.* at 814.

Despite the continual efforts of the South to challenge the free speech rights of those who spoke or wrote against slavery, the abolitionists supported the free speech rights of those who supported slavery, even though they found a pro-slavery position morally indefensible: "It was their faith that ideas of liberty would defeat slavery so long as persuasion and argument were the only weapons allowed in the contest. . . . Abolitionists saw calls for censorship as a confession of weakness."[25] The South, however, saw calls for censorship as a necessary defense against Northern publications they believed threatened their safety and their livelihood. This became readily apparent at the end of 1829 with the appearance of David Walker's *Appeal*. Like no other publication that came before it, *Walker's Appeal* would illustrate just how differently the North and South viewed free speech rights when it came to determining protective standards for abolitionist speech.

DAVID WALKER AND HIS *APPEAL*

In October 1829, a free black man from Boston named David Walker published and distributed a pamphlet called *Walker's Appeal in Four Articles, Together with a Preamble to the Colored Citizens of the World, But in Particular and Very Expressly to Those of the United States*. As the Reverend Henry Highland Garnet[26] wrote nearly 20 years later:

> This little book produced more commotion amongst slaveholders than any volume of its size that was ever issued from an American press. They saw that it was a bold attack upon their idolatry, and that too by a black man who once lived amongst them. It was merely a smooth stone which this David took up, and yet it terrified a host of Goliaths.[27]

Walker's Appeal, as it was commonly called, was an unusual pamphlet because it was considered incendiary in nature by both slaveholders and abolitionists: "Walker's solution of the problem of the Negro was insurrection and violence. The articles were expositions of the four causes for the wretchedness of the colored race: slavery, ignorance, religious teaching, and the colonization scheme."[28] The only supporters of Walker's message were blacks and a few radical abolitionists like William Lloyd

---

[25]*Id.* at 868–869.

[26]Garnet was an influential black minister and abolitionist who wrote that *Walker's Appeal* greatly influenced his work and thoughts about slavery. Garnet became prominent in abolitionist circles during the 1840s. *See* GARNET, *supra* note 5.

[27]GARNET, *supra* note 5, at 1.

[28]TYLER, *supra* note 5, at 484.

Garrison, who supported Walker's right to publish his pamphlet and express his views but who qualified his support for Walker's message.[29] As a pacifist, Garrison did not support Walker's militant message, writing in the *Liberator* that "we depreciate the spirit and tendency of this Appeal. . . . we do not teach rebellion—no, but submission and peace."[30]

Walker's Appeal was one of the first written assaults upon slavery to come from a black man in the United States.[31] In the pamphlet, Walker specifically attacked several political solutions to slavery, most notably the colonization movement. Walker wrote that "America is more our country than it is the whites—we have enriched it with our blood and tears."[32] Walker challenged Thomas Jefferson's claim that blacks were innately inferior to whites, and he placed some of the burdens of slavery on his own people for tolerating the ignorance and cruelty forced upon them.[33] He also showed

> a profound pride in his people and a deep awareness of their militancy and their discontent. In that sense, his words and his call—and his very being—are blasting replies to those of the past, and of the present, who find—or say they find—some special docility or passivity in Negro people, as contrasted with all other peoples in the world.[34]

Walker made it clear in his pamphlet that his hatred was directed at slave owners specifically, and not all whites.[35] The main point of the pamphlet was that slavery is anti-human and that the persistence in continuing slavery would eventually bring about destruction.[36] On the specific use of violence, Walker was sometimes ambiguous: He wrote that his position grew out of the Declaration of Independence, which he believed repudiated both pacifism and terrorism:

> See your Declaration Americans!! Do you understand your own language? Hear your language, proclaimed to the world, July 4th, 1776—"We hold these truths to be self evident—that ALL men are created EQUAL!! That they are *endowed by their creator with certain un-alienable rights;* that among these are life, *liberty* and the pursuit of happiness!!"

---

[29]William Lloyd Garrison, *Walker's Appeal No. 1*, LIBERATOR, Jan. 8, 1831, at 2.
[30]*Id.*
[31]See HINKS, *supra* note 5, at 107.
[32]DAVID WALKER, WALKER'S APPEAL IN FOUR ARTICLES, TOGETHER WITH A PREAMBLE TO THE COLORED CITIZENS OF THE WORLD, BUT IN PARTICULAR AND VERY EXPRESSLY TO THOSE OF THE UNITED STATES 77 (3rd ed.) (1830).
[33]*Id.*
[34]APTHEKER, *supra* note 5, at 56-57.
[35]WALKER, *supra* note 32, at 77.
[36]*Id.*

Compare your own language, above, extracted from your Declaration of Independence, with your cruelties and murders inflicted by your cruel and unmerciful fathers and yourselves on our fathers and on us—men who have never given your fathers or you the least provocation! !!!!! Hear your language further! "But when a long train of abuses and usurpation, pursuing invariably the same object, evinces a design to reduce them under absolute despotism, it is their right, it is their duty, to throw off such government, and to provide new guards for their future security."[37]

In other passages, Walker more clearly advocated violent overthrow as a strategy for achieving freedom, especially if no other alternative exists. In the *Appeal*, Walker seemed to state that violence, even if it came in the form of a white massacre, was not an ideal strategy and should be avoided, but that such a strategy was at least understandable.[38] For example, Walker tells the story of a small group of slaves who murdered a few white slave dealers in order to gain their freedom. Another slave reported them to the white authorities, and the freed slaves were recaptured.[39] Wrote Walker:

We must remember that humanity, kindness and the fear of the Lord, does not consist in protecting devils. . . . What has the Lord to do with a gang of desperate wretches, who go sneaking about the country like robbers—light upon his people wherever they can get a chance, binding them with chains and handcuffs, beat and murder them as they would rattle-snakes? Are they not the Lord's enemies? Ought they not be destroyed? Any person who will save such wretches from destruction, is fighting against the Lord, and will receive his just recompense.[40]

Walker's impassioned thoughts about slavery did not grow out of his own experiences as a slave, but rather out of his observations of slavery.[41] He was born a free black man in Wilmington, N.C., on September 28, 1785.[42] His mother was a free black and his father was a slave who died a few months before he was born.[43] Garnet writes that Walker's hatred of slavery was very early developed:

When yet a boy, he declared that the slaveholding South was not the place for him. His soul became so indignant at the wrongs which his father and

---

[37]*Id.* at 77.

[38]*Id.* at 24.

[39]*Id.* at 25.

[40]*Id.*

[41]*See* APTHEKER, *supra* note 5, at 41; GARNET, *supra* note 5, at 2.

[42]GARNET, *supra* note 5, at 2.

[43]*Id.* Walker's son was also posthumous.

kindred bore, that he determined to find some portion of his country where he would see less to harrow his soul. Said he "If I remain in this bloody land, I will not live long. As true as God reigns, I will be avenged for the sorrow which my people have suffered."[44]

Walker traveled through parts of the South and eventually headed north, ending up in Boston by late 1825 or early 1826.[45] In 1827, he began working in the second-hand clothing business on Boston's busy Brattle Street, which was located near the seaports. It was Walker's position as a small business owner that "facilitated his entrance into established black Boston."[46] Walker had become a leading member of Boston's black community, not only because of his business but also because he was actively involved in black Boston's social and political gatherings. Walker was a leader of the General Colored Association of Boston, a member of the African Lodge, and an agent for the newly published *Freedom's Journal.*[47] By 1828, Walker had become a respected speaker and organizer.[48] In December 1828, the text of one of Walker's addresses to the General Colored Association of Boston appeared in the *Journal.*[49] Even before his *Appeal*, Walker was advocating the unification of the black population and the use of any option to end slavery and improve conditions for blacks in America:

> It is necessary to remark here, at once, that the primary object of this institution [the GCA], is to unite the colored population so far, through the United States of America, as may be practicable and expedient; forming societies, opening, extending, and keeping up correspondences and not withholding any thing which might have the least tendency to meliorate our miserable condition—with the restrictions, however, of not infringing on

---

[44]GARNET, *supra* note 5, at 2.

[45]*See* APTHEKER, *supra* note 5, at 41; HINKS, *supra* note 5, at 13-15. Aptheker suggests that Walker taught himself to read and write once he arrived in Boston; Hinks makes a stronger argument that Walker was secretly educated through the efforts of the AME Church as a child in North Carolina. It was common for churches, both black and white, to educate free blacks, and sometimes slaves, so that they could read the Bible and have a stronger religious understanding.

[46]HINKS, *supra* note 5, at 67.

[47]*See* HINKS, *supra* note 5, at 74. *Freedom's Journal*, the first newspaper published by free blacks, began publication in 1827 in New York City. *See* FREEDOM'S JOURNAL, Mar. 16, 1827, at 1. For additional, comprehensive information about *Freedom's Journal*, see DONALD M. JACOBS, ANTEBELLUM BLACK NEWSPAPERS: INDICES TO NEW YORK'S FREEDOM'S JOURNAL (1827-1829), THE RIGHTS OF ALL (1829), THE WEEKLY ADVOCATE (1837), AND THE COLORED AMERICAN (1837-1841) 3 (1976); Bella Gross, *Freedom's Journal and the Rights of All*, 17 J. OF NEGRO HIST. 277 (1932).

[48]*Id.*

[49]David Walker, *Address to the General Colored Association of Boston*, FREEDOM'S JOURNAL, Dec. 19, 1828, at 1.

the articles of its constitution, or that of the United States of America. . . . It is indispensably our duty to try every scheme that we think will have a tendency to facilitate our salvation and leave the final result to that.[50]

Walker continued to speak about the condition of blacks, both free and slave, at GCA and at other free black meetings. He wrote the first of three revised editions of his *Appeal* and distributed it in October 1829.[51] Walker typically delivered his pamphlet through the mails and by way of individuals who carried copies, particularly on ships.[52] Because Walker lived and worked near the sea, and maritime employment was common for free blacks, most people speculated that this was the primary means by which Walker distributed the *Appeal*. Some white men also served as distributors of the pamphlet.[53]

REACTION TO *WALKER'S APPEAL*

Walker's Appeal was discovered in the South almost immediately after its publication.[54] Many states quickly passed legislative measures to try to stop its perceived effects, namely slave insurrections, none of which had been attributed to *Walker's Appeal* by the end of 1829.[55] The pamphlet was also disseminated in the North, but few people paid it much attention in 1829. William Lloyd Garrison and Benjamin Lundy, two of the leading abolitionist publishers and writers at the time, had received copies of the pamphlet as early as November 1829, but did not write any substantial comments about it until early 1830, after the South had swiftly

---

[50]*Id.*

[51]*See* APTHEKER, *supra* note 5, at 45; HINKS, *supra* note 5, at 116.

[52]*Id.*

[53]For a detailed account of the distribution of *Walker's Appeal*, *see* HINKS, *supra* note 5, at 116-195.

[54]*See* Clement Eaton, *A Dangerous Pamphlet in the Old South*, 2 J. OF S. HIST. 325 (August, 1936); William Lloyd Garrison, *Black List: Singular Panic*, GENIUS OF UNIVERSAL EMANCIPATION, Jan. 15, 1831, at 147. Benjamin Lundy edited the *Genius of Universal Emancipation*, and the paper often did not contain formal bylines. All subsequent citations to the *Genius* include bylines when the author is known or listed, article titles (when included) and page numbers (which ran consecutively throughout each year). Some of the subsequent publication dates include only the month and year since the *Genius* switched from a weekly publication to a monthly publication in April 1830. Lundy wrote most of the paper's content. Garrison was responsible for editing and writing the "Black List" section of the newspaper during the time he worked there between 1829 and 1830. The "Black List" was a weekly feature that highlighted and detailed particularly egregious behavior by the government or individuals towards slaves and free blacks.

[55]See Eaton, *supra* note 54, at 325; Garrison, *supra*, note 54, at 147.

responded with legislation aimed at curbing the effects of such incendiary writing.[56] *Walker's Appeal* became one of the first indications that the North and the South did not, and would not, agree on the magnitude of free speech protections for strongly worded abolitionist messages.

One of the first places the pamphlet appeared in the South was the Georgia port city of Savannah. In May 1829, just a few months before *Walker's Appeal* appeared in Savannah, "[A] disastrous fire swept the [nearby] city of Augusta which consumed nearly all the arms of the local militia. A suspicion was aroused that the conflagration was the handiwork of slaves who were plotting an insurrection, especially since fires broke out in various parts of the city."[57]

By October, rumors of slave uprisings across the entire state of Georgia had not quieted down. The appearance of *Walker's Appeal* further aggravated southern fears. In December, William T. Williams, the mayor of Savannah, wrote Georgia Governor George Gilmer to inform him that a slave who was found possessing dozens of Walker's pamphlets had been arrested, although, according to the mayor, the slave was later discharged because he appeared "ignorant of the contents."[58] Williams urged Gilmer to use his influence to convince the Georgia delegation in Congress to pass legislation that prohibited printing incendiary publications similar to *Walker's Appeal*.[59] Gilmer agreed and sent a copy of the *Appeal* to former Georgia Governor John Forsyth, who had recently been elected to the U.S. Senate, urging him to convince Congress to take some action against such incendiary writings.[60] Forsyth "refused to urge the Georgia delegation in Congress to initiate the desired legislation." In a letter addressed to Williams, Forsyth told him that the federal government did not have the power to pass such legislation, but "[T]he authority of the state was competent to pass all necessary laws relating to slavery."[61]

Williams took Forsyth's advice of turning to the state, and he asked Gilmer to present their case to the Georgia legislature. In his December 1829 speech to the legislature, Governor Gilmer mentioned receiving a letter from the Savannah mayor "informing me that sixty pamphlets of a highly seditious character had been seized by the police of the city."[62] Gilmer and Williams suggested that *Walker's Appeal* threatened the safety of the white residents of the state, and the Georgia state representatives

---

[56]*See* Reynolds, *supra* note 5, at 602.
[57]Eaton, *supra* note 54, at 326.
[58]*Id.*
[59]*Id. See also* Garrison, *supra* note 54, at 147.
[60]*Id.*
[61]*Id.* at 326–327.
[62]APTHEKER, *supra* note 5, at 46.

agreed, quickly passing several laws designed to stop the distribution of the *Appeal*.[63]

One of the newly passed laws quarantined black sailors on boats coming into Georgia harbors to prevent their having shore leave, since they were considered a primary means of distribution for the pamphlet.[64] If black sailors attempted to disembark, they would be put in jail for the duration of the ship's stay in port.[65] Another law held that anyone found guilty of introducing or circulating any publication for the purpose of exciting a revolt among slaves in the state could face the death penalty.[66]

In addition to lobbying the state legislature, Williams and Gilmer wrote separate letters to Mayor Harrison Gray Otis of Boston, telling him that his city was the source of Walker's "highly inflammatory" work.[67] Williams begged Otis to do something to stop Walker from publishing his work. Mayor Otis sent an emissary to Walker's second-hand clothing shop to find out more about the pamphlet.[68] Walker admitted to writing the *Appeal* and said he intended to continue printing and distributing it. Otis then issued a warning to ships' captains sailing out of Boston to be on the lookout for seditious cargo, referring to *Walker's Appeal* even though he did not mention it by name.[69] Otis also wrote letters to Williams and Gilmer explaining that Walker had violated no federal or Massachusetts law and "therefore—much as all sensible people regretted what he wrote and what he was doing—he could not be stopped legally."[70]

Some Boston newspapers had heard of Williams' and Gilmer's letters to Otis and reported on the actions that the Georgia legislature had taken against the *Appeal*.[71] The editor of the Boston *Columbian Centinel* observed that the Georgia laws did seem "at first blush violent and sanguinary." He continued:

> On nearer approach, however, it appears necessary to the immediate safety of whites. We have seen the pamphlet, which is doubtless here alluded to

---

[63] JOURNAL OF THE HOUSE OF REPRESENTATIVES OF THE STATE OF GEORGIA, 1829-1830, 353-354 (1830).

[64] *Id. See also* Garrison, *supra* note 54, at 147.

[65] *Id.*

[66] *Id. See also* APTHEKER, *supra* note 5, at 48; WENDELL PHILLIPS GARRISON & FRANCIS JACKSON GARRISON, 1 WILLIAM LLOYD GARRISON: THE STORY OF HIS LIFE TOLD BY HIS CHILDREN 161-162 (1885); TYLER, *supra* note 5, at 485; Garrison, *supra* note 54, at 147.

[67] APTHEKER, *supra* note 5, at 46.

[68] *See id.*

[69] *See id.*

[70] *Id.*

[71] *See* Benjamin Russell, BOSTON COLUMBIAN CENTINEL, Jan. 16, 1830, at 1.

and do not hesitate to pronounce it one of the most wicked and inflammatory productions that ever issued from the press. Its character is entirely mischievous, without one redeeming quality. . . . It reveals a disposition that would exult to see the white population slaughtered in their beds.[72]

Despite the fact that the citizens of Boston, and Otis as an individual, seemed to understand Georgia's legislative action, as a public official Otis was unwilling to infringe upon Walker's rights to free speech or to propose legislation he thought would infringe upon those rights. As Garnet relays the event:

His Honor replied to the Southern Governor that he had no power nor disposition to hinder Mr. Walker from pursuing a lawful course in the utterance of his thoughts. A company of Georgia men then bound themselves by an oath that they would eat as little as possible until they had killed the youthful author. They also offered a reward of a thousand dollars for his head, and ten times as much for the live Walker.[73]

As a result of the North's lack of interest in attempting to silence writings like Walker's, several Southern states followed Georgia's lead and passed legislation to insulate their slaves "from the contamination of such noxious pamphlets."[74] Heavy penalties were allowed for the circulation of publications inciting slaves to rebellion. It was made illegal to teach a slave to read or write,[75] and blacks were not permitted to travel without white escorts, nor could they assemble in large groups unless a white person was present.[76] According to the biography of William Lloyd Garrison written by Garrison's children, the laws that the Georgia legislature passed and that served as the southern example of how to handle the *Appeal*, "were rushed through in a single day on the discovery of Walker's incendiary pamphlet."[77]

Between the end of 1829 and the spring of 1831, a substantial amount of legislation "of a precautionary nature" was enacted in the South.[78] In 1830, North Carolina law prohibited the dissemination of publications that "tended to produce slave revolt or dissension" and made it a crime to

---

[72]*Id.*

[73]GARNET, *supra* note 5, at 2.

[74]Garrison, *supra* note 54, at 147. *See also* TYLER, *supra* note 5, at 485.

[75]*See id.* at 147. Georgia was the first state to enact this law in 1829. *See* TYLER, *supra* note 5, at 485.

[76]*See* APTHEKER, *supra* note 5, at 48; GARRISON & GARRISON, *supra* note 66, at 161; TYLER, *supra* note 5, at 485; Garrison, *supra* note 54, at 147.

[77]GARRISON & GARRISON, *supra* note 66, at 161

[78]*Id.* at 161-162.

teach slaves to read.[79] And, as noted in the Georgia laws, since free blacks on ships were strongly suspected of distributing incendiary publications, North Carolina also decided to provide for the temporary imprisonment of free black sailors who came into Southern ports.[80]

In Louisiana in 1830, the legislature passed two acts directed toward stopping the spread of the *Appeal*, one of which threatened death or life in prison to anyone who would "write, print, publish, or distribute any thing having a tendency to create discontent among the free colored population of this state, or insubordination among the slaves therein."[81] The second act was designed, like others in the South, to reinforce penalties for teaching slaves to read or write.[82]

Many of the newly passed laws were the result of secret legislative sessions, so few of them are documented in the session law books of 1829–1831. In some cases, like that of North Carolina, the laws are documented, but the discussions that preceded them are not.[83] Many of the accounts of the laws came from newspapers in the various states, and Virginia was no exception to the "newspaper exposure" phenomenon when it started to consider the passage of a "no reading and writing" law.[84] Garrison and Lundy heard of the proposed bill after reading an account of the Virginia House of Delegates' secret session in the Richmond *Whig*.[85]

The details of the bill appeared under the regular *Black List* feature, written by Garrison in Lundy's abolitionist newspaper the *Genius of Universal Emancipation*:

> A bill has passed the Virginia House of Delegates by a vote of 81 to 80, which prohibits the *instruction of free negroes, mulattoes or slaves*, either in religious or secular knowledge, under the most aggravated penalties. This abominable act owes its origin to the circulation of a stirring pamphlet, addressed to all colored people, by David Walker of Boston—a most injudicious publication, yet warranted by the creed of an independent people. It is, says the Richmond *Whig*, "as far as our knowledge extends, the most

---

[79]Act to Prevent Circulation of Seditious Publications, Ch. 5, 1830 N.C. Session Laws 10.

[80]Act Passed by the General Assembly of North Carolina, Ch. 30, 1831 N.C. Session Laws 29.

[81]Hinks, *supra* note 5, at 150.

[82]See id.

[83]See Eaton, *supra* note 54, at 331-32. Eaton noted that some citizens of North Carolina were concerned about the secrecy with which the legislative sessions were conducted.

[84]William Lloyd Garrison, *Black List: Astounding Legislation*, Genius of Universal Emancipation, Feb. 26, 1830, at 195.

[85]Id.

highly penal (law) of any that has been enacted by any American Legislature. It is indefensible." We believe it can never be executed.[86]

Garrison and the *Whig* were temporarily correct. The Virginia State Senate rejected the bill 11-7, but by the end of 1831 the law would resurface and pass. For "history's sake," the *Genius* printed the provisions of the bill in their entirety in the March 5, 1830, edition.[87]

In that same edition, Lundy noted that additional state attempts to thwart the circulation of *Walker's Appeal* continued. He relayed that an editor at a Kentucky newspaper was arrested but later discharged for possessing twenty copies of the pamphlet.[88]

Discussion of *Walker's Appeal* continued in the *Genius* during the spring and summer of 1830.[89] Lundy continued to monitor the effects of the *Appeal* and comment on its contents. Although most people were familiar with the pamphlet's existence, few had read it or understood its contents. In April 1830, Lundy offered the first glimpse of his thoughts on the *Appeal*.[90] He wrote that "a more bold, daring, inflammatory publication, perhaps, never issued from the press, in any country. I can do no less than set the broadest set of condemnation upon it."[91] Lundy focused his attack of the *Appeal* on the means by which Walker advocated the end of slavery—through rebellion, if necessary. Lundy avoided the question of whether speech such as Walker's should be protected.[92]

The subject of Walker was not broached by Lundy or Garrison again until Garrison began publishing the *Liberator* in 1831, where *Walker's Appeal* received its most favorable treatment. A discussion of its effects was ongoing in the newspaper, and Garrison continually supported its right to exist as free speech, even though he disagreed with violence as a means to end slavery.[93]

---

[86]*Id.*

[87]William Lloyd Garrison, *Black List*, GENIUS OF UNIVERSAL EMANCIPATION, Mar. 5, 1830, at 203.

[88]Benjamin Lundy, *More on the Pamphlet*, GENIUS OF UNIVERSAL EMANCIPATION, Mar. 5, 1830, at 202.

[89]Direct discussion of the content of the *Appeal* was rare in mainstream Southern newspapers such as the Richmond *Whig* and the Richmond *Enquirer*. An analysis of the two newspapers in 1829 and 1830 indicates they made scant mention of the *Appeal* and provided no information about the content.

[90]Benjamin Lundy, *Walker's Boston Pamphlet*, GENIUS OF UNIVERSAL EMANCIPATION, Apr., 1830, at 15.

[91]*Id.*

[92]*Id.*

[93]Garrison, *supra* note 29, at 2.

In the third issue of the *Liberator*, a letter from "A Colored Bostonian" questioned the circumstances of Walker's death on June 28, 1830.[94] "The most I can learn is, that some one or more, recently from the south, spread a report in this city that a reward of $1,000 was offered by southern planters to anyone who would take the life of Walker."[95] Garrison replied that he heard the sum was as high as $30,000.[96] Although Walker's cause of death was never determined, speculation that he was poisoned eventually subsided and most agreed that he died of natural causes.[97]

In the next week's *Liberator*, a man named "Leo" offered criticism of *Walker's Appeal* because of its marked effects in the South.[98] "I am opposed to the pamphlet, therefore, in the second place because I believe it to be at the bottom of the recent enactments of severe laws in the southern states, such as are too notorious to be mentioned."[99] Garrison replied, "We have repeatedly expressed our disapprobation of [the *Appeal's*] general spirit. It contains, however, many valuable truths and seasonable warnings."[100] Still, few questioned that the reading and writing laws and the incendiary publication laws—among others—grew out of rebellion fears that Southerners traced directly to *Walker's Appeal*.[101]

In that same edition of the *Liberator*, Garrison reprinted a column from the Greensborough, N.C., *Patriot* which noted: "From what we can learn of this incendiary and sanguinary production, we depreciate its circulation and cheerfully accord with those who are taking measures to suppress it," but later added, "If the Legislatures of the southern states wish to guard effectually against insurrection, they cannot do it by abridging the already limited privileges of the slave."[102]

Discussions of *Walker's Appeal* by many readers of the *Liberator* continued through the end of February 1831. In April and May, Garrison printed a series of articles that reprinted sections of the *Appeal* that were accompanied by letters from a man who signed his writings only with the letter "V." This compelling series showed how much the reputation *of Walker's Appeal* had subverted its content. For example:

> I have often heard, and constantly believed, that *Walker's Appeal* was the incoherent rhapsody of a blood-thirsty, but vulgar and very ignorant fa-

---

[94]*Death of Walker*, LIBERATOR, Jan. 22, 1831, at 1.
[95]*Id*.
[96]*Id*.
[97]*Id*.
[98]*Walker's Appeal*, LIBERATOR, Jan. 29, 1831, at 1.
[99]*Id*.
[100]*Id*.
[101]*Id*.
[102]*Walker's Pamphlet*, LIBERATOR, Jan. 29, 1831, at 4.

natic, and have therefore felt no little astonishment that it should have created so much alarm in the slaveholding states. . . . I have now read the book and my opinions are changed. It is vain to call him incendiary, ruffian, or exciter of sedition. Let those who hold him such, imagine the circumstances of the two classes of our population reversed, and those who now rise up and call him cursed will build him a monument, and cry hosannah to the patriot, the herald of freedom. . . . The further I have read his pamphlet, the less has been *my* surprise that he is regarded among his people as a man inspired.[103]

In a subsequent issue, "V" observed that many sections of the *Appeal* were "written in a sincere and patriotic spirit. Let those who believe in the mental inferiority of the blacks read it and acknowledge that *if* their theory is true, David Walker was an exception to it."[104]

THE EFFECT OF THE APPEAL
ON GARRISON AND LUNDY

If *Walker's Appeal* had seemed incendiary to the South, the first issue of Garrison's *Liberator* in January 1831 was also a "summons to every agency of self-defense, for it was the cry of the outraged conscience of the white North, and with its passionate assertion there could be no compromise" regarding slavery.[105] By publishing the *Liberator*, one of the most popular early abolitionist newspapers, Garrison would soon find himself in the company of Walker as far as southern laws were concerned.

By September 1831, the South claimed it had correctly identified *Walker's Appeal* as incendiary and had added Garrison's *Liberator* and Lundy's *Genius of Universal Emancipation* to its list of illegal publications after the Southampton slave insurrections.[106] A large number of slaveholders, newspaper editors and public officials in the South directly attributed the August 1831 slave insurrection led by Nat Turner to Walker, Garrison and other abolitionists.[107] Early on the morning of August 22, 1831, Turner and a group of rebels began an insurrection in Southampton County, Virginia, that lasted only a few hours but left at least 55 white men, women and children dead, some gruesomely massacred.[108] It did not take long for news of the insurrection to spread, and

---

[103]*Walker's Appeal No. 2*, LIBERATOR, May 14, 1831, at 2.

[104]*Walker's Appeal No. 3*, LIBERATOR, May 28, 1831, at 1.

[105]TYLER, *supra* note 5, at 488.

[106]*See* Charles Edward Morris, *Panic and Reprisal: Reaction in North Carolina to the Nat Turner Insurrection*, 112 N.C. HIST. REV. 29 (January 1985).

[107]*See id.*

[108]*See id.*

only a few hours after the murders took place, residents of nearby North Carolina were already facing a state of emergency. The militia and citizens were called to arms, and North Carolina Governor Montfort Stokes was receiving urgent requests for weapons and ammunition from all corners of the state, where fear had taken over.[109]

After the fact, *Walker's Appeal* and abolitionist newspapers like Garrison's were assigned a large part of the blame for Turner's actions.[110] Many southern slaveholders believed these publications had incited their slaves to rebel and, because of this, they clearly identified abolitionist speech as incendiary and illegal. Many historians have attempted to document a connection between Turner and *Walker's Appeal*, but none has been found.[111] Historian Peter P. Hinks suggests that historians can only speculate on whether Turner had read or been exposed to the *Appeal*, but he notes that the historical record clearly shows that the slave society in which Nat Turner lived was a world in which the *Appeal* would most likely be favorably received.[112] Walker himself encouraged "all colored men, women and children of every nation, language and tongue under heaven," to copy, distribute and read the *Appeal* or have it read to them in the preamble of the pamphlet.[113]

Some historians have suggested a connection between Turner and *Walker's Appeal* because some newspapers and societal leaders asserted that a connection existed.[114] One of those leaders was Lundy, who found the content of the *Appeal* offensive.[115] Lundy was also well aware of the Southern reaction to the *Appeal* because the *Liberator* and his own *Genius of Universal Emancipation* were often included in the same category. This frustrated Lundy. He did not consider his or Garrison's newspapers to be in the same category as the *Appeal* because neither advocated violence as an acceptable way to end slavery.[116] In a diary entry regarding a Turner connection to the *Appeal*, Lundy wrote that "[t]he pamphlet of David Walker, which [Turner] had probably seen, had professed much religious zeal, and urged insurrection on the alleged authority of the New Testament."[117]

Walker's Appeal, the *Liberator* and, to a lesser extent, Lundy's *Genius*—combined with the insurrection—caused the severity of the additions to

---

[109]*See Causes of Slave Insurrections*, LIBERATOR, Sept. 17, 1831, at 3. *See also* HINKS, *supra* note 5, at 160-161, 163-164; Morris, *supra* note 106, at 31.

[110]*See id.*

[111]*See* HINKS, *supra* note 5, at 169.

[112]*See id.*

[113]*See* WALKER, *supra* note 32, at 1.

[114]*See* TYLER, *supra* note 5, at 488. *See also* BENJAMIN LUNDY, THE LIFE, TRAVELS AND OPINIONS OF BENJAMIN LUNDY 249 (1847).

[115]*Id.*

[116]*Id.*

[117]LUNDY, *supra* note 114, at 249.

the slave codes in many states and furthered the general suppression efforts toward anti-slavery sentiment.[118] For example, after Nat Turner's insurrection, in all slave states except Maryland, Kentucky, Tennessee and Arkansas, it was against the law to teach a slave to read or write.[119] The laws were an especially peculiar way Southerners attempted to thwart the penetration of the *Appeal* and other incendiary publications. Scholars who have studied slave literacy have suggested that only about one of every ten slaves was literate; the abolitionists themselves frequently challenged the slave literacy laws making a similar argument—so few slaves could read that they believed the laws were absurd.[120] Many of the devoutly religious abolitionists especially opposed the reading and writing laws because most efforts to educate slaves were tied to religious instruction.[121] The most common way slaves learned to read and write was instruction by whites who believed it was their moral duty to teach them how to read the Bible.[122] Other opportunities for slaves to learn to read and write were available as well. Some secretly used hidden readers or other "devious tactics" to try to gain instruction from unsuspecting whites.[123] Some favored slaves were selected by their masters to learn how to read, and slaves and free blacks who were literate often shared their knowledge. Despite these various avenues, literacy among slaves was still not common.[124]

Literacy was uncommon, but Southerners still had three central fears relating to slave literacy that fueled the anti-reading and writing laws most states passed in 1830 and 1831: Teaching blacks to read was simply inherently dangerous; black preachers were typically literate, and they posed a threat because they could provoke revolt; and, literate blacks who would read to large groups of illiterate slaves and free blacks could facilitate revolt as well as foster the spread of information through underground channels.[125] These fears were not entirely unfounded. Walker suggested this approach to reading the *Appeal* and urged, in the preamble to the third edition, "All I ask is for a candid and careful perusal."[126] Hinks

---

[118]*See* TYLER, *supra* note 5, at 488.

[119]*See* CLEMENT EATON, THE GROWTH OF SOUTHERN CIVILIZATION, 1790-1860, 77 (1961).

[120]*See* LEONARD, *supra* note 18, at 68. *See also* JANET DUITSMAN CORNELIUS, WHEN CAN I READ MY TITLE CLEAR: LITERACY, SLAVERY AND RELIGION IN THE ANTEBELLUM SOUTH 8-10 (1991).

[121]*See* CORNELIUS, *supra* note 120, at 8.

[122]*See id.*

[123]HINKS, *supra* note 5, at 156 (noting that Frederick Douglass was the most famous slave who learned to read and write using this method).

[124]*See* CORNELIUS, *supra* note 120, at 37-58; HINKS, *supra* note 5, at 156.

[125]*See* HINKS, *supra* note 5, at 157.

[126]WALKER, *supra* note 32, at 1.

quotes the Reverend Amos Beman of Middletown, Connecticut, to show how common and powerful public readings were. Beman wrote that a public reading of the *Appeal* and the *Liberator* facilitated political organization in Middletown:

> It was in Middletown that we saw the first number of the Liberator, and its clarion voice sank deep into our mind. That paper, and *"Walker's Appeal,"* and the Address of Mr. Garrison, and his "Thoughts on Colonization," were read and re-read until their words were stamped in letters of fire upon our soul.—The first time we ever spoke in a public meeting was in that city, in behalf of the Liberator, and against the Colonization Society.[127]

Although Southerners had taken legislative action to try to prevent similar scenes, they still faced a serious challenge in preventing the spread of the *Appeal* and the *Liberator* and other abolitionist newspapers in their states because the North refused to pass similar laws.[128] Boston newspapers noted that by the end of 1830 Walker had succeeded in widely circulating his pamphlet into the farthest reaches of the South, despite the laws that prohibited such circulation.[129] In Virginia, Governor John Floyd voiced the opinion of many Southern governors when he expressed his frustration with Northern public officials who tolerated incendiary speech.[130] He wrote in his diary on September 27, 1831:

> I have received this day another number of the Liberator, a newspaper printed in Boston, with the express intention of inciting the slaves and free negroes in this and the other States to rebellion and to murder the men, women and children of those states. Yet we are gravely told there is no law to punish such an offense. The amount of it then is this, a man in our States may plot treason in one state against another without fear of punishment, whilst the suffering state has no right to resist by the provisions of the Federal Constitution. If this is not checked it must lead to a separation of these states. If the forms of law will not punish, the law of nature will not permit men to have their families butchered before their eyes by their slaves and not seek by force to punish those who plan and encourage them to perpetrate these deeds. I shall notice this in my next message to the General Assembly of this State. Something must be done and with decision.[131]

[127]*Id.* at 154. Hinks is quoting Beman from the Beman Private Papers Collection a the Beinecke Rare Book Library, Yale University.

[128]*See* HINKS, *supra* note 5, at 151 (quoting BOSTON DAILY COURIER, May 21, 1830; RICHMOND ENQUIRER, Mar. 30, 1830).

[129]*Id.*

[130]*See* JOHN FLOYD, THE DIARY OF JOHN FLOYD 38-39 (reprinted in CHARLES H. AMBLER, THE LIFE AND DIARY OF JOHN FLOYD, GOVERNOR OF VIRGINIA, AN APOSTLE OF SUCCESSION, AND THE FATHER OF THE OREGON COUNTRY 161-162 (1918)).

[131]*Id.*

Consistent with his diary entry, Floyd raised the issue in his message to the Virginia Senate and House of Delegates on December 6, 1831.[132] He told his audience:

> There is much reason to believe, that the spirit of insurrection was not confined to Southampton. . . . From the documents, which I have herewith lay before you, there is too much reason to believe those plans of treason, insurrection and murder, have been designed, planned and matured by unrestrained fanatics in some of the neighbouring States, who find facilities in distributing their views and plans amongst our population, either through the post office, or by agents sent for that purpose throughout our territory.[133]

The Southern legislatures continued to pass laws restricting the rights of slaves with the intent of squashing ideas of insurrection that publications like *Walker's Appeal* and the *Liberator* were allegedly encouraging, and the presses of the South began to join the cause. In Washington, D.C., the *National Intelligencer* appealed to the people of New England, specifically to the mayor of Boston, to find some way to suppress the *Liberator* after the Tarborough, N.C., *Free Press* wrote that "[a]n incendiary paper, The *Liberator*, is circulating openly among free blacks of this city. . . . It is published in Boston or Philadelphia by a white man, with the avowed purpose of inciting rebellion in the South."[134] The article, reprinted in the *Liberator*, added that Garrison had "secret agents" distributing the paper to slaves, so "[I]f you catch them, by all that is sacred, you ought to barbecue them."[135] Lundy responded to the charge in the *Genius* by offering a quote from Garrison, who said, "We have circulated no papers extra in any part of our country. We have not a single white or black subscriber south of Potomac."[136] Garrison wrote in the *Liberator*, "The charge of the Washington libeller, respecting the circulation of the *Liberator* by 'secret agents' is as silly as it is false."[137]

The *National Intelligencer* called on the Massachusetts Legislature to "provide a durable remedy" to stop publication of the *Liberator*.[138] The pa-

---

[132]*See* HENRY IRVING TRAGLE, THE SOUTHAMPTON SLAVE REVOLT OF 1831: A COMPILATION OF SOURCE MATERIAL 432 (1971) (quoting THE JOURNAL OF THE VIRGINIA HOUSE OF DELEGATES (Dec. 6, 1831)).

[133]*Id.*

[134]*Incendiary Publications*, LIBERATOR, Oct. 8, 1831, at 1; Benjamin Lundy, *"Incendiary Publications,"* GENIUS OF UNIVERSAL EMANCIPATION, Sept. 1831, at 70.

[135]*Id.*

[136]Lundy, *supra* note 134, at 71.

[137]William Lloyd Garrison, *To the Editors of the National Intelligencer*, LIBERATOR, Oct. 15, 1831, at 1.

[138]*Id.*

per wrote that "surely if the Courts of Law have no power, public opinion has to interfere" until the Massachusetts Legislature takes action.[139] Lundy's *Genius of Universal Emancipation* also received some attention from Southern papers—specifically the *National Intelligencer;* the Charleston, S.C., *Mercury;* the Macon, Ga., *Messenger;* and the Tarborough, N.C., *Free Press*—as another incendiary publication that needed to be controlled.[140]

Garrison responded to the pointed attack by the *Intelligencer:* "Your 'appeal to the worthy Mayor of the City of Boston' and to 'the intelligent Legislators of Massachusetts,' to interpose their authority, and prevent the publication of the *Liberator* is so ineffacably ridiculous that I may justly term it the incoherence of madness."[141] He added, "Ye accuse the pacific friends of emancipation of instigating the slaves to revolt. Take back the charge as foul slander. The slaves need no incentives at our hands."[142]

Garrison and the editors of the *National Intelligencer* continued to argue in each paper about whether the *Liberator* was an incendiary publication, and Garrison printed, with very limited commentary, dozens of excerpts from Southern newspapers supporting the *Intelligencer's* claim that his paper was incendiary and directly responsible for the Southampton insurrection.[143] Much of Garrison's motivation for publicly replaying the voices of his critics was based on principle—to protect his own rights to speak and write about slavery by allowing critics to respond.[144] Garrison was absolute in his claim to free speech rights. He believed his opponents enjoyed the same degree of freedom of expression and supported the idea that sound, rational ideas would prevail in any political debate.[145]

In October 1831, Garrison continued to receive harsh reprimands from his Southern press brethren and learned, from the Charleston, S.C., *Mercury*, that the Vigilance Association of Columbia had offered a $1,500 reward for the "apprehension and prosecution to conviction, of any white person [who] may be detected in distributing or circulating within the state either the *Liberator, Walker's Appeal*, or any other publication of a seditious tendency."[146] In the same issue of the *Liberator*, Garrison pub-

---

[139]*Id.*
[140]*Id.*
[141]*Id.*
[142]*Id.* at 2.
[143]*See* William Lloyd Garrison, *Three Curiosities*, LIBERATOR, Oct. 22, 1831, at 2.
[144]*See* Reynolds, *supra* note 5, at 595-605.
[145]*See id.*
[146]*See* Garrison, *supra* note 143, at 2.

lished an article from a Raleigh, N.C., newspaper that claimed a North Carolina grand jury had indicted Garrison and his publishing partner Isaac Knapp for the felony offense of circulating an incendiary publication in the state, punishable by whipping, imprisonment and hanging.[147] The newspaper account further stated that "we suppose the accused would be demanded by the Governor of this State, but whether they will be surrendered or not by the Executive of Massachusetts is a matter about which we are not prepared to hazard a conjecture."[148]

Just a week before, Garrison had written his brother-in-law, Henry Benson, and alluded to the trouble that was brewing in the South. "The *Liberator* is causing the most extraordinary movements in the slave States among the whites, as you are doubtless already aware," Garrison wrote. "I am constantly receiving anonymous letters, filled with abominable and bloody sentiments . . ."[149]

The end of 1831 did not see any clear end to the dispute between the North and the South about what constituted incendiary speech and whether it should be protected. In general terms, the South viewed any writing that challenged the legitimacy of slavery as incendiary.[150] The North had not formalized a definition of what constituted incendiary speech, but behaved through its legislatures as if its definition did not include the abolitionists' rhetoric. The climate that was created after the Nat Turner insurrection in 1831 clarified the significant differences, however, in the northern and southern viewpoints—abolitionist speech was protected in one arena and legislated against in the other.

BEYOND *WALKER'S APPEAL*

As previously indicated, Walker died of natural causes in 1830. His son, Edwin Walker, would become the first black elected to the Massachusetts state legislature in 1866.[151] After the events that surrounded the publication and distribution of *Walker's Appeal*, Garrison and Lundy continued to remain active in the abolitionist cause. Garrison became one of the best-known abolitionists in the United States for his so-called "fanatical" and radical ideas,[152] and Lundy faded into the background to work on his

---

[147]*Id.*

[148]*Id.*

[149]WILLIAM LLOYD GARRISON, 1 THE LETTERS OF WILLIAM LLOYD GARRISON, 1822-1835, 139 (1971).

[150]*See* APTHEKER, *supra* note 5, at 41.

[151]*See id.*

[152]*See The Libel Suit*, LIBERATOR, Jan. 15, 1831, at 1.

Texas colonization plan.[153] During the remainder of the 1830s, continued attempts to suppress abolitionist speech were heightened in the South. Mob violence became more common in "enforcing" and "creating" incendiary speech laws that did not exist in the North.[154] The Postal Campaign in 1835 sought to further punish anti-slavery writing that was sent through the U.S. mails.[155] And Garrison remained an outspoken critic of slavery, one of several abolitionists who helped frame the debate about slavery in America as a debate about the liberty of all American citizens.[156] Garrison, like other abolitionists, maintained the argument that the rights of free expression were given to all men by God, and that although the federal Constitution did not create these rights, it secured them in the United States.[157]

In 1834, Garrison revisited his criminal and civil libel trials[158] and wrote a second preface to his *Brief Sketch of the Trial of William Lloyd Garrison* that reflected on the importance and influence of both the libel case and the Southern condemnation of the *Liberator* in his life and his views about liberty and free speech.

Garrison explained, that "[s]ince I have had the charge of the *Liberator*, I have been freely branded as a madman and incendiary, and my language has been deemed harsh and violent; but if any person will turn to a file of the Genius of Universal Emancipation, he will discover that I was no less denunciatory and fanatical in 1829 than I am in 1834."[159] Garrison noted that it was not until he challenged the Colonization Societies that he was effectively branded a madman; yet, despite all of the attempts to suppress his speech, Garrison believed he would prevail in the struggle for liberty to all Americans.[160] The wide swing in public opinion about

---

[153]For more on Lundy's plans for Texas colonization *see* BENJAMIN LUNDY, THE WAR IN TEXAS: A REVIEW OF THE FACTS AND CIRCUMSTANCES SHOWING THAT THIS CONTEST IS THE RESULT OF A LONG PREMEDITATED CRUSADE AGAINST THE GOVERNMENT, SET ON FOOT BY SLAVEHOLDERS, LAND SPECULATORS, &C. WITH THE VIEW OF RE-ESTABLISHING, EXTENDING AND PERPETUATING THE SYSTEM OF SLAVERY AND THE SLAVE TRADE IN THE REPUBLIC OF MEXICO 1 (1836). *See also* Fred Landon, *Benjamin Lundy, Abolitionist, 1789-1839: A Sketch Prepared on the Occasion of the Centenary of his Death*, in A MEMORIAL TO BENJAMIN LUNDY, PIONEER QUAKER ABOLITIONIST, 1789-1839, 7 (1939).

[154]*See* LEONARD, *supra* note 18, at 69.

[155]*See* Curtis, *supra* note 8, at 859.

[156]*See* Reynolds, *supra* note 8, at 605.

[157]*See* Curtis, *supra* note 8, at 859, 860.

[158]Garrison was convicted of both criminal and civil libel in 1830 for an 1829 article he wrote in the *Genius of Universal Emancipation* that criticized a well-known Massachusetts businessman for allowing his ships to be used to transport slaves from Boston to New Orleans. For a detailed account, *see* Reynolds *supra* note 5, at 590-607.

[159]WILLIAM LLOYD GARRISON, A BRIEF SKETCH OF THE TRIAL OF WILLIAM LLOYD GARRISON FOR AN ALLEGED LIBEL ON FRANCIS TODD OF MASSACHUSETTS 1 (1834).

[160]*See id.*

Garrison and his anti-slavery views as well as the response to his writings helps provide some early background about the importance the role the first abolitionist movements played in defining free speech issues as early as the late 1820s.

First Amendment historian Michael Kent Curtis notes that "the history of the Sedition Act shaped the debate of free speech in the 1830s at the height of Northern and Southern demands of suppression of abolitionist expression. But what was the moral? Was it that no government had the power to suppress speech about public men and public measures or was it simply that the federal government lacked such power?"[161]

Walker's, Garrison's and Lundy's experiences show that in 1829–1831 the moral was that the power to suppress speech still clearly remained with the states. But, public opinion was ahead of the law, and as Curtis notes in his study of the abolitionists and anti-slavery speech in 1835–1837, a broad support of the value of free speech in the North is what helped protect Garrison, Walker, Lundy and others from Northern state suppression of their speech.[162] This was as true in 1829 and 1831 as it was in 1835 and 1837. As a result, the events that attempted to interfere with the free speech rights of Walker, Garrison and Lundy served to strengthen the belief in a Constitutional guarantee to free expression.

A large body of First Amendment law exists to shed more light on the interplay of threatened violence, political and social stability and freedom of expression in a democracy. Despite the vast number of Supreme Court First Amendment-related decisions over the past 80 years that provide more and clearer protection for unpopular political speech, both government and public efforts to silence expression based on perceived threats of violence or social unrest have still surfaced since the abolitionists struggled to assert their free speech rights.[163] The catalyst of efforts to suppress is often the presence of a threat to power and a heightened sense of public fear based on a perceived threat to national security. Or, in the words of First Amendment scholar Harry Kalven, "This problem complements the problem of a reflexive disorder. . . . Speech is seen as a stimulus to undesirable action; censorship is seen as part of a strategy for controlling that action."[164] When these conditions exist, like they did for Walker, Garrison and Lundy, the relationship between government censorship and asserting a First Amendment right to expression become more public and contentious.

---

[161]Curtis, *supra* note 8, at 796.

[162]*See id.* at 866.

[163]For a good overview of significant First Amendment cases since 1907 *see* WILLIAM W. VAN ALSTYNE, FIRST AMENDMENT CASES AND MATERIALS (2ⁿᵈ ed.) (1995).

[164]KALVEN, *supra* note 3, at 119.

For example, in the early and mid-twentieth Century the red scare of Communism resulted in multiple convictions under the Espionage Act of 1917, the Smith Act of 1940 and a variety of state anti-criminalism syndicate laws.[165] Courts convicted individuals and groups for the expression of unpopular ideas that included advocating the use of violence as a necessary means to promote political change. All of the cases that arose from these episodes had significant free speech implications and reinforced the idea that speech is a powerful force in a democratic society. The speech at issue in these cases challenged government power and the existing political or social order in the same way that Walker, Garrison and Lundy did nearly a century earlier.

This same tension between political speech and threats of violence exists today. Since September 11, 2001, the government and the public have again shown a willingness to limit free expression under certain circumstances.[166] For example, the USA PATRIOT Act, passed six weeks after the September 11 terrorist attacks, provided additional tools for the government to combat terrorist activity.[167] But the bill also gave the government broad latitude to prosecute and investigate people based solely on their speech and associations with unpopular political groups.[168] Other recently passed, as well as pending, legislation aimed at curbing terrorism has broad free speech implications that run the risk of repeating history.[169]

What can be learned from the controversy that surrounded *Walker's Appeal?* The stir the pamphlet caused hit at the heart of a significant political question that Americans wrestled with in the mid- to late-1830s:

---

[165]*See e.g.*, Abrams v. United States 250 U.S. 616 (1919); Debs v. United States, 249 U.S. 211 (1919); Frohwerk v. United States, 249 U.S. 204 (1919); Schenck v. United States 249 U.S. 47 (1919); Whitney v. California, 274 U.S. 357 (1927); Dennis v. United States, 341 U.S. 494 (1951).

[166]*See* Reynolds & Barnett, *supra* note 4, at 129-146.

[167]147 CONG. REC. S10990 (daily ed. October 25, 2001).

[168]*See* terrorism definitions in the USA PATRIOT Act of 2001, H. R. 3162, 107th Cong. Section 411 (a) (2001) (enacted). For a current and regularly updated list of pending and/or recently passed legislation and other free speech-related actions and events since September 11, 2001, see the American Civil Liberties Union "Safe and Free" Web site at http://www.aclu.org/SafeandFree.cfm?id=12942&c=207. According to the web site, "Hundreds have been arrested for exercising their constitutionally protected freedoms; some have lost their jobs or been suspended from school. Some government officials, including local police, have gone to extraordinary lengths to squelch dissent wherever it has sprung up, drawing on a breathtaking array of tactics—from censorship and surveillance to detention, denial of due process and excessive force."

[169]Homeland Security Act, H. R. 1158, 107th Cong. (2002) (enacted); Surveillance Oversight and Disclosure Act, H. R. 2429, 108th Cong. (2003); Domestic Security Enhancement Act, Section-by-Section Analysis, Aug. 13, 2003, *available at* http://www.pbs.org/now/politics/patriot2-hi.pdf.

How much power does the government have to stop the criticism of the legal institution of slavery? How much power should it have? In broad First Amendment terms, how free is unpopular and potentially dangerous political speech? Although the question seems simple, it is "both the most important and most difficult" of First Amendment issues to resolve.[170]

Some of the value of studying history comes in improving the understanding of the relationship between the past and the present as well as the potential relationship of the present and the future.[171] Understanding the struggles of political dissenters like Walker, Garrison and Lundy can strengthen both the legal and popular perceptions of the significant role free speech plays in a democracy. The moral of this story for contemporary times is that government efforts to silence "dangerous" speech in a democracy should have the unintended consequence of strengthening a society's understanding of the fundamental power and value of free expression. Just as Garrison re-framed part of the slavery debate as one that had as much to do with protecting the liberties of all Americans, political dissenters in 2003 are re-framing part of the combating terrorism debate as a debate about protecting the civil liberties of all Americans, including rights to free expression, in times of national crisis.

---

[170]*See* KALVEN, *supra* note 3, at 119.
[171]*See* MICHAEL KAMMEN, SELVAGES AND BIASES, THE FABRIC OF HISTORY IN AMERICAN CULTURE 55 (1987).

Introductory Comments to Chapter 15

Elon University

Cable franchising first peaked my interest as a doctoral student at the University of Georgia. I was taking a Telecommunications Policy course with Dr. William Lee, who had published an influential article in the *Vanderbilt Law Review*, "Cable Franchising and the First Amendment." Professor Lee is an excellent writer, and in that article, as well as in others, he persuasively argued that municipal regulation of cable TV abridged the First Amendment rights of cable operators. Drawing comparisons between newspapers and cable TV, Professor Lee maintained that in the same way newspaper editors selected stories and then placed those stories in a news bin on a public sidewalk, a cable operator selected networks for carriage and utilized the public right of way to lay cable to the subscriber's home. Blending quotes in his copy from zealous municipal regulators who had little appreciation for First Amendment issues made a compelling argument.

In class, I can recall feeling uncomfortable with the notion that a newspaper editor and a cable TV operations manager could call on parallel First Amendment protections. Having worked in and studied the broadcast industry, cable TV's largely monopolistic presence in American cities felt more parallel to spectrum scarcity. With a finite amount of spectrum available to those interested in broadcasting, not everyone who desired access could have access. As a result of spectrum scarcity and the pervasiveness of over-the-air broadcasting, the broadcast industry is accountable to the public interest as interpreted by the Federal Communications Commission (FCC). In the same way, cable companies have a contract with cities, a franchise, to utilize the public right of way and are accountable to the public interest as interpreted by municipalities.

My differences of opinion with Professor Lee led to lively class discussions and made salient the difficult task of operationalizing notions of public interest without interfering with the First Amendment rights of the media.

When I finished that class, I decided to further pursue cable franchising and the First Amendment as the topic of my dissertation, and I asked Dr. Lee to chair my committee. I was specifically interested in how local needs and interests (i.e., the public interest) were presented during cable franchise renewals. Working in conjunction with the National League of Cities and the National Association of Telecommunication Officers and Advisors, I surveyed elected city officials and municipal employees to test models of cable TV oversight and notions of public interest. Interestingly, most city officials responsible for negotiating cable franchises reported being unclear about what constitutes the public interest. As a result, the cable TV industry is in the difficult position of negotiating more than 10,000 unique cable franchises. For an industry that has concentrated itself into a handful of companies, this task is especially cumbersome. So, one might ask—Why can't all the cities operate under one national franchise?

In my mind, this would go against the fundamental essence of the public interest. A national franchise would ignore the specific qualities of each community. Local communities are unique, and each should have its own relationship with cable TV to determine what the public interest is within that community. A tangible power exists in local citizens being able to "talk" to local media providers and have those "talks" result in responsive representation as to how the media will function in that community.

This chapter discusses the tangible, social science of cable franchise negotiations, when cities use the federally sanctioned cable TV franchising negotiation to create cable systems that respond to their community needs. In a world where the public interest is difficult to articulate and even more difficult to enforce, there is something meaningful about a data collection process that creates a dialog about a local community's idea of public interest and how the cable company might serve those needs.

After all, the audience is what makes the TV industry a profitable one. A monopolistic cable industry complicates this model by disenfranchising the audience, as it becomes a given rather than something that has to be competitively won. Cable TV's use of the public right of way empowers the audience "to speak" in cable TV franchising negotiations.

Since earning my doctoral degree, I have worked with cities assisting in their needs and interests ascertainments during franchise renewal. The First Amendment is a constant presence during these negotiations; the First Amendment rights of community stakeholders desiring to speak and the First Amendment rights of the owner of the distribution system. Determining the appropriate balance is the tenuous part. During a focused discussion with cable franchising attorneys representing the major cable companies, one attorney commented that cities and cable companies would never have amicable cable franchise negotiations because they did not value the same things. The observation has resonated with me over the years. Cable companies are accountable to shareholders and cities to constituents. Rather than debating the commonality, perhaps cable franchising is an opportunity to embrace the difficult task of compromise in an effort to bring the public interest to the table.

The following chapter illustrates four cases where community needs were challenged by the cable company, and the data collection used to support those needs came under the scrutiny of the court.

The People and the Cable Guy: Federally Empowered Public Interest Standards

Constance Ledoux Book

Attempts to define, quantify, and enforce notions of *public interest* have pervaded the legal atmosphere of broadcast, cable, and satellite since their invention. The Federal Communications Commission's (FCC) immediate past chairman, Michael Powell, struggled with the meaning of the words since first taking office. He told a group of communications attorneys shortly after he took office: "The night after I was sworn in, I waited for a visit from the angel of the public interest. I waited all night, but she did not come. And, in fact, five months into this job, I still have had no divine awakening and no one has issued me my public interest crystal ball" (Powell, 1998). Powell's predecessor, Bill Kennard, conducted his own year-long investigation into the public interest obligations of broadcasters, just a few months after Vice President Al Gore's public interest advisory committee spent 18 months doing the same thing and failed to enact or quantify public interest requirements. In short, the study of the public interest has received significant attention as the government attempted to determine how to make the concept more tangible and, perhaps more important, what concepts of public interest could be enforced and later upheld in the courts. During the last 70 years, public interest has focused on three areas: localism, children's TV programming, and political broadcasting (Sarver, 2004).

In this chapter, the legal arena of cable TV franchising is explored, specifically looking at how social science data have been and are utilized by local franchising authorities (LFAs), typically municipalities, to define local needs and in turn the public interest. Four areas are discussed: the regulatory framework of cable TV's presence in America (federal, state, and local); the cable TV franchise renewal process and the criteria established for nonrenewal, needs, and interests ascertainments; cases of nonrenewal; and employment of the judicial handbook for social science data to evaluate data collected for the purpose of cable franchise decision making in the courts.

CABLE TV OVERSIGHT

Inherent in each of the previous attempts to define the *public interest* is an assumption that it can be articulated in words and corporate behavior. Krugman and Reid (1980) attempted to decipher the FCC's definition of public interest by conducting long interviews with staff at the FCC about cable TV. The researchers believed that those who carry out policy related to public interest would likely be the most able to define the concept. The focus of the interviews was on cable TV public interest and policy. In the late 1970s, cable TV was quickly becoming a cultural and commercial force. The two researchers concluded that FCC policymakers took a preferred reactive approach to operationalizing the public interest as it dealt with the new phenomenon of cable TV. As strategic business moves were made by commercial entities, the FCC mediated and engaged public response, creating the *public interest*.

One can consider the energy between these forces triangularly (see Fig. 15.1). The foundation of the triangle consists of commercial interests, equally anchored by the FCC, and the decision making that bubbles to the surface is the *public interest*. One colleague jokingly described the relationship as the "holy trinity" of electronic media (Book, 2004).

Cable TV is a much-regulated phenomenon in the United States, regulated at the local, state, and federal levels. Three localities declare themselves the home of the first cable system. So rather than choose, the National Cable Television Association declares the "simultaneous" development of cable TV in 1948 in Arkansas, Oregon, and Philadelphia. In all three communities, community antenna television (CATV) was developed because geographical conditions created poor terrestrial distribution of TV. Using coaxial cable, entrepreneurs were able to collect TV signals at one point (e.g., a hilltop) and then distribute, via cable, programming to local homes. Local governments play the primary regulatory role because cable TV utilizes the public right of way (PROW) to lay wires for the delivery of TV programming. The PROW is the land that runs adjacent to the road, a bridge so to speak, between public and privately owned property. Use of the PROW allows cities to negotiate franchise agreements with the cable

PUBLIC INTEREST

Business/Corporate   FCC

Broadcast
Cable/Satellite
Consumer Electronics Industry
Content Producers
Wireless/Mobile/Personal

FIG. 15.1. The "Holy Trinity" of Broadcasting and Cable.

company. Franchise terms typically run 10 to 15 years, forcing the cable operator into a renewal process much more intimate than the federal government's postcard renewal used with broadcasters. In nine states, local cable TV franchises are negotiated by state agencies rather than individual municipalities.[1] Today, more than 11,000 individual franchise agreements are working to bring cable TV services to 67 million American households (National Cable Television Association, 2004).

At the federal level, the FCC regulates cable TV because the courts determined that cable TV provided services ancillary to broadcast TV. A federal regulatory relationship exists with cable—not because of any physical element like the broadcast spectrum, but because in the FCC's oversight of broadcasting the government is responsible for maintaining a free, over-the-air distribution system. Cable TV has the potential to threaten that system because consumers rely on cable TV's retransmission of broadcast signals. The authority of the FCC to regulate cable TV was upheld on this basis in 1968 by the Supreme Court in the *United States v. Southwestern Cable Co.* (1968).

---

[1]The states of Alaska, Connecticut, Delaware, Nevada, New Jersey, Rhode Island, and Vermont regulate cable TV at the state public utility level. In Hawaii, regulation of cable TV is the responsibility of the Department of Regulatory Agencies; and in Massachusetts, cable TV oversight is conducted by an advisory board.

During the development years of cable TV, the franchising process was conducted on a case-by-case basis without systematic procedures. As the cable industry went from a locally owned business structure in the 1960s to powerful multiple system operators (MSO) in the 1980s, the cable industry began to resist local franchising and complained to the FCC about municipal franchising practices. In 1984, Congress responded to those complaints and adopted what is now known as the Cable Act. The Cable Act better defined regulatory procedures and placed primary regulatory responsibility at the state and local levels. The Act was intended to "establish franchise procedures and standards which encourage the growth and development of cable systems and which assure that cable systems are responsive to the needs and interests of the local community" (47 U.S.C. § 521).

Being responsive to local needs and interests required some type of data gathering effort be used to create franchise agreements tailored to local public interests. As a result, social science data become the frequent basis for regulatory decisions.

THE CABLE FRANCHISE RENEWAL PROCESS

While the Cable Act of 1984 detailed a formal franchise renewal process, a majority of the cable TV franchises in the United States are negotiated using an informal process. This informal process was recognized in the language of the Cable Act, but few guidelines or parameters for informal renewal negotiations are discussed. The Cable Act does require that if a franchise is negotiated informally, the local franchising authority (LFA) must notify the public and provide an opportunity for the public to comment on the new franchise before it is adopted (47 U.S.C. § 546(h)).

Formal negotiations are more expensive for LFA's and the cable operator because the negotiations require adherence to the Federal Code of Regulations and mean the involvement of several attorneys. However, the cable operator is deeply invested (as well as the LFA) in the franchise being renewed, so both parties frequently begin an informal and formal process simultaneously. In other words, if informal negotiations fail to create a franchise contract both parties can accept, the formal process will be underway and ultimately will end with a decision by a specified date.

The formal renewal process is initiated when either the cable operator or the LFA submits a written notice to each other requesting the commencement of formal renewal proceedings. Notification of the formal renewal must occur in the 30- to 36-month window before the franchise is scheduled to expire. Most cable franchises today are negotiated for 10 to

15 years, so written notice would occur in the 7th year of a 10-year franchise or in the 12th year of a 15-year franchise.

The formal cable TV renewal process has four phases:

Phase I: The Cable Act directs the LFA to begin a process of identifying community needs and interests related to cable TV services and review the past performance of the cable operator. The "needs and interests" and "past performance" ascertainment can be performed using a variety of data gathering tools, including public hearings, telephone or written surveys, focus groups, long interviews, and audits of the cable operator's past performance (47 U.S.C. § 546(a)). Consultants and attorneys frequently assist cities with first-phase requirements, bringing to the table a national perspective and comparative data. A detailed report outlining and typically prioritizing cable-related needs and interests of the community is produced using the collected data.

Phase II: When the ascertainment is complete and the report filed, the LFA can issue a formal request for a renewal proposal to the cable operator. That request normally includes franchise requirements based on the public interest obligations identified in the evidence gathered, such as customer service provisions; TV facilities and equipment; public, educational, and government (PEG) channels; and network support (47 U.S.C. § 531, 544(b)). The cable company has a window of opportunity to respond to the proposed franchise requirements.

Phase III: When the LFA receives the cable operator's response, it has 4 months to make a decision to either renew or issue a preliminary denial of renewal. During this 4-month period, more than likely, the LFA will try to negotiate with the cable company to create a successful franchise agreement—one that meets the identified public interest requirements to some degree to avoid Phase IV, an administrative hearing. The length of a franchise term can frequently be a significant bartering tool. The majority of franchise agreements and communities are typically between 10 and 15 years (Head et al., 2001).

Phase IV: If the LFA chooses not to renew the cable franchise and no compromise seems forthcoming, the cable company can require that the LFA begin an administrative hearing before making a final decision (47 U.S.C. § 546(c)(1)). During this window, the cable operator typically introduces evidence that challenges the LFA's data gathering process and subsequent public interest requirements.

The purpose of the administrative proceeding is to determine whether:

- the cable operator has complied with the material terms of the existing cable franchise and applicable law;

- the quality of the cable operator's service has been reasonable in light of community needs;[2]
- the cable operator has the financial, legal, and technical ability to provide services;
- the proposal is reasonable to meet the future cable-related community needs and interests identified during the ascertainment, taking into account the cost of meeting such needs and interests.

The local franchising authority can deny a cable operator's request for renewal if it finds that the operator is not compliant in any one of the four areas. When the administrative proceeding is completed, the cable operator must be notified of the LFA's decision in writing and the reasons for denial if that is the determination (47 U.S.C. § 546(c)(3)).

The cable operator can appeal the LFA's decision in federal or state courts within 120 days after receiving notice of the decision. The reviewing court can grant "appropriate relief" from the LFA's decision if the court finds that the LFA failed to comply with the procedural requirements of the Cable Acts (1984, 1992) or the cable operator demonstrated that the data collected and used by the LFA were not supported by a preponderance of the evidence (47 U.S.C. §§ 546(e)(1), 555). When the data are challenged, the use of social science research practices as a way to define local public interest obligations for cable TV operators is often questioned too.

THE CABLE TV NEEDS AND INTERESTS ASCERTAINMENT

Inherent in conducting a needs and interests ascertainment to identify local needs is that not all communities are the same. Notions of localism as a measuring stick for the public interest are bedrocks of terrestrial broadcasting and cable, and they set broadcasting and cable apart from satellite TV competitors. For example, cable subscribers in Dayton, Ohio, receive six local access channels as part of their basic cable package. Two of the channels are operated by a nonprofit public access corporation, Dayton Access Television (DATV). Farther south in Virginia Beach, one of the largest cable systems in the United States, three access TV channels are available in the basic cable package dedicated to education and government programming, but the city has not had a grassroots movement to provide public access programming. Adjacent to Virginia Beach is Nor-

---

[2]This implies that it is incumbent on the cable operator to have an understanding of community needs and interests throughout the course of the franchise.

folk, Virginia, where local leaders have decided city council meetings will *not* be shown on the cable system. In Greensboro, North Carolina, the educational access channel is used to cablecast the school lunch menu and job openings, and the government access channel programs traffic cameras from four major intersections during the morning. Each community is different, and these differences are readily apparent in the local access TV programming provided on the cable system.

When the federal government codified the cable TV needs and interests ascertainment as a key component of Phase I of franchise renewal in the Cable Act of 1984,[3] it was already familiar with ascertainments as part of license renewal processes from its oversight of broadcasting.

In the late 1950s, the FCC was concerned that local broadcasters were simply conduits for lackluster network programming and were not utilizing licensed spectrum (or millions of dollars in profits) to provide the local programming desired in the individual communities served and as a result not operating in the public interest. In an effort to improve the quality of local broadcast programming, the FCC passed a new policy that found, "In fulfillment of his obligation the broadcaster should consider the tastes, needs and desires of the public he is licensed to serve in developing his programming and should exercise conscientious efforts not only to ascertain them, but also to carry them out as well as he reasonably can" (Federal Communications Commission, 1960, p. 28). Fourteen categories of programming (see Table 15.1) were identified as "major elements usually necessary to the public interest" and included showcasing local talent, local sports, local news, local weather, and agricultural news (Federal Communications Commission, 1960, p. 29).

In the years following the 1960 Statement, the broadcast industry began the practice of utilizing professional consultants to aid in gathering local data. Using focus groups and surveys, consultants assisted broadcasters in developing more responsive programming and offered proof to the FCC that local public interest was being served (Allen, 1996).

In the 1980s, just as broadcasting was being deregulated under the leadership of President Ronald Reagan and the required community ascertainment no longer enforced, Congress took a much different stance with cable TV and required a local needs assessment. When conducting local cable TV ascertainments, selected municipal employees are typically assigned the task of coordinating participation from local stakeholders, such as operators of access TV channels, business leaders, the educational

---

[3]Congress would also pass cable legislation in 1992, the Cable Television Competition and Consumer Protection Act. Although the new legislation did not alter the process outlined in the Cable Act of 1984, it did enhance the LFA's ability to temporarily regulate cable rates and enforce more stringent customer service standards.

TABLE 15.1
FCC's 1960 Programming Policy Statement
Fourteen "Major Elements Usually Necessary to the Public Interest"

1. Opportunity for local self-expression.
2. Development and use of local talent.
3. Programs for children.
4. Religious programs.
5. Educational programs.
6. Public affairs programs.
7. Editorialization by licensees.
8. Political broadcasts.
9. Agricultural programs.
10. News programs.
11. Weather and market services.
12. Sports programs.
13. Service to minority groups.
14. Entertainment programming.

community, city employees, and the general public. Data gathering efforts frequently include qualitative and quantitative measures. Sue Buske, president and founder of the cable TV consulting company, the Buske Group, has conducted several ascertainments. She describes the process as several months of fact finding that lead to the establishment of franchise renewal goals (Buske, 2004). Using the data collected during the ascertainment process, the Buske Group has successfully assisted cities in negotiating cable franchises that required the cable operator to build a broadband network for local schools, to make funds available to local nonprofits for video and audio equipment to support local access TV, and to establish customer service standards that if not met by the operator can lead to fines.

DENIAL OF CABLE TV FRANCHISE RENEWAL

During franchise renewal proceedings, the cable operator remains in a better negotiating position than the LFA simply because of the corporate, multiple system operating structure of the cable industry. For example, the city of San Jose, California, is attempting to resolve a franchise renewal dispute with Comcast. The city's cable TV needs and interest ascertainment, conducted using focus groups and surveys, found significant local interest in a community access TV studio (accessible to students and nonprofit groups) and a fiber optic network that would move video and data between government buildings and schools (Bazeleyc, 2003). As part of the cable franchise renewal, San Jose officials would like Comcast to help support capital costs with the establishment of these services. Comcast, using its staff of corporate attorneys, is fighting the requirement. The Comcast attorneys are working on several franchise renewal projects, including neighboring San Mateo County, California. Because Comcast has an understanding of the provisions it has made in each of its separate franchises, it has a better snapshot of the breadth and scope of cable franchises nationwide. Inherently, this puts Comcast in a better negotiating position than the city of San Jose with primarily an understanding of what its city needs and wants.

Little case precedence exists in the denial of cable TV franchises based on the data gathered under the ascertainment umbrella. Only a few cities can afford to fight the seemingly unlimited resources of the powerful cable TV industry. Bunnie Reidel, executive director of the Alliance for Community Media in Washington, is watching the San Jose case closely: "We want legal precedence on it, obviously. It's only places like San Jose [reference to legal funding] that can stand up to Comcast" (Bazeleyc, 2003, p. C1). Four cable cases challenging the validity of local decisions merit discussion.

Morganton, North Carolina

Cable TV service in Morganton, North Carolina, made headlines when the city decided to deny TCI's franchise in 1985 on the basis that the cable company had failed to meet local needs and interests. As a result, the city desired to construct its own cable system. TCI sued in federal district court in *Madison Cablevision v. City of Morganton* (1989) on the grounds that the city of Morganton's decision violated the cable company's First and Fourteenth Amendment rights (Thompson, 1991b). The court found that the cable franchising process did impose some acceptable limits on a cable operator's First Amendment rights. TCI lost an appeal of the decision, but the court gave little reason behind its decision in its one-paragraph ruling (Thompson, 1992a).

TCI decided to invest in collecting enough local signatures to bring the renewal decision to a public referendum, barring Morganton from constructing its own cable system. Two thousand signatures were collected, and TCI hired a political consultant to advance a campaign before the election, "Citizens Opposed to City-Owned Cable." Lobbying was aggressive on both sides of the issue. Ultimately, the voters decided not to renew TCI's cable franchise and that the city should be allowed to construct its own cable system.

TCI continued to advance its First Amendment argument to the Supreme Court, but its petition for review was denied (Thompson, 1992b).

Rolla, Missouri

In *Rolla Cable System v. City of Rolla* (1991), the court upheld the city of Rolla's decision not to renew the cable franchise when the consultants hired by the city found that the cable operator's technical staff was not competent to run the cable system. An engineer and building inspector testified that grounding work to bring the cable system in compliance with the 1987 National Electric Code was done improperly, and the cable operator had not used standard system design procedures when conceptually creating the system. The nonrenewal came after 11 years of complaints regarding signal quality—specifically, poor reception of the cable system's retransmission of over-the-air networks (Thomson, 1991a).

Sturgis, Kentucky

Several residents in the small town of Sturgis, Kentucky (population 2,184), participated in public hearings in 1995 when the local cable provider, Union CATV, came up for franchise renewal. The evidence gathered using long interviews and focused discussions included future needs related to the wiring of an elementary school to receive cable TV and allowing subscribers the ability to use their VCRs to modulate the cable signal as an additional cable outlet in the home. Residents also asked for a payment drop facility and the provision of news and weather in the basic cable service tier. The city determined that a 5-year franchise was appropriate, although the cable operator was requesting a 20-year franchise term.

The city's denial of renewal was upheld in *Union CATV, Inc v. City of Sturgis, Kentucky* (1997). The court found that the city of Sturgis' cable TV needs assessment demonstrated a "preponderance of evidence" for nonrenewal. Cities celebrated the decision as affirmation of the needs and interests ascertainment process, and cable operators became concerned that the door had been opened for a host of unreasonable demands by cities. However, 1 year later, the U.S. Court of Appeals for the 6th Circuit, while upholding the decision of the lower court, rejected language in the decision that would have blocked any judicial review of a franchising authority's judgment as to a community's cable-related needs and interest. Allowing the cable company to challenge the city's data during a judicial review ensured cable operators that unsubstantiated demands could be rejected during franchise negotiations. The judicial review in turn requires the city to be certain of the reliability and validity of its data gathering efforts (Lloyd, 1997).

Brunswick and Brunswick Hills Township, Ohio

The most significant case to challenge social science data collected and utilized during cable TV franchising is *Cablevision of the Midwest, Inc. v. City of Brunswick* (2000). The city of Brunswick and Brunswick Hills Township, both located in Northern Ohio, had about 10,000 cable subscribers in 1994. The city and township worked together on franchise negotiations. Cablevision owned the Brunswick systems, and the renewal process began with a formal request by Cablevision in January 1994. Six months later, the city contracted with the consulting firm, The Buske Group, to conduct the local community needs and interests analysis. Ad Hoc Advisory Committee of Brunswick community leaders assisted the consultant and city staff.

Over the course of the next 18 months, the Buske Group conducted the following assessment activities to complete the needs and interests ascertainment:

1. conducted a technical/engineering review of the cable system, physically inspecting the current condition of the cable plant and how well the system had been maintained;
2. conducted a financial review of Cablevision to determine the company's financial performance in the Brunswick franchise area and whether the appropriate franchise fee payments had been made;
3. conducted six focus groups with community stakeholders to identify community cable-related needs and interests;
4. conducted written surveys among representatives of community groups, organizations, institutions, and government agencies to identify community cable-related needs and interests;
5. conducted a written survey to determine current institutional network uses and identify future cable-related needs and interest specific to telecommunications;
6. analyzed materials and documentation provided by local schools, local government agencies, nonprofit community organizations, and the local libraries;
7. conducted an audit of the availability and quality of current public, educational and governmental ("PEG") access equipment, facilities, and services;
8. and reviewed testimony and documents submitted during public hearings.

Once information was gathered, the Buske Group submitted four separate reports to the city: a Cablevision Franchise Compliance Review preliminary report, a Financial Performance and Franchise Fee Report, a cable system technical audit, and a preliminary report on Ascertainment and Recommendations Regarding Public, Educational, and Governmental Access for Brunswick, Ohio.

On two occasions, the reports were presented during public hearings where the public could comment on the findings. In addition to presenting current needs and interests in the report filed with the City, the Buske Group, during long interviews, focus groups, and onsite visits, found that the cable operator was not compliant with the *existing* franchise agreement in the following areas:

- Cablevision failed to provide a production facility to be used for public access and local programming origination purposes located in Brunswick as required by the franchise;
- Cablevision refused to provide a separate channel for public access as required by the franchise (a shared public/local origination channel has been provided instead);
- Cablevision failed to provide 20 hours per week of locally produced programming as required by the franchise;
- Cablevision failed to provide and maintain the system so that it is two-way activated (i.e., capable of sending a signal from the cable system headquarters to subscriber and back from subscriber to cable system headquarters) as required by the franchise; and
- Cablevision failed to make a local access production specialist available in Brunswick as required by the franchise.

In September 1996, the city of Brunswick adopted a resolution to accept the findings in the Buske Group's Franchise Compliance Report that Cablevision was not in compliance with the cable franchise agreement and directed Cablevision to provide a detailed plan of action to address the areas of noncompliance within 30 days of the adoption of the Resolution. The cable operator was late filing a response and, when the response came, it was painfully inadequate. In two pages, the cable operator argued that, because it had purchased the cable system from another operator during the course of the previous franchise, the city had waived its rights to enforce the provisions of that franchise. Cablevision did not produce any documentation to support its position. The city decided to take further action.

After several attempts to work with the cable operator, the city and township decided that their efforts were not going to result in a productive cable franchise agreement and decided to preliminarily deny the cable operator's renewal proposal. Under the procedural process outlined in the

Cable Act of 1984, an administrative hearing was held. During this hearing, the data collected in Brunswick was challenged. Sue Buske (2004) recalled the administrative hearing as "an intense four days of cross examination by the cable operator's attorneys" where the procedures of data collection were dissected for the hearing examiner, a locally retired judge. Under questioning, the attorneys for the cable operator argued that the focus groups and interviews conducted were partial to the consultant's bias and did not reflect the community needs and interests.

Other than requiring notice be given and opportunity for participation, the Cable Act does not detail how community needs and interests should be conducted, but instead requires only that the renewal process be orderly and fair (47 U.S.C. §§ 601(5)).

To challenge the cable operator's argument that the Buske Group's ascertainment process was biased, a professor from the University of Michigan was hired to serve as a validity check on the process. He employed the standards published by The Federal Judicial Center in a *Reference Manual on Scientific Evidence* (Federal Judicial Center, 2000). The *Manual* was written to assist judges in managing evidence presented in court, primarily in cases involving issues of science or technology. Although the *Manual* contains a specific chapter on survey research, it does not include evaluation of data collected in focus groups, and perhaps this made them the most vulnerable data in the Brunswick needs assessment. However, the *Manual* does take into consideration other forms of qualitative data collection, such as expert testimony. The focus group data did nonetheless become a focal point for the cable operator's attorneys.

Brunswick demonstrated that the focus group methodology was the appropriate choice when ascertaining future community cable-related needs and interests. By focusing on local stakeholders, decision makers, local persons with businesses and services linked to technology, and the Brunswick PEG access community, Brunswick gained important information concerning community needs and interests. The outside auditor found that the Buske Group's assessment was creative, valid, and in keeping with standard practices of qualitative research.

To challenge the Buske Group's findings, the cable operator submitted data it collected using a telephone survey of cable subscribers. The auditor did find that the cable operator's data were not in compliance with the standards set forth in the *Reference Manual on Scientific Evidence*. For example, the *Reference Manual* makes clear the need for adequate survey documentation stating, "instructions [provided to interviewers] should be made available to the opposing party and to the trier of fact." The *Manual* also states that a survey report should contain "copies of interviewer instructions, validation results and codebooks" and "copies of all questionnaires should be made available upon request so that the opposing party may have an opportunity to evaluate the raw data" (Federal Judicial Center, 2000, pp. 264, 272). The cable company never provided these documents.

The hearing examiner, however, continued to be critical of the city's use of focus group data and found in favor of renewal of the cable franchise as proposed by the cable company. The city disagreed and chose to reject the hearing examiner's findings and proceed with the denial of the franchise. The cable company challenged on the grounds that the hearing examiner's decision should be upheld, but lost that argument on appeal. The city of Brunswick's denial of franchise renewal based on its data gathering efforts has created a strong affirmation of the ascertainment process' ability to determine public interest obligations that sustain the test of judicial review (*Cablevision of the Midwest, Inc. v. City of Brunswick*, 2000).

GOING FORWARD

Attempting to create tangible measures surrounding notions of the *public interest* is not a simple task, but an important one if policymakers in the United States want to create media systems responsive to the communities they service. The process of defining local public interest is inherently an intimate process. One can appreciate why large media structures would find the process burdensome and at odds with their own national, streamlined corporate behavior. However, media consumption is a local phenomenon supported with local dollars, and each community is different. For the United States to maintain a media culture responsive to the individual community's needs, data gathering at the local level has to be conducted.

The local needs and interests ascertainment process is not without its flaws. For example, in 1997 in Jackson, Mississippi, the city council voted 4 to 3 not to renew Time Warner's cable franchise. Shortly after the vote, Time Warner received a call from a local car dealership owner saying that if the cable company paid $150,000, he was sure he could get the vote to go in their favor. Time Warner contacted the FBI and, after an undercover operation was completed, one of the local city councilmen was found guilty of conspiring to bribe the cable company in exchange for his vote and influence to approve the cable franchise (*United States v. Williams*, 2001).

Adding systematic processes to the cable TV needs and interests ascertainment helps to ensure that local biases are not included in the determination of the public interest, but in fact that the totality of the public's opinion is on the table. Although not a perfect system, the opportunity for judicial review does help create more opportunity to have the data challenged and discussed.

The Federal Judicial Center's *Reference Manual on Scientific Evidence* and other similar tools developed by the legal system are valuable in that they provide a common measuring stick for researchers engaged in data collection. These standards of practice also provide reassurance to hearing examiners, judges, and attorneys when relying on the data to uphold what can be costly and difficult decision making.

The FCC has been largely unsuccessful in attempts to define public interest. Even the 1960 policymaking that led to the categories of programming presented in Table 15.1 were problematic in that it created a menu of programming. No one could say for certain that the programming categories offered were inherently good for all communities, not without engaging in some type of local ascertainment. Rather than attempting to define the public interest, perhaps the FCC's efforts should be in defining standards and practices for local needs assessments that in turn help to partially define the public interest. Such an effort would recognize the impossibility of a federal agency being able to create such important local definitions, as well as help codify the important role social science can have in the complex media puzzle of the public interest.

REFERENCES

Allen, C. (1996). *Mandate to news consult: The untold story of the FCC's 1960 community ascertainment policy*. Paper presented at the annual meeting of the Association for Education in Journalism and Mass Communication, Anaheim, CA.

Bazeleyc, M. (2003, October 26). California squares off with Comcast over community access programming. *San Jose Mercury News*.

Book, C. (2004). *DTV: Digital television and consumers*. Cedar Rapids, IA: Blackwell.

Buske, S. (2004, July 11). Telephone interview.

The Cable Communications Act of 1984. Pub. L. No. 98–549, 98 Stat. 2779 (47 U.S.C. § 521 et seq.) (1984).

Cable Television Consumer Protection Act of 1992 ("1992 Cable Act" or "the Act"), Pub. L. No. 102–385, 106 Stat. 1460 (codified in scattered sections of 47 U.S.C.) (1992).

Cablevision of the Midwest, Inc. v. City of Brunswick, 117 F. Supp. 2d 658 (N.D. Ohio 2000).

Federal Communications Commission. (1960). *Programming policy statement* (FCC 60-970). Washington, DC: Author.

Federal Judicial Center. (2000). *Reference manual on scientific evidence* (2nd ed.). Washington, DC. Retrieved from http://www.fjc.gov

Head, S., Spann, T., & McGregor, M. (2001). *Broadcasting in America* (9th ed.). Boston: Houghton Mifflin.

Krugman, D., & Reid, L. (1980). The "Public Interest" as defined by FCC policy makers. *Journal of Broadcasting, 24*(3), 311–325.

Lloyd, F. (1997, March). *Cities' cable needs assessments held subject to judicial review. Cable TV and New Media Law & Finance*. New York: American Lawyer Media.

Madison Cablevision v. City of Morganton, 325 N.C. 634, 386 S.E. 2d 200 (1989).

National Cable Television Association. (2004). "History of cable television." Retrieved from www.ncta.com

Powell, M. (1998, April 5). *The public interest standard: A new regulator's search for enlightenment*. Presented to the American Bar Association Annual Legal Forum on Communications Law, Las Vegas, NV.

Rolla Cable System, Inc. v. City of Rolla, 761 F. Supp. 1398, 1409 (ED Mo. 1991).

Sarver, D. (2004). In the public's interest. In E. Erickson & W. D. Sloan (Eds.), *Contemporary media issues* (2nd ed., pp. 49–66). Northport, AL: Vision.

Thompson, R. (1991a, April 22). Court upholds city council's firing of Rolla. *Multichannel News*.

Thompson, R. (1991b, December 21). TCI loses N.C. appeal, pushes referendum. *Multichannel News*.

Thompson, R. (1992a, March 16). Morganton, NC voters thrash TCI. *Multichannel News*.

Thompson, R. (1992b, April 27). TCI denied Morganton review. *Multichannel News*.

Union CATV, Inc. v. City of Sturgis, 107 F.3d 434 (6th Cir. 1997).

United States v. Southwestern Cable Co., 392 U.S. 157 (1968).

United States v. Williams, 264 F.3d 561 (2001).

Introductory Comments to Chapter 16

Michael Hoefges
University of North Carolina at Chapel Hill

Kent Lancaster
University of Miami

Class action lawsuits are widely used to adjudicate similar claims made by a defined group of plaintiffs against a common defendant or group of defendants. As a procedural mechanism, the class action device allows litigation of such claims in a single court proceeding. The device was developed to facilitate judicial economy and efficiency in handling groups of similar claims as opposed to requiring a separate lawsuit for each individual claim.

The class action mechanism clearly facilitates judicial economy and efficiency. However, these systemic policy grounds may not be used by courts to override constitutional due process rights of individual class members. Provisions in the Fifth Amendment of the U.S. Constitution generally prohibit government from depriving individuals of "life, liberty, or property without due process of law." Typically, due process issues arise in class action proceedings because a portion of the class—the absentees—are not named as parties and usually have no knowledge of the lawsuit or their legal rights and obligations in the litigation being conducted on their behalf (see Conte & Newberg, 2002, §8:1, p. 163). In most class actions, absentees have rights to be notified and to exclude themselves from the litigation, and these rights are grounded in due process requirements.

Often absentee class members are provided individual notice by targeted, direct mail when their names and addresses are known. In addition, mass media advertising is often used to supplement direct mail campaigns and, more important, to reach absentees who cannot be identified through reasonable efforts for purposes of individual notice (see Conte & Newberg 2002, §8.34, p. 270). Class action notice plans utilizing mass media advertising typically include an array of media vehicles across various media categories, including newspapers, magazines, TV, radio, and, recently, the Internet. For instance, in a national class action filed on behalf of Vietnam veterans who were exposed to the chemical defoliant known as "Agent Orange," an array of national print and broadcast media were utilized in addition to direct mail to provide notice to absentee class members (*In re "Agent Orange" Product Liability Litigation*, 1983).

Issues surrounding the use of mass media advertising to provide legal notice in class actions have been largely ignored by mass communication scholars. However, with billions of dollars of claims being litigated each year in class action proceedings and with courts frequently ordering notice plans that include mass media advertising campaigns with multimillion dollar media schedules, the topic is worthy of exploration by mass communication scholars who can provide unique insights to legal professionals and scholars. Specifically, for instance, advertising media planning theories, methods, and data can be utilized to create class action notice plans that effectively and efficiently reach a sufficiently substantial percentage of absentee class members to meet the requirements of constitutional due process and court rules that govern class action proceedings in state and federal courts.

This chapter focuses on class actions brought under subdivision (b)(3) of Federal Rule of Civil Procedure 23 ("Rule 23"), which is the most common form of class action and the most likely to be used for large consumer class actions seeking primarily monetary damages. Created in 1966, this form of class action allows a class of plaintiffs to recover damages from one or more common defendants who cause similar harm to class members. Subdivision (b)(3) was added to Rule 23 to cover situations such as a fraudulent scheme that causes similar damages to many individuals (*1966 Advisory Committee's Note*). As studied and reported by Hoefges (1998), the types of class actions recently certified by courts under subdivision (b)(3) have expanded beyond the category of fraud cases (Wright, Miller, & Kane, 2005, §§1781–1783).

Over the years, courts have used Rule 23(b)(3) to certify classes in product liability, securities fraud, antitrust, and Federal Truth-in-Lending cases, among others (American Bar Association, 1976). In one of the most widely publicized class actions filed under Rule 23(b)(3), the U.S. Court of Appeals, Second Circuit, ultimately approved a $180 million settlement reached on behalf of nearly 250,000 Vietnam veterans exposed to Agent Orange (*In re Agent Orange*, 1987). In 1998, however, the

Supreme Court overruled the certification of a sprawling class action filed on behalf of millions of individuals who had been exposed to asbestos because their claims were too diverse and dissimilar to be handled in class action proceedings (*Amchem Products, Inc. v. Windsor*, 1997; Wright, Miller, & Kane, 2005, §1783 for general discussion of mass tort cases under Rule 23(b)(3)).

To certify a class action under subdivision (b)(3) of Rule 23, the presiding court must make two general findings. First, this subdivision requires that there exist "questions of law or fact [that are] common to the members of the class [and] predominate over any questions affecting only individual members." Second, Rule 23(b)(3) requires that, in any given case, the class action mechanism must be "superior to other available methods for the fair and efficient adjudication of the controversy." Clearly, these requirements seek to balance the rights of individuals to pursue their claims with the interests of judicial economy and efficiency in handling similar claims collectively.

The chapter uses legal research methods to identify the constitutional and procedural role of mass media advertising in class action notice plans. The purpose is to demonstrate how legal research can identify an issue for further exploration and explication with mass communication research. Then we further explain how advertising media planning theories, procedures, and methods can be used to evaluate class action notice plans that utilize mass media advertising. We then demonstrate the application of these theories, procedures, and methods using typical data used by professional media planners. For purposes of simplicity and clarity, the demonstration uses a sample schedule of national print vehicles that courts have utilized routinely for publication of class action notices. This chapter follows up on a similar and more detailed study published by Hoefges and Lancaster (2000), which analyzed an actual mass media notice plan used in a federal class action, and a subsequent study conducted by Hoefges and Hoy (2002) that content-analyzed a sample of class action notices for consumer readability.

As mentioned, the issues explored in this chapter have constitutional ramifications for courts that utilize mass media advertising to provide legal notice in class action litigation. In such cases, meeting due process requirements often hinges on the effectiveness of the notice plan in terms of reaching a sufficient percentage of the absentee class members. The chapter concludes that advertising media planning methods can help courts ensure that absentee class members are adequately notified with effective media plans, and that the due process rights of absentee class members have been preserved in the process. Courts that utilize constitutionally and procedurally inadequate notice plans compromise the integrity of class action judgments by leaving them subject to subsequent invalidation in court challenges filed by absentee class members who claim they were never legally notified (Conte & Newberg, 2002, §§8:25–8:30).

REFERENCES

Amchem Products, Inc. v. Windsor, 521 U.S. 591 (U.S. 1997).

American Bar Association. (1976). *Class actions: In the wake of Eisen III and IV*. Chicago, IL: American Bar Association Section of Litigation.

Conte, A., & Newberg, H. (2002). *Newberg on class actions* (4th ed.). St. Paul, MN: Thomson West.

Federal Rule of Civil Procedure 23 (through 2003 amendments).

Hoefges, R. M. (1998). Legal notice by mass media publication in federal rule 23(b)(3) class actions: The role of advertising media planning concepts and methods. *Dissertation Abstracts International, 59*(09), 3622.

Hoefges, R. M., & Hoy, M. G. (2002, May). *Readability evaluations of class action advertising: Legal and public policy implications*. Poster session presented at the Marketing and Public Policy Conference, Atlanta, GA.

Hoefges, R. M., & Lancaster, K. M. (2000). The critical role of advertising media planning in federal "Rule 23" class action notice. *Journal of Public Policy and Marketing, 19*(2), 201–212.

In re "Agent Orange" Product Liability Litigation, 100 F.R.D. 718 (E.D. N.Y. 1983).

In re "Agent Orange" Product Liability Litigation, 818 F.2d 145 (2d Cir. 1987).

1966 Advisor Committee's Note, 39 F.R.D. 69 (1966).

Wright, C. A., Miller, A. R., & Kane, M. K. (1986). *Federal practice and procedure* (2nd ed.). St. Paul, MN: West.

Utilizing Mass Media Advertising for Legal Notice in Class Action Lawsuits

Michael Hoefges
Kent Lancaster

Although this chapter focuses on class actions filed under the federal class action rule, it bears mention here that most states also have procedural court rules that govern class actions in state courts. However, the focus on the federal rule is justified here for two reasons. First, federal constitutional requirements that govern class action procedures—including notice plans—apply equally to class actions filed in both federal and state courts. Second, many state class action rules are patterned after the federal rule (Florida Rule of Civil Procedure 1220, 2004). Thus, the constitutional and procedural requirements of the federal rule, along with the various federal court opinions that interpret these requirements, are instructive in class actions governed by federal and state procedural rules. Specifically, the requirements of constitutional due process are important to the conduct of all class actions whether conducted under state or federal courts rules.

CONSTITUTIONAL SIGNIFICANCE OF NOTICE IN RULE 23(b)(3) CLASS ACTIONS

Under Rule 23, courts must give notice to class members in subdivision (b)(3) cases along with a subsequent opportunity to opt out from the class proceedings (Federal Rule of Civil Procedure 23(3)(2)). As described by Yeazell (1987), notice and the right to opt out give class members the "chance to vote with their feet by withdrawing from the class" (p. 248). Class members who fail to exclude themselves—or opt out—before a deadline set by the court must abide by any judgment rendered in the case, whether favorable to them or not (Federal Rule of Civil Procedure 23(c)(2)).

Arguably, for the opt out right to be meaningful, absentee class members need to be notified about the litigation and advised of the class description, claims being made, existence of the right to opt out, ramifications of failing to opt out, and opt-out deadline (see e.g., Wright, Miller, & Kane, 2005, §1786, p. 188). In addition to complying with Rule 23, the requirements of notice and the right to opt out are grounded in constitutional due process and must be met before absentee class members in Rule 23(b)(3) cases can be constitutionally bound by a class judgment (Wright, Miller, & Kane, 2005, §1786, p. 189).

The notice and opt-out requirements for subdivision (b)(3) class actions were added to Rule 23 when it was substantially amended in 1966 (*1966 Advisory Committee's Note*). The federal advisory committee that drafted the amendments concluded that notice and the right to opt out were necessary to meet constitutional due process requirements (*1966 Advisory Committee's Note*, 1966; see also Conte & Newberg, 2002, §8:4). As grounds, the advisory committee relied on two Supreme Court opinions—*Hansberry v. Lee* (1940) and *Mullane v. Central Hanover Bank & Trust* (1950; *1966 Advisory Committee's Note*, 1966).

In *Hansberry v. Lee* (1940), the Supreme Court held generally that class litigation must be conducted fairly as to the rights of absentee claimants. The *Hansberry* Court concluded that due process requires the named parties in class litigation have a duty to "fairly represent" the "common interests" of absentee claimants. To satisfy due process requirements, the *Hansberry* Court concluded, class proceedings must "insure full and fair consideration" of these common interests (p. 43). Thus, the *Hansberry* opinion is important for establishing general due process requirements that require courts to consider and protect the rights of absentee claimants in the face of the individual interests of the named parties as well as systemic concerns of judicial economy and efficiency (Gray, 1975).

Ten years after deciding *Hansberry*, the Supreme Court addressed the issue of what constitutes constitutionally adequate notice to absentee claimants in group litigation proceedings such as class actions. In *Mullane* (1950), the Supreme Court held that legal notice by newspaper publication is not a constitutional substitute for individual notice to claimants whose names and addresses are known. In that case, a state banking statute allowed for final judicial settlement of trust accounts that was binding on all beneficiaries. The statute only required prejudgment notice to potential beneficiaries by newspaper publication. The Supreme Court held that such publication notice violated the due process rights of the potential beneficiaries who are known and can be reached individually with notice.

In addressing the notice issue, the *Mullane* Court wrote:

> It would be idle to pretend that publication alone . . . is a reliable means of acquainting interested parties of the fact that their rights are before the courts. . . . *Chance alone brings to the attention of even a local resident an advertisement in small type inserted in the back pages of a newspaper, and if he makes his home outside the area of a newspaper's normal circulation the odds that the information will never reach him are large indeed.* (p. 315; italics added)

However, the *Mullane* Court explained, publication can be a sufficiently constitutional means of providing legal notice depending on the "practicalities and peculiarities" of a particular case (p. 314). On this point, the opinion says:

> This Court has not hesitated to approve of *resort to publication* as a customary substitute . . . where it is not reasonably possible or practicable to give more adequate warning. *Thus it has been recognized that, in the case of persons missing or unknown, employment of an indirect and even a probably futile means of notification is all that the situation permits and creates no constitutional bar to a final decree foreclosing their rights.* (p. 317; italics added)

In light of this somewhat ambivalent endorsement of legal notice by publication, the *Mullane* Court provided additional guidance for courts considering publication notice plans in class litigation contexts. The *Mullane* Court wrote that such plans must be "reasonably calculated in all circumstances to apprise interested parties of the pendency of the action and afford them an opportunity to present their objections," which requires more than a "mere gesture" (p. 317).

Taken together, the *Hansberry* and *Mullane* decisions indicate that absentee class members must be treated fairly in class action litigation and are entitled to individual notice if they are reasonably identifiable under constitutional due process principles. In addition, the *Mullane* decision stands for the proposition that publication notice can be a sufficiently constitutional means of notifying *unidentifiable* absentee class members so long as the notice plan is "reasonably calculated" to apprise them of their rights and the proceedings present an opportunity for them to present objections. However, after *Mullane*, the "reasonably calculated" standard remained vague and has not been further clarified by the Court. In addition, what is not clear from either of these decisions are the constitutional standards for determining whether a publication notice plan in class action litigation complies with constitutional due process requirements or the notice requirements that were added to Rule 23 after the Supreme Court's decisions in *Hansberry* and *Mullane*. In this light, the next section looks more specifically at the mandatory notice provisions of Rule 23.

MANDATORY NOTICE IN RULE 23(b)(3) CLASS ACTIONS

Rule 23 includes mandatory notice provisions that apply to subdivision (b)(3) class actions. Under these provisions, courts must notify absentee class members at two junctures in the case. First, prior to class certification, courts must notify absentees about the existence of the case and their legal rights and responsibilities in the litigation ("certification notice") (Federal Rule of Civil Procedure 23(c)(2)). Second, courts must notify all class members before approving any agreement by the named parties to settle claims made in the case ("settlement notice") (Federal Rule of Civil Procedure. 23(e)(1)(B)). In cases where the named parties have reached a settlement *before* the case is filed or certified ("settlement classes"), courts often combine certification and settlement notice into a single round of notice to absentees ("combination" or "simultaneous" notice).

A current class action practice guide describes the use of publication notice plans in federal class actions as varying "from largely perfunctory legal notices to aggressive advertising campaigns involving television and radio spots, full-scale newspaper advertising, and posting notice on products involved in the lawsuit" (Rossman & Edelman, 2002, p. 136). In Rule 23(b)(3) class actions, federal courts have utilized an array of media including print media such as newspapers, magazines, and trade publications, as well as broadcast media such as radio and TV (see Conte & Newberg, 2002, §8:24; Wright, Miller, & Kane, 2005, §8:38). Commentators have described and even advocated using the Internet, including Web sites and electronic mail, for purposes of delivering notice to class members (Fischer, 1996; Ginsberg, 2003; Mingus, 1999; Rossman & Edelman, 2002). This section looks at when and under what circumstance courts may appropriately utilize publication notice in subdivision (b)(3) class actions.

Certification Notice

Under Rule 23, judges in subdivision (b)(3) class actions are required to notify absentee class members using the "best notice practicable under the circumstances, including individual notice to all members who can be identified through reasonable effort" (Rule 23(c)(2)). Until legally sufficient notice occurs, the absentees are merely considered "passive beneficiaries" with no legal obligation to take any affirmative action with regard to the litigation (see *Bedel v. Thompson*, 1992). More important, as mentioned, legally sufficient notice and an opportunity to opt out of the class are constitutional prerequisites to binding absentee class members with a judgment in subdivision (b)(3) cases (Wright, Miller, & Kane, 2005, §1786; Federal Judicial Center, 2004).

There are two important legal considerations in designing and evaluating a certification notice plan in a 23(b)(3) class action. First, the content of the notice must adequately inform class members of their relevant rights and responsibilities. Second, known and reasonably identifiable class members must be notified individually by direct mail for instance, and unidentifiable class members must be notified by some other means such as mass media publication. Summarizing these two general considerations, one federal court wrote that a class action notice plan first must "convey its message in a meaningful way" and second "must . . . reach the affected parties" (*In re Domestic Air Transportation Antitrust Litigation*, 1992, p. 553; see also Wright, Miller, & Kane, 2005, §1786). These two steps are analogous to the advertising processes of planning the advertising creative content and then devising the media plan for message delivery to a defined target audience.

In subdivision (b)(3) cases, Rule 23 describes the required content for certification notice. The notice must inform class members about the nature of the action; the definition of the class; the claims, issues, and defenses raised on behalf of the class; the right of class members to appear individually with their own attorneys; the right of class members to exclude themselves from the class and not be bound by any judgment; and the binding effect of a class judgment on class members who do not opt out (Federal Rule of Civil Procedure 23(c)(2)(B)).

The mandatory notice provisions of subdivision (c)(2) were amended in 2003 and now require that certification notices be clear, concise, and utilize "plain, easily understood language" to facilitate communication with absentee class members. The amendment was prompted in part by empirical research, which found that consumers often were confused by complex legal terminology used in typical class action notices (Federal Judicial Center, 2003a). To demonstrate the plain language requirement, the Federal Judicial Center—the official research and education agency of the federal court system—published various model notices as examples for judges, lawyers, and communication professionals in subdivision (b)(3) class actions and included a model certification notice in a hypothetical employment discrimination case (see Federal Judicial Center, 2003b).

Clearly, the requirement for "plain, easily understood language" focuses on message content and seeks to avoid the use of complex legal terminology that absentees are likely to find perplexing and inaccessible (Federal Judicial Center, 2003a; Hoefges & Hoy, 2002). Thus, the requirement and accompanying model notices provide content and layout guidance for notices in subdivision (b)(3) cases filed under Rule 23. However, the rule and accompanying federal judicial guidelines are less clear and instructive with regard to the means of notice delivery and, specifically, actually reaching absentee class members with the required notice.

Turning to notice delivery issues in Rule 23(b)(3) class actions, subdivision (c)(2) requires the "best notice practicable under the circumstances," including "individual notice" to reasonably identifiable absentee class members. However, the terms *individual notice* and *reasonable effort* are not defined or explained. In addition, the rule is virtually silent on the means of notice to absentee class members who cannot be identified through reasonable means. On this point, the authors of a prominent class action practice guide wrote:

> While the language of [subdivision (c)(2)] itself makes notice mandatory in a Rule 23(b)(3) damages suit, the nature and extent of how that mandate is to be carried out are not predetermined in the rule. Thus, from a practitioner's point of view, a controversial aspect of Rule 23(c)(2) has been the determination of the proper construction of the requirement for "the best notice practicable under the circumstances. . . ." *Unfortunately, no single set of rules or factors has yet emerged, and courts continue to revisit and refine the illusive issue of reasonable notice.* (Conte & Newberg, 2002, §8:2, pp. 164–165; italics added) (footnotes omitted)

With murkiness in the mandatory notice provisions of Rule 23, determining the means of delivering certification notice in subdivision (b)(3) cases largely rests within the discretion of federal trial judges (see e.g., Conte & Newberg, 2002, §8:2; Wright, Miller, & Kane, 2005, §1786). In light of constitutional due process issues related to certification notice, one prominent federal practice guide recommended that judges handle notice issues cautiously in these cases (Wright, Miller, & Kane, 2005, §1786). Not surprisingly, that same federal practice guide described the "manner in which notice is given" as the most significant issue related to mandatory certification notice (Wright, Miller, & Kane, 2005, §1786). Similarly, another prominent practice guide recommended that courts and lawyers use "their 'cooperative ingenuity' in determining the most suitable notice in each case, given the estimated size of the class, the ratio of known to unknown class members, and the cost of reasonable effort in identifying the class members" (Newberg, 1992, §8.04, pp. 8–15).

In class actions, at least some and perhaps all of the absentee class members often are known or identifiable for purposes of individual notice. Determining the absentees who are entitled to individual notice is a "key finding" in devising notice plans in subdivision (b)(3) cases (*In re Franklin National Bank Securities Litigation*, 1978). Federal judicial guidelines indicate that first-class mail can be a legally sufficient means to deliver individual certification notice to identifiable class members (Federal Judicial Center, 2004). Many federal courts indeed have utilized direct mail for this purpose.

The Supreme Court has held that publication notice may not be employed as the exclusive means of providing certification notice to identifiable class members (*Eisen v. Carlisle & Jacquelin*, 1974). In that case, the trial court had approved publication notice in several national newspapers as opposed to requiring individual, and far more costly, mailed notice to more than 2 million class members who could be identified in computerized records. The Supreme Court held that the failure to utilize individual notice under these circumstances violated the individual notice requirement of Rule 23(c)(2) (*Eisen v. Carlisle & Jacquelin*, 1974). Thus, in subdivision (b)(3) cases, courts often utilize publication notice to supplement—but not replace—individual certification notice mailed to identifiable absentees to compensate for the estimated percentage of undelivered notices resulting from incorrect addresses, lost or misdelivered mail, and failure of recipients to open or read their notices (Conte & Newberg, 2002, §8:35).

Often in Rule 23(b)(3) class actions, many and sometimes most of the absentee class members are not reasonably identifiable for purposes of individual notice (Conte & Newberg, 2002, §8:35, note 1). In these circumstances, courts have utilized various forms of mass media publication to deliver certification notice to absentees who cannot be reached by individual means such as direct mail (*In re "Agent Orange" Product Liability Litigation*, 1993). Federal class action practice guides recommend the use of publication notice under these circumstances (*In re Domestic Air Transportation Antitrust Litigation*, 1992).

The size of the class in a subdivision (b)(3) case varies from case to case as does the percentage of the absentee class members who are identifiable for purposes of individual notice. A recent analysis of 1990–1997 federal court notice orders and appellate opinions indicated that the decision to utilize publication notice often is dependent on two primary factors: (a) The number of class members, and (b) the expected percentage of absentees who will not be reached by individual notice (Hoefges, 1998). This analysis also demonstrated that federal courts have been inconsistent in their application of the "best notice practicable" standard to publication notice plans in class action cases and often order publication plans without analyzing expected reach among absentee class members (Hoefges, 1998). Class action research has indicated that the greater the number of absentee class members and the larger the expected percentage of them who will not be reached by individual notice, the greater the need for a publication plan that effectively reaches a legally and constitutionally sufficient percentage of absentees class members with publication notice (Hoefges, 1998; Hoefges & Lancaster, 2000).

Courts have held that neither Rule 23 nor constitutional due process requirements mandate actual notice receipt by every absentee class member (see e.g., *In re Prudential Insurance Co.*, 1997; *In re Domestic Air Transportation*, 1992). However, the Supreme Court's holdings and language in *Hansberry, Mullane,* and *Eisen* strongly suggest that a notice plan should be designed to minimize the number of absentee class members who will not be reached by a notice plan.

Settlement Notice

In class actions certified under Rule 23(b)(3), the named parties may not settle or dismiss any of the class claims without court approval and prior notice to all class members (Federal Rule of Civil Procedure 23(e)(1)) (referred to here as "settlement notice"). Under the relevant provisions of the rule, the trial court in a Rule 23(b)(3) class action "must direct notice in a reasonable manner to all class members who would be bound by a proposed settlement, voluntary dismissal, or compromise" (Federal Rule of Civil Procedure 23(e)(1)(B)). The rule contains no further explanation of the settlement notice requirement. Thus, what constitutes a "reasonable manner" is largely undetermined except by study of court decisions. Seemingly, the settlement notice provisions of subdivision (e) are not as stringent as the certification notice provisions of subdivision (c)(2) (see Conte & Newberg, 2002, §8:18). For instance, the settlement notice need only be in such a "manner as the court directs" (Federal Rule of Civil Procedure 23(c)(2)) while the certification notice must be the "best notice practicable under the circumstances" (Federal Rule of Civil Procedure 23(e)).

Rule 23(e) does not spell out the criteria that federal district judges should consider when deciding whether to approve a class action settlement or compromise of claims. However, federal appellate courts have developed criteria for judging the fairness and reasonableness of class action settlements (*Girsh v. Jepson*, 1975; *Reed v. General Motors Corp.*, 1983). Significant to the notice issue, one of the factors that federal appellate courts agree on is the value of feedback from class members, including the absentees (*Girsh v. Jepson*, 1975; *Reed v. General Motors Corp.*, 1983). Thus, the mandatory settlement notice to the absentees is important to the court's ability to obtain such feedback and to fully consider the fairness and reasonableness of a proposed settlement. Rule 23 does not describe the required content for settlement notices (Conte & Newberg, 2002, §8:21), nor does the "plain language" requirement for certification notice apply explicitly to settlement notices. However, according to current federal judicial guidelines, settlement notices in Rule 23(b)(3) cases should accomplish the following:

> [D]escribe the essential terms of the proposed settlement; disclose any special benefits provided to the class representatives; provide information regarding attorneys' fees . . . ; indicate the time and place of the hearing to consider approval of the settlement; describe the method for objecting to (or, if permitted, for opting out of) the settlement; explain the procedures for allocating and distributing settlement funds, and, if the settlement provides different kinds of relief for different categories of class members, clearly set out those variations; . . . and prominently display the address and phone number of class counsel and the procedure for making inquiries. (Federal Judicial Center, 2004, p. 295)

Combination Notice in Settlement Classes

In some class actions, the parties may have reached a settlement agreement before the class is even certified (*In re Beef Industry Antitrust Litigation*, 1979; *Weinberger v. Kendrick*, 1982; *West Virginia v. Chas. Pfizer & Co., Inc.*, 1971). Federal courts have certified these so-called *settlement classes* and authorized the use of a single round of notice that provides simultaneous notice of certification and settlement to absentee class members in Rule 23(b)(3) cases (Hoefges, 1998).

Settlement class actions are not explicitly authorized by Rule 23 and, despite their frequent use by federal courts, have been controversial as a procedural mechanism (Yeazell, 1997). The Supreme Court has tacitly approved the use of settlement classes, describing them as "stock devices" in federal civil procedure (*Amchem Products, Inc. v. Windsor*, 1997, p. 618). Likewise, Rule 23 neither authorizes nor prohibits simultaneous certification and settlement notice. However, current federal judicial guidelines note that when a federal class action "is certified and settled simultaneously, a single notice is generally used" (Federal Judicial Center, 2004, p. 289).

Combination notice plans in Rule 23(b)(3) class actions must meet the mandatory notice requirements for certification notice under subdivision (c)(2) and those for settlement notice under subdivision (e)(1)(B) of Rule 23 (Federal Judicial Center, 1995; see also Conte & Newberg, 2002, §8.21). In addition, current federal guidelines suggest that the combination notice should be clear that certification and settlement are separate issues (Federal Judicial Center, 2004). As one federal court of appeals described, the combination notice presents a "threefold opportunity to class members: (1) to file a claim; (2) to state a desire for exclusion or (3) to object to the settlement" (*Greenfield v. Villager Industries, Inc.*, 1973, p. 833). Clearly, the need for an effective means of notifying absentee class members is especially critical in settlement classes where the goal is simultaneous notification of certification and settlement.

EVALUATING MASS MEDIA NOTICE

When publication and other mass media notice is necessary, whether for certification, settlement, or combination notice plans, there are many factors that should be considered. The procedures for developing and evaluating publication and mass media notice programs can range from relatively general approaches, which offer the courts only a vague idea of class coverage, to more comprehensive approaches, which provide greater insight into the likely communication effectiveness of notice options.

What follows is a review of major media planning concepts that are relevant to developing and evaluating mass media notice programs. These concepts are then applied to a national publication schedule to illustrate how such a plan can be evaluated and how likely it is that notice will reach potential class members.

Key Concepts

Those preparing and evaluating class action notice media plans have ample data, methods, and procedures to assist them. Recent overviews of media planning theory and practice, for example, can be obtained from Kelley and Jugenheimer (2004) and Sissors and Baron (2002), among others. Many key media planning procedures have been described and applied to class notice in substantial detail by Hoefges and Lancaster (2000) and are not repeated in this chapter. The goal here is to summarize these key concepts and tools and apply them to an example mass media notice plan. The example illustrates the gap between the number of class members receiving and reading mass media publications that contain a class notice, and the often much smaller number of them who actually see and read the notice somewhere within the pages of that publication.

Thus, a class member might be among the readership of a print vehicle carrying a relevant class action notice, but might not even find or see the notice and then read it. The example underscores the importance of esti-mating the likelihood that class members will actually see and read pub-lished notices in mass media vehicles because exposure to the published notice, *in addition to exposure to the publication generally*, is necessary to actually inform class members about their rights. As previously dis-cussed, the Supreme Court pointed out that in the context of legal notice by newspaper publication, "[c]hance alone brings to the attention [of a reader] an advertisement in small type inserted in the back pages of a newspaper" (*Mullane v. Central Hanover Bank & Trust*, 1950, pp. 106–107).

Generally the class definition should be the target audience for a notice plan that utilizes mass media publication. However, when the class defi-nition is too narrow for available audience information, the target audi-ence definition should be broad enough to encompass the class definition. For instance, an employment discrimination class action filed on behalf of adult women who worked for a large southern grocery chain from 1991 to 1997 could be covered by a publication plan with a target audience of adult women in four southern states (*Shores v. Publix Super Markets, Inc.*, 1997a, 1997b, 1997c). The target audience is broad enough to include the class description as a subset, but recognizes that published audience data are not typically cross-tabulated with such narrow employment de-mographics as grocery store employment.

Media selection should be based on the media usage habits of the target audience. Large quantities of audience data that are useful for media se-lection are published regularly for all major media categories at the na-tional and local levels (see e.g., Hoefges & Lancaster, 2000). Direct mail often is required when the names and addresses of class members can be obtained with reasonable effort. Newspapers, magazines, and Web sites are especially suited for full-length and complex class notices. Abbrevi-ated notices on TV and radio can serve to prepublicize print notice (Newberg, 1992), and to more broadly reach class members who do not regularly read newspapers or magazines or who do not have access to the Web. To enhance effectiveness, broadcast notices often contain additional information leading class members to the full notice, including a toll-free telephone number, Web address, and postal address (Hoefges & Lancas-ter, 2000).

Many syndicated research services provide data on publication circula-tion and readership for various target audiences. Some well-known com-panies include Mediamark Research Inc. (MRI), Mendelsohn, Scar-borough, Simmons Market Research Bureau (SMRB), Audit Bureau of Circulations (ABC), Bacon's, and Standard Rate and Data Service (SRDS), among several others (Hoefges & Lancaster, 2000). Similar information is available for TV and radio in the form of network, daypart, station, and program ratings. Companies that provide this type of information include Arbitron, Nielsen Media Research, RADAR, and Strategic Accuratings (Hoefges & Lancaster, 2000). Although these are necessary data for evaluating the likely delivery of a mass media notice plan, alone they are not sufficient for analyzing the probability that the notice will be seen and read.

Message audience measurement services must be used for such information based on norms for messages of similar size, length, use of color, product category, and publication type, for example. These data help determine the proportion of publication readers or broadcast program viewers or listeners who also attend to the advertisements contained in the publication or program. Companies that provide such information include Gallup & Robinson, Harvey Research Organization, Readex, and RoperASW, among many others (Hoefges & Lancaster, 2000).

For purposes of this chapter, *reach* is defined as the number or percentage of class members who are likely to see and read the notice. It can be estimated by evaluating the vehicle (i.e., publication, TV program) and message (i.e., class notice) audience delivery of all media in the class notice plan. Media planning software generally is used for this purpose to also account for the duplication within and between vehicles. This software is available from Interactive Market Systems and Telmar Information Services Corp, for example, among many other systems often provided by the various audience measurement services (Hoefges & Lancaster, 2000).

Generally, the larger the class size, the more it will cost to reach them. Planners can help ensure that they are getting the greatest practical notice for a given expenditure by focusing on cost-per-thousand (CPM) impressions. CPM is obtained by dividing the cost of notice in a particular publication—for example, by the total number of readers of that publication, in thousands. Choosing vehicles with relatively low CPM, in comparison to alternatives with relatively high CPM, will help boost the overall delivery of the notice plan for a given total class notice expenditure.

Practical Application

What follows is a practical application of these concepts and procedures to an example class action notice schedule. This schedule assumes a national class of U.S. adults who can be efficiently reached with full- and half-page, black-and-white notices in five top U.S. publications that are frequently used to deliver notice for a large variety of class actions. These publications include two Sunday newspaper supplements, *Parade* and

USA Weekend. The schedule also includes three national newspapers, *USA Today*, *The New York Times*, and *The Wall Street Journal*. Publication details on circulation, readership, and notice cost are provided in Table 16.1.

The relatively small list of publications in Table 16.1 is intended to support a schedule that distributes notices in three separate issues of each publication. This schedule also assumes that one full-page notice will be published in three different issues of *Parade* magazine, for example, while one half-page notice will be published in three different issues of *USA Today*. Three insertions in each publication are utilized to increase the probability that the notice will be seen and read.

Given a fixed amount of notice content using a standard 10-point type size for the main text of the notice, a full-page notice in *Parade* and *USA Weekend* newspaper supplements would require only one half-page notice in the remaining standard size newspapers.

The Starch Readership Service has been measuring the editorial and advertising readership of publications for more than 75 years. Such readership data have clearly established that only a portion of those who receive and read a publication also see and read the typical advertisements contained in the publication. For example, *2001 STARCH Adnorms* reports these averages for full- and half-page, black-and-white advertisements, among many other message characteristics. Data in the report indicate that only approximately 43% of publication readers are likely to notice the typical full-page, black-and-white advertisement, whereas only 35% are likely to notice the typical half-page, black-and-white advertisement.

This advertisement readership information, applied to class action notices, can be analyzed along with the data in Table 16.1 using any standard media planning software. Telmar's InterMix (www.etelmar.com) is used here because of its sophisticated procedures for simultaneously evaluating both vehicle and message delivery, and because it is available world wide.

TABLE 16.1
Several U.S. Publications Often Used for Class Action Notice

Publication	Circulation (000)	Readership (000)	Notice Size (Page)	Cost ($)
Parade	35,507	78,657	Full	614,700
USA Weekend	21,755	49,295	Full	448,400
USA Today	2,610	5,694	Half	89,300
The New York Times	1,672	5,086	Half	62,622
The Wall Street Journal	1,890	3,689	Half	86,233
Total	63,433	142,421		1,301,255

Sources: *Marketer's Guide to Media 2003*, *SRDS Newspaper Advertising Source*, April 2003.

Results of Schedule Evaluation

The analysis indicates that three issues of each of the five publications in the schedule are likely to reach approximately 55% of U.S. adults. However, only about 33% of the target audience is likely to see the class notice. This gap of 22% includes approximately 4.6 million adults who would receive or read one or more of the publication issues in the schedule, but who nevertheless are not likely to also see or read the notice contained in the publications. Consequently, they are not likely to be informed of their rights in the litigation. Therefore, approximately 45% of U.S. adults will not receive a publication containing the notice, whereas approximately 67% are not likely to see or read the notice. Assuming for this example that adult absentee class members are distributed randomly throughout the adult population, then one can presume that this notice plan is likely to reach less than one third of the absentees with at least one exposure to a published notice.

These limited results underscore the substantial cost necessary to achieve national reach. In this example, the $3.9 million expenditure delivers only 33% notice reach. Because of the generally diminishing returns to reach due to increased media expenditures, a much greater expenditure would be required to reach a substantial proportion of U.S. adults with the typical class action notice. Doing so would require the use of additional publications, as well as additional media categories, such as TV, to reach those who do not or cannot regularly read newspapers and magazines.

The level of notice reach that is necessary to meet due process requirements has never been established with any clarity by the courts. However, as pointed out by Hoefges and Lancaster (2000), a federal court of appeals approved a notice plan in *Grunin v. International House of Pancakes* (1975), although approximately one third of the class did not receive notice according to evidence in the case. The lowest limit of notice reach that would still satisfy constitutional due process and the procedural requirements of Rule 23 remains undetermined. However, in their study, Hoefges and Lancaster (2000) recommended that courts strive for a notice reach level of at least 75% among the absentee class members to meet these requirements.

Further Considerations

This example schedule has been presented and evaluated to illustrate key media planning concepts and procedures using publications that frequently carry class action notices. However, this schedule does not take into consideration many other potential characteristics of a class.

For example, publications targeting minorities often are required, including Hispanics, African Americans, and Asians, among others. Often multiple languages are necessary in print and broadcast notices and on the Web. However, courts have ordered publication plans that seemingly fail to reach significant percentages of minority audiences among which class members are dispersed (see e.g., *Jackson v. Motel 6 Multipurposes, Inc.*, 1997).

In addition, many broad class definitions include a substantial number of individuals who are functionally illiterate. Such class members are not likely to read newspapers and magazines, let alone detailed and complex class action notices including those that meet the new "plain language" requirements of Rule 23. Television and radio notices may be the most important means of reaching these class members.

SUMMARY AND CONCLUSIONS

This chapter provided a brief introduction and overview of class actions and the types of class action notification that are supported by Federal Rule 23. These include certification, settlement, and combination notices. Certification notice informs potential class members that a class has been established by the court, the nature of the litigation, and the procedures to follow to remain in or be excluded from the class. Settlement notice informs class members of the potential resolution of the litigation, the proposed nature of the settlement, and the procedures to follow to challenge or participate in the settlement. Combination notice includes elements of both certification and settlement notice.

When the names and addresses of class members cannot be obtained through reasonable effort, courts often approve mass media notification that includes newspapers, magazines, TV, radio, and the Internet, among other media. Mass media planning data, methods, and procedures can be utilized to determine the likely communication effectiveness of the notice program. The media schedule can be evaluated using vehicle and message audience estimates in conjunction with media planning computer software that accounts for the duplication within and between vehicles. Such software typically produces estimates of vehicle and message reach and frequency, among many other well-established media evaluation factors. These help estimate the number of class members who are likely to receive one or more vehicles utilized to distribute the notice, as well as the number of class members who are also likely to see and read the notice.

A class notice schedule was presented and evaluated. This class notice schedule includes several publications that are often used to reach a national class. The example illustrates the media weight that is necessary to reach a substantial portion of a national class with both vehicles and messages. The example also highlights the large gap that often exists between vehicle and message delivery. This gap underscores the importance of evaluating mass media class notice schedules in terms of message delivery, not just the broader vehicle delivery, if courts are to have a realistic understanding of the extent to which class members are likely to see and read the notice.

REFERENCES

Amchem Products, Inc. v. Windsor, 521 U.S. 591 (1997).

American Bar Association. (1976). *Class actions: In the wake of Eisen III and IV*. Chicago, IL: Author.

Bedel v. Thompson, 1992 U.S. App. LEXIS 3751 (6th Cir. 1992).

Conte, A., & Newberg, H. (2002). *Newberg on class actions* (4th ed.). St. Paul, MN: Thomson West.

Eisen v. Carlisle & Jacquelin, 417 U.S. 156 (U.S. 1974).

Federal Judicial Center. (2004). *Manual for complex litigation, fourth*. Washington, DC: Federal Judicial Center.

Federal Judicial Center. (2003a). *Detailed discussion of methodology*. Retrieved January 23, 2004, from http://199.0.74.114/newweb/jnetweb.nsf/pages/816

Federal Judicial Center. (2003b). *The Federal Judicial Center's "illustrative" forms of class action notices*. Retrieved January 23, 2004, from http://www.fjc.gov/newweb/jnetweb.nsf/pages/376

Federal Rule of Civil Procedure 23 (through 2003 amendments).

Fischer, J. M. (1996, July 1). Internet seen as means of providing legal notice. *National Law Journal*, p. C3.

Florida Rule of Civil Procedure 1220 (2004 edition).

Ginsberg, J. S. (2003). Class action notice: The internet's time has come. *University of Chicago Legal Forum*, pp. 739–772.

Girsh v. Jepson, 521 F.2d 153 (3d. Cir. 1975).

Gray, W. (1975). Recent case. *Emory University Law Review*, *24*(2), 533–548.

Greenfield v. Villager Industries, Inc., 483 F.2d 824 (3d Cir. 1973).

Hansberry v. Lee, 311 U.S. 32 (1940).

Hoefges, R. M. (1998). Legal notice by mass media publication in federal rule 23(b)(3) class actions: The role of advertising media planning concepts and methods. *Dissertation Abstracts International*, *59*(09), 3622.

Hoefges, R. M., & Hoy, M. G. (2002, May). *Readability evaluations of class action advertising: Legal and public policy implications*. Poster session presented at the Marketing and Public Policy Conference, Atlanta, GA.

Hoefges, R. M., & Lancaster, K. M. (2000). The critical role of advertising media planning In federal "Rule 23" class action notice. *Journal of Public Policy and Marketing*, *19*(2), 201–212.

In re "Agent Orange" Product Liability Litigation, 100 F.R.D. 718 (E.D. N.Y. 1983).

In re "Agent Orange" Product Liability Litigation, 818 F.2d 145 (2d Cir. 1987).

In re "Agent Orange" Product Liability Litigation, 996 F.2d 1425 (2d Cir. 1993).

In re Beef Industry Antitrust Litigation, 607 F.2d 167 (5th Cir. 1979).

In re Domestic Air Transportation Antitrust Litigation, 141 F.R.D. 534 (N.D. Ga. 1992).

In re Franklin National Bank Securities Litigation, 599 F.2d 1109 (2d Cir. 1978).

Jackson v. Motel 6 Multipurposes, Inc., 1997 U.S. Dist. LEXIS 18534 (M.D. Fla. 1997).

Kelley, L. D., & Jugenheimer, D. W. (2004). *Advertising media planning: A brand management approach*. Armonk, NY: M. E. Sharpe.

Marketer's guide to media 2003 (vol. 26). New York: VNU Business Media.

Mingus, J. (1999). E-mail: A constitutional (and economical) method of transmitting class action notice. *Cleveland State Law Review*, 47(1), 87–113.

Mullane v. Central Hanover Bank & Trust, 339 U.S. 306 (1950).

Newberg, H. B., & Conte, A. (1992). *Newberg on class actions* (3rd ed.). Colorado Springs, CO: Shepard's/McGraw-Hill.

Reed v. General Motors Corp., 703 F.2d 170 (5th. Cir. 1983).

Rossman, S. T., & Edelman, D. A. (2002). *Consumer class actions: A practical guide* (5th ed.). Boston, MA: National Consumer Law Center.

Shores v. Publix Super Markets Inc., No. 95–1162-CIV-T–25E (M. D. Fla. Jan. 27, 1997a) (preliminary order approving consent decree).

Shores v. Publix Super Markets, Inc., Case No. 95–1162-CIV-T–25E (M. D. Fla. May 23, 1997b) (order approving consent decree).

Shores v. Publix Super Markets, Inc., No. 95–1162-CIV-T–25E (M. D. Fla. May, 8, 1997c) (defendant's verified report on completion of notice process).

Sissors, J. Z., & Baron, R. D. (2002). *Advertising media planning* (6th ed.). New York: McGraw-Hill.

SRDS newspaper advertising source. (2003, April). Des Plaines, IL: Standard Rate and Data Service.

2001 STARCH Adnorms. (October). New York: RoperASW.

Weinberger v. Kendrick, 698 F.2d 61 (2d Cir. 1982).

West Virginia v. Chas. Pfizer & Co., Inc., 440 F.2d 1079 (2d Cir. 1971).

Wright, C. A., Miller, A. R., & Kane, M. K. (1986). *Federal practice and procedure* (2nd ed.). St. Paul, MN: West.

Yeazell, S. (1987). *From medieval group litigation to the modern class action*. New Haven, CT: Yale University Press.

Yeazell, S. (1997). The past and future of defendant and settlement classes in collective litigation. *Arizona Law Review*, 39(2), 687–726.

Contributors

David S. Allen is an associate professor in the Department of Journalism and Mass Communication at the University of Wisconsin-Milwaukee. His most recent book is titled *Democracy, Inc.: The Press and Law in the Corporate Rationalization of the Public Sphere* (2005, University of Illinois Press). His research has appeared in journals such as *Communication Law & Policy, Journal of Mass Media Ethics*, and the *Free Speech Yearbook*. He is the co-editor, with Robert Jensen, of *Freeing the First Amendment: Critical Perspectives on Freedom of Expression.*

Brooke Barnett (PhD, Indiana University) is an assistant professor in the School of Communications at Elon University where she teaches law and broadcast courses. Prior to teaching, she worked as a journalist in public and commercial TV. Her work has appeared in *Journalism & Mass Communication Quarterly, Journalism and Mass Communication Monographs, Journal of Broadcasting and Electronic Media, Visual Communication Quarterly*, and the *Federal Communications Law Journal.*

Constance Ledoux Book is an associate professor of communications at Elon University in North Carolina. Book's research includes the first national assessment of municipal officials' attitudes toward cable TV oversight. She has conducted quantitative and qualitative assessments of cable TV service in some of the nation's largest cable systems. She has also explored the pivotal role TV plays in American society and public policy. She is the author of the recently published *Digital Television: DTV and Consumers*, the first book dedicated to understanding how our nation's transition to digital TV impacts the general consumer. Book's research has been published in academic and legal journals and has been recognized in several competitive settings, including the National Cable Television Association and the National Association of Broadcasters.

Sandra Braman has been studying the macrolevel effects of the use of new information technologies and their policy implications since the mid-1980s. Current work includes *Change of State: An Introduction to Information Policy* (2006, MIT Press) and the edited volumes *Communication Researchers and Policy-makers* (2003, MIT Press), *The Emergent Global Information Policy Regime* (2004, Palgrave Macmillan), and *The Metatechnologies of Information: Biotechnology and Communication* (2004, Lawrence Erlbaum Associates). With Ford Foundation and Rockefeller Foundation support, Braman has been working on problems associated with the effort to bring the research and communication policy communities more closely together. She has published over four dozen scholarly journal articles, book chapters, and books; served as book review editor of the *Journal of Communication*; is former Chair of the Communication Law & Policy Division of the International Communication Association; and currently sits on the editorial boards of six scholarly journals. During 1997–1998, Braman designed and implemented the first graduate-level program in telecommunication and information policy on the African continent, for the University of South Africa. Currently Professor of Communication at the University of Wisconsin-Milwaukee, Braman earned her PhD from the University of Minnesota in 1988 and previously served as Reese Phifer Professor at the University of Alabama, Henry Rutgers Research Fellow at Rutgers University, Research Assistant Professor at the University of Illinois-Urbana, and the Silha Fellow of Media Law and Ethics at the University of Minnesota.

Jon Bruschke earned his BA and MA from CSU, Fullerton and his PhD from the University of Utah. He is an associate professor and the Director of Forensics at CSU, Fullerton. Bruschke publishes in the area of legal communication, with an interest in quantitative approaches to the study of legal decision making. He recently published *Free Press vs. Fair Trials: Examining Publicity's Role in Trial Outcomes* with Bill Loges. He is a lifelong New York Mets fan.

Fred H. Cate is a Distinguished Professor and director of the Indiana University Center for Applied Cybersecurity Research. He is the author of many articles and books, including *Mass Media Law* (6th ed.) with Marc

Franklin and David Anderson, *The Internet and the First Amendment*, and *Visions of the First Amendment for a New Millennium*. Cate is the faculty advisor to the *Federal Communications Law Journal*. Previously he served as a senior fellow and Director of Research and Projects for The Annenberg Washington Program in Communications Policy Studies. A Senator and Fellow of the Phi Beta Kappa Society, Professor Cate is an elected member of the American Law Institute.

Bill Chamberlin is the Joseph L. Brechner Eminent Scholar of Mass Communication in the College of Journalism and Communication and affiliate professor of the College of Law at the University of Florida. He also is chair of the Marion Brechner Citizen Access Project, which uses a variety of research methods to rate open meetings and public records laws. The project received the 2003 Sunshine Award from the Society of Professional Journalists for contributions to FOI research. In 2004, Chamberlin received the Applied Research Award from the International Communication Association. Chamberlin is co-author of the textbook *The Law of Public Communication*, as well as the author of articles and conference papers studying media law issues through the use of social science research methods, in addition to several research book chapters and articles using legal research.

Jeremy Cohen is Associate Vice Provost for Undergraduate Education, Chair of the Bachelor of Philosophy Program, and Professor of Communications at Penn State University. He is editor of *Journalism & Mass Communication Educator* and is the author of *Congress Shall Make No Law: Oliver Wendell Holmes, The First Amendment and Judicial Decision Making*, and co-author with Timothy Gleason of *Social Research in Communication and Law*. Cohen's current work focuses on the relations of democracy, education, and freedom of expression.

Robert Drechsel is Professor of Journalism and Mass Communication and an affiliated professor of law at the University of Wisconsin-Madison. He received his MA and PhD in mass communication from the University of Minnesota. His research has focused on journalists and sources in the judiciary and on tort law affecting mass communication, and has appeared in a variety of communication, law, and political science journals.

Robert M. Entman is J. C. and Maurice Shapiro Professor of Media and Public Affairs at George Washington University. He earned his PhD in political science as a National Science Foundation Fellow at Yale and taught at Duke from 1980 to 1989 and Northwestern from 1989 to 1994. His most recent books include *Projections of Power: Framing News*,

Public Opinion, and U.S. Foreign Policy (University of Chicago, 2004); *Mediated Politics: Communication in the Future of Democracy* (Cambridge, edited with L. Bennett), which will be published in Chinese translation by Tsinghua University Press in 2005; and *The Black Image in the White Mind: Media and Race in America* (University of Chicago, 2000, with A. Rojecki), which won Harvard's Goldsmith Book Prize and the Lane Award from the American Political Science Association, among other awards. He is currently writing *Media Bias Scandals* and, with Clay Steinman, is editing *Key Works in Communication Studies*. He edits the book series Communication, Society and Politics (with Lance Bennett) for Cambridge University Press. He served previously on the faculties at Duke, Northwestern, and North Carolina State.

Anthony L. Fargo has taught journalism at Indiana University since 2004. He previously taught at the University of Nevada, Las Vegas, and the University of Rhode Island. He earned his PhD in mass communication and his master's degree in mass communication from the University of Florida. He earned his bachelor's degree in English and journalism at Morehead State University. Before entering graduate school, Fargo was a reporter and editor at four newspapers in Kentucky and Florida. His scholarly work on journalists' privilege issues has been published in the *Cardozo Arts & Entertainment Law Journal*, *Communication Law and Policy*, *Free Speech Yearbook*, *Journal of Broadcasting & Electronic Media*, and *Newspaper Research Journal*.

Tim Gleason is Professor and the Edwin L. Artzt Dean of the School of Journalism and Communication at the University of Oregon. He holds his PhD in Communications from the University of Washington. Gleason's research and teaching focus is communication law and ethics. He is the author or co-author of two books and has published articles in communication and legal journals, as well as written numerous op-ed articles for newspapers. Gleason has served as the guest editor of *Communication Law & Policy* and is on the editorial boards of *Communication Law & Policy*, *Journalism History*, *American Journalism*, *Mass Communication and Society*, and *Journalism Educator*.

Tom Grimes holds the Ross Beach Chair in broadcast research at Kansas State University. He received his MS from Columbia University and PhD from Indiana University in mass communication. Professor Grimes' research areas include human information processing, with special emphasis on memory and attention processes.

Michael Hoefges is an assistant professor in the School of Journalism and Mass Communication at the University of North Carolina at Chapel

Hill. He teaches media law, and his research interests include advertising law and regulation, class action notice plans, lawyer advertising, regulation of corporate communication, freedom of information and access law, and privacy issues in advertising and marketing contexts. He has published sole-authored and co-authored articles in *Communication Law and Policy, Hastings Communication and Entertainment Law Journal, Journal of Marketing and Public Policy,* and *William & Mary Bill of Rights Journal.* In addition, he has presented numerous papers at regional and national academic conferences. He has taught a variety of mass media and advertising courses at the University of Tennessee, Trinity University, and the University of Florida. Prior to joining academia, Hoefges was in private law practice for 9 years in Florida. He holds JD and PhD degrees from the University of Florida.

Robert Jensen is an associate professor in the School of Journalism at the University of Texas at Austin, where he teaches courses in media law, ethics, and politics. Prior to his academic career, he worked as a professional journalist for a decade. He is the author of *Citizens of the Empire: The Struggle to Claim Our Humanity* (City Lights, 2004) and *Writing Dissent: Taking Radical Ideas from the Margins to the Mainstream* (Peter Lang, 2002); co-author with Gail Dines and Ann Russo of *Pornography: The Production and Consumption of Inequality* (Routledge, 1998); and co-editor with David S. Allen of *Freeing the First Amendment: Critical Perspectives on Freedom of Expression* (New York University Press, 1995).

Kent Lancaster teaches at The University of Miami. He was previously a Professor of Advertising in the College of Journalism and Communications at the University of Florida, where he also served as the Gannett Distinguished Visiting Professor of Advertising; he was also an associate professor of Advertising at the University of Illinois. His PhD in mass media and MA in advertising are from Michigan State University, and his BS in Business Administration (Advertising) is from Ferris State University. Lancaster's research focuses on advertising media and the economics of advertising. He has written more than 50 research reports, which have appeared in a variety of advertising, marketing, and business journals and proceedings. He has also written several texts and microcomputer software packages, some of which are distributed worldwide by Telmar Information Services Corp.

Glenn Leshner's areas of research include political communication, health communication, and mass media effects. Recently, his attention has focused on the cognitive and emotional effects of health communication messages and the relationship between campaign media and citizen outcomes, including voting, political learning, and community participation. His research has appeared in scholarly journals such as *Journal of Communication, Communication Research, Journalism and Mass Communication Quarterly, Political Communication,* and *Journal of Broadcasting and Electronic Media.* He teaches graduate-level theory and research methods. He earned his PhD at Stanford in 1994, prior to joining the journalism faculty at the University of Missouri. He worked in radio and TV in North and South Carolina as a photographer, field producer, and reporter. He holds a master's degree in journalism from the University of South Carolina and a bachelor's degree from Rutgers.

Cristina Popescu is a doctoral student in the College of Journalism and Communications at the University of Florida, with a concentration in public relations. Popescu teaches public relations principles and research methods. Her research focuses on evaluation measurements in public relations and corporate social citizenship. Popescu is a native of Romania and holds an undergraduate degree in theatre management.

David Pritchard is a professor of journalism and mass communication at the University of Wisconsin-Milwaukee. In 1984, he received his PhD in mass communications with a minor in law from UW-Madison. Before moving into the academic world, Pritchard was a newspaper reporter for 7 years. Professor Pritchard has been a visiting professor at the French Press Institute in Paris, a Fulbright scholar and visiting professor at Laval University in Canada, and head of the law division of the Association for Education in Journalism and Mass Communication. He has published two books: *Les journalistes canadiens: Un portrait de fin de siècle* (Presses de l'Université Laval, 1999) *and Holding the Media Accountable: Citizens, Ethics, and the Law* (Indiana University Press, 2000). He also has authored numerous scholarly articles and has done consulting for media corporations, law firms, and government agencies in both Canada and the United States.

Amy Reynolds is an assistant professor in the School of Journalism at Indiana University in Bloomington. Reynolds' research interests broadly include media and democracy, political dissent, First Amendment history, multidisciplinary approaches to the study of communication law, and media sociology/creation of media content. Her work has been published in *Communication Law and Policy, Journalism & Mass Communication Quarterly,* and *Journal of International Communication.* Reynolds has authored a half-dozen book chapters, and she is the co-editor (with Max McCombs) of *The Poll with a Human Face: The National Issues Convention Experiment in Political Communication,* as well as co-author of a forthcoming primary source reference volume, *The Civil War, North and South* (2005), which explores media coverage of the Civil War. Reynolds has a PhD from the University of Texas at Austin and an MA from the Indiana University School of Journalism. Previously, she taught at the University of Oklahoma and Miami University of Ohio.

Michael Weigold is an associate professor in the Department of Advertising at the University of Florida. He received his PhD in psychology from Florida in 1989 and teaches both undergraduate and graduate courses in persuasion and research methods. His research interests include science and health communication and political advertising.

Author Index

A

Abel, R. L., 49, 50, 53, 58, 60
Abraham, H. J., 184, *200*
Adams, J. B., 184, 185, 189, *200*
Aday, S., 24, *37*, *203*
Addison, A., 99, *108*
Ajzen, I., 194, *200*
Alexander, G., *159*
Alfini, J. J., 80, *83*, *84*
Allen, C., 339, *347*
Allen, D. S., xix, *xxv*, *137*, *158*
Allport, G. W., 270
Ambler, C. H., 320
Anderson, D. A., 17, 20, 21, *47*, 269
Anderson, J., 49
Andreasen, A. R., 53
Aptheker, H., 302, 305, 307, 308, 309,
    310, 311, 312, 313, 323
Arpan, L. M., 24, *37*
Ashcroft, J., 276, *292*
Ax, J., 95, *107*

B

Bachrach, P., 135, *135*
Baldwin, M., 94, *107*

Barbaree, H. E., 99, *108*
Barber, S., 48
Bargh, J. A., 236, 237, *250*
Barnett, B., 234, 238, 247, *250*, 274,
    292, 302, 326
Baron, J., 234, *251*
Baron, R. D., 362, *369*
Baron, S. S., 269
Barron, J. A., 46
Bartlett, F. C., 270
Barton, A. H., 64, 65, 80, *85*
Bazeleyc, M., 340, 341, *347*
Becker, H. S., 139, *157*, *159*
Becklen, R., 270
Beckmann, M. N., *203*
Bennett, W. L., 45
Bergen, R. K., 100, *107*
Berger, C. R., *136*
Bern, S. L., 270
Besirevic, J., 62, *85*
Best, A., 53
Bezanson, R., 40, *41*, 49
Bix, B., 15, *21*
Blackman, H., 127, 164, 169, 172, 176
Blanchard, M. A., 303
Blascovich, J., 62, 65, 75, *85*
Blasi, V., 30, 32, *37*, 54, 183, 188, *200*,
    276, *292*
Blau, P. M., *159*

379

Blumberg, A. S., 55
Boayue, S., *250*
Bobo, L., 207
Bogle, K. A., 100, *107*
Book, C., 334, *347*
Boon, J. C. W., 270
Bork, R. H., 114, 115, *136*, 302
Bornstein, B. H., 65, 69, 72, 76, *82*, *86*
Boulding, K. E., 146, 154, *157*, *178*
Boyle, J., 116, *136*
Boyle, K., 98, *107*
Boyte, H. C., 131, *136*
Braman, S., 140, 141, 146, 150, 157, *158*, *178*
Brand, J. E., 234, *251*
Brandeis, L. D., 28–29, 31, 124, 183, 278, *292*, 295
Brennan, W., 30, 110, 115–116, 133–134, *136*, 163, 164, 167, 171, 173, 176
Brigham, J. C., 236, *250*
Bright, S. B., 81, *82*
Brock, B., *84*
Brockway, J. P., 270
Brotman, S. N., 150, *159*
Brown, C. J., xviii, *xxv*, 303
Bruce, R. R., 150, *158*
Bruschke, J., 63, 64, 65, 68, 70, *82*, *83*
Bryant, J., *83*, 100, *108*, *251*
Buddenbaum, J. M., xviii, *xxv*, 48
Bunker, M. D., xviii, xix, *xxv*, 6, 7, 24, 33, *37*
Burger, W. E., 170
Burke, T. M., 63, 65, 78, *83*
Burns-Melican, D., *250*
Bush, C. R., 48
Buske, S., 340, 345, *347*

C

Callahan, C., 278, *292*
Calvert, C., 120, *136*
Campbell, C., 233, *250*
Cardozo, B. N., 149, *158*
Carmines, E. G., 239, *251*
Carroll, J. S., 62, 64, 65, 75, 76, 80, *83*, *84*
Carroll, R., 211, 213
Carter, D. B., 270
Carter, T. B., 46, 55

Cate, F. H., 17, 20, *21*
Cavanagh, R., 56
Chaffee, S. H., xvii, *xxvi*, 47, 69, 75, *86*, *136*, 139, *158*
Chaiken, S., *250*
Chamberlin, B. F., 269, 303
Chance, J. E., 270
Chartrand, T. L., 236, 237, *250*
Chitty, N., 302
Chmielewski, D. L., 270
Chung, Y., 24, *37*
Cisin, C. Y., xvii, *xxvi*
Clarke, J., 122, 208
Cleveland, H., 185, 186, *200*
Coates, D., 50
Cofer, C. N., 270
Cohen, J., xiii, xiv, xv, xix, xx, *xxv*, 3, 4, 7, 8, 24, *38*, 132, *136*, 183, *200*, 269
Cohen, J. D., 241, *250*, 258
Cohen, J. R., 119, 120, *136*
Cohen, M. L., 46
Cole, S., 105, *107*
Condit, C., 217
Connors, M. M., 48
Constantini, E., 69, 75, *83*
Conte, A., 349, 350, 352, *352*, 354, 356, 358, 359, 360, 361, *368*, *369*
Cook, P., 213
Corbin, J., 189, *200*
Cornelius, J. D., 319
Cover, R. M., 119, *136*
Cranberg, G., 40, *41*, 49
Critcher, C., 208
Croce, C., *250*
Crocker, J., 270
Cunard, J. P., *158*
Curtis, M. K., 296, *298*, 303, 304, 305, 324, 325
Cutler, B. L., 62, 64, 69, 75, 76, 78, *83*, *84*

D

D'Alessio, D., 24, *37*
Dalglish, L., 278, *292*
Davenport, J. L., 85
Davidson, J. W., 298, *298*
Davies, G. M., 270
Davis, R. W., 65, 79, *83*

de Coteau, N. J., *203*, 233, *251*
Delgado, R., xix, *xxv*, 23, *37*, 119, 134, *136*
Delia, J., 118, *136*
Dennis, E. E., xiii, xix, *xxvi*, 47–48, 49
Devine, P. G., 236, 237, *250*
Dexter, H. R., 65, 78, 80, *83*, 85
Dezalay, Y., 150, 151, *158*
Diamond, S. S., 80, *86*
Dickerson, D. L., 303
Dillehay, R. C., 75, *84*
Dines, G., 101, 103, *107*, *108*
Director, M. D., *158*
Domke, D., 234, *250*
Doob, A. N., 65, 69, 78, *83*
Douglas, W. O., 31
Douglass, F., 304
Dovidio, J., 206, 209, 224, *231*, 237, 240, *250*
Downing, J., 208
Doyle, A. C., 45
Drechsel, R. E., 57
Driscoll, P. D., 279, *292*
Duff, K., *84*
Dunn, D., 57
Dunton, B. C., 237, *250*
Dworkin, A., 96, 97, 100, *108*
Dworkin, R., 116, 117, *136*

E

Eaton, C., 310, 311, 314, 319
Edelman, D. A., 356, *369*
Ehrlich, H. J., 236, *250*
Eimermann, T., 69, 75, 76, *85*
Eisenstein, E. L., 149, *158*
Elliot, A. J., 236, *250*
Emerson, T. I., 54, 276, *292*
Entman, R. M., xvi, xxiii, *xxvi*, 202, *203*, 209, 210, 211, 213, 224, 226, 229, *231*, 233, 234, 235, 236, 238, 247, 249, *250*
Erickson, E., *348*
Evans, N., 237, 240, *250*
Evans, P., *159*
Eveland, W. P., Jr., 24, *37*

F

Fairman, D. L., 5, *8*
Fandel, M. H., 150, *158*
Farber, D., 133, *136*
Farley, M., 94, *108*
Farrar, R. T., 59
Fazio, R. H., 237, *250*, 271
Fein, S., 70, 76
Feldman, S. M., 25, 26, 27, *37*
Feldman, V., *83*
Felstiner, W. L., 49, 50, 53, 58
Fischer, G., 209, 234, 235, *251*
Fischer, J. M., 356, *368*
Fiske, J., 119, *136*
Fiss, O. M., 23, *37*, 302
Fitzgerald, J., 49, 53
Flatt, B., 241, *250*
Floyd, J., 320
Ford, P. L., 12, *21*
Frable, D. E. S., 270
Frank, J., 54, 116, *136*
Franklin, M. A., 17, 20, *21*, 46, 47, 49, 53, 55, 183, *200*, 269
Frasca, R., 75, *83*
Frederick, J., 75, *84*
Freedman, J. L., 63, 65, 78, *83*
Freedman, M. H., 81, *83*
Freeman, G., 53, 55
Friedman, L. M., 53, 56
Frye, M., 104, *108*
Fujioka, Y., 239, *250*
Fulero, S. M., 62, 63, 64, 65, *83*, *85*

G

Gaertner, S., 206, 209, 224, *231*
Galanter, M., 53, 56, 57, 59
Gandy, O. H., 234, *250*, *251*
Gans, H. J., 57
Garnet, H. H., 302, 306, 308, 309, 313
Garrison, B., 279, *292*
Garrison, F. J., 312, 313
Garrison, W. L., 296, 297, 304, 307, 310, 311, 312, 313, 314, 315–316, 317–323, 324–325, 327
Garrison, W. P., 312, 313
Gaziano, C., 47
Gerber, R. J., 81, 82, *83*
Gerbner, G., 72, *83*

Gibbons, J. A., 254, *255*
Gibson, D. C., 62, *83*
Giddens, A., 145, *158*
Gilbert, R., *86*
Gilens, M., 234, *251*
Gilliam, F. D., Jr., 202, *203*, 233, 234, *251*
Gillmor, D. M., 46, 47–48, 140
Ginsberg, J. S., 356, *368*
Giroux, H. A., 119, *136*
Gitlin, T., 57
Gittler, I., 94, *108*
Glasser, T. L., *178*
Gleason, T. W., xii, xiv, xx, *xxv*, 3, 4, *8*,
    183, *200*, 258, 269, 296, 303
Glendon, M. A., 121, *136*
Glock, C. Y., xvii, *xxvi*
Goldberg, H., 278, *292*
Goldstein, A. G., 270
Gomery, D., 213
Graber, D., 215
Graber, M., 28, *37*
Graesser, A. C., 270, 271
Gray, H., 208
Gray, W., 354, *368*
Greenberg, B. S., 234, *251*
Greene, E., 73, *83*
Greenwald, A. G., 242, *251*
Gressett, L. A., 45
Grimes, T., 254, *255*, 269
Groscup, J. L., *85*
Gross, B., 309
Gross, K., 24, *37*
Gross, L., 72, *83*
Grossberg, L., *136*
Gunther, A. C., *8*, 269
Gutierrez, F., 233, *251*

H

Habermas, J., 109
Hage, G. S., 49
Hale, F. D., 47, 54
Hall, S., 121, *136*, 208
Haltom, W., 45
Halverson, C. F., 270
Hamilton, D., 209
Hanrieder, W. F., *158*
Hans, V. P., 48, 65, 69, 78, *83*
Harrison, B., 224
Hart, J. R., *178*

Hartley, E. L., 270
Hartmann, P., 208, 225
Head, S., 337, *347*
Heise, M., 36, *37*
Heisenberg, D., 150, *158*
Herman, C. A., 270
Hess, S., 213
Higgins, E. T., 270
Hinks, P. P., 302, 307, 309, 310, 314,
    318, 319, 320
Hirsch, P., 226
Hochheimer, J. L., 45
Hoefges, R. M., 351, *352*, 358, 359, 360,
    361, 362, 363, 364, 366, *368*
Hoffman, Y., 84
Hoiberg, B. C., 76, *83*
Holmes, O. W., xix, *xxvi*, 5, *8*, 25–26,
    28, *37*, 122–123, 124, 132, 173,
    296, 301
Holsinger, R. L., xviii, *xxv*
Hoy, M. G., 351, *352*, 358, *368*
Hoyt, J. L., 48
Huber, P. W., 148, *158*
Hunt, G., 276, *292*
Hurwitz, J., 233, *251*
Husband, C., 208, 225
Hvistendahl, J. K., 76, *84*

I

Imrich, D. J., 73, 75, *84*
Insko, C. A., *251*
Iorio, S. H., 185, 189, *200*
Iyengar, S., 202, *203*, 233, 234, *251*

J

Jackson, J. R., 237, *250*
Jackson, R., 125
Jacob, H., 53
Jacobs, D. M., 309
Jaffee, D., 99, *108*
Jamieson, K. H., *203*, 233, *251*
Jefferson, T., 208
Jenkins, H., 120, *136*
Jensen, R., xix, *xxv*, 101, 103, 105, *107*,
    108, 131, *136*, *137*, *158*
Jimenez-Lorente, B., 62, *85*
Johnson, R. F., 302, 304, 305
Jones, E. E., 270

Jones, R. M., 64, 65, *84*
Judson, J. T., 62, 69, 75, 76, *86*
Jugenheimer, D. W., 362, *369*

K

Kahin, B., 151, *158*
Kairys, D., 54
Kaiser, R., 78, *84*
Kalven, H., Jr., 32, *37*, 132, *136*, 302, 325, 327
Kamhawi, R., xv, *xxvi*
Kammen, M., 327
Kane, M. K., 350, 351, *352*, 354, 356, 357, 358, *369*
Kang, J., 202, *203*
Kaplan, M. F., 63, 78, *84*
Kari, N. N., 131, *136*
Kassin, S. M., 69, *85*
Katz, P., 206, 207, 208, 216
Katz, P. A., 236, *251*
Kelley, L. D., 362, *368*
Kellogg, M. K., 148, *158*
Kendrick, A., 207
Kennedy, A., 111, 121
Kenner, B., *250*
Kent, D. R., 235, *251*
Kerr, N. L., 62, 63, 65, 76, 78, 79, 80, *83*, *84*
Kerwin, J., 68, 70, 78, *84*
Kimmel, M. S., *107*
King, J., 69, 75, *83*
Klapper, I. T., xvii, *xxvi*
Klein, B., 53
Kochman, T., 210, 223
Kohles, C., 235, *251*
Kornhauser, L., 56
Koss, M., 99, *108*
Kovera, M. B., 64, 72, 73, 78, *84*
Kramer, G. P., 63, 65, 67, 75, 76, 78, 79, 80, *84*
Kritzer, H. M., 55, *58*
Krueger, J., 239, *251*
Krugman, D., 334, *347*
Kuhn, T. S., 44, 45, *58*
Kulish, M., 64, *84*
Kutchinsky, B., 99, *108*
Kyvig, D. E., 298, 299

L

Ladinsky, J., 49, 50, 51, 53, 57, 58
Lambright, W. H., 149, *158*
Lancaster, D., 48
Lancaster, K. M., 351, *352*, 360, 361, 362, 363, 364, 366, *368*
Landon, F., 324
Lane, F. S., 89, *108*
Lang, A., 24, *37*
Langdell, C. C., 25–26
Langford, R. H., *250*
Larsen, R. J., 270
Lasorsa, D. L., 24, *37*
Lavallee, M., 270
Lawrence, D. H., 103, *108*
Lazarsfeld, P. F., *159*
Lederer, L., *108*
Lee, A., 151, *159*
Lee, S., 24, *37*
Leiholdt, D., *107*
Lempert, R., 25, *37*
Leonard, T. C., 304, 319, 324
Lessig, L., 7, 8, 121, *136*, 146, *159*
Lester, P., 208
Levine, J., 239, *251*
Levy, G. D., 270
Lewis, D., 211
Liben, L. S., 270
Lichty, L., 213
Lindman, R., 62, *84*
Linville, P., 209, 216, 234, 235, *251*, 270
Linz, D., 73, 75, *84*
Lloyd, F., 342, *347*
Loftus, E. F., 73, *83*
Loges, W. E., 63, 64, 65, 68, 70, 73, 82, *83*
Loh, W. D., 47
London, K., 68, 69, 70, *84*
Lorde, A., 107, *108*
Lundy, B., 304, 310, 314, 315, 317–323, 324–325, 327
Lustig, R. J., 123, *136*
Lytle, M. H., 298, *298*

M

Macaulay, S., 49, 53, 54, 55, 56, 57
MacCoun, R. J., *83*
MacDonald, J. F., 209

Machlup, F., 153, *159*, *178*
MacKinnon, C. A., 23, *37*, 96, 97, 100, 104, *108*
Macoby, E. E., 270
MacWhinney, B., 241, *250*
Madison, J., 275
Maisel, R., xvii, *xxvi*
Malamuth, N. M., 99, *108*
Maric, A., 99, *108*
Marindale, C., 208
Marsh, D., 151, *159*
Marshall, T., 30, 31, 166, 167, 173, 174, 175
Martin, C. K., 65, *83*
Martin, C. L., 270
Marty, M. A., 298, *299*
Mason, A. T., 28, *37*
Mason, L., *8*, 269
Massing, M., 55
Matabane, P., 209
Mather, L., 50
McBain, H., 114, *136*
McCloskey, A. L., 70, *83*
McCombs, M., xvii, *xxvi*, 65, 76, 86
McConahay, J. B., 75, *84*, 206, 207, 224, 225, 229, *231*
McCoy, K., 234, *250*
McGhee, 242, *251*
McGregor, M., *347*
Mehra, A., 47
Meiklejohn, A., 32, *37*, 276, *292*, 302
Melnitzer, J., 80, *86*
Melton, G. B., 62, *84*
Menand, L., 123, 124, *136*
Merrit, C., *250*
Merritt, B., 209
Merton, R. K., 149, *159*
Meyer, P., 238, *251*
Middleton, K., xvii, *xxvi*, 75, *86*, 269
Miller, A. R., 350, 351, *352*, 354, 356, 357, 358, *369*
Miller, G. R., 47
Miller, L. E., 63, 78, *84*
Miller, R. E., 50
Millhollon, M., 277, 278, *292*
Mills, C. J., 270
Milton, J., 132, *136*
Mingus, J., 356, *369*
Mnookin, R. H., 56
Monahan, J., 24, *37*, 47
Monteith, M. J., 236, 237, *250*
Moore, S. F., 53, 58

Moran, G., 62, 64, 69, 70, 72, 75, 76, 78, *83*, *84*
Morgan, M., 72, *83*
Morgan, S. J., 76, *83*
Morris, C. E., 317, 318
Mota, V. L., 65, *83*
Mullin, C., 73, 75, 79, *84*
Mullin, C. J., 75, *84*
Munoz, I., *250*
Murdock, M., 47
Murray, C. B., 78, *84*
Mutz, D., *8*, 269

N

Nass, C., *8*, 269
Neisser, U., 270
Nelson, C., *136*
Nelson, H. L., 46
Nemeth, N., 40, *41*
Netteburg, K., 48
Newberg, H., 349, 350, 352, *352*, 354, 356, 358, 359, 360, 361, 363, *368*, *369*
Newcomb, H., 226
Newcomb, T. M., 270
Newman, L. S., 70, 78, *84*
Newsom, A., 64, *84*
Nietzel, M. T., 75, *84*
Noam, E. M., 150, *159*
Noelle-Neumann, E., 225
Norton, M. I., 76, *83*
Nunez, N., 68, 69, 70, *84*

O

O'Connor, S. D., 128–129, 167
Ogloff, J. R. P., 62, 69, 70, 75, 76, *84*, *85*
Oliver, M. B., 234, *251*
Otsuki, T. A., 235, *251*
Otto, A. L., 65, 76, *85*
Overbeck, W., 46, 54
Owen, B. M., 154, *159*

P

Padawer-Singer, A. M., 64, 65, 80, *85*
Padgett, G. E., 47

Padilla, M., 62, *83*
Paletz, D., 226
Paper, L. J., 28, *38*
Pathak-Sharma, M. K., 65, *85*
Pedrosa, G., *86*
Peffley, M., 202, *203*, 233, 234, 235, *251*
Pelletier, R., 270
Pember, D. R., 46, 65, *85*
Penrod, S., 50, 69, 78, *86*
Penrod, S. D., 62, 64, 65, *85*
Pepper, R., 150, 159
Perry, D. K., xviii, xix, *xxv*, 6, *8*, 24, 33, 37
Peters, C., 57
Peterson, R. D., *159*
Petty, C. W., *159*
Piazza, T., 207
Pines, A. M., 101, *108*
Plante, R. F., *107*
Poe, E. A., 43
Posner, R. A., xiii, xix, *xxvi*, 25, 27, 32, 38
Post, R. C., 132, *137*
Postman, L. J., 270
Potter, S., 276, *292*
Potter, W. C., 152, *159*
Powell, L. F., 164, 167, 170
Powell, M., 333, *348*
Price, M., 150, *159*
Price, V., *8*, 269
Priest, G. L., 53
Pritchard, D., xxi, *xxvi*, 39, 40, *41*
Provost, J., 241, *250*
Pullen, R. D., 46, 54

R

Rabban, D. M., 296, 297, *299*, 303
Ragin, C. C., 139, *159*
Rajki, M., 69, 72, *82*
Raman, A., *250*
Raney, A. A., 24, *37*
Ravaja, N., 24, *38*
Raymond, J. G., *107*
Rehnquist, W., 114, *137*
Reid, L., 334, *347*
Renaud, J., 150, *159*
Reynolds, A., 297, *299*, 302, 303, 304, 305, 311, 322, 324, 326

Rehnquist, W., 113–114, 133–134, 165, 172, 173, 174
Richards, L. L., 304
Riedel, R. G., 73, *85*
Riley, S. G., 62, 65, 69, 72, 75, 76, *85*
Rimmer, T., xvii, *xxvi*, 75, *86*
Robbennolt, J. K., 65, *85*
Roberts, B., 208
Roberts, C., 234, *251*
Rojecki, A., 202, *203*
Rollings, H. E., 62, 65, 75, *85*
Romer, D., 201, 202, *203*, 233, *251*
Rosati, J., 152, *159*
Rosenberg, M., *159*
Roshco, B., 57
Roskos-Ewoldsen, D. R., 271
Rossman, S. T., 356, *369*
Roth, B. M., 207
Rueschemeyer, D., *159*
Rush, R. R., 302
Russell, B., 312
Russell, D. E. H., 100, *108*
Russo, A., 101, 103, *108*
Ryan, M. P., 298, *299*

S

Sack, R. D., 269
Salem, G., 211
Salovey, P., 209
Salwen, M. B., 279, *292*
Sampson, M., 152, *159*
Sanders, C., 40, *41*
Sanders, J., 25, *37*
Sanford, E., 124
Sarat, A., 49, 50, 53, 56, 58
Sarver, D., 333, *348*
Scalia, A., 113–114, 128, 130–131, *137*
Schauer, F., 7, *8*
Scheppele, K. L., 119, *137*
Schlegel, J. H., 46
Schneider, W., 236, *251*
Schnopp-Wyatt, N., *84*
Schoenfein, L., 270
Schopler, J., *251*
Schwartz, J. L. K., 242, *251*
Schwartz, N., 24, *37*
Schwartz, T., 47
Sears, D., 206, 207, 208
Sedikides, C., *251*

Seidman, E., 270
Seizer, J. A., 217
Semati, M., 302
Sentman, M. A., 208
Seto, M. C., 99, *108*
Shaffer, D. R., 68, 70, 78, *84*
Shaffer, R. A., 69, *85*
Shields, T., *203*, 233, 234, 235, *251*
Shiffrin, R. M., 236, *251*
Sigal, L. V., 57
Signorella, M. L., 270
Signorielli, N., 72, *83*
Silbert, M. H., 101, *108*
Simon, A., 234, *251*
Simon, R. J., 63, 64, 69, 75, 76, *85*
Singer, A., 80, *85*
Singer, A. N., 65, *85*
Singer, R., 80, *85*
Singer, R. L. J., 65, *85*
Sissors, J. Z., 362, *369*
Skocpol, T., 149, *159*
Slater, D., 48
Sloan, T., 151, *159*
Sloan, W. D., *348*
Smith, D. A., 270, 271
Smith, R., 208
Smith, R. E., *86*
Smythe, D. W., 152, *159*
Sniderman, P. M., 207, 239, *251*
Sohn, A. B., 69, 75, *85*
Soloski, J., 40, *41*, 49
Soma, J. T., 150, *159*
Sommers, S. R., 69, 76, *83*, *85*
Spann, T., *347*
Spears, S., *8*, 269
Spero, J., 151, *159*
Splichal, S. L., 279, *292*
Statsky, W. P., 46
Steblay, N. M., 62, 63, *85*
Stempel, G. H. III, 47
Stevens, J. D., 59
Stevens, J. P., 126–127, 129, 166, 168,
        171, 172, 174, 176
Stewart, P., 30–31, 276
Stires, L. K., 76, *83*
Strauss, A., 189, *200*
Strauss, D. A., 64, *85*
Strauss, M. A., 99, *108*
Streeter, T., 110, 119, *137*
Stroman, C., 209
Studebaker, C. A., 62, 64, 65, *85*
Sue, S., 70, 76, 78, *86*

Sullivan, D., 278, *292*
Sullivan, K. M., 3, *8*
Sunder, M., 120, *137*
Surette, R., 67, 72, *86*
Susmilch, C., 49, 50, 51, 53, 57, 58
Sussman, B., 211, 223

T

Tanford, S., 69, 78, *86*
Tankard, J. W., xvii, *xxvi*, 75, *86*
Tans, M. D., xvii, *xxvi*, 69, 75, *86*
Tate, C. N., 53
Taylor, D., 206, 207, 208, 216
Taylor, S., 78, *84*
Taylor, S. E., 270
Teeter, D. L., Jr., 46
Teske, P., 150, *159*
Tetlock, P. E., 207
Thomas, C., 129
Thompson, M., 150, *159*
Thompson, R., 341, 342, *348*
Thompson, S., 235, *251*
Thorndyke, P. W., 269, 270
Thorne, J., 148, *158*
Tomlinson, T. M., 70, *83*
Torres, M., 234, *250*
Tragle, H. I., 321
Traxel, N. M., 254, *255*
Treichler, P., *136*
Tribe, L., 117, *137*, *178*
Troller, T., 209
Trope, Y., *250*
Trubek, D. M., 53
Tsfati, Y., 24, *38*
Tuchman, G., 57
Turner, E. L., 270
Tushnet, M. V., 45, 46, 58
Tyler, A. F., 302, 305, 306, 313, 317,
        318, 319
Tyler, R. B., 237, 240, *250*
Tyrell, D. J., 270

U, V

Urofsky, M. I., 28, *38*
Valentino, N. A., *203*
Van Alstyne, W. W., 325
van Dijk, T., 208, 225, 226

Vidmar, N., 62, 65, 69, 70, 75, 76, 80, 85, 86
Visher, C. A., 63, 78, 86
Vogl, R. J., 254, 255

W

Wade, R., 73, 83
Walker, D., 297, 298, 301–302, 304, 306–323, 325, 327
Walker, L., 24, 37, 47
Wall, S., 150, 159
Walton, J. A., 67, 86
Warren, J., 270
Warren, S. D., 278, 292
Watkins, W. J., Jr., 277, 292
Weaver, D. H., xv, xviii, xxv, xxvi, 40, 41
Weaver, F. M., 83
Webb, E. J., 53
Wechsler, H., 29–30, 38, 114, 137
Weinberg, S., 55
White, B., 171, 172, 173, 276
White, G. E., xix, xxvi
White, J. B., 118, 137
Wilcox, W., xvii, xxvi, 48, 65, 76, 86
Wildman, S. S., 154, 159
Wilhoit, G. C., 40, 41

Williams, B., 203, 233, 234, 235, 251
Williams, C. J., 237, 250
Wilson, C. C. II, 233, 251
Wilson, J. R., 65, 72, 76, 86
Winter, S. L., 116, 117, 137
Wright, C. A., 350, 351, 352, 354, 356, 357, 358, 369
Wright, J. B., 46, 55
Wright, O., 234, 251

Y

Yeazell, S., 353, 361, 369
Yekovich, F. R., 269, 270
Yngvesson, B., 50
Young, D. G., 24, 38

Z

Zanna, M. P., 270
Zick, T., 24, 38
Ziesel, H., 80, 86
Zillmann, D., 83, 100, 108, 251
Zinn, H., 295, 298, 299
Zuwerink, J. R., 236, 250

Subject Index

A

Abrams v. United States, 122–123, 132, 135, 296, 298, 301, 302, 326
access to information, 275–278, 283–292
  see also state access laws, state open meeting laws
advertising, 350–351, 356, 357
  see also class action lawsuits
Akron v. Akron Center for Reproductive Health, 170
Amchem Products, Inc. v. Windsor, 352, 361, 368
American Booksellers v. Hudnut, 34, 36, 96
Ashcroft v. Free Speech Coalition, 35, 37, 96, 107
Atkins v. Parker, 166, 171

B

Barnes v. Glen Theater, 34, 37
Bateman Eichler, Hill Richards, Inc. v. Berner, 170
Bedel v. Thompson, 357, 368
Bethel v. Fraser, 165

Boag v. MacDougall, 165
Board of Education, Hendrick Hudson Central School District v. Rowley, 164, 165
Boy Scouts of America v. Dale, 133, 136
Branzburg v. Hayes, 30–32, 37, 292
Brown v. Board of Education, xix, xxv, 28–30, 31, 36, 37, 183, 200
Burdine v. Johnson, 82, 83
Burnett v. Collins, 82, 83

C

Cable franchising, 329–330, 333–347
  needs and interest ascertainment, 338–340
  oversight, 334–336
  renewal process, 336–338, 340–346
  see also Federal Communications Commission, public interest
Cablevision of the Midwest, Inc. v. City of Brunswick, 343, 346, 347
Capital Cities v. Crisp, 150, 158
Capital Square Review and Advisory Board v. Pinette, 127–129, 131, 136

Chandler v. Florida, 184, 200

Cibenko v. Worth Publishers, 271

Citizens against Rent Control/Coalition for Fair Housing v. Berkeley, 172

City of Erie v. Pap's A.M., 34, 37

City of LaDue v. Gilleo, 126, 127, 136

City of Renton v. Playtime Theaters, Inc., 5, 6, 7, 34, 37

Clark v. Community for Creative Non-Violence, 175

Clark v. American Broadcasting Companies, Inc., 269, 270

Class action lawsuits, 349–352, 353–369
    constitutional significance of notice, 353–356
    evaluating mass media notice, 362–367
    mandatory notice, 356–362
        certification notice, 356–360
        combination notice, 361–362
        settlement notice, 360–361
    see also advertising

Coble v. Texas, 79, 83

common and civil law systems, 10–15

communication policy, 142–143

communication research, 45–48

Community Television of Southern California v. Gottfried, 165

contemporary media practice, 147–148

content analysis, 189–191, 202, 205, 210–211

content neutrality, 175

convergence, 144–145

County of Allegheny v. ACLU, 127, 136

courts and social science, 27–30, 65–67

critical legal studies, 14
    see also critical legal theory

critical legal theory, 27, 109–110

critical race theory, 15

cultural studies, 118–121

cumulative remedy hypothesis, 68

D

Dairy Barn Stores v. ABC, 269

Debs v. U.S., 123–124, 136, 296, 298, 302, 326

democracy and free expression, 4, 6, 325, 327

democratic society, 3, 26–27, 109, 112–113, 118–120, 132, 134–135, 275

Demouchette v. Texas, 72, 83

Dennis v. United States, 326

Dirks v. Securities and Exchange Commission, 170

Dobbert v. Florida, 66, 83

due process, 349–350, 354–356

Duncan v. WJLA-TV, 269

E

economic analysis of law, 13–14, 27

Eisen v. Carlisle & Jacquelin, 359, 360, 368

Ellis v. Brotherhood of Railway, Airline & Steamship Clerks, 166, 167

Espionage Act cases, 122–124, 295–296, 302

experimental design, 237–241, 254, 261–263

explication, 139–140, 351

F

FBI v. Abramson, 169

FCC v. League of Women Voters of California, 174

Federal Communications Commission, 16–17, 95, 140, 155, 330, 333, 334, 335, 336, 339, 347

Federal Trade Commission v. Grolier, 169

feminist legal studies, 14, 27, 96, 104, 107

Finnegan v. Leu, 167

First National Bank of Boston v. Bellotti, 32, 37

flag burning, 111

flexible structuration, 145–146

focus groups, 342–346

free expression in the nineteenth century, 301–327
    abolitionists and free speech, 304–306, 325
    suppression of abolitionist speech, 311–317
    see also Garrison, William Lloyd, Lundy, Benjamin, Walker, David, Walker's Appeal

free speech and war, 121–127
freedom of association, 133–134
Freedom of Information Act, 169, 276
Frohwerk v. United States, 296, 298, 302, 326

G

Geary v. Goldstein, 271
Gilbert v. Minnesota, 124, 136
Ginsberg v. New York, 34, 37
Girsh v. Jepson, 360, 368
Gitlow v. New York, 124, 136, 302
Greenfield v. Villager Industries, Inc., 362, 368
grounded theory, 187
Grunin v. International House of Pancakes, 366

H

Hansberry v. Lee, 354, 360, 368
Hartman v. Meredith Corporation, 269
Hill v. Ozmint, 72, 83
H.L. v. Matheson, 170

I

incendiary speech, 305, 318–320, 322–323
information policy, 139–140, 153–155, 161–162
   see also law and technology
information production, 155–157
In re "Agent Orange" Product Liability Litigation, 350, 352, 359, 368
In re Beef Industry Antitrust Litigation, 361, 368
In re Domestic Air Transportation Antitrust Litigation, 357, 359, 360, 368
In re Franklin National Bank Securities Litigation, 359, 369
In re Prudential Insurance Co., 360
In re RMJ, 170
institution-centered paradigm, 46–47
Interactive Digital Software Association v. St. Louis County, 33–34, 37
Interactive Software Association v. St. Louis County, 33, 37

International Longshoremen's Association, AFL-CIO v. Allied International, 168

J

Jackson v. Motel 6 Multipurposes, Inc., 367, 369
James v. Meow Media, 33, 37
Journalists' privilege, 30–32
   see also Branzburg v. Hayes

K

Kelly v. Texas, 72, 74, 79, 84
Kleindienst v. Mandel, 145, 158
Korematsu v. United States, 29, 37

L

laboratory research, 64–65, 239–247, 261–263
Lal v. CBS, Inc., 269
law and communication, xvi–xxv, 4–7, 44–48
law and creation of meaning, 112–118, 121–135
   active citizenship, 110, 130–131
   active public sphere, 110, 132–135
   control of meaning, 131–132
   see also cultural studies
law and history, 295–298, 301–304, 327
law and science, 5–6, 44–45, 110–111
law and social science, xiii–xvi, xxi–xxv, 23–24, 57–59, 61–62, 67–73, 183–185, 203, 253–255, 268–269, 273–274, 333, 340–347
   see also courts and social science, law and communication, law and science, Marion Brechner Citizens Access Project, social science and the First Amendment
law and society, 15
law and socioeconomic class, 162–178
   Supreme Court cases, 163–177
      class stratifications, 166–168
      economics of information processing, 172–174
      informational rights, limits and responsibilities, 169–171

law and technology, 143–144, 146
  see also information policy
legal formalism, 11–12, 25, 110–111
  see also legal positivism, 11–12
legal methodology, xxiii–xxv, 10, 15–21,
    57–58, 351
  codified rules, 16–17
  policy analysis, 17–19, 148–153
  precedent, 16
  procedural analysis, 19–20
legal philosophy
  see legal formalism, legal process the-
    ory, legal positivism, legal realism,
    nonoriginalism, originalism
legal process theory, 26–27
legal realism, 13, 25–26, 59, 116
libel, 20, 32, 40–41, 49, 55, 120–121,
    254, 257–258, 261, 267–269, 324
  *see also New York Times Company v.
    Sullivan*, media-related disputes
local television news, 201–203, 205,
    208–209, 212–227, 229–230
Lochner v. New York, 28, 37
Los Angeles v. Taxpayers for Vincent, 176
Lowe v. SEC, 171

M

Madison Cablevision v. City of Morgantown,
    341, 347
Marion Brechner Citizens Access Project,
    182, 183, 187–200
  data manipulation, 193–194
  limitations, 197–199
  rating procedures, 191–193
  results, 194–197
marketplace theory, 117, 123, 131–132
mass communication behavior, 44
Martinez v. Bynum, 164
media and race, 201–203, 205–227,
    229–230, 233–250, 258–260
  black portrayal in the press, 208–209,
    214–225
    blacks and crime, 219–220
    white hostility and black crime news,
      214–218
    white rejection of black politics,
      221–223
  dehumanizing depictions of race,
    233–250

perceived guilt and story credibility,
    246–247, 248–249
  media and racism, 206–208, 223–225
  stereotypes and schema, 209–210, 230,
    234–238, 242–243
    cultural stereotyping, 236–237, 243
    response latency and stereotyping,
      237–238, 242
media effects, 23–24, 33–36
media-related disputes, 49–59
  dispute process, 49–52
  theory and methodology, 57–59
Metromedia v. San Diego, 176
Miller v. California, 95, 108
*Minnesota State Board for Community Col-
  leges v. Knight*, 167
Missouri v. Holland, 114, 137
modern racism, 205–214, 229, 237
  definition, 211
Mullane v. Central Hanover Bank & Trust,
    354, 360, 363, 369
Muller v. Oregon, xix, xxvi, 28, 38, 183,
    200

N

*National Association for the Advancement of
  Colored People v. Claiborne Hardware
  Co.*, 168
*National Labor Relations Board v. Hendricks
  County Rural Electric Membership
  Corp.*, 167
natural law, 12–13
Near v. Minnesota, 303
neutral principles, 29–30, 114
New York v. Ferber, 96, 108
New York Times Company v. Sullivan, 18,
    20, 21, 32, 38
nonoriginalism, 114–118

O

Ohio v. Lundgren, 66, 74, 77, 80, 85
Ohio v. Nobles, 66, 70, 79, 80, 85
Ohio v. Ritchie, 66, 71, 80, 85
Ohio v. Yarbrough, 66, 74, 77, 85
originalism, 112–114, 130

P

Pacifica Foundation v. FCC, 32, 34, 38
Parnell v. Booth Newspapers, Inc., 271
Philadelphia Newspapers, Inc. v. Hepps, 20, 21
Plyler v. Doe, 163
pornography, 87–107
　child pornography, 95–96
　definition, 98
　feminist research, 91, 104–107
　indecency, 95
　see also Pacifica Foundation v. FCC
　law, 95–98, 102–104
　obscenity, 95–96
　social science, 97–98, 99–101
pretrial publicity, 61–64, 68–82
　future research, 73–80
　high-profile defendants, 80–82
　see also media and race
privacy, 273–274, 278–280
Pruett v. Norris, 68, 71, 77, 79, 85
public interest, 330, 333–336, 337, 339, 346–347
public sphere, 109–110, 118–121, 121–127, 127–130
Puckett v. American Broadcasting Companies, 269

R

R.A.V. v. City of St. Paul, 32, 38
Red Lion Broadcasting Co. v. FCC, 276, 293
Reed v. General Motors Corp., 360, 369
religious symbols, 127–130
Reno v. Condon, 278, 293
Richmond Newspapers v. Virginia, 276, 293
Ritchie v. Rogers, 71, 77, 85
Roberts v. United States Jaycees, 13, 137
Rolla Cable System, Inc. v. City of Rolla, 342, 348

S, T

schema theory, 254–255, 258–261, 264–269
　gender and schema, 254, 258–260, 264–266
　memory, 266–267

　see also media and race
Schenk v. U.S., 122, 137, 296, 298, 302, 326
Scott v. Sandford, 5, 7
seditious speech, 305
Sheppard v. Maxwell, 48
Shores v. Publix Super Markets, Inc., 363, 369
social science and the First Amendment, 30–36
sociological approach to media law, 39–41
Southern Air Transport v. ABC, 269
spectrum scarcity, 329–330
Spence v. Washington, 125, 137
state access laws, 181–182, 183, 187–191, 195–199, 276
　"security and safety" records, 195–197
state open meeting laws, 181–182, 183–187
survey research, 273–274, 279, 280–282
Texas v. Johnson, 111, 137

U

Union CATV, Inc. v. City of Sturgis, 342, 348
United Brotherhood of Carpenters & Joiners of America v. Scott, 168
United Reporting Corp. v. Los Angeles Police Department, 278, 293
United States v. Allee, 66, 77, 79, 85
United States v. Bieganowski, 71, 78, 85
United States v. Blom, 66, 68, 71, 72, 74, 77, 80, 85
United States v. Carolene Products, 32, 38
United States v. Faul, 66, 68, 71, 72, 77, 78, 80, 85
United States v. Microsoft, 156, 159
United States v. Nelson, 68, 70, 85
United States v. Progressive, Inc., 156, 159
United States v. Smith, 32, 38
United States v. Southwestern Cable Co., 335, 348
United States v. Williams, 346, 348
United Steelworkers of America v. Sadlowski, 166, 168
Upjohn v. US, 169
U.S. v. Arthur Young, 169

U.S. Department of Justice v. Reporter's Committee for Freedom of the Press, 278, 293
U.S. ex. rel. Milwaukee Social Democratic Publishing Co. v. Burleson, 173
U.S. Postal Service v. Greenburgh Civic Association, 173, 177
USA PATRIOT Act, 7, 326
utilitarianism, 12–13

V

Virginia v. Black, 33, 38
Virginia State Board of Pharmacy v. Virginia Citizens Consumer Council, 32, 38

W

Walker's Appeal, 297, 301–302, 306–323, 325
   reaction to, 310–317
Walters v. National Association of Radiation Survivors, 172
Watts v. United States, 125–126, 137
Weinberger v. Kendrick, 361, 369
West Virginia State Board of Education v. Barnette, 137
West Virginia v. Chas. Pfizer & Co., Inc., 361
White, Byron, 171, 172, 173, 276
Whitney v. California, 326
Wilhoit v. WCSC, Inc., 269

For Product Safety Concerns and Information please contact our EU
representative GPSR@taylorandfrancis.com
Taylor & Francis Verlag GmbH, Kaufingerstraße 24, 80331 München, Germany